ATLANTIC CROSSROADS IN LISBON'S NEW GOLDEN AGE, 1668–1750

IBERIAN ENCOUNTER
AND EXCHANGE
475–1755 | Vol. 12

SERIES EDITORS
Erin Kathleen Rowe
Michael A. Ryan

The Pennsylvania State
University Press

The Iberian Peninsula has historically been an area of the world that fostered encounters and exchanges among peoples from different societies. For centuries, Iberia acted as a nexus for the circulation of ideas, people, objects, and technology around the premodern western Mediterranean, Atlantic, and eventually the Pacific. Iberian Encounter and Exchange, 475–1755 combines a broad thematic scope with the territorial limits of the Iberian Peninsula and its global contacts. In doing so, works in this series juxtapose previously disparate areas of study and challenge scholars to rethink the role of encounter and exchange in the formation of the modern world.

ADVISORY BOARD
Paul H. Freedman
Richard Kagan
Marie Kelleher
Ricardo Padrón
Teofilo F. Ruiz
Marta V. Vicente

OTHER TITLES IN THIS SERIES
Thomas W. Barton, *Contested Treasure: Jews and Authority in the Crown of Aragon*

Mercedes García-Arenal and Gerard Wiegers, eds., *Polemical Encounters: Christians, Jews, and Muslims in Iberia and Beyond*

Nicholas R. Jones, *Staging* Habla de Negros: *Radical Performances of the African Diaspora in Early Modern Spain*

Freddy Cristóbal Domínguez, *Radicals in Exile: English Catholic Books During the Reign of Philip II*

Lu Ann Homza, *Village Infernos and Witches' Advocates: Witch-Hunting in Navarre, 1608–1614*

Adam Franklin-Lyons, *Shortage and Famine in the Late Medieval Crown of Aragon*

Sarah Ifft Decker, *The Fruit of Her Hands: Jewish and Christian Women's Work in Medieval Catalan Cities*

Kyle C. Lincoln, *A Constellation of Authority: Castilian Bishops and the Secular Church During the Reign of Alfonso VIII*

Ran Segev, *Sacred Habitat: Nature and Catholicism in the Early Modern Spanish Atlantic*

A. Katie Harris, *The Stolen Bones of St. John of Matha: Forgery, Theft, and Sainthood in the Seventeenth Century*

Nicholas R. Jones, *Cervantine Blackness*

ATLANTIC CROSSROADS IN LISBON'S NEW GOLDEN AGE, 1668–1750

CACEY BOWEN FARNSWORTH

THE PENNSYLVANIA STATE UNIVERSITY PRESS
UNIVERSITY PARK, PENNSYLVANIA

Library of Congress Cataloging-in-Publication Data

Names: Farnsworth, Cacey Bowen, author.
Title: Atlantic crossroads in Lisbon's new golden age, 1668–1750 / Cacey Bowen Farnsworth.
Other titles: Iberian encounter and exchange, 475–1755 ; v. 12.
Description: University Park, Pennsylvania : The Pennsylvania State University Press, [2024] | Series: Iberian encounter and exchange, 475–1755 ; vol. 12 | Includes bibliographical references and index.
Summary: "Explores Lisbon's transition to Atlantic-centered trade during the early modern era by examining the city's social, economic, religious, and political evolution during a period of upheaval and transformation in Portugal, Europe, and the broader Atlantic World"— Provided by publisher.
Identifiers: LCCN 2024040041 | ISBN 9780271098869 (hardback)
Subjects: LCSH: Lisbon (Portugal)—History—17th century. | Lisbon (Portugal)—History— 18th century. | Lisbon (Portugal)—Civilization—17th century. | Lisbon (Portugal)— Civilization—18th century. | Lisbon (Portugal)—Civilization—Foreign influences.
Classification: LCC DP762 .F37 2024 | DDC 946.9/42032—dc23/eng/20241031
LC record available at https://lccn.loc.gov/2024040041

Copyright © 2024 Cacey Bowen Farnsworth
All rights reserved
Printed in the United States of America
Published by The Pennsylvania State University Press,
University Park, PA 16802–1003

The Pennsylvania State University Press is a member of the Association of University Presses.

It is the policy of The Pennsylvania State University Press to use acid-free paper. Publications on uncoated stock satisfy the minimum requirements of American National Standard for Information Sciences—Permanence of Paper for Printed Library Material, ANSI Z39.48–1992.

To my wife, Phoebe; my daughters, Ruby, Daphne, and Camilla; and my son, Cacey, for their patience and encouragement that saw this dream come true. To my father, for instilling his love of history in me. Lastly, I cannot forget to thank my mother for her strength when difficulties arose.

1 Nephi 18:2–3

Contents

LIST OF ILLUSTRATIONS   ix

ACKNOWLEDGMENTS   xi

A NOTE CONCERNING ORTHOGRAPHY   xiii

Introduction: A City Transformed   1

1   Black Influences in Atlantic Lisbon   15

2   The English in Atlantic Lisbon   39

3   Keeping Lisbon Catholic   71

4   Economic Change in Atlanticized Lisbon   97

5   Atlantic Opulence and the Local Manifestations of
    a Developing Royal Absolutism   123

Conclusion: A City Lost   159

NOTES   165

BIBLIOGRAPHY   199

INDEX   219

Illustrations

Figures

1. Francisco Zuzarte, *Vista de Lisboa en se reprezenta o Palacio. . .* , view of the Terreiro do Paço before the earthquake   13

2. Characters and designs from the *bolsa de mandinga* contained in the Inquisition papers of José Francisco Pedroso   95

3. Filippo Juvarra, *Projeto de Juvarra para o Palácio Real de Lisboa* (Juvarra's project for the Royal Palace of Lisbon), 1717   156

4. Jacques Philippe le Bas, *Praça da Patriarcal* (The Patriarchal Square), 1757   162

Map

1. Lisbon before 1755   12

Acknowledgments

I am deeply indebted to the many individuals who made this book what it is. I would first like to thank my advisor Ida Altman at the University of Florida for her years of coaching and unfailing support for me and my work. Jeffrey D. Needell was also a well of confidence during that time. I would be remiss if I did not extend a heartfelt thanks to Pedro Cardim at the Universidade Nova de Lisboa for his guidance during both the research and writing phases. I also wish to thank Dauril Alden, professor emeritus at the University of Washington, and Bill Donovan of Bellarmine University for their input. I am grateful to Fernanda Olival, Francisco Zamora Rodríguez, Carla Vieira, Sara Ceia, Walter Rossa, Delminda Rijo, Jorge Fonseca, Arlindo Caldeira, and countless others in Portugal for their useful tips and leads. Jim Sweet and Thiago Krause were kind enough to read portions of this book and offer valuable feedback, for which I am grateful. Matthew Restall also deserves particular mention for his many hours offering advice. The project itself would not have been possible without the generous support of the Fulbright Student Program and the Instituto Camões, both of which allowed me to spend an academic year in Lisbon. Their trust in the value of the project was a welcome source of encouragement. I cannot forget the library staff at both Brigham Young University and the University of Florida and their efforts at securing materials along the way. Mark Christensen, my dear colleague and friend, merits as much recognition as anyone for his role as a much-needed sounding board during our swim workouts. Last of all, I will be eternally indebted to Dr. Paulo Tremoçeiro and the rest of the staff at the Arquivo Nacional da Torre do Tombo for training and inspiring me all those years ago.

A Note Concerning Orthography

Both the Portuguese and English languages have evolved over time. So too has their spelling. As such, and thinking of the reader, I have standardized spelling throughout the text. In that same spirit, I have opted for a modern rather than literal translation in many instances. All translations are mine unless noted otherwise.

INTRODUCTION

A City Transformed

Land! land! although it might better be said, heaven! heaven! for we are without a doubt at the famous port of Lisbon.

—Miguel de Cervantes, 1617

Sir John Huxtable Elliott once described Atlantic history as "the creation, destruction, and re-creation of communities as a result of the movement, across and around the Atlantic basin, of people, commodities, cultural practices, and ideas."[1] Considering these factors, Lisbon for much of its history has been an Atlantic city.

Certainly, the Portuguese overseas empire had its genesis in the Atlantic sphere in the fifteenth and sixteenth centuries. That said, the focus of the empire was primarily India. Yet, as Portugal's global holdings shrank before the growing strength of the Dutch and others, the Portuguese increasingly turned to the Atlantic. This turn impacted Lisbon in new ways. Atlantic world historiography, however, continues to focus overwhelmingly on the Anglo North Atlantic sphere.[2] The dearth of scholarship in English on Lisbon is especially glaring considering the important relations between England and Portugal. It is true that Atlantic studies that include Iberia have appeared, yet these are almost entirely devoted to Spain. This book injects Portugal into the discussion through an examination of the Atlantic influences and changes that occurred in Lisbon. Simply put, this book demonstrates the prominent role of the Atlantic world in Lisbon.

The Portuguese empire, long dependent on India and the spice trade in Asia, suffered serious setbacks as the Dutch and others seized key regions and destroyed commercial monopolies during the period of political union with Spain (1580–1640). The year 1640 brought not only the restoration of a Portuguese monarch in João IV (1640–56) but also the start of a twenty-eight-year conflict for independence that drained the country of precious revenue and manpower. By the time peace was declared in 1668, the Portuguese had become utterly dependent on the Atlantic to support their imperial revival. In the following years, Lisbon experienced intensifying Atlantic influences that combined with local developments to transform the city's social fabric and in turn alter the metropole in racial, diplomatic, religious, economic, and structural ways. Demographic changes occurred as shifts in the Atlantic slave trade reverberated in the capital and affected intermixing and racial composition. Diplomatic alterations followed as England became Portugal's trusted ally in defense of the resurgent Atlantic empire. Religious influences penetrated Lisbon from both the North and South Atlantic as shifting economic fortunes brought diverse beliefs together. And the city itself bore witness to these broader metamorphoses as it was utterly transformed along baroque (in the sense of grandeur and complexity) and absolutist lines by Brazilian wealth. The exact nature of these changes is the overarching focus of this study.

Whereas the Atlanticization of the Portuguese empire began earlier in the seventeenth century, its fullest iteration with the most lasting effects came to fruition during the reigns of Pedro II (1668–1706) and João V (1706–50)—a foundational, yet understudied, period for such processes. Of course, Atlantic influences by their very nature are not always readily apparent in the short term. Tracing these elements in a given locale presents a particularly difficult task and, therefore, requires an expansive chronology and broad scope. While Lisbon did experience a change on multiple levels, it is inaccurate to argue that these changes were wholly attributable to Atlantic influence. However, because Portugal, when compared to other European powers, was among the most dependent on its overseas empire, it naturally follows that any shift in that framework should be traceable in the imperial center.[3] In other words, Atlantic history need not always be confined to broad scopes and macroanalyses. Rather, "localized" versions of Atlantic history, as defined by Trevor Burnard and Cécile Vidal, more fully reveal the diversity present in the Atlantic world as a variety of scales are considered alongside Atlantic influence.[4]

This book, then, is a response to Patrick Griffin's call for "a new Atlantic history," in which he declares that the large comparative frameworks so fashionable in the field tend to favor uniformity while neglecting the very element of distinctive response to Atlantic influence that proved so influential in the trajectory of the whole.[5] Overall, the resulting research demonstrates that the Atlantic played a crucial, but not exclusive, role in many of the changes to Lisbon and its society between 1668 and 1750 as the city became a crossroads where colonial developments intermingled with metropolitan and global influences to produce something novel among contemporary European port capitals. In short, Cervantes's heaven was about to become Atlanticized.

The Atlantic World

While the concept of Atlantic history has existed for quite some time, its consideration as a full-fledged field of historical study is relatively new. Admittedly, some of the first practitioners of Atlantic history in the 1960s considered it merely as a useful perspective. Institutionalization of the subject at the university level only began in the 1990s. Since then, the field of Atlantic history has interjected novel insights into a plethora of previous historical subfields and topics for the better part of three decades. While valid criticisms have arisen, the approach remains overwhelmingly popular among students and scholars alike.[6]

Alison Games has outlined the benefits of such an approach, declaring, "Atlantic perspectives deepen our understanding of transformations over a period of several centuries, cast old problems in an entirely new light, and illuminate connections hitherto obscured."[7] Emma Rothschild offers a similar assessment by arguing that Atlantic history reveals what other models cannot.[8] Therefore, with the Atlantic acting simultaneously as an organizing principle and the connective tissue, this work builds on the existing scholarship of those who have studied Lisbon through various perspectives during the period.[9] Albeit useful, these studies largely fall short of drawing out and analyzing the developing Atlantic linkages and their consequences for the Portuguese capital. Thus, this book demonstrates that Lisbon underwent a series of changes from 1668 to 1750 as it became a booming Atlantic city at the center of a resurgent Portuguese empire.

By employing a cisatlantic perspective (national or regional history within an Atlantic context) as defined by David Armitage, Lisbon remains the focus throughout the chapters—not as a surrogate for the rest of the country but as a city with a particular Atlantic experience.[10] The contributions of accomplished scholars like April Lee Hatfield and Alejandro de la Fuente provide a welcome road map for this process by demonstrating that to fully understand the development of a single place, one must look beyond local conditions and examine complex interactions.[11] Yet, unlike their work, the present study reverses the metropole-to-colony framework by asking how the Atlantic experience effected change in the heart of empire. As such, it proves that Atlantic history need not always favor margins and peripheries. By so doing, this work is a response to the current and valid argument among critics that Europe remains neglected and is a "blind spot" within the Atlantic world.[12]

The field of Atlantic history has more recently come under heavy criticism for its failure to see "the global dimensions of certain processes" and has been scrutinized as an artificially limited view that often "blinds" historians to developments and conditions that are important to the understanding of their "little corner of the world."[13] Critics have even argued that Atlantic history has been reduced to a buzzword.[14] While a critique of Atlantic history is warranted, particularly the idea that everything is Atlantic history, this book demonstrates that employing an Atlantic perspective can reveal heretofore unknown processes and connections. Furthermore, the idea that global history is a superior lens through which to view historical change is seriously challenged in the case of Lisbon during the period. The following chapters demonstrate that from the middle of the seventeenth century onward, the Portuguese global empire had been largely reduced to an Atlantic sphere with a focus on Brazil and the African slave trade. It was this withered empire reborn in the Atlantic, not the hollowed shell of the former global enterprise based in India, that had lasting economic, social, and cultural impacts in the Portuguese metropole during the period. However, it must be remembered that despite the primacy of the Atlantic world for Portugal at the time, it was never a sealed-off system entirely separate from outside influence. Global impacts were still felt in the city. The reverse is also true, as Atlantic developments began to foster metropolitan aspirations for a reinvigorated global empire. Thus, Bernard Bailyn's assertion that Atlantic history "illuminates the history of everything to the east of it" proves correct at least in the case of Lisbon and the Portuguese empire during the period under study.[15]

In sum, this project provides a new way to consider the history of Lisbon as it demonstrates the impact of the Atlantic world on a specific locale. As such, it recenters that world as it uncovers a history of the Atlantic in a relatively understudied period and place. Overall, Lisbon became a unique crossroads of encounter and exchange where North and South Atlantic met, the African and European Atlantics converged, and Atlantic diversity was both accepted and rejected. The city was, therefore, unique among Atlantic spaces.

An Introduction to Lisbon

Lisbon and the Atlantic became integral parts of the new imperial vision of the Bragança dynasty after the restoration war against Spain as Pedro II and João V both sought to rebuild the empire and elevate Portugal in the eyes of Europe by modernizing their capital city. Contemporary descriptions laud Lisbon for its natural beauty. Visiting in 1729, the Frenchman Charles Alexandre de Montgon declared that he "did not tire in admiring it."[16] The span of the city, according to another visitor, extended about one French league (roughly three miles) in length along the Tagus River, with a width a quarter of that distance.[17] At the beginning of the eighteenth century, the Englishman John Stevens described Lisbon's harbor as "the most convenient for the trade of the world" with a "wonderful capaciousness such as might with ease contain ten thousand ships all riding in safety and without encumbering one another."[18]

Yet the city itself was a complicated mixture of medieval and modern in its design and function. The center consisted of tortuous streets that made transit difficult, particularly after the introduction of the coach during the previous period of Spanish Union. Litters and sedan chairs were the normal form of transportation for the upper classes.[19] Commoners went on foot. The narrow streets fostered the buildup of rubbish, which consisted of all manner of filth, including human waste that was routinely dumped from the upper windows to the street with a shout of "água vai."[20] According to the English merchant Thomas Cox, simply strolling through the city in the evening required expert caution to avoid having a pail of excrement or other garbage poured on one's head.[21] The streets were cleaned only every three to four days unless a religious procession or other public festivity was to occur.[22] During these events whole portions of the city transformed as the streets were cleaned, incense burned, and draperies hung to honor the day.

Trash buildup became such a problem that at one point residents complained they could no longer see out of their windows.[23] The debris from the streets ended up in the Tagus River near the royal palace, routinely clogging the city's shipyards immediately to the west.[24] A good rain was often the best solution to the urban muck, but it also could make conditions worse.[25] John Stevens decried, "Whilst the violence of the rain lasts there is often no crossing a street without wading above mid-leg."[26]

To complicate matters, pigs roamed about feeding on whatever they could find. To eliminate the problem the city council ruled, to little avail, that anyone could kill or claim pigs found wandering the streets.[27] Pests and disease flourished, and people routinely purchased perfumes to cover up the unbearable stench.[28] Overall, Thomas Cox described Lisbon as "the dirtiest place I ever came into. Several old commanders of ships have assured me that it is the dirtiest sea port town in Europe and I believe them."[29] A more nuanced description was offered by François de Tours, who recognized that the streets of Lisbon were dirty, but argued, "This does not mean that some are not very beautiful, particularly the streets where the goldsmiths and silversmiths have shops named *Rua do Ouro* and *Rua da Prata*, which are full of works illustrating their art."[30] However dirty, and despite the colorful foreign depictions stating otherwise, it is likely that Lisbon was not much worse than contemporary Madrid, London, or Paris.[31]

The buildings in the city center occupied by the wealthier residents were themselves basic, usually consisting of two or three levels, with the first reserved for stables, servants, and enslaved people.[32] For the most part, the structures were whitewashed and unadorned except during popular festivals or religious processions.[33] Multilevel residences for the working classes also existed. Each floor was divided into two separate units with an average size of roughly forty-nine square meters. The interiors of these living spaces often featured one partition, and residents slept on mattresses on the floor.[34]

At the beginning of the eighteenth century, the average dwelling in Lisbon housed between seven and eight people—a considerable increase from the four to five during the previous century.[35] Family members and relatives were the most common residents of each living space, but servants, enslaved people, and apprentices who emigrated to the city to train or work in artistic and commercial trades were also present in some households.[36] Much of Lisbon's population spent most of their time in the streets where they came in constant contact with others.[37] Whether in their homes or in the streets, the people of Lisbon, like the residents of other early modern European cities, lived in close proximity to one another.

While population estimates for the period have ranged as high as 250,000 by 1730, a more accurate number according to the analysis of various sources by Helena Murteira is somewhere between 150,000 and 190,000 on the eve of the devastating 1755 earthquake.[38] Lisbon's population naturally increased overall during the period under study, at times even spectacularly. An augmented population in the capital was in many ways the result of rural flight and the influx of foreigners as Brazilian commerce continued to expand.[39] Put another way, Lisbon was ranked the fifth most populous European city in 1700. By comparison, the Spanish Atlantic cites of Seville and Cádiz were ranked seventeenth and thirty-ninth, respectively.[40] Growth further reinforced Lisbon's role as the demographic center of Portugal, with the next largest city of Porto enjoying only about a quarter of Lisbon's population.[41]

Scholars have estimated that the rate of urbanization in Portugal in 1706 near the beginning of João V's reign was 10.3 percent of the total population. At the same time, an estimated 33.6 percent of the Dutch population lived in cities while England stood at 13.3 percent. That figure was 9 percent for Spain. Even more interesting is the fact that the rate of urbanization in Portugal declined slightly over the course of the eighteenth century, yet Lisbon and Porto both saw periods of significant growth. During the period, these two cities, with Lisbon by far outstripping Porto in population terms, were the exceptions to an otherwise weaker percentage in Portugal of labor reallocation to urban centers in comparison with Northern Europe.[42]

As Lisbon's population steadily increased, the city grew in a haphazard and organic fashion, which only added to the disorderly nature of the urban space.[43] By the 1750s, the city was divided into thirty-eight parishes with a total of twelve neighborhoods, the eight most principal being Limoeiro, Santa Catarina, Bairro Alto, Remolares, Castelo, Ribeira, Rossio, and Rua Nova.[44] The neighborhoods or *bairros* of the popular classes were Alfama, Mouraria, and Bairro Alto.[45] The central parishes and commercial heart of the city near the river included Sé, Alfama, São Julião, São Nicolau, Mártires, Sacramento, and Santa Catarina. Just beyond these were the mixed residential and commercial parishes of Mercês, Santa Justa, Santiago, and Salvador. Peripheral parishes included Ajuda, Santa Isabel, Anjos, São Sebastião, São José, and Santa Engrácia and were the center of manufacturing installations. The outlying parishes produced cereals and other agricultural goods that were sold in the city.[46] The dirtiest areas were those nearest the river.

City life revolved around two public squares, the Terreiro do Paço and Rossio. The first was situated on the banks of the Tagus and was completely enclosed by the royal palace to the west, residences to the north, and the customs house to the east.[47] Here, royally sponsored spectacles transpired as bullfights, fireworks, and inquisitorial shows of public penance, or *autos-da-fé*, occurring under the watchful eye of king and court. While the Terreiro do Paço was the political center of the city, the other great square of Rossio, located a short distance to the north, was the heart. It was here that the bustle of daily life and activity transpired. Bullfights put on by the city council and other popular entertainments were a common occurrence.[48] These events were accompanied by a weekly flea market where various wares were bought and sold.[49] Many residents paid handsomely in precious silver for the best spot to observe the *autos-da-fé* and other events from the windows of the houses surrounding the Rossio square.[50] The famed Portuguese literary figure D. Francisco Manuel de Melo (1608–1666) described the space: "The best part of the world is Europe; the best part of Europe is Spain; the best part of Spain is Portugal; the best part of Portugal is Lisbon; the best part of Lisbon is Rossio; and the best part of Rossio are the houses of my father in the middle where you can watch the bulls in the shade."[51]

Various groups occupied different areas of the city. Germans lived primarily in the parish of São Julião,[52] the French in São Paulo,[53] and the Italians in Nossa Senhora do Loreto.[54] Noble residences dotted the city but were particularly concentrated in the Bairro Alto.[55] Large numbers of Africans (both freed and enslaved) and other working-class individuals often congregated in the Mocambo neighborhood in the western part of the city.[56] Occupations varied among residents with the popular classes largely consigned to manual labor. Those with skills found work in the shipyards, quarries, or workshops. African men worked under artisans, became artisans themselves, plastered homes, or toiled on the docks as porters and stevedores. Black women hawked goods in the streets and carried all manner of waste and garbage to the river. Both served as domestic servants for the wealthy. Portuguese artisans, petty merchants, and shopkeepers constituted the middle sort of society.

Lisbon was especially full of Catholic clergy; mendicant friars, nuns, priests, and other ecclesiastics abounded in every quarter. At the beginning of the eighteenth century alone there were an estimated 1,296 friars and 1,166 nuns.[57] By the 1740s, the city and its hinterland had eighty-five convents.[58] Stevens wrote, "If we were to speak of all the churches and monasteries in Lisbon it would furnish matter enough for a particular treatise of itself."[59] Little wonder historian Charles Ralph Boxer (not without a touch of prejudice) described Portugal around that time as "more priest-ridden than . . . any other country in the world, with the possible exception of Tibet."[60]

Lisbon was a particularly dangerous city after dark, in part due to the lack of adequate lighting. Melo composed a poem concerning the perils of nightfall and exhorted residents to

Carry a cross against the Devil
And against men a sword!
Oh! What darkness!
What infested corners!
All are crossroads
Property of demons and thieves![61]

Those demons and thieves came from every social group and standing. Murderous gangs roamed the darkness, some consisting entirely of nobles and members of the royal family.[62] As a result, no man who owned arms left home without his sword or dagger and a long black cape.[63] Those who could afford to do so armed their lackeys with pistols.[64] The clergy were among the worst perpetrators of violence. The English chaplain John Colbatch claimed that "it is equally dangerous to deal with a friar by night, as with a *fidalgo* [nobleman] by day. The reason usually given for it is: that in a night-scuffle the friar will be sure to stand as stoutly to it, because he is not known, as a *fidalgo* would in the daytime because he is."[65] The most dangerous sections were the parishes of São Sebastião da Pedreira and Santa Catarina along with the dock areas where Portuguese miscreants and rowdy foreign sailors mingled. Public spaces like city fountains where enslaved people and others of the poorer classes congregated were also risky.[66] The lack of a modern police force contributed to the disorder—but in fairness, London and Paris suffered from similar problems at the time.[67]

Lisbon notoriously lacked an adequate water supply for its growing population. While there were various fountains throughout the city, the vast majority were in the lower *baixa* valley, which necessitated difficult or costly transport. Even more problematic, the fountains regularly ran dry during the hot summer months.[68] Food was consistently lacking and expensive. The problem of supply stemmed from the underdeveloped nature of the infrastructure. The Tagus was unnavigable for long distances, and the country suffered from a severe dearth of adequate roads.[69] Some went so far as to claim that travel from Lisbon to India or Brazil was easier than from Lisbon to Porto. Under these circumstances, food often reached the capital from the interior already spoiled.[70] These factors combined with the development of cash crops for export, competitive prices from abroad, and a ban on exporting grain to discourage cereal production beyond local consumption.[71] Considering all this, the Italian visitor Lorenzo Magalotti's epigram for the city in 1669 was probably quite accurate: "Watching from afar, without detail, [Lisbon] appears much more magnificent than in fact it really is."[72]

Lisbon's Post-1668 Atlantic Transformation

Lisbon's urban space underwent a profound transformation during the last quarter of the seventeenth century until the middle of the eighteenth century in large part as a result of increased Atlantic involvement. Lisbon benefited greatly from the outset of the imperial shift toward Brazil during the second half of the seventeenth century, effectively shoring up its leading role as Portugal's main commercial port—a role that to some extent had begun to plateau in relation to Porto.[73] This change was largely due to royal sponsorship of the Brazil company, which centralized the organization of the Brazil fleets in Lisbon. Distinct advantages arose for businesses and others located in the capital. All these factors transformed Lisbon into the main hub of colonial commerce, a position that had not been as clearly defined during the previous century.[74]

Lisbon's commanding economic position as the center of colonial commerce after the restoration in turn allowed it to attract the lion's share of foreign trade to the detriment of other Portuguese ports.[75] For example, in 1685 the capital city was by far the most diverse seaport with regard to shipping and trade, as it was responsible for 77 percent of all imports to the country and 75 percent of exports.[76] The expansion of trade with Brazil only exaggerated Lisbon's commercial dominance. However, as the city became utterly dependent on Brazilian products and the associated African slave trade, it was left dangerously exposed by the 1670s to economic fluctuations throughout the Atlantic world. The result was a sharp economic downturn caused by growing imperial and economic competition from the English, French, and Dutch. The already close relationship between the capital city and the Atlantic empire became increasingly intertwined as large gold (and later diamond) deposits were discovered in the Brazilian backlands at the end of the seventeenth century. The astronomical influx of gold alone consisted of more than half the world flow at the time.[77] Such wealth led friar António Rosário to declare that "the East-Indies for many years, as a result of sins and injustices, is no longer India; Brazil through its cane [and] by its sacks of diamonds that are shipped in thousands of crates every year, is the true India and Mina of the Portuguese."[78]

By the first decades of the eighteenth century, the Brazil trade merged with the windfall of gold and diamonds to once again make Lisbon an important European center for commerce as foreigners flocked to the city, eager to share in the burgeoning profits.[79] In essence, as Portugal's Atlantic empire became more important, so did Lisbon. This fact is reflected in Lisbon's custom revenues, which in 1632 equaled 34 percent of the entire kingdom's total. By 1716, that share had more than doubled to an enormous 77 percent.[80] No wonder the Englishman Arthur Costigan described Portugal as "one of that sort of spiders which has a large body, containing all the substance (the capital), with extremely long, thin, feeble legs, reaching to a great distance, but are of no sort of use to it, and which it is hardly able to move."[81]

Portugal's second largest port city, Porto, also increased in importance with the growing focus on the Atlantic, but merely as a regional port due to a growing linkage to England through the developing wine trade.[82] In short, as a result of Atlanticization, Lisbon became an outward-looking port focused on Brazilian trade while Porto increasingly depended on its hinterland.[83] Amsterdam, in contrast, drew its wealth from a variety of sources that included not only colonial trade but also industry, shipping, finance, and control of the intra-European "mother trade" in Baltic grain.[84] London operated on a similar structure and rose to commercial prominence as a key junction between rapidly expanding provincial and global overseas markets.[85] Seville and Cádiz offer the closest comparisons to Lisbon as both were overly reliant on colonial commerce. Yet while Seville has traditionally been the Spanish port most compared to Lisbon, during the period under study it was a city in serious decline as its former anteport Cádiz gradually, and then officially, overtook its function as the center of the Indies trade.[86] Therefore, as stated previously, if overseas empire consistently played a greater role for Portugal than any other European power, any changes to that network would be clearly reflected in Lisbon.[87]

Lisbon's growing dependence on Brazil is woven throughout the book, with each chapter treating one of the major effects of Lisbon's Atlanticization. The first chapter examines the changing agency, role, and legacy of people of African descent in Lisbon as developments in the Atlantic slave trade reverberated in the Portuguese capital. The second focuses on the long-standing Anglo-Portuguese relationship and its impacts in Lisbon. The overarching argument is that a major part of the Atlanticization of Lisbon resulted from a growing reliance on the English. The third chapter emphasizes the increasing (and overlapping) influences of the North and South Atlantic spheres, which together led to a resurgence of the Inquisition. The penultimate chapter highlights the economic intricacies of Atlantic dependency in Lisbon and Portuguese efforts to combat it. The closing chapter treats the political transformations incurred by expanding Atlantic wealth and their wider consequences, including the development of royal absolutism, a robust urban transformation, and impressive cultural renovation. Other topics

INTRODUCTION

Map 1. Lisbon before 1755. Commissioned by author. Created by the Geospatial Services and Training Lab of Brigham Young University.

mentioned in each chapter include Lisbon's continued (albeit diminished) global ties and the foundational nature of the period in shaping the subsequent reforms of the Marquis of Pombal.

While each chapter treats different Atlantic impacts, a sense of interconnectedness pervades the work as many of these influences interacted with local developments to foster additional changes that together transformed Lisbon. Additionally, comparisons with other Atlantic cities in Europe are occasionally drawn. Doing so underscores Lisbon's transformation and showcases its understudied role as an early forerunner of the integration of, and adaptation to, Atlantic influences. Only a handful of European metropoles offer appropriate comparisons, given that Lisbon was simultaneously the

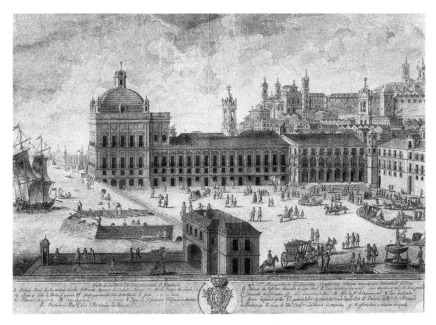

Fig. 1. Francisco Zuzarte, *Vista de Lisboa en se reprezenta o Palacio*. . . . View of the Terreiro do Paço before the earthquake, looking west. Museu de Lisboa (MC.DES.0837). Coleção do Museu de Lisboa / EGEAC / Câmara Municipal de Lisboa.

imperial capital and Portugal's largest port city.[88] London and Amsterdam are the logical choices, but the inclusion of Seville is warranted because of its importance as a center for Atlantic commerce that experienced a sharp decline vis-à-vis Cádiz during the same period. Porto is also touched upon to further highlight the extent and pace of Lisbon's metamorphosis within Portugal.

Taken together, the source material is segmented and heterogeneous, requiring extensive archival work in the Arquivo Nacional da Torre do Tombo, Biblioteca Nacional de Portugal, Biblioteca Pública de Évora, Biblioteca Pública Municipal de Porto, Biblioteca da Ajuda, Arquivo Histórico Ultramarino, the British Library, and the National Archives, among others. Some of the sources gleaned from these repositories have never been looked at before, while others have been examined through a new lens considering their biases and limitations. Altogether, the archival evidence produces a clear understanding that Lisbon at the middle of the eighteenth century was distinct from Lisbon in 1668 at the end of the restoration war, in large part as a result of the Atlanticization of the Portuguese empire—something that generations of scholars have noticed in passing but never fully examined and illustrated.

As a pioneer and participant in the formation of the wider Atlantic world, Lisbon reflected increased Atlantic involvement as the Portuguese rebuilt their empire with new elements during a new "golden" age. In consequence, the heart of that empire underwent a significant transformation as Africans arriving from Brazil introduced new cultural and religious practices, the English brought commercial and religious pressures, the Inquisition responded vigorously to a plethora of perceived threats, pioneering economic endeavors began, and the rise in royal absolutism with growing wealth led to the complete cultural and urban makeover of the capital. In sum, Lisbon became a crossroads where a considerable mixing of cultures and economies occurred. These changes converged during the period to recast Lisbon's image as the center of a powerful Atlantic empire, an image that would be upheld during the subsequent Pombaline era despite the devastating earthquake that destroyed the city on 1 November 1755.

I

BLACK INFLUENCES IN ATLANTIC LISBON

In May 1706, the inquisitors of the Holy Office in Lisbon heard the confession of an enslaved Afro-Brazilian woman named Grácia Luzia. Grácia declared that she was thirty years old, born in Bahia, and currently living in the city. She related that on one occasion, at the behest of her previous mistress (the prioress of the Anunciada convent), she went to the house of the mariner José Francisco to be examined for purchase and transport to Brazil. It was then that she "renounced her faith in Christ our Lord and in His Blood . . . as well as the Holy Trinity and the purity of the Virgin Mary, and repeating these various times, she took off the rosary that she wore around her neck and threw it on a chair while declaring that she did not want to be a Christian." The reason behind this outburst, according to Grácia Luzia, was her "having served the said convent satisfactorily for many years, yet they did not want to grant her freedom despite her insistence and offer of payment." She declared that her blasphemous declarations should not be taken seriously because she had always been a devout Christian, but she had uttered her comments in a moment of great passion. She further noted that the goal of these shocking statements was to "intimidate the said mariner from purchasing her," which proved successful.[1] Overall, the outcome was something of a Pyrrhic victory, as Grácia's outburst achieved her desired goal of avoiding sale to Brazil but also landed her in Lisbon's inquisitorial dungeon.

This chapter highlights the vital role people of African descent—enslaved persons, free people of color, and mulattoes—played in the Atlanticization of

Lisbon and the effects of that particular role in their own lives. The number of enslaved Africans in Lisbon began to diminish during the second half of the seventeenth century as growing demand in Brazil diverted traffic away from the metropole. Enslaved Afro-Lisboans were particularly affected by the shift as the threat of sale to Brazil increased. As a result, many individuals like Grácia employed inventive means to avoid the possibility. Others joined the growing number of Black brotherhoods in the capital. These demographic changes had additional consequences as Lisbon's African population became increasingly sustained not by new arrivals but by natural reproduction. Natural reproduction in the capital, or Iberianization, meant an increased degree of intermixing with the broader Portuguese culture and the intensification of racial prejudice. While the few scholars who have studied the Afro-Lisboan experience during the period have provided key insights on the topic, none have highlighted the important link between the Atlanticization of Lisbon and the increasing Iberianization of its Afro-descended population.

Lisbon was further influenced by the Atlanticization of the slave trade as diminishing numbers saw prices for enslaved individuals in the city rise. This dynamic meant that households with multiple enslaved persons became increasingly concentrated among the upper classes. However, by the beginning of the eighteenth century, the expansion of the Atlantic slave trade combined with the arrival of Brazilian wealth in the capital to increase the importation of enslaved Africans for a time. More importantly, these new arrivals came predominantly from Brazil rather than Africa. While their numbers were never enough to reverse the steady decline as a result of Brazilian demand, the new arrivals proved impactful in other ways as they mingled with Iberianized individuals and introduced novel cultural and religious practices from the South Atlantic world. In other words, despite a steady population decline due to a shift in the slave trade, Lisbon easily remained Europe's most African city in both demographic and cultural terms as a result of the interplay between Atlanticization and Iberianization. In the end, Afro-Lisboans like Grácia were neither passive nor voiceless in the face of larger changes occurring in the capital. Rather, they proved influential in the formation of popular culture and identity in the very heart of the empire.

Changing Demographics

The growing Atlantic focus of the Portuguese empire after the restoration led to significant transformations among the lowest strata in Lisbon as fluctuations in the slave trade reverberated throughout the Portuguese capital. Having sustained the independence movement during the restoration war with Spain (1640–68), Brazilian revenues became even more important for Pedro II, given the loss of much of the Asian spice trade to the Dutch and others. The intense focus on Brazil naturally led to a strengthening of contacts between Africa and the American colony that, combined with greater demand in the Caribbean holdings of various European powers after the sugar revolution, led to an amplification of the Atlantic slave trade.[2] The total number of enslaved persons shipped across the Atlantic to Brazil and the Caribbean ballooned from roughly 488,065 in 1651–75 to 1,471,725 in 1726–50.[3] This intensification of the trade led to major transformations throughout the Atlantic during the second half of the seventeenth century as the new slaving ports of Liverpool, London, Bristol, and Nantes developed in the North Atlantic. In the South Atlantic, a bilateral trade emerged between various Brazilian and African ports that sustained roughly 95 percent of the slave voyages to Portuguese America.[4]

These developments naturally affected Lisbon as the arrival of slave ships (already declining in the sixteenth century) diminished to a trickle during the seventeenth and eighteenth centuries.[5] Stiff Caribbean competition only compounded the situation in Portugal as the price for enslaved individuals effectively doubled during the period between 1640 and 1680. Combined, these factors led to a decline in Lisbon's enslaved population during the last quarter of the seventeenth century.[6] However, Lisbon continued to play a critical role in the South Atlantic slave trade as a major financier even though the vast majority of slaving voyages now commenced and terminated in Brazilian ports.[7]

The trade was further transformed after the discovery of Brazilian gold during the 1690s when miners in Brazil's southern captaincies began to compete with planters in the northeast precisely at a time when sugar was rebounding as a result of disruptions to the Caribbean markets of the English and French during the Nine Years' War.[8] The inevitable consequence was an even greater expansion of the Atlantic slave trade in the eighteenth century and even higher prices in Lisbon.[9] In the sixteenth century, the value of an enslaved adult in Portugal was equivalent to that of four oxen; during the seventeenth century, it was closer to six oxen.[10] By the eighteenth century an enslaved person in Portugal cost as much as nine oxen.[11] Rising prices led many in Lisbon to sell their slaves (or those kidnapped from others) to Brazil.[12]

Lisbon's enslaved population had fallen to such a point in the last decades of the seventeenth century that the city council petitioned Pedro II to allow the resignation of one of the city's slave brokers due to falling revenue from the position.[13] Furthermore, commerce had declined so sharply that by the second half of the seventeenth century the title itself had changed from simply slave broker to slave and livestock broker, and only three had any regular activity.[14] The Jesuit Balthazar Tellez declared in 1587 that Lisbon was full of Africans representing twenty nations.[15] By the eighteenth century, only three African nations had a meaningful presence in Lisbon.[16]

Economic realities recast slave ownership in Lisbon. In contrast to previous eras, when individuals from almost every social station (including prostitutes) owned enslaved people, decreasing arrivals at the end of the seventeenth century and soaring prices effectively put slave ownership out of reach for many.[17] Those who could no longer afford Africans but needed help at home or in a trade began to depend on wage-labor.[18] In the modest households that could still afford enslaved individuals, it became rare to have more than one. One of the more populous parishes in the city, Santa Justa, witnessed an overall decrease in households owning enslaved persons from 8.4 percent to 6.2 percent in the span of one decade (1693–1702).[19] Put another way, 139 households in the parish owned enslaved people in 1693 compared to 106 in 1702. Additionally, households employing waged servants during the same period went from 250 to 355. Households on the wealthier streets of the parish, however, maintained an elevated number of enslaved people during the same period.[20] This pattern holds true for various parishes across the city.[21]

Nevertheless, the arrival of Brazilian bullion and the expansion of the Atlantic slave trade led to a small uptick in importations of enslaved individuals during the first half of the eighteenth century, which, when combined with natural reproduction, slowed the overall decline of the late seventeenth.[22] The baptismal records of multiple parishes across the city reflect the change.[23] To be clear, these numbers by no means signal a return to the rates of previous centuries nor a complete reversal of the overall decline. Using the Trans-Atlantic Slave Trade Database, Filipa Ribeiro da Silva established that an average of 260–325 enslaved individuals arrived legally in Portugal each year during the first half of the eighteenth century. Her study also reveals that during most of the seventeenth century, that number was 500.[24]

The only slavers to arrive during the period were the occasional Portuguese vessel from Cabo Verde or India and English ships that changed course, intentionally or not, for Lisbon.[25] In September 1727, the weekly *Gazeta de Lisboa Occidental* advertised the sale of recently arrived enslaved Africans from Cacheu. Those interested were directed to the house of Patrício

(Patrick) Nolan in the Bairro Alto.[26] In July 1723, the same paper trumpeted the arrival of a Portuguese vessel returning from Cabo Verde with 144 enslaved Africans, as well as an additional English ship that unloaded another 94 from the Guinea coast.[27] A separate publication in October 1731 mentions a slave ship from Cacheu with a cargo of ivory and two hundred enslaved Africans, of whom only sixteen made it to Portugal alive after the ship was lost at sea.[28] Altogether, seven Portuguese slavers disembarked a total of 1,092 enslaved individuals in the capital directly from Cacheu between 1725 and 1755 alone. In the same period, ten English ships delivered nine hundred captives from Senegambia, Sierra Leone, and the Gulf of Guinea.[29]

The decline in slave ship arrivals meant that Africans arrived through other means during this period. The majority accompanied their masters to the capital at the conclusion of their service as colonial officials or merchants.[30] Others came as a portion of the salary paid to sailors and soldiers returning from Portuguese Africa.[31] Partial or even total exemption from import duties on enslaved individuals brought to the metropole by captains and clergy further incentivized many who crisscrossed the Atlantic to bring enslaved persons with them as they made their way to Lisbon.[32] As was the case with one of Pedro II's enslaved servants, some were disembarked after being captured from Moorish pirates on the high seas.[33]

Others interested in purchasing enslaved Africans often did so through commercial agents in Brazil as the slave trade between that colony and Africa intensified. The correspondence of the Lisbon merchant Francisco Pinheiro reveals as much, as he repeatedly petitioned his agents to procure enslaved Africans in Brazil and remit them to the capital for himself and others.[34] While enslaved individuals at times arrived in Lisbon directly from Africa, an interesting transformation occurred as the majority came from Brazil during the period, a natural evolution considering the preponderance of the bilateral trade that developed. An Englishman living in Lisbon in 1701 wrote, "There are among them a great number of blacks who are slaves in this country though they are baptized. They are generally brought from Angola, a kingdom in Africa, to the Brazils and when persons come home they bring these blacks with them."[35] Multiple accounts in Lisbon's gazettes record the presence of Africans alongside gold and other products shipped to the capital on the yearly Brazil fleets. One of the larger shipments contained 360 enslaved individuals as part of its cargo.[36]

Together with occasional arrivals from Brazil and Africa, natural reproduction bolstered the population of enslaved persons in Lisbon.[37] All this meant that Lisbon's African population was becoming increasingly home-grown and integrated in comparison to earlier eras. The visible number of Africans and Afro-descendants in the city after the turn of the eighteenth century caused the Italian traveler Giuseppe Baretti to remark "One of the things that most surprise[s] a stranger as he rambles about this town is that great number of Negroes who swarm in every corner. Many of these un-happy wretches are natives of Africa, and many born of African parents ei-ther in Portugal or in its ultramarine dominions. No ship comes from those regions without bringing some of either sex, and, when they are here, they are allowed to marry not only among themselves, but also with those of a different color."[38] While foreign accounts are notoriously exaggerated in this regard in comparison to the extant demographic data, Baretti makes it clear that Africans remained a visible presence in Lisbon during the eighteenth century despite increasing Brazilian demand for enslaved persons.

Estimates of the enslaved population in the city during the period have varied, yet most scholars cite a general decline in the overall number from previous eras.[39] In 1551 Cristovão Rodrigues de Oliveira estimated that Lis-bon had 9,950 enslaved persons out of a population of 100,595—roughly 10 percent. Almost a century later, Nicolau de Oliveira calculated the popu-lation in 1620 at 165,878 inhabitants with 10,470 enslaved individuals, or about 6 percent.[40] It is safe to say that with the economic downturn in the Portuguese Atlantic during the second half of the seventeenth century this percentage gradually declined but was bolstered by renewed importations during the first half of the eighteenth century and by natural reproduction. It is therefore probable, as scholars have surmised, that the proportion of en-slaved people in Lisbon's overall population hovered around 5 percent dur-ing the period, or around ten thousand individuals in 1750. Combined with the free African-descendant population of around twenty thousand, it has been estimated that as much as one-fifth of the city consisted of people of color.[41] When compared with other Iberian port cities like Cádiz, which had a free and enslaved population of all ethnicities and backgrounds of roughly 15 percent between 1682 and 1729, the conclusion that Lisbon was Europe's most African city is only strengthened.[42] In other words, even as the propor-tion of Africans and African-descended people in Lisbon declined, contem-poraries continued to think of the city as strongly Africanized. Reaching beyond Iberia to the port capitals of Northern Europe only reinforces the heavy weight of African slavery in the Portuguese metropole that was not present elsewhere. Enslaved Africans in London were just above 2 percent of the total population during the decades after the middle of the eighteenth century, while the Black community was meager in Amsterdam considering slavery did not legally exist in that city.[43]

The ethnic background of Lisbon's servile population was also transformed as new arrivals increasingly originated from the African region just east of the Gold Coast known as Mina despite the overall greater availability of enslaved individuals from Portuguese-controlled Angola.[44] The change occurred when miners and merchants in Brazil's southern captaincies were unable to secure adequate numbers of enslaved persons from Angola and began looking elsewhere to bolster their trade.[45] The inability of Brazilian slavers to secure sufficient cargo may well have been due to an epidemic that swept through Portuguese Angola beginning in 1687.[46]

Brazilian slaveowners at the time were not in agreement concerning which ethnicities of enslaved persons were best, but many preferred individuals from Mina who were perceived as stronger, resistant to disease, better workers, more intelligent, and particularly adept at discovering gold.[47] These same considerations made enslaved Africans from Mina popular in Lisbon from the middle of the seventeenth century on.[48] Parish records in the city clearly reveal this trend by the beginning of the eighteenth century. In Santa Catarina, on the western side of Lisbon, the number of enslaved Africans from Mina not born in the parish was listed at 111. The next largest group was 25 individuals from unknown ethnic backgrounds. Other parishes demonstrate similar trends.[49] When taken as a whole, these records reveal that during the same span, 17.5 percent of all enslaved Africans—both Black and mulatto—were born in Lisbon, 16 percent were originally from the Congo and Benguela regions, 13 percent from the Costa da Mina, and 13 percent from other parts of Africa, the Americas, and Asia.[50] The predominance of enslaved people from Angola and Mina was a direct consequence of the Angola market functioning as a trade hub for *gerebita* or *cachaça* (alcoholic by-products of Brazilian sugar), whereas the Mina traders provided a market for lesser-quality tobacco sweetened with molasses.[51]

While Lisbon's servile population was overwhelmingly African during this period of imperial Atlanticization, there are occasional mentions of the arrival of enslaved Indigenous Brazilians.[52] Additionally, there was a continued presence in Lisbon, albeit minor, of enslaved people from the Estado da Índia, who often returned to the capital with their masters.[53] These individuals were labeled in parish registers alongside those labeled Blacks, Moors, Turks, Indians, and Chinese, among others, and served as a real reminder in the city of the diminished but unbroken global connections of the Portuguese empire in an Atlantic age.[54]

The Lives of Africans in Baroque Lisbon

While owning multiple enslaved individuals had always been a status symbol among the wealthy in Portugal, the arrival of Brazilian riches and the associated aspirations to baroque ostentation only amplified the trend in Lisbon as successful merchants and others sought to do the same.[55] Through his examination of the life of Francisco Pinheiro, Bill Donovan has argued (as have others) that for merchants to penetrate the upper echelons of society in Lisbon they needed to live in a noble manner, which always meant owning enslaved Africans.[56] Foreigners in the city also increasingly used Africans. As English merchants poured into the capital after the discovery of Brazilian gold, they brought with them enslaved Africans from the English colonies in the Atlantic, whom they preferred due to their command of the English language. Yet as time went on, English merchants also began purchasing enslaved people from Portuguese Africa as social requirements demanded a large retinue of enslaved persons and other servants.[57] The royal family set the pattern by owning large numbers of enslaved people.[58] Visiting in the 1720s, the Swiss-born Charles Frédéric de Merveilleux declared, "In every noble house there are more than a hundred servants, including blacks."[59] Another observer noted that "black slaves" were a majority in wealthier households and that they were preferred over white servants because they were considered "more docile, having become meek through the fear of being sold to work in the [Brazilian] mines."[60]

Enslaved Africans were not only popular as domestic servants during the period, but they also became integral showpieces as bullfighting—long viewed as one of the major pastimes for the city's residents and as a means of aristocratic self-promotion—increasingly employed Africans as the baroque took hold of Lisbon. While Africans no doubt played some part in bullfighting before the period, at the end of the seventeenth century and the beginning of the eighteenth, their role began to change.[61] First, Africans began to participate in greater numbers in the grand entry of the noble *cavaleiros* (gentlemen). For example, on the first day of the 1686 bullfights celebrating Pedro II's forthcoming second marriage, to Maria Sofia de Neuburg, the Count of Atalaia made four separate entries into the ring, each with fifty people representing a different corner of the global empire. In one of these spectacular entries, fifty Black people armed with bows and arrows accompanied the count.[62] Before a bullfight held in honor of João V's marriage to Maria Anna of Austria in 1708, the Viscount Ponte de Lima appeared in the ring with twenty-four Africans whom he had purchased and dressed richly before granting each their freedom.[63] A Portuguese diplomat at the time, José da Cunha Brochado, remarked in a letter to a friend that such "liberality" was not advisable considering "the land [was] already full of chocolatiers and did not now need this poor recruitment."[64] The assertion is revealing considering that the term "chocolatiers" was likely a euphemism for Black people, betraying the perception that Africans were abundant in Lisbon.

Bullfights became not only more elaborate but also more common as Brazilian wealth flooded Lisbon and the pastime took on a popular and professional character. Designated bullfighting plazas with paid admission arose during the first half of the eighteenth century, and the roles of Africans shifted once more, from serving as mere preshow ornamentation to actors providing intermission spectacles or even as auxiliary participants.[65] The English merchant Thomas Cox remarked at the beginning of the eighteenth century that whenever there was a bullfight in the capital, Africans entered the ring and entertained the crowd with African music and dancing and "[fought] with armor such as they use[d] in their own country and [made] several odd postures."[66] Altogether, Africans became such an integral part of public entertainments during the period that rare was the occasion in which they did not participate.[67]

While enslaved Africans owned by the nobility and wealthy were used primarily as servants or for ostentation, enslaved individuals belonging to more modest households were often employed as *escravos de ganho*, or wage earners, in the city. These enslaved Africans soon came to dominate entire trades and monopolize specific tasks. African men were commonly seen carrying and selling baskets of fish or charcoal in the city markets. Women sold water and vegetables.[68] One French visitor in 1730 was astounded at the practice, exclaiming that in Lisbon, one sees many Black women whose masters "[put] them to work throughout the city, [and receive] as payment [their] wages." The account further explains that the enslaved individuals received a portion of their daily earnings to feed and clothe themselves and that after a few years they could purchase their freedom.[69]

A group of these *escravos de ganho* continually congregated on the steps of the hospital in the Rossio square to sell products and with their profits "pay their masters for their upkeep, [as well as that] of their husbands and children, and even [pay] for their confraternities and liberties."[70] Others were rented out for their labor or skills. The Englishman Henry Fielding rented an enslaved couple in 1754 for a pound sterling a week.[71] Lisbon's gazettes reveal a wealth of information concerning the artistic trades of Africans in the city as worried masters placed ads in these papers describing the skills of the enslaved who had fled, ranging from blacksmith and coach driver to cook and musician.[72] Enslaved Africans and freedmen were also needed on the docks of the Tagus and as members of the crews sailing the Atlantic due to the growing emigration of Portuguese men to Brazil during the goldrush.[73] The same occurred to a lesser degree in Portugal's second city, Porto.[74]

By the eighteenth century, Afro-Lisboans were used almost exclusively for certain jobs in the city such as whitewashing homes.[75] For a fee, African women carried human waste and other garbage to the river for disposal. Yet, despite the efforts of these women, large parts of the city continued to be filthy as many residents were unwilling or unable to pay to have their chamber pots emptied.[76] While resigned to this disgusting work, Black women did at times raise their voices. In 1717 after the city council attempted to enforce an income tax on the group, they marched to the royal palace in protest and delivered a petition to the queen and prince. They were aided by a nobleman who was perturbed that the women had not appeared at his home to provide their services. Three of the women with the best command of Portuguese presented the petition personally after the nobleman, a palace courtier for the queen, allowed them access. The queen and prince agreed and issued a mandate that the city council should not insist on the tax. Overjoyed with their victory, the women ran through the streets in large groups with their shawls made into flags. Some of the women were arrested after city officials deemed their celebration a riot.[77]

This episode is remarkable considering that women and Africans occupied lowly places in Lisbon's social hierarchy. Moreover, the fact that they were admitted by a nobleman into the presence of the queen and prince demonstrates acknowledgment by the highest organs of power of the vital role these women played in society. That the three best Portuguese speakers were chosen to present the group's case reveals the existence of a vibrant African culture and language in the capital despite declining overall numbers. This small episode speaks volumes about the determination and agency of Lisbon's African population in the face of widespread injustice.[78]

Even the city council came to recognize the crucial role of these women in the effective functioning of the city, and by 1744, decided to send gangs of them throughout the capital, including the neighborhoods farthest from the river where they usually did not appear, to clean the filth that was constantly piling up.[79] The employment of African women for sewage removal is further attested to by the *Folheto de Lisboa* in July 1740, which mentioned jocularly, "Yesterday a black woman near the cross of *Cata-que-farás* on her way to dump a vat of human waste at the beach, slipped into the container up to her shoulders, with her head, mouth, and eyes full of waste, which caused so much laughter among the commoners that it seemed like the day of a bullfight."[80]

These activities and trades led to greater contact among Africans and Lisbon's working class. At times the interactions extended beyond their labors. The city council noted in 1689 that "negroes" and the working classes were visiting the same taverns.[81] However, relations between the two groups were not always cordial. In 1703, the city council asked Pedro II to uphold the previous ban on enslaved persons becoming goldsmiths due to the "great inconveniences and loss that could result for the republic [if] the above-mentioned practice the office of goldsmith poorly, by reason of the great thefts, falsifications, and deceit that they could use in an office of such importance and credit."[82] It was an interesting complaint, considering that enslaved individuals were almost certainly taught by the goldsmiths themselves. During the period, many of the most severe laws regulating slavery in the city went largely unenforced or were forgotten altogether as the number of enslaved people declined overall. Still, prejudices behind such laws continued.[83]

Africans were also employed for more sinister purposes in Lisbon at the time. In 1699, the Capuchin friar François de Tours mentioned in particular that the Portuguese often had their enemies "killed by a black or a moor . . . and they perform[ed] these errands willingly for little money."[84] In 1731, the countess of Prado ordered her enslaved mulatto to kill her husband, the count. The mulatto revealed the plot to the authorities and was exiled to India. No action was taken against the countess.[85] The soldier Luís Álvares de Andrade e Cunha was executed in October 1734 for ordering his enslaved mulatto to murder his wife.[86]

Free and enslaved Africans of all stripes played a part in the general danger and disorder of Lisbon during the period as highlighted by excerpts from the *Folheto de Lisboa Occidental*. In August 1741, the paper reports on the continuous battles of "stone-throwing" between different neighborhoods and consisting of both Black and white men.[87] Besides killing individuals on occasion, the battles often got so out of hand that no one could pass through the neighborhoods in which they took place.[88] Danger was ever-present, and everyone went armed with swords in the city. For greater protection, the upper classes transformed their servants and enslaved individuals into personal bodyguards who themselves were armed despite repeated legislation against the practice.[89] Furthermore, the nobility themselves often participated alongside their enslaved Africans in criminal pursuits. The weekly *Mercúrio de Lisboa* announced in January 1747 that "seven thieves were

BLACK INFLUENCES IN ATLANTIC LISBON

arrested in the house of the curate of the church of Our Lady of Relief . . . and among them was a person of distinction with his mulatto."[90] Even Pedro II was often found running with gangs of mulattoes and engaging in street fights after nightfall.[91]

In the eyes of some, enslaved Africans were transformed by their increasing association with the aristocracy as many began to adopt the attitudes and demeanor of their masters. In 1687, the city council complained that Africans who served the upper classes were becoming insolent. Worse yet, by illegally carrying arms, these enslaved individuals were becoming a disturbance and causing fights.[92] These instances outraged the naturalized French Padre Raphael Bluteau, who in 1723 bemoaned that the city was overrun (according to his estimation) by both noble and Black criminals.[93]

The intimate details of the lives of Lisbon's enslaved population were varied and complex. Under ecclesiastical and civil law, they were allowed to marry, and masters were not to impede them.[94] While the Catholic Church encouraged the enslaved to marry, masters at the time largely opposed such unions, considering them a risk for a variety of reasons, including the fear that enslaved individuals who were married would be harder to sell in light of previous doctrinal clarifications from the archbishop of Lisbon prohibiting such abominable transactions. Marriage to a freed person only complicated matters, and many masters feared it would more easily open the doors to eventual manumission. An additional concern was the unwillingness of masters to give up sexual access to enslaved females.[95] Sexual access was easy considering most enslaved people lived in the master's home or in an adjoining annex, often sharing a bed with other enslaved persons of the same sex or sleeping on the floor.[96] Runaways from these conditions found refuge in the tortuous streets and alleyways of the city or congregated alongside freed persons who occupied the Mocambo neighborhood in the western parish of Santa Catarina.[97]

Some masters believed that marriages among enslaved individuals created a sense of independence and identity that threatened their authority.[98] Marriages, however, increased overall during the period. Parish records demonstrate that matrimony was most common among individuals who were both enslaved.[99] Marriage between freedmen or freedwomen and the enslaved, while it did occur, appeared to be less common.[100] Increasing rates of marriage during the period were tied to some degree to the general decline of the enslaved population. As a result, enslaved people in Lisbon were more likely to be second and third generation and thus were more integrated into the wider community despite the boost in importations during the first half of the eighteenth century.[101] As much as they were able, the enslaved formed families in the capital, and natural increase combined with the uptick in the slave trade to bolster the servile population in the eighteenth century.[102] Nonetheless, enslaved individuals were less likely to form official families than freedmen and freedwomen.[103]

Nonmarital relations were another matter and were common among people from all ranks of society. In 1683, a woman named Catarina Taboado was denounced by Domingos Soares for being *amançebada* (in concubinage) with the slave of Diogo Lopes Moreno.[104] A similar occurrence was recorded in 1707 when the slave Tomás Pereira was admonished to cease his relations with Maria de Fonçequa.[105] That same year, the widowed fisherman Manoel Botelho was chastised for his relations with the mulatta Leonor.[106] It was also commonly reported that Pedro II was particularly fond of African women, a passion his son João V apparently shared.[107] Pedro II's nocturnal liaisons even yielded mixed-race children, the majority of whom were sent to the colonies.[108]

Although Africans' white sexual partners were drawn from all social classes, these relations most often occurred among those on the margins of society.[109] Marriages between white and Black people, while rare, did occur. The Italian Baretti declared, "These cross-marriages have filled the country with different breeds of human monsters . . . to such a degree [that] the original breed is here depraved."[110] He continued, "These strange combinations have filled this town with such a variety of odd faces, as to make the traveler doubt whether Lisbon is in Europe."[111] These assertions of Lisbon's African nature were shared by many a foreign visitor to the Portuguese capital.

In a baroque society obsessed with social status, *limpeza de sangue* (blood purity) became even more important in the face of increased intermixing. As such, to call someone a mulatto was considered as offensive as it was to brand someone a Jew, and pretending to sneeze at Black people in the streets as they passed became a common insult.[112] Various foreigners in Lisbon noted that if the Portuguese wanted to convey that they were men of honor, they declared they were *branco*, or white.[113] These developments resulted from changing social perceptions of Africans rather than their actual behavior. Thus, as the African population declined overall and became more integrated in comparison to previous centuries, overt social fears among the upper classes over religious and cultural differences were progressively joined by concerns about racialization and intermixing.

Changing perceptions led to an evolution of racial qualifications for social advancement as the previous notion of blood purity based on Jewish or Moorish mixing was compounded by a focus on African contamination.[114]

Thus the growing integration, or Iberianization, of the African population in Lisbon merged with the intensification of African slavery throughout the Atlantic world during the period to make mulattoes and others of African descent suspect.[115] For example, the stain of being a mulatto was such that mixed-race men were often not permitted to serve as bailiffs of the Inquisition because of social anxieties rather than religious concerns.[116] The Catholic brotherhood of *Nosso Senhor dos Passos* in 1708 allowed individuals both male and female from the noble and trade classes to join with the exception of those who were Jewish, Moorish, or African.[117] Pedro II mandated in 1671 that because individuals with impure blood were serving in public offices, there would be a renewed investigation into everyone before they obtained any office so as to determine whether they "[were] part New Christian, Moor, or mulatto."[118]

Although the social stigma placed on mulattoes by blood-purity requirements appears to have been based on race, in reality it was a system built on descent and belief that African blood was associated with servility and dubious conversion to Christianity, which were linked to a host of undesirable traits, including rebelliousness and vice. In essence, mulattoes were not categorized as lacking in blood purity because of their race per se but rather were thought to lack the social qualities necessary to hold public office, military commanderies, and other positions of social prestige.[119] Despite the increasing stigma, however, mulattoes in Lisbon had a greater chance of social advancement compared to freed Black people and enslaved Africans in the city during the period, especially if they were lucky enough to have a wealthy white father and a history of service to the Crown.[120] Such was the case with André Ferreira da Costa, who was the bastard son of a sergeant-major and his enslaved mulatta. Even in the face of these obstacles, Ferreira da Costa had no difficulties securing his knighthood in the Order of Christ in 1710.[121] The perceived social threat of *mestiçagem* (racial mixing) grew during the period and reached its zenith under the reign of João V, precisely at a time when Lisbon's African population was becoming more Iberianized and established in the city.[122]

African Agency and Action

Increasing social exclusion was merely one effect of the Atlanticization of Lisbon's African community. An equally concerning development was the growing possibility of being sent from the capital to the mines and plantations of Brazil as the slave trade convincingly shifted toward that colony. One of the main defenses against both obstacles was to join a Black confraternity or brotherhood. For Africans, these organizations provided both protection and sociability in an increasingly exclusive society.[123] Black brotherhoods therefore effectively doubled in Lisbon between the last decade of the seventeenth century and the first two decades of the eighteenth, totaling eight by that time.[124] By comparison, Porto had one, or possibly two, Black brotherhoods and another for the surrounding regions just beyond the city.[125] Further afield, Seville had only a single Black brotherhood that survived past the middle of the seventeenth century.[126] The same was true for Cádiz.[127] Salvador de Bahia, at the beginning of the eighteenth century, had six Black Rosary brotherhoods with an additional five composed entirely of mulattoes, not to mention others under different patronage.[128] Another reason behind the rapid expansion of Black brotherhoods in Lisbon was the slight rise in slave imports discussed previously during the first decades of the eighteenth century and the reluctance of some established Black confraternities to accept new arrivals from different African *nações*, or ethnicities.[129]

Catholic confraternities in general in the Portuguese Atlantic were often formed around a specific social caste, descent group, or occupation but also could be open to all, including women. Their main pillar was mutual assistance in times of sickness, captivity, poverty, and death.[130] Wives and legitimate children also enjoyed benefits.[131] Brotherhoods paid the burial expenses of needy members, which for an enslaved person in 1700 could cost upward of 500 *réis*.[132] These, along with sociability, were the attractions for Africans in Lisbon. Additionally, there is some evidence that Africans favored certain organizations due to the parallel attributes of the brotherhood's patron saint and a particular African deity.[133] Furthermore, the corporate nature of confraternities elevated the voices of their members in the ears of judicial authorities or the Crown, meaning they often received the right to petition.[134] Enslaved people and freedmen who were not members of a confraternity were otherwise left to plead their case before the monarch in one of his weekly public audiences.[135]

The vast majority of Black confraternities in the Portuguese Atlantic world were formed under the patronage of Our Lady of the Rosary.[136] Rosary confraternities in theory accepted any Christian, male or female, regardless of social station.[137] Africans also might have been attracted to the Rosary confraternities because these organizations placed no limit on the number of *confrades*, and the weekly recitation of the Rosary (150 *Ave Marias* and 15 *Pater Nosters*, which could be divided into thirds, or *terços*) was the main responsibility of members.[138] Lisbon's first Black Rosary brotherhood was initially founded in the mid-fifteenth century. White people were eventually allowed to join. As a mixed organization, conflicts arose and Black members attempted to form their own separate organization.[139] However, the creation and expansion of Black brotherhoods in the capital was also the result of population changes.[140] Other mixed confraternities developed, and enjoyed substantial participation from Black, mulatto, and white people in the capital. On one specific occasion, a brotherhood was formed by white people in Lisbon under the title *Homens Pretos* (Black men) due to its mixed membership.[141] Black people joining mixed confraternities is further proof of the internal divisions within the Black community in Lisbon as new arrivals were not always so easily absorbed.[142] While the records are not clear, Lisbon may or may not have had a single confraternity for mulattoes during the period despite their large presence in the city. The only specific reference to such an organization appeared previously in 1613.[143] By contrast, there was a mulatto brotherhood in Porto during the period.[144] Spanish Cádiz had a single brotherhood for mulattoes that disappeared by 1675.[145] In Rio de Janeiro, Brazil, however, several mulatto brotherhoods existed.[146]

Each confraternity was governed by *compromissos*, or statutes, recognized by either the Crown or an ecclesiastical authority. Black confraternities in Lisbon for the most part had two types of membership. Members of the first type were mere *confrades* who could elect members to certain positions within the confraternity but largely could not be elected themselves. *Irmãos*, or brothers, on the other hand, could vote and hold office. The separation between the two was largely based on social status as the enslaved were routinely excluded from becoming brothers and holding offices due to the perception by freedmen of their dishonest and disorderly nature.[147] A surviving book of *compromissos* from the Irmandade de Nossa Senhora do Rosário dos Homens Pretos in 1565 provides a glimpse of what limitations existed for enslaved people in Lisbon's confraternities during the period under study. It states that "no captive slave [could] be an official or have control in the confraternity."[148] Other Black confraternities allowed enslaved individuals to hold positions, but this was a rare occurrence given fears that they might use funds to secure their own freedom or concerns over the possibility that they might be sold at any time. All Black confraternities allowed equal place and benefits to wives, and some even allowed them to hold offices.[149] Not all Black brotherhoods and confraternities, however, were composed entirely of Africans; some allowed white people to join.[150] Yet even these organizations comprised mostly Black members. The Black brotherhoods and confraternities of colonial Brazil, in contrast, were often completely separated by color.[151]

Of the various offices in the brotherhood, the treasurer was responsible for collected funds; the secretary maintained the entry books, voting roles, accounting, and statutes of the confraternity; and the *procurador* begged alms in the street, called brothers to meetings, and cared for the chapel. The judge was in charge of disputes between members and managed other affairs of the confraternity.[152] This last office was at times honorific and held by respected persons. For example, D. Manuel, brother to King João V, was judge of the Black confraternity of Nossa Senhora do Rosário Resgatada in 1714.[153] Black brotherhoods in Lisbon almost always chose someone of high status as their protector, possibly a noble or member of the royal family.[154]

Another responsibility of the members of various confraternities was electing kings and queens to represent the organization in Lisbon's important religious processions.[155] Similar to what occurred in colonial Brazil, as Black confraternities grew in number some eventually developed into representative institutions for Africans from a given ethnic background, or *nação*.[156] By the eighteenth century, Lisbon had a confraternity representing individuals from Angola and another for those from Mina.[157]

In Lisbon, Black brotherhoods maintained individual chapels in churches or convents; by comparison, Rio de Janeiro had two churches owned by Black brotherhoods in 1740.[158] While established as a separate place for Africans, Black brotherhoods in Lisbon often still relied on white people for the functioning of the confraternity. The offices of scribe and treasurer were largely exercised by white males due to the requirements of these positions, which demanded levels of proficiency in reading and writing that the majority of the African population in the capital lacked.[159] The same Irmandade de Nossa Senhora do Rosário dos Homens Pretos discussed previously required in 1565 that their scribe be "white, noble, and respectable."[160]

The lives of members of Lisbon's Black confraternities and brotherhoods were transformed as royal recognition became common during the last quarter of the seventeenth century.[161] Didier Lahon, one of the leading scholars on the topic, and others have argued that recognition came precisely when the importation of enslaved Africans to the capital began increasing in 1680.[162] Yet, as discussed previously, demographic data shows a clear decline in the enslaved population at the end of the seventeenth century. The fact that already extant Black brotherhoods were officially recognized is not, therefore, a sign of a growth in population. Rather, it is a sign of increasing Iberianization and diversification. Yet Lahon is certainly correct in arguing that some of the expansion was due to an uptick in importations.

Beginning in 1688, Pedro II renewed many of the privileges previously enjoyed by Black confraternities in the city and decreed that they had the right to purchase enslaved members who were to be sold to Brazil, where they fetched a higher price.[163] The privilege came about as the brotherhoods complained that such sales were seriously impinging on the functioning and devotion of their organizations.[164] The brothers further argued that when they had tried to purchase members, masters asked exorbitant prices. For example, in 1738 a *negro bruto* (a newly arrived individual who spoke a different language) from the west African region of Cacheu was sold in the city for 79,200 *réis*, or sixteen and a half gold coins.[165] Pedro II then ruled that the confraternities would be able to buy enslaved members after a "just evaluation" of their price had been carried out by an independent assessor.[166] In effect, between 1688 and 1714, six established brotherhoods enjoyed these privileges to varying degrees, while two additional brotherhoods established later did not.[167] Black brotherhoods in Spain, Brazil, and Spanish America obtained similar concessions, but only in the Portuguese metropole were some organizations allowed for a short time to purchase enslaved individuals from masters in cases of proven abuse.[168] This privilege disappeared quickly in Lisbon, but the right to purchase an enslaved member destined for sale in Brazil was consistently renewed.[169]

The ban on sales was viewed as the most valuable privilege, given that the common (and most feared) punishment for the enslaved who proved recalcitrant during the period was the threat of sale to Brazil.[170] To facilitate purchases, both Pedro II and João V consistently granted royal permission for brotherhoods to ask alms in the city streets. These funds made up a considerable portion of the annual revenue of the brotherhoods in Lisbon, but they were not their only income.[171] In 1742, for example, João V renewed the 1518 privilege of collecting 500 *réis* on every caravel returning from the Mina coast for the Irmandade de Nossa Senhora do Rosário dos Homens Pretos based in the Dominican church of Salvador in Lisbon.[172] Additional cash flows came from annual membership dues, which financial obligations made necessary.[173] The membership fees ranged, but one brotherhood in 1745 required an annual payment of 240 *réis*.[174] To give an idea of the purchasing power of 240 *réis*, in 1688 roughly one pound of tobacco (one *arratel*) in the city cost 70 *réis*.[175] João V had prints of his 1749 pragmatic law sold for the price of 240 *réis* throughout the city.[176]

Some confraternities received generous endowments. The Black confraternity of Jesus, Maria, José dos Homens Pretos was protected by João V, who was also named perpetual judge and donated 10,000 *réis* annually to the organization.[177] The monarch's queen, Maria Anna of Austria, also gave generous annual contributions.[178] The brotherhood itself had more than two thousand members of both sexes and enjoyed an annual income of an estimated 500,000 *réis*.[179] Other brotherhoods discovered additional revenue streams in Brazil, particularly by the eighteenth century, as Black confraternities of the same invocation in the colony sent gold remittances to Lisbon.[180] Altogether, funds spent purchasing the liberty of enslaved members were regularly recouped as those individuals were then beholden to the confraternity until they had paid back their debt in full.[181]

Pedro II's concern for Africans in the capital went beyond those who were members of a confraternity. He was personally unhappy about the expanding trade and issued a decree attempting to ameliorate conditions for captives on Portuguese slave vessels.[182] His confessor Padre Sebastião de Magalhães extolled the monarch's efforts, given that he had purchased and freed a number of enslaved Black people throughout his reign. According to the Jesuit, the result of such royal favor was that a countless number of Africans complained to the king about their masters and that "his majesty [sent] these petitions to the *corregidor* of the court . . . who, with great Christian piety, [examined] their complaints, and finding those that [were] just, he [remedied] them. Those that [were] not just he [made] peace between them and their masters."[183] Perhaps Pedro II's most lasting impact on the enslaved community came at his death, whereupon he freed all his slaves. This act alone set a strong social precedent that became popular during the reign of his son, João V.[184]

While the privileges of Black confraternities reached a high point under Pedro II, they began to decline during the reign of the "Magnanimous" João V. After about 1740, the monarch became less and less likely to renew these privileges, particularly the ban on selling enslaved Africans to Brazil.[185] One official remembered that João V eventually came to view these privileges negatively.[186] This attitude carried into the reign of José I, and by the 1750s, there were calls for that monarch not to extend the same privileges granted to those of the Rosary of Salvador because such favors impeded slaves from being transported to Brazil where they were in high demand. Some complained that the privilege led to a growing number of Black people in Portugal who were "very harmful" because they lived "without masters."[187] Thus, the growing hesitation of João V to renew privileges of Black confraternities very much coincided with the expansion of mining and the revitalization of Brazilian plantation exports at a time when concerns over racialization and the Black presence were steadily increasing.

Not everyone was able, or allowed, to join a Black confraternity in Lisbon. The financial requirement that developed no doubt made membership difficult for many of the enslaved who lacked disposable income. Others were impeded by masters who correctly perceived these organizations as a potential threat to their control. As the case of Grácia Luzia demonstrated at the opening of this chapter, individuals who for these or other reasons were not able to join devised other channels of achieving some of the same desired outcomes secured by Black religious organizations. Others, like the mulatto cook that Francisco Pinheiro wanted to send to Brazil, simply fled before they could be embarked.[188] Clearly, it is inaccurate to paint Africans solely as passive victims who were helplessly pushed and pulled by Atlantic influences in the Portuguese capital. Rather, they became not only inventive resisters to the greater changes affecting their lives but also active participants in some of these processes as they owned a bit of their religious experience via Black brotherhoods.

African Cultural Influence in the Metropole

An Atlantic perspective on Lisbon's African community further enlightens our understanding of the city's history as it uncovers various cultural contributions of Africans during the period. Africans were actively involved in developing Lisbon's unique and exotic nature at the time. From at least the seventeenth century on, Africans began to exercise significant influence on popular culture in Lisbon. That influence only continued during the first part of the eighteenth century as more enslaved Africans arrived via Brazil. Afro-Brazilian influences in the Portuguese capital were felt in a variety of ways but were most significant in popular entertainments.[189] Music and musical tastes in Lisbon were particularly affected by Afro-Brazilian styles and instruments that increasingly penetrated the city during the period.[190] Africans in Lisbon were excellent musicians in their own right. Not only did they master their own instruments, but they were proficient in European ones as well.

Lisbon in the era of baroque ostentation and increasing luxury saw the employment of enslaved Africans as musicians for the aristocracy. The Count of Ericeira asked Francisco Pinheiro to sell an enslaved African of his in Brazil who was "a good trumpet player."[191] African musicians were also highly visible in public spectacles, often playing horns and other instruments at bullfights.[192] At the beginning of the eighteenth century, the Englishman Dr. Cox Macro recorded that Black musicians often played the music for religious processions and popular festivals.[193] Afro-Brazilian instruments also became conspicuous in the public square. One observer highlighted their presence alongside Portuguese instruments at a popular religious festival in 1730.[194] Dr. Macro described the nature and origin of some of these instruments which resembled a type of marimba: "Several Blacks played upon an instrument made of a sort of pumpkin and there are little pieces of board, about a foot long and about an inch broad, laid over the pumpkin; on which has one end cut off and by striking with two little sticks upon the boards they made an odd noise which is very soft; these instruments come ready made from Angola." The whole scene as described by the Englishman was attended by a multitude of people who had come to see the Africans play and dance.[195]

In 1730, the gazette *Folheto de Ambas Lisboas* mentioned the immense popularity in the central neighborhood of Alfama of a certain style of Afro-Brazilian dance known as the *fofa*. The dance became popular among Lisbon's lower classes as enslaved Afro-Brazilians began arriving in greater numbers at the beginning of the eighteenth century. The mention of the *fofa* in a city publication clearly signifies that the dance was performed in Lisbon's streets well before 1730. The dance had become so popular that some foreigners actually mistook it for a native dance of Portugal.[196] One went so far as to label it the national dance of the Portuguese.[197] All recalled the fondness for the dance among the popular classes due to its suggestive style.[198] Such declarations demonstrate the impact of Lisbon's Afro-descendants on popular culture and clearly reinforce the idea of increasing integration. Other Afro-Brazilian dances, like the *gandu*, arrived during the same period.[199] The *cumbé* was danced by Africans in 1730 in celebration of the feast of Our Lady of the Rosary, and there were warnings against Portuguese women dancing the African *sarambeque*.[200] A Portuguese source described the Atlantic influence on popular dance in poetry:

> From Brazil in procession
> The sounds arrive barefoot,
> Breed there, they grow up there,
> And from there they pass
> Gradually to the *chulas* [lower-class women],
> Step by step to the mulattoes.[201]

In essence, as Afro-Brazilian dances arrived in the city, they mingled with native cultural elements and spread rapidly not only among mixed-race individuals but also the popular classes.[202]

Not everyone in the city welcomed African musical and artistic influences. In 1730, just outside of Lisbon, a bystander who witnessed a musical celebration by a group of Black people prayed, "God free us from these."[203] Charles Frédéric de Merveilleux mentioned the dances as part of a bullfight in the 1720s, noting, "Two black kings appeared with their courts of black men and women who danced for quite some time those lascivious and infamous dances that everyone knows, and which annoy me. The Portuguese, however, were enthusiastic."[204] For the Africans themselves, the dances were much more than simplistic entertainments; they were meant as a transmitter to teach younger captive Africans something about their culture.[205] For the Portuguese, they were a means of escaping the hardships of life and the impediments of an increasingly exacting religion. Some of the dances were outlawed, but others continued.[206] As such, the dances in some ways were a means of resistance for even the Portuguese. Popular dances thus became a powerful example of how Lisbon was becoming more and more African.

The dances were performed everywhere, it seemed, including religious processions with Black confraternities being regular participants. The confraternities of different African "nations" contributed to the dissemination of musical and artistic influences as they danced, sang, and played in the city streets. In 1730, the elected king of the confraternity representing the Angolan nation in Lisbon sent a letter to the king of the Mina confraternity inviting him and his people to dance in the celebration of Our Lady of the Rosary.[207] As historian James Sweet has argued, the letter contained in the previously mentioned *Folheto de Ambas Lisboas* was more than likely composed by a Portuguese person rather than an African. The fact that the publication is written in the style of speech known in Lisbon as the *lingua de negro* (Black tongue) demonstrates that African ideas and culture had permeated Lisbon, even among the literate and learned, once again reflecting just how African Lisbon had become. Sweet further notes that Afro-Brazilian influences in the city even reached the royal family, who endorsed Black religious celebrations in a variety of ways. As recorded in the royal gazette, King João V and his queen appeared at the feast of the Black confraternity of Nossa Senhora de Guadalupe in 1744. This appearance, according to Sweet, "[signaled] the king's embrace of African Catholicism to his mostly white metropolitan subjects . . . [and] in this way an absolutist crown sometimes served as both master and protector of African interests in the heart of the metropole."[208] Altogether, the extent of Afro-Brazilian cultural influence in the capital was such during the period that José Ramos

Tinhorão has rightly asserted that the baroque period in Lisbon should not be considered as a time when only French styles were all the rage and on the rise but African ones as well.[209]

Examining the lives and experiences of Lisbon's African population of enslaved people, freedmen, and mulattoes through an Atlantic perspective reveals their considerable role in transforming the sociocultural and racial fabric of a major European capital. The heightened focus on Brazil and the consequent shift in the Atlantic slave trade away from Lisbon had profound impacts as for the first time in the city's history enslaved Africans came predominantly from Brazil rather than Africa. There were further reverberations as the numbers of captives originating from the Mina coast grew rapidly in Lisbon due to preferences among slave owners in Brazil. Together, these alterations had a profound impact on Lisbon's popular culture as new practices were introduced.

However, the diversion of slave traffic and declining arrivals overall meant that Lisbon's African population during the period was increasingly sustained by natural reproduction within Portugal. This process of Iberianization also meant a degree of physical and cultural intermixing among the lower classes precisely at a time when new arrivals from Brazil were introducing novel influences in Lisbon. Afro-Lisboans, both bound and free, were themselves profoundly impacted by these processes as their role within society began to change as the baroque became fashionable, the threat of sale to Brazil exploded, and intermixing led to the intensification of racial prejudice.

Individuals actively developed methods to combat these effects of Atlanticization and exercise some control over their own lives. Many turned to Black religious brotherhoods and confraternities for relief. These organizations shielded the enslaved from sale to Brazil and provided freedmen a valuable social avenue. In some ways, they were also a means of asserting the adoption of Iberian culture among the city's African residents. The relationship established between these organizations and the structures of power vacillated as Atlantic developments initially led to the granting of generous privileges as well as their withdrawal. However, the fact that Black confraternities effectively doubled during the period is a further testament to the long reach of Lisbon's Atlanticization during the period and the active role of Afro-Lisboans in that process.

Overall, Lisbon's African population left a deep and abiding imprint on the capital. The complex interplay between Atlanticization and Iberianization among this group led to many of the sociocultural changes that utterly transformed the heart of empire and made Lisbon strikingly different from other European metropoles of the day. Understanding all this, one may rightfully argue that in some sense Baretti was right. Lisbon was not necessarily European. It was Atlantic.

2

THE ENGLISH IN ATLANTIC LISBON

English merchant ships were a common sight in Lisbon's harbor. Most came and went without incident. On occasion, however, English vessels and their crew became embroiled in conflicts with the Portuguese authorities and populace. Often violent, these occurrences quickly developed into diplomatic skirmishes between the two Atlantic kingdoms as each endeavored to make their historic, yet uneasy, alliance more advantageous. One such episode occurred in the summer of 1749 when a certain Captain Stepney was apprehended in Lisbon by Portuguese authorities after resisting a search of his warship for fugitive slaves from the city. Shockingly, the arrest was ordered by the Portuguese judge conservator of the English nation—a position secured by treaty to ensure the protection of English citizens in Portugal.

The whole fiasco caused such an international stir that the secretary of state for the Southern Department, the Duke of Bedford, presented the affair to King George II himself. Bedford then relayed the monarch's instructions on the matter to the English consul and envoy-extraordinaire in Lisbon, Abraham Castres. Those instructions warned Castres of the seriousness of the incident and reminded him that "the insult of arresting his Majesty's officer for slaves having taken refuge aboard the King's ship is of so serious a nature and so derogatory to the Law of Nations, and the King our Master's honor, that it is His pleasure you should make the strongest remonstrances thereupon to the Portuguese minister." The demands were that the judge conservator be removed and that in no cases should English ships "be searched either for fugitives, or upon any other account whatsoever."[1] After a period of deadlock, English pressure finally secured the dismissal of the judge, but only on the grounds of having lost the confidence of the group of organized merchants known as the English factory who financially supported him—not for his actions in regard to Captain Stepney.[2] Despite the uproar, the English continued to harbor fugitive slaves.[3]

The Stepney affair is merely one example of Portuguese attempts to curtail the extraordinary treaty privileges granted to the English during the period and the resulting consequences in Lisbon. Those attempts and the resultant conflicts form the backbone of this chapter. The privileges enjoyed by the English in Lisbon first arose in consequence of Portugal's increasing dependence on Brazil and the Atlantic during the previous restoration period (1640–68). The need for a powerful ally who could defend Portugal and its Atlantic interests from both Spanish reprisal and Dutch expansion was the driving force behind a series of lopsided treaties between the two countries. The effect of such high-handed concessions was a developing English ascendancy in Lisbon over other trading nations precisely at a time when Brazilian wealth began to pour into the city at the end of the seventeenth century. While Lisbon already relied on the Brazil trade, the discovery of gold and diamonds made that commerce an equally important focus for the English merchants in the city who benefited greatly. While the Portuguese did much to limit the privileges of the English, those gains were largely wiped out at the outbreak of the War of the Spanish Succession with the signing of the Methuen Treaty in 1703, which saw Portugal receive English military aid in return for additional economic privileges.

Previous scholars interested in Portugal's Atlantic turn have rightly highlighted the increased focus on Brazil and its imperial consequences. Others have even studied the growing reliance on England as a result. However, within this context, the developing vital role of Lisbon for both the English and the Portuguese and the contentious relationship that resulted remain largely unexamined. Thus, studying the Atlanticization of Lisbon provides a better understanding of the Anglo-Portuguese relationship. In short, Lisbon became a crossroads where much of the benefit of the renewed Portuguese empire in the South Atlantic flowed north and the convergence of Atlantic interests created a situation in which tensions flared and confrontation became commonplace among otherwise allies.

The English Commercial Rise

Lisbon after the restoration was a city with a large number of foreigners as Portugal's imperial shift included a greater reliance on the nations of the North Atlantic. In 1721, the Portuguese friar Agostinho de Santa Maria described the cosmopolitan feel of the capital and declared, "Truly the city of Lisbon is the common homeland of all foreigners . . . because those who enter her forget so much of their former lands, that they elect to stay perpetually."[4] While the Portuguese eventually secured treaties with the French, Dutch, and Spanish, it was the renewed alliance with England that helped preserve the empire in the South Atlantic and proved most transformative for society in Lisbon. English merchants, officials, and sailors all made their way to the city in ever-greater numbers (particularly after the discovery of Brazilian gold) to take advantage of Portuguese economic weakness coming out of the seventeenth century and to engage in the lucrative Brazil trade. The period was marked not only by the growing commercial dominance of the English, who eventually managed to outpace even the Dutch, but also by the decline of French interests in Lisbon.[5] Shipping statistics from the first decades of the eighteenth century bear this out, when it was estimated that by 1732 almost 75 percent of Lisbon's port traffic was English![6] Arguably, one of the major effects of the Atlanticization of Lisbon was the increasing arrival and ascendancy of the English.

Notwithstanding Portugal's official alliance with England since 1386, the Anglo-Portuguese relationship broke down during Portugal's sixty-year union with Spain.[7] The partnership was revived during the restoration war through various treaties as Portugal sought allies in its twenty-eight-year struggle for independence. Indeed, along with assistance from the French, English military aid proved vital in securing Portuguese freedom from Habsburg rule in 1668. The Duke of Bragança, and eventual king of Portugal, D. João IV (1640–56) first secured a peace treaty with Charles I of England in 1642.[8] The need to solidify the agreement increased after the English Civil Wars deposed Charles I in 1649 in favor of Oliver Cromwell and the English Commonwealth. Diplomatically pinned, João IV grudgingly agreed to a heavy-handed commercial treaty with Cromwell in 1654 after he had unwisely supported the failed royalist cause.[9] The 1654 treaty, as one historian described it, "set the pattern of the alliance for the next hundred years [and] can fairly be described as a diktat."[10] And as late as 1726, a Portuguese nobleman described the treaty as "the most pernicious ever made with a crowned head."[11]

The treaty granted the English several privileges, including the right to a judge conservator, freedom from imprisonment unless caught in flagrant crime, and freedom of conscience. The guarantee of religious freedom allowed for individual worship in the home, a cemetery in the city, and protection from inquisitorial harassment. By the so-called secret article, the customs ceiling on English imports was set at a maximum of 23 percent ad valorem (proportionate tax according to the estimated value of the goods), while traders from other nations were forced to pay 26 percent.[12] The English ambassador in 1752 stated that under such terms, English merchants in Lisbon "allow that our evaluations are so underrated that we do not [really] pay above fourteen percent, on any of the material articles."[13]

In addition, there was always the common use of corruption and force. One Frenchman described this practice and asserted that in Lisbon "tis easy to evade the customs, if one has a right understanding with the guards, who are a parcel of knaves that the sound of a pistol will make as flexible as you can wish."[14] Still, the English envoy in Lisbon, when speaking of the commercial advantages of the treaty overall, stated in 1683, "It cannot be denied but that several things in the treaty [of 1654] were obtained with a high hand, and that his majesty's subjects enjoy in some particulars rather greater privileges than the natives, which with some reason may make them uneasy."[15]

Further concessions were granted under the subsequent marriage treaty of 1661 by which Charles II (restored to the English throne only a year earlier) agreed to marry João IV's daughter Catarina in exchange for a considerable dowry of 2 million Portuguese *cruzados*, the cession of the North African outpost of Tangier, and the Indian base at Bombay, all of which made it the largest dowry in Europe to that date.[16] The acquisition of Tangier helped secure English domination in the Mediterranean, and the possession of Bombay effectively opened up eastern trade.[17] In addition to upholding all the privileges of the 1654 treaty, the marriage treaty allowed four English merchants to settle in each of the Brazilian ports of Pernambuco, Rio de Janeiro, and Bahia. Allowing foreigners into the Brazil trade solidified the growing reliance on foreign manufactures as metropolitan production proved inadequate to supply the growing colonial market. This allowance effectively transformed the Portuguese South Atlantic economy from a triangular trade into a quadrangular network in which the benefits of empire increasingly flowed to London rather than Lisbon.[18] These generous privileges were more than enough for Charles II to agree to anchor an English fleet in the Tagus to defend the Brazil trade and protect the interests of Portugal.[19] The guarantee of diplomatic and military aid at home and abroad in exchange for commercial privileges secured Portuguese acceptance of these treaties. The calculations paid off as English efforts brought both the Dutch and Spanish to the table, effectively ending the conflicts of the restoration.[20]

Regarding the French, as a result of their own war with Spain at the beginning of the restoration, they saw in Portugal an ally that would divide Habsburg forces. Even after signing the Treaty of the Pyrenees in 1659, which allowed Spain to fully focus on retaking Portugal, French interest in the restoration cause persisted. By continuing the fight, the Portuguese kept Spain in check for the French and the two nations signed a treaty in 1667 agreeing to continue hostilities despite English attempts to bring the war to a close.[21] The advantages of the conflict for the French were such that they backed Pedro II's seizure of his feeble brother Afonso VI's throne (and his French bride) in 1667 after the latter had attempted to end the war.[22] The plan failed as the Portuguese *côrtes*, or parliament, forced Pedro II, now ruling as prince regent, to end the struggle with Spain.[23] Thus, from the restoration until the War of the Spanish Succession, Franco-Portuguese relations dramatically declined while those with England only intensified.[24] As one scholar has put it, for the Portuguese, a "weakened Spain was no longer as dangerous as an overly powerful France."[25]

The French position in Lisbon continued to deteriorate as result of internal issues. The French factory, already declining at the end of the seventeenth century, was dealt a crushing blow by Louis XIV's 1685 Edict of Fontainebleau declaring Protestantism illegal. Many Huguenots then sought naturalization and protection as English or Dutch citizens and began trading under those nations. Such a loss was highlighted by the French ambassador the Marquis of Saint-Romain, who declared that the Huguenots in Lisbon made up "most of our good merchants."[26] Furthermore, the French, of all the foreign groups in Lisbon, were among the most inclined to intermarry in the capital and many became naturalized Portuguese citizens. These unions had commercial benefits, as naturalized Frenchmen claimed freedom from certain taxes imposed on other French merchants in the absence of a commercial treaty. The continual loss of French merchants to Portuguese naturalization hindered the functioning of the factory as they often refused to pay certain duties. To make matters worse, a French decree of 1716 excluded children of mixed marriages from enjoying the rights and privileges of the French nation, which led to further decline as an increasing number of commercial firms were passed to sons from those mixed marriages and, therefore, fell outside of the bounds of the French factory. The French ambassador Mornay noted in 1717 that under such a ruling, out of seven hundred merchants in

Lisbon only thirty would qualify for French privileges. The effect of the decree on French commerce was far-reaching. As late as 1746, consul François Du Vernay was complaining that the ordinance had become a "great obstacle to the augmentation of the French nation in Portugal and to our commerce" and, while intended to protect French interests, "[the ordinance] produced the contrary effect."[27]

Despite reaching a peace with João IV in 1642 concerning their conflict in Europe, the Luso-Dutch struggles continued to play out in the Atlantic and Asia. Peace would come in 1661 when the Dutch secured many of the same commercial privileges (such as the establishment of merchant families in the main ports of Brazil) as the English as well as an indemnity payment of 4 million *cruzados*—500,000 of which was to be levied in Brazil.[28] In a final shift toward Atlantic imperial interests over global pretensions, the Portuguese also forfeited any claim to territories taken by the Dutch in the East in exchange for formal recognition of the Portuguese reconquest of Dutch holdings in Brazil only a few years earlier.[29] These, and other, privileges were reaffirmed in 1669.[30]

Even though the Dutch secured some advantageous commercial liberties akin to those the English enjoyed, the English factory eventually surpassed that of the Dutch and others in Lisbon by the beginning of the eighteenth century, expanding in size and commercial importance.[31] The reason behind English commercial dominance in Lisbon, according to a Swiss visitor in 1730, was that the English "enjoy privileges that no other nation does. It is estimated that in one year more English ships enter the Tagus than those of the Portuguese and the other nations combined."[32]

Besides their own extraordinary privileges, the English nation in Lisbon further benefited from the fact that France never secured a commercial treaty with Portugal, the Hamburghers had no powerful state behind them, and the Dutch were never well liked due to their imperial conquests at Portuguese expense.[33] Repeated conflicts with Spain along with a competing export economy all but eliminated Spanish merchants from Lisbon after the restoration period.[34] The era has therefore been described as "the zenith of the English ascendancy over Portugal."[35] Notwithstanding their privileges, the English in Lisbon were subject to continuous attempts to scale back their liberties as a deepening reliance led many Portuguese to conclude that "all trade carried on by foreigners is of the utmost prejudice to this country."[36] Or, as one contemporary put it, "Where now is the ancient honor and truth of the Portuguese nation, that we have become favorers of strangers, of the English, the worst and the most insolent of all strangers?"[37]

Lisbon's Atlantic Dependency

The concessions to foreign powers reflected the new imperial focus on the South Atlantic for the Portuguese after the restoration. The cession of Bombay and Tangier, along with recognition of Dutch power in the decaying Estado da Índia, in many ways marked the end of the old global empire. That Brazil and the Atlantic had become the de facto post-restoration focus was further reinforced in Lisbon as an economic depression took hold by the 1670s due to English, French, and Dutch efforts to ban or discourage Brazilian tropical exports in their own countries as a means of stimulating production from the Caribbean and North America. In 1689 the Englishman Edward Littleton summed up the economic drain from Brazilian reexports in England: "Heretofore we had all our sugars from Portugal: and it is computed, that they cost us yearly about four hundred thousand pounds. Now that great leak is stopped: and we hardly buy any Portugal or Brazil sugars, being plentifully supplied by our own plantations."[38] The effects in Lisbon were devastating.

As reexports from Lisbon plummeted due to market closures in Europe, prices in the Portuguese capital for Brazilian goods tumbled as commodities piled up and supply outpaced demand.[39] Tobacco, for example, suffered a price free-fall of 65 percent on the Lisbon market between 1650 and 1688.[40] Just as Portuguese colonial reexports were declining in Lisbon, the incursion of foreign traders and merchandise was increasing.[41] As these economic developments in the Atlantic continued to cripple society in Lisbon, the Portuguese dug in their heels and attempted to whittle away costly foreign privileges in the city with particular regard to the Brazil trade, which envoy Charles Fanshaw described as "the apple of their eye, it being the only navigation left them, which they think strangers would wholly carry from them."[42] Frustration only grew as the English and, to a lesser extent, other nations came to dominate trade with Lisbon and Brazil through the importation of foodstuffs and manufactures.[43]

Worsening trade imbalances led to a short-lived effort to curtail foreign imports with protective legislation and the beginning of a domestic manufacturing program (discussed in chapter 4). These attempts damaged English trade in Lisbon and all but destroyed that of the French. Fear of even stricter measures led the English to insist on a new commercial treaty, which became a necessity after the eruption of the War of the Spanish Succession during the first decade of the eighteenth century. However, the Anglo-Dutch failure to provide agreeable terms to the Portuguese combined with Philip V's threat of reconquering Portugal to push Pedro II into the arms of France for protection. Under French influence, Spain set aside those designs, and the Portuguese officially joined the Franco-Hispanic alliance in 1701.[44] According to the Count of Povolide, religion was also a factor for many who advocated that the Portuguese side with the Catholic nations of Spain and France against the Protestant English and Dutch.[45]

Fear gripped the English community in Lisbon after the signing of the French treaty as war became certain. The envoy Paul Methuen offered his assistance to English merchants and their families who desired to leave the capital. Many availed themselves of the offer and left aboard English naval vessels. To those who desired to stay, he cautioned that the repeated assurances from the Portuguese government of protection were "hardly to be trusted."[46] Still, some remained, having "made their applications to the king of Portugal and his ministers for a protection to stay . . . and continue their trade if there should be a war with England." Methuen warned these that he did not believe the applications would be respected "unless they are resolved to change their religion," which would inevitably make those who did not convert even greater targets for the Portuguese.[47]

Pedro II's actions stunned the English and Dutch, who began sending envoys in 1702 to win back the Portuguese.[48] Still the process was difficult. Paul Methuen grew frustrated by the failure to secure Portuguese allegiance exclaiming, "All the attempts we have made to open the eyes of this court, and make them sensible of their true interest, have been rather prejudicial than otherwise, and served only to increase the natural pride and vanity of these haughty people."[49] He further emphasized the degree to which the alliance with England had deteriorated, noting that every day he discovered "more and more the servile complacency of these people to the French and their ill will towards us."[50] The ambassador John Methuen declared that if his mission to secure a new treaty alliance with Portugal failed, he would encourage the merchants in Lisbon to leave and return to England, which he thought "would cause the whole people of this city to fall upon the ministers who have advised the alliance with France." Paul Methuen underscored the magnitude of his father's threat, noting that "the people of this country would be strangely concerned, it being impossible for them to subsist without the English and Dutch trade."[51]

Pedro II finally abandoned the alliance when the French failed to provide a response to the punitive Anglo-Dutch fleet sent to attack Cádiz in August 1702.[52] The lack of a French naval response highlights the influence of the Atlantic on Portugal's decision to rejoin the Grand Alliance, as the English and the Dutch were clearly the only powers capable of defending Lisbon and its South Atlantic empire.[53] English promises to help secure the Brazilian colony of Sacramento from Spanish aggression and Dutch forgiveness of much of the remaining debt from their 1669 treaty also aided the process.[54] Ultimately, three treaties were signed in 1703 between England and Portugal—one commercial and two concerning military matters and support for the Grand Alliance.[55] The commercial agreement, which ultimately became known as the Methuen Treaty, favored Portuguese wines over French varieties on the English market in exchange for the revocation of sumptuary legislation on English woolen goods in Portugal and a strict enforcement of the 23 percent customs duty.[56] The readmission of English manufactures merged with the increasing availability of Brazilian gold to destroy the nascent manufacturing program and fundamentally transform the Portuguese economy into one reliant on viniculture.[57]

The Methuen Treaty was a critical turning point for English fortunes in Lisbon and a reset for the alliance as the agreement renewed English commercial dominance after some of their previous privileges had been granted to others in varying degrees.[58] John Methuen complained before the signing of the treaty that the French, even without an expressed commercial treaty, "do here enjoy all privileges granted to the English."[59] That renewed dominance came at the perfect time as Brazilian gold began to arrive in Lisbon. By 1711 the Genoese consul in the city remarked, "Commerce, therefore, is almost wholly in the hands of the English, who are quite numerous; and these collect all the gold and silver of this country, to say nothing of what they have already drawn out."[60] Access to the Portuguese Atlantic through Lisbon was proving to be an increasingly worthwhile endeavor to the English.

The English in Lisbon: The Good and the Bad

In 1715 the English factory at Lisbon described the vital importance of the Brazil trade to their interests in the city and their displeasure at attempts to limit their participation. According to the English merchants, their woolen trade to Portugal had grown by two-thirds over the previous thirty years primarily as a result of increasing demand in Brazil after the discovery of gold. The Brazil trade was equally important for the Portuguese, which led to significant tensions in Lisbon between the two Atlantic empires.

Understanding the attraction of Brazilian trade after the discovery of gold, the Portuguese authorities in Lisbon continuously endeavored to limit and control foreign participation. Even though the English were allowed by treaty to settle four merchants in all the major Brazilian ports, the English factory complained in 1715 that the Portuguese "make great difficulties in giving that liberty to any, and do not only almost refuse it, but also begin to hinder our merchants from trading thither though in Portuguese ships."[61] Serious efforts began even earlier during the War of the Spanish Succession in which significant Atlantic developments had occurred, including the brief French seizure of Rio de Janeiro in 1711. The Portuguese attempted, therefore, to limit all foreign trade with the colony or as the English *chargé d'affaires* Thomas Leffever remarked in 1711, the Portuguese court "resolved to throw us entirely out of the Brazil trade."[62]

One of the first measures taken by the new monarch, João V, was to issue repeated decrees outlawing foreign vessels from illegally entering Brazilian ports.[63] In 1715, the Portuguese further petitioned the English to give up the privilege of settling four merchants in the ports of Brazil, threatening to extend the concession to the French if they did not agree.[64] In 1716, the Portuguese ambassador in London formally requested the withdrawal of English merchants from Brazil, but nothing came of it. The Portuguese found that the most efficient way to achieve their objective was to delay or deny residence permits for English and Dutch merchants in Brazil, arguing that citizens of these nations who were Catholic and had naturalized and married into the local population already fulfilled the levy of four merchants per major port. Still other means were devised. The English merchant in Rio de Janeiro, Ralph Gulston, was expelled under false charges of having committed a crime in 1716. The Dutch suffered similar attacks as the governor of Pernambuco went so far as to jail two merchants of that nation. They were released only after signing a statement declaring they would not return to the colony.[65] João V even adopted a policy of strict enforcement of the Methuen Treaty at home to get the English to give up the constant pressure of breaking into the Brazil trade for themselves. In essence, if João V continued to favor English woolens in Portugal, he could more effectively pressure the English to honor their promise of not engaging in direct trade with Brazilian ports—a threat issued candidly to João V by Lord Galway.[66]

The result of the prohibition on foreign merchants from establishing themselves in the Portuguese colony was that the English, Dutch, and others began trading even more heavily through Portuguese intermediaries in Lisbon.[67] Writing over a decade after the death of João V, consul Edward Hay described the transatlantic relationship that had developed in the city between merchants and factors as the Portuguese in the Brazil trade became for the most part "but commissaries for other people."[68] The Portuguese diplomat

D. Luís da Cunha remarked, "It is a pure falsehood to suppose that the English do not have businesses in Brazil, if not directly then indirectly, that is the businesses have Portuguese names but they are no more than mere commissaries of the English."[69] In 1700, diplomatic correspondence recorded that the cargo of the Brazil fleet was 70 percent English cloth.[70] The deepening dependence had already become so apparent, according to the French ambassador Abbe René de Mornay Montchevreuil, that by 1715, the English provided over 50 percent of the imports for Portugal and Brazil while the rest lay in the hands of Dutch, French, and other foreign merchants.[71] The Italian Lorenzo Magalotti claimed while visiting Porto in 1668–69 that all the traffic in manufactures in that port was in the hands of foreigners, the English in particular.[72] Considering the excellent work produced by Bill Donovan on the Portuguese trader Francisco Pinheiro during the period, these are clearly overestimations, but not by much.[73] Even more damaging than the overreliance on foreign goods was the hemorrhaging of Brazilian wealth needed to pay for them in Lisbon.

Having already limited direct foreign participation in the Brazil trade, João V also began to curtail the export of gold from the capital.[74] Although the practice had been illegal since medieval times, foreigners continuously shipped gold out of port as trade boomed during the first half of the eighteenth century. The English and Dutch were the worst offenders.[75] During João V's reign, foreign manufactured goods and necessary foodstuffs were increasingly paid for with Brazilian gold and diamonds as Portuguese wines and salt failed to balance trade. The resultant economic imbalance fulfilled the prophetic warning of the governor general of Brazil at the beginning of the eighteenth century, who declared that the greatest evil that could result from the discovery of Brazilian gold would be for that same gold to leave the Tagus soon after it entered as foreigners reaped the benefits much like they had with Spain's silver.[76]

Consul John Milner outlined in detail the utter dependence on Brazilian wealth that had developed among the Portuguese in Lisbon when he stated, "The greater part of that vast treasure in gold brought home by their last Brazil fleet is feasibly gone, and I fear there will be even an apparent want before the arrival of another, and if that should miscarry . . . the kingdom would be in danger of sinking at once." Milner further remarked that the English shipping gold from the city at such a time "incenses the generality of the people against us, and the great men who never were friends to the alliance increase and aggravate this ill disposition by telling the people that the war [of the Spanish Succession] is the occasion of all their misery and that the

English will ruin them."[77] Yet the consul was dumbfounded by the popular resentment considering that "all strangers do the same, both Dutch, Hamburghers, and Italians, and even their own [Portuguese] merchants who are rich."[78] While the English justified themselves, the French consul Jacques Montagnac wrote, somewhat exaggeratedly, "[The English] are the masters in Portugal and remove all the gold from Brazil at the arrival of each fleet."[79]

From the 1690s onward, gold was often exported by the English on merchant vessels. By the beginning of the eighteenth century, they also began using the secure postal service of packet boats that developed between England and Portugal as a result of cooperation during the War of the Spanish Succession.[80] Enjoying diplomatic immunity from search, these vessels were among the largest carriers of bullion to England. This fact was not lost on the hordes of Moorish pirates operating in the Atlantic whose continual threats caused English merchants in Lisbon to petition London for bigger and better armed vessels to defend themselves against the "Sallé rovers."[81] Envious of the profitability of the packet-boat system, the French endeavored to establish their own service but failed.[82]

The other main culprits were English naval vessels that also enjoyed immunity from search (contrary to what occurred in the case of Captain Stepney at the beginning of this chapter). Lord Tyrawly, the English envoy-extraordinaire to Portugal in 1734, declared:

> There is not an English Man-of-War homeward bound from almost any point of the compass that does not take Lisbon in their way home, and more especially if it be at a time that the Portuguese Rio de Janeiro and Bahia fleets are expected, the reason of this is in hopes that when the effects of these fleets are given out, that they may pick up some freight by carrying part of it to England . . . everybody knows that a Man-of-War can have no other business in life here but to carry away money and generally go about it so awkwardly that I have often wondered they are not caught in the fact. The ships of Newfoundland station constantly touch here on their way home, how many leagues it is out of their way, I need not tell your grace.[83]

The navies of other nations also plotted Lisbon in their course for the same reason. In 1741, the French consul Du Vernay noted the presence of a Dutch man-of-war in the harbor with the same intent.[84] That very year the English envoy Charles Compton reported the presence of two French men-of-war on the Tagus, a situation all the more remarkable "because none of that nation have appeared here these many years, what they are designed for I cannot learn, but have heard the French ambassador write to advise their coming in hopes they might fall in the way of carrying money."[85]

Under these conditions, the illegal export of Brazilian wealth became a lucrative and widespread affair during the first half of the eighteenth century. English consul Thomas Burnett wrote in 1720 that "the Dursley Man-of-War sailed from hence, with forty-thousand *moedas* [coins] on board for England."[86] Lord Tyrawly recorded the case of a naval vessel carrying one hundred thousand coins, and another with twenty thousand.[87] He later added, "[The] greater part of the diamonds that come from the Brazils have hitherto gone to London, from whence they are distributed to the rest of Europe."[88]

Exporting such vast quantities of bullion and gemstones primarily to England had a profound influence on the North Atlantic kingdom. Between 1710 and 1714 alone, the London mint transformed over a million Portuguese coins into English specie. Moreover, Portuguese gold coins circulated widely in England and Ireland, at times to the exclusion of the national currency. One Englishman announced in 1713, "We have hardly any money current among us but Portugal gold."[89] Portuguese coinage was so common in England that the coins were often referred to colloquially as "Jo's" after João V.[90] Portuguese coins were even found as far afield as British North America and the Caribbean well into the nineteenth century.[91] Additionally, significant amounts arrived in Italy via the grain and other Mediterranean trades as Italian merchants sold to English and French vessels out of Lisbon.[92] Portuguese gold arrived in Italy during the period in such quantities that Portuguese coins known as *Lisboninas* circulated throughout the country until the nineteenth century.[93]

Put another way, while the annual output of the Brazilian mines for the first half of the eighteenth century ranged somewhere between 3 and 4 million English pounds sterling, roughly half of that went to England and Ireland.[94] The total amount of gold imported into England during the period was such that it measured three times the amount already in circulation. These imports proved enormously transformative for English commerce as they were foundational in the country's shift from the silver to the gold standard and influential in establishing London as the foremost financial market of the period.[95] Considering this evidence, it becomes clear that an accurate picture of English economic and diplomatic history must, by necessity, at least acknowledge the important role of Lisbon and the Portuguese South Atlantic.

While the practice of exporting money was technically illegal, Portuguese officials at times recognized it as necessary in order to balance trade deficits.

Writing in 1728, Lord Tyrawly described the temper of the Portuguese regarding the illegal trade as "a state of connivance that almost amounts to a toleration."[96] Issues arose only when the Crown needed money or foreigners acted indiscreetly. An anonymous Portuguese poem from 1713 lambasted officials for their apathy in the matter:

> Here comes every foreigner
> Each one trading
> Gold and silver taking
> Leaving us lacking money
> There being no gifted councilor
> To ascertain an understanding
> And apply a remedy
> So that the kingdom
> Is not deprived of this metal
> This is the good government of Portugal.[97]

With such apparent toleration, the English resisted efforts by the Portuguese Crown to legalize the trade by proposing a 3 percent tax on exported gold.[98]

The increasingly open nature of illegal exports in coin and bullion during the first half of the eighteenth century clearly betrays the extent of foreign reliance on Lisbon. Speaking of the relationship, the English merchant Thomas Leffever declared, "Tis plain these people live by us and cannot live without us."[99] For their part, the popular classes in the capital were incensed at the practice, constantly throwing stones at the naval skiffs in harbor and starting brawls with English sailors in port. João V repeatedly lost patience with the English for their "breaking in so plain and bare faced a manner upon the prohibition of carrying money and gold dust out of his country."[100] Even the regularly pugnacious Tyrawly lamented the carelessness of English merchants in Lisbon, saying, "[They] talk as publicly upon the exchange of what money they have shipped for England, and with as little secrecy send it on board as they do a chest of oranges." He further warned the English that "if people will be so indiscreet, they must take their suffering for the reward of their indiscretion."[101]

English indiscretion eventually spread beyond Lisbon to London's various gazettes, which began publishing the arriving quantities (usually embellished) of Portuguese gold. In 1716 consul William Poyntz decried the publications while noting that the information from the English papers was subsequently transcribed into the Lisbon gazette "with a malicious design

(I do not doubt) of enraging the populace against us that are livers here, who were already too much our enemies on account of the jealousy they entertained of our merchants carrying off their bullion, and now they see it confirmed in our own, as well as their prints, [and] are ready to rise against us."[102] The outrage against English papers was raised again by Lord Tyrawly in 1738 and by consul John Russell in 1749.[103] Alongside English gazettes, the French, Dutch, and papal diplomats all regularly reported the latest numbers coming from Brazil.[104] As much as the English would have liked the practice to remain discreet, it was no small secret among merchants and monarchs that Brazilian wealth had transformed Lisbon into Europe's El Dorado.

The use of Brazilian wealth to pay for imports also made Lisbon during João V's absolutist reign a city increasingly reliant on foreign traders. The Earl of Sandwich, who stayed in the capital for a month as part of his broader tour of the Mediterranean in 1738–39, described the extent to which the Portuguese economy had slumped, noting that they produced no manufactures and underutilized their lands: "Hence they are obliged to apply to foreigners both for their food and raiment; who, by assisting them in their necessities, enrich their own countries at the expense of an indolent nation."[105] The haughty charge of indolence might well be suspected from an English traveler unaware of the nuances of commerce in Lisbon and the growing economic deficits during the first decades of the eighteenth century after the influx of Brazilian bullion and the signing of the Methuen Treaty.[106]

Recognizing that the massive losses could not continue, João V revived some of the manufacturing programs implemented during the last quarter of the seventeenth century.[107] Further changes occurred at the tail end of João's reign as the king issued a pragmatic on certain imported goods a year before his death in 1749 in an attempt to ameliorate the situation.[108] Speaking of the decree, the French consul Du Vernay declared, "Our commerce will suffer more than all that of the other nations combined. . . . The damage to the French houses established in Lisbon is irreparable, and our commerce with Portugal almost annihilated for the future."[109] In the decade leading up to the publication of the pragmatic, the French ambassador Chavigny appealed directly to João V's growing religious fanaticism in an effort to pry him away from England. He warned that unless English dominance were put in check, what they had done to the Catholics in Ireland would be but a "forerunner of England's vast designs to overthrow Catholicism and establish on its ruins the predominance of Protestantism."[110] Despite these concerns, the manufacturing push during the first half of the eighteenth century under João V was a testament to the deepening Portuguese reliance on the English as these efforts for the most part were not intended to seriously harm the interests of England.[111]

Conflict and Confrontation

The economic reality of growing English dependence after the restoration combined with stringent efforts to limit costly privileges to create an atmosphere of considerable tension with, and contempt for, foreigners previously unseen in Lisbon.[112] While varying degrees of tension between natives and foreigners were a recurring theme in other European port cities, Atlantic commerce bred a degree of religious tolerance in both London and Amsterdam as traders from all over Europe flocked to those emporia. Importantly, no single foreign group overwhelmingly dominated trade in either location to the same degree as in Lisbon.[113] In the case of Cádiz, it was the Catholic French, Italians, and Irish who were the most numerous and powerful brokers.[114] Put simply, Lisbon remained unique in terms of its foreign population, their religious affiliation, and its participation in commerce.

Conflict of various degrees resulted as the city became a node of competing commercial and religious economies from the North and South Atlantic. The disdain seemed to be shared by almost all, including city authorities who repeatedly harassed and jailed Englishmen without written consent of their judge conservator. In 1672 an English merchant named Joseph Hardwick was imprisoned by order of the city council for refusing to confess to whom he had sold his merchandise. According to consul Thomas Maynard, the reasoning behind the action was to harm English trade in the city by punishing Portuguese retailers who were dealing in English goods.[115] The council defended its actions, claiming Hardwick had been flagrantly guilty of contempt and had used various "indecencies" while refusing to confess.[116] The English merchant Mr. Noah Houssaye was imprisoned on the pretense that his weights on the Lisbon market had not been properly certified.[117] Envoy-extraordinaire Henry Worsley eventually had the man freed but feared that the English would be "daily subjected to many innovations of this nature" in an effort to curtail their privileges.[118]

Another particularly thorny issue was carrying firearms in the city. Although this concession was granted to the English even before the restoration and marriage treaties were signed, it was illegal for all other residents of Lisbon. City officials, therefore, took matters into their own hands, at times harassing and arresting Englishmen for carrying arms. Envoy Thomas Lumley reported in 1723 that an English sailor was jailed for sporting a pistol. Despite Lumley's complaints against the illegality of the arrest, he despaired, "They will be ready to lay hold of any pretext to prove this man a criminal, and evade acknowledging us this right." Lumley argued that having firearms in the city was vital, considering that the people viewed English sailors "as the persons principally concerned in carrying off their money" and also because "they are sensible it is a very extraordinary privilege, and what must be disagreeable to their own people, who are forbid under the severest penalties to carry any sort of firearms."[119] The arbitrary application of the law led the English merchant Anthony Corbiere to lament, "We have everyday occasion to see how little regard these people have to our privileges and how difficult it is to obtain a redress when they are diminished."[120]

Negligence or deceit by the judge conservator who was appointed to defend English interests was even more disappointing.[121] In 1670, consul Maynard claimed that the judge conservator, Luís Álvarez Ribeira, had become "most horridly impudent in debauching of seamen [through drunkenness or other diversions] and selling them into the king of Portugal's service."[122] Lord Tyrawly reported that the consul Charles Compton received an unexpected answer from the conservator when he complained that English privileges were not being upheld, to which the judge responded, "This was no time for the English to talk of their privileges, and that possibly a time might come when they would explain our privileges to us." The quick-tempered Tyrawly responded that such attitudes developed among the Portuguese when the English were "too mealy mouthed with them."[123] The ultimate blow came in 1742 as the increasingly absolutist João V (discussed in chapter 5) decreed that any economic disputes between English merchants and the Portuguese be settled by the municipal council rather than through the judge conservator. Despite the chorus of complaints, the new policy stood firm.[124]

The unwillingness of city officials to recognize or enforce foreign privileges extended to naturalized subjects of foreign nations. These individuals, discussed previously, who were most often French Huguenots who had become English or Dutch citizens in the aftermath of the 1685 Edict of Fontainebleau, were persecuted in the city due to their religious leanings and their liminal economic position.[125] The envoy George Delaval complained in 1712 that the court continued "to vex the naturalized French Protestants by repeated demands of the tithe, and lately laid an embargo upon what effects they have in their debtor's hands."[126] He later reported that others were required to pay additional taxes on their goods, seeing as they were not

"English born."[127] Compton recorded similar treatment in 1730, despite Portuguese law exempting foreigners from such payments.[128] English frustrations largely stemmed from their belief that their privileges were often less respected than those of other trading nations. Consul Maynard complained years earlier of "the great injustice that we daily meet with from these ministers" and contended that "it were better that we had no articles than to be so imposed upon; being the Genoese, Hamburgers, and others that trade upon the general laws and customs of nations without any capitulations, fare better than we do."[129] The fact that the English received the brunt of the abuse, even if according to their own estimations, reaffirms their developing stranglehold on trade in the city in the aftermath of Portugal's Atlantic turn.

Despite various attempts to limit the privileges of the English, their participation in Lisbon's commerce exploded. The merchants associated with the factory alone numbered around 90 individuals in 1717. By the earthquake of 1755, there were 150.[130] The English factories of both Seville and Cádiz at the time were comparatively smaller and dominated by the Irish Catholics.[131] According to Lord Tyrawly, by the middle of the eighteenth century, the English factory in Lisbon had become "rich, opulent, and every day increasing their fortunes and enlarging their dealings."[132] Success fostered attitudes of superiority and social isolation as the English grew wealthy through commerce while looking down on both Irish Catholics and the Portuguese, whom they deemed socially inferior.[133] The high lifestyle exhibited by English men and women combined with haughty attitudes and illegal endeavors to breed widespread discontent in the city. It became a common barb and insult among the Portuguese at the time to call someone an "English sot" if drunk and disorderly.[134]

Englishmen were also subjected at times to physical violence, being assaulted and murdered in the streets. Consul Maynard reported in 1670 that five English seamen were murdered. Although the guilty were apprehended, there was insufficient evidence against them and they were set at liberty.[135] In 1707, a Portuguese chronicler recorded a fight between an English sailor and a Portuguese man that ended with a brawl and the death of the Englishman from a blow by a stone.[136] According to the Portuguese diplomat José da Cunha Brochado, after the death of three English seamen in 1707 as a result of a skirmish, the ambassador Paul Methuen complained that the same thing had occurred over one hundred times.[137] Whether Methuen's complaint is numerically accurate is beside the point. Rather, the grievance reveals the atmosphere of tension that existed between the Portuguese and English in Lisbon during the period.

Resentment of the English overtook the entire city when a fleet of Hamburg ships was mistaken for an English fleet sent to force Pedro II to break his alliance with France. Fear reigned before the vessels were accurately identified, and, according to Paul Methuen, "several of the soldiers and common people laid hold on that opportunity to show their hatred and malice to the English, calling them heretic dogs and threatening to assault some of their houses."[138] The hatred grew to such a point over the years that the merchants later petitioned João V for protection against "the robberies and insults they [were] exposed to."[139] A particularly raucous clash occurred in 1731 between an English sailor and Portuguese porter. After exchanging blows, the sailor retired to his boat with other members of his crew while the Portuguese went and "raised a mob upon them."[140] The sailors began firing their muskets in defense, wounding two and killing one before they were arrested.[141]

Days later, members of the same crew were engaged in another brawl with a Portuguese throng on the riverfront. The event occurred when the men were taking a Sunday swim near the palace and one of them began to drown. The man was first passed over by a nearby Portuguese skiff before being rescued by his crewmates.[142] While pulling him aboard the ship, the men were taken by surprise when, "the Portuguese, according to their want and custom, began to fling stones very furiously." Portuguese witnesses claimed that while the man was being rescued and held upside down by his heels to induce vomiting, a crowd gathered, to which the sailors took offense and "presented a musket at them." The men were arrested and when the complaint reached the Portuguese secretary of state, Diogo de Mendonça Corte-Real, he expressed "the utmost concern that these little quarrels so frequently happened."[143] Lord Tyrawly in turn warned that if nothing were done with the "Portuguese rabble" who were "very unruly, and insolent to the boats . . . there would be eternal squabbles between our people and theirs."[144] Considering all the presented evidence from both British and Portuguese archives, it is clearly inaccurate to reduce the Anglo-Portuguese relationship in Lisbon, as previous scholars have done, to mere "flare-ups" and occasional "pin-pricks."[145]

The repercussions of the affair continued to reverberate throughout the city. Charles Compton lamented, "These disputes have raised so much ill blood in the Portuguese against [us]" and led to "several merchants [being] insulted in the streets."[146] Not long after, the English were again targeted when the muster call in the city was mistaken for English cannons. According to the formal, if not somewhat embellished, complaint of the factory merchants, "No other names could be heard out of their mouths but those of insolent, heretics, and dogs . . . and that whoever would begin to murder the English they should not want a second to support them."[147] Merchants and sailors alike were mobbed and abused as the attacks worsened. Tensions reached such a point that one of the biggest merchants in Lisbon, along with others, left the country.[148]

While attacks did occur, Tyrawly was skeptical of the threats of murder, writing, "Though I believe in general that the Portuguese have ill will enough to the English nation, which they are apt to let drop in conversation . . . yet I cannot learn from all the enquiry I can make underhand either amongst the Portuguese or English, that any such words were spoken."[149] However, considering the strained relationship in the capital between the Portuguese and the English, it is no wonder Tyrawly exclaimed in a letter to the Duke of Newcastle, "I hope your grace will be so good to remember me, or even remove me to any court, for I believe your grace won't be surprised if I say that I am pretty weary of this."[150]

The English were not always innocent victims in the rising tensions of the day. In 1741, the envoy Compton mentioned that an English sailor had killed a woman when he threw a two-pound shot at the captain of a Portuguese vessel that collided with his packet-boat on the river.[151] The reaction to the event escalated to such a degree that João V placed an embargo on the vessel for over a year.[152] Even English diplomats complained of English behavior in the city. In 1668, Maynard recounted that on one occasion the merchants of the factory refused to pay their judge conservator's wages. The judge fell sick and eventually died. The callousness was not taken well by the Portuguese.[153] Describing the English merchants, Captain James Jenefer said, "[They are] like our coffer breed in England, who, no longer than they are choked with privileges and riches cannot endure to speak well of any government . . . when I came to converse with them, I could not gain the advantage of one passage in ten to any satisfaction."[154] In his journal, Augustus Hervey wrote that he preferred not to spend his time in Lisbon with the English merchants, whom he very much disliked.[155] In 1729, Lord Tyrawly labeled the group as "a parcel of the greatest jackasses I ever met with. Fops, beauxs, drunkards, gamesters, and prodigiously ignorant, even in their own business."[156]

Tyrawly himself was not without blame. On one occasion in 1733, while in his coach, he came upon a religious procession. His coachmen, who were Catholic, wanted to pay their respects but the English diplomat demanded they drive on. A mob then attacked the coachmen for their disrespect, for which Tyrawly filed a complaint with the secretary of state.[157] Tyrawly was involved in a similar scuffle, this time in 1741, when a large crowd had gathered in the streets, making passage difficult. Tyrawly's coach soon came upon the coach of a Portuguese nobleman. When Tyrawly insolently tried to proceed first, the other driver began whipping Tyrawly's mules. Finally, managing to maneuver around the other coach, Tyrawly asked "who they were, and if they knew that he was the English envoy? They responded they did, and that they were Portuguese *fidalgos*, and that here such people were given more respect than in England." Tyrawly wisely let the matter drop; otherwise, as Portuguese sources recorded, "it is understood that had they come to blows, there would have been an uproar throughout the city, and not only the envoy, but all the English that they could find would suffer the wrath of their passion."[158] Altogether, the mixture of English actions and increasing economic dependency created a situation in which varying levels of confrontation with foreign Protestants in one of Europe's most Catholic cities became increasingly common.

Portuguese Catholics vs. English Protestants

Certainly, religious strife existed in Lisbon before the baroque period.[159] Yet, from the closure of Portuguese society in the aftermath of the Catholic Reformation and the Council of Trent, individual Protestants did not have a large presence in the city until the outbreak of the restoration and the need for powerful maritime allies to defend the Atlantic empire.[160] As a result, and as supported by archival documents, the city was marked from the second half of the seventeenth century on by a considerable amplification of religious tensions. Essentially, expanding commercial dealings and military alliances in the wake of the restoration led to greater contact in many aspects of daily life between the Portuguese and conspicuous Protestants—the English in particular, who arrived in increasing numbers and were proud to "enjoy [their] Protestant religion and civil liberties; even in the midst of popery and arbitrary power."[161]

For example, shortly after peace was declared with Spain, a parish church near Lisbon was desecrated in 1671. Although a New Christian was eventually apprehended for the crime, some among the Portuguese initially ran through the streets blaming the "English or French heretics."[162] Other issues arose over the public practice of Protestantism. In the absence of a church, English diplomats strained to hold religious services in their homes, especially when increasing numbers of Englishmen flocked to the city as Brazilian gold began pouring in at the end of the seventeenth century.

The Portuguese were not at all happy about the swelling ranks of Protestants in the city. Father Raphael Bluteau (himself a naturalized foreigner) echoed these thoughts in a 1723 sermon warning that Protestant traders brought not only their merchandise to the city, but also "the vices of their lands together with the errors of their sects, which they publicly profess."[163] George Delaval, the envoy in 1711, attested that because of the large number of worshippers in his house, his Portuguese landlord made him "pay a hundred pounds a year more than he did my predecessor Galway."[164] The year before, the factory had petitioned Queen Anne for money to rent a house large enough for five hundred worshippers.[165] Almost two decades later, Lord Tyrawly complained of the difficulty of holding services in his home for "seven hundred of his majesty's Protestant subjects in this place, besides masters of ships, and sailors" and petitioned for permission to secure a large enough house to accommodate everyone. In addition to being of adequate size, the house, he suggested, should also be "a little out of the way for fear of disputes and accidents that might attend the meeting of so great a concourse of Protestants amongst such a bigoted mob in a more frequented part of the town."[166] By the time of the earthquake, the number of English residents numbered in the thousands, with individuals practicing a variety of trades ranging from merchants and factors to hairdressers and cobblers. Many English Catholics had also moved to Portugal.[167] Other problems associated with increasing numbers arose. A visitor in 1730 decried the lack of available lodgings for foreigners in the city, claiming with some exaggeration, "When a foreigner arrives in Lisbon they have to seek out lodging with a French or Englishman (a Portuguese would not receive them)."[168]

Protestant burials were another sticky issue. Despite the 1654 treaty promising a cemetery plot in the city, it would be over sixty years before it came to fruition. According to the opinions of some of the king's advisers at the time of the treaty, the concession could not be granted because "clearly it could not be a church, or churchyard; [and] giving them a field among the plots where they are, other than the inconvenience of having it become a sacred place, it would also be a novelty and something which until now no other nation has been granted."[169] The denial of a Protestant cemetery created unique burial procedures among the English in the city. The merchant Thomas Cox observed that when English Protestants expired in Lisbon, they "put the coffin in a sugar chest and in the evening pretty late, carry it aboard some English ship."[170] An integral part of this secretive ritual included burying the body on the other side of the Tagus River between the tide marks on the beach.[171] Reverend John Swinton claimed that if these practices were not followed and the Portuguese discovered the burial site, they would "afterwards take up the body and expose it in the open air to be devoured by birds and beasts."[172]

The practice of secretive burials ceased when João V finally assented to an English cemetery in 1717. The chosen parcel of land was later hidden from view by tall trees.[173] A cemetery was yet another reason for concern over religious contamination in Lisbon. One Portuguese chronicler feared that the English would eventually be granted a church, which was the only thing lacking before "some declare themselves Anglicans."[174] The English at times protested the limitations quite openly. The envoy Charles Fanshaw was stunned in 1683 when he recorded a host of Englishmen carrying a corpse through the streets during the day, "which provoked the people to give them many ill names." Fanshaw sternly warned the minister and factory to avoid such affronts considering the treaty articles supported no such behavior.[175]

Daily life in the city was further complicated by religious gestures and strife. For instance, when church bells rang around noon and Catholics kneeled in the streets and recited their prayers, Protestants were required to at least remove their caps or they were likely to be punished for disrespecting the church.[176] When he asked a friend about the practice, a visitor learned that there was considerable tension between the Portuguese and the English, Dutch, and other Protestants in the city for "I don't know how many years" and that the Portuguese wanted to force all the Protestants to kneel. The king ultimately interfered, allowing the Protestants simply to remove their caps and remain quiet. Everyone accepted the king's wishes, yet many continued to murmur about the practice.[177]

According to Charles Frédéric de Merveilleux, who visited Lisbon in the 1720s, the public *autos-da-fé* were particularly difficult for foreigners in Lisbon who struggled to "cross the streets full of people without hearing insults from the commoners, snarling between their teeth, which generally signified that these heretics should also be accountable to the Holy Office."[178] His suggestion for avoiding the abuse demonstrates just how deeply religious ill-feeling had taken hold among the populace, as he judged it best for a foreigner to "sit alone in a window, without speaking to anyone, having in hand one of the printed sheets relating the names of disgraced penitents. . . . Being thus occupied with such literature one can avoid obtrusive and useless questioning."[179]

Religious bigotry and persecution manifested themselves in other ways. Portuguese lawyers made various attempts to reject Protestant testimony in court.[180] Although the Crown routinely blocked these efforts, the danger was worrisome to Protestant merchants, who would have been unable to recover debts from their Portuguese debtors if their accounts on the matter were ruled invalid.[181] Complaining of the lack of justice for foreigners, Lord Tyrawly exclaimed that when the English Protestants obtain "justice of the court of Portugal, it has been by bribery here," they being otherwise "left to themselves to sink or swim."[182] The English agent Francis Parry noted that there was even a proposal at one point that English Protestants in the city carry a certificate declaring them heretics.[183]

The fact that the Crown often sided with foreign interests in opposition to such schemes led various visitors to conclude erroneously that "the common people about the city are not observed to be guilty of any rudeness towards the English, on account of their religion."[184] Yet the same account highlights the absolute nature of royal rule at the time, noting, "It is true, that opprobrious language to strangers is so severely prohibited, that upon complaint made against any that shall call an Englishman heretic, no punishment short of death or the galleys will be thought too great for the offense."[185] All these factors combined to make Lisbon during the baroque period into a city in which the English were said to have only "limited dealings with [the Portuguese] except in matters of business, and even then it is with care so that they are not cheated."[186] The English factory at Porto enjoyed better relations with the Portuguese, no doubt a direct result of fewer numbers.[187]

Religious life was only made more complicated by the large numbers of English or Irish friars and nuns in Lisbon who continually sought to convert their countrymen. Some of the most notorious were the seminarians at the English College of St. Peter and St. Paul. Colloquially known as the *Inglesinhos*, this group was funded in part by Catholics in England.[188] While visiting Lisbon in 1672–73, Captain James Jenefer wrote that these seminarians "are bred up to trouble [us]; doubtless the design is deeply laid in culling out such choice lads, for I never saw any [others] of their years defend an argument so smartly."[189] The efforts of these and others paid off with continual conversions of foreign Protestants during the period. The weekly *Gazeta de Lisboa Occidental* records a spectacular show of conversion that occurred in May 1733 when an English Quaker named Thomas David along with Andrew Kennedy, a Scottish Presbyterian, and John Peebles, an Irish Protestant, received baptism after being taught by the Irish Dominicans in Lisbon.[190]

English Protestants were not the only target for conversion as the religious houses of various other nations in the city worked to achieve the same purpose. For example, the *Gazeta de Lisboa Occidental* mentions the conversion of a German Calvinist and a Dutch Lutheran in 1722.[191] Moreover, records from the period show that during the period from 1642 to 1700, 195 German Protestants converted to Catholicism in the city.[192] Conversion at times was a cause for celebration. The nobility threw a banquet in 1738 after the German military engineer João Henrique de Braun abjured his Lutheranism.[193]

Some English men and women found in Lisbon a haven to practice their Catholicism openly. Allen Hutchinson claimed in the 1670s that he had gone to Portugal to become a Catholic. He even received a pension from Pedro II, despite his having killed a fellow English merchant in Lisbon. The pension, according to Hutchinson, was granted due to the sacrifice of his large estates in England in order to convert and live in Lisbon. His sister was granted permission soon after to come to the city for the same reasons.[194] Other Protestants no doubt saw conversion in the capital as an opportunity. This was the case with Florence Angovi, the former maid and mistress to the English merchant John Compton. Compton fathered a child with Angovi in 1709 before dying in 1712. Compton drafted a will while living that paid Angovi a sum and sent their son to England to be brought up in the Anglican faith. When Compton passed, Angovi sued his executor before the judge conservator for the return of her child and the entirety of Compton's estate. Her reasoning was that, according to the laws of Portugal, natural children inherit all in default of legitimate offspring. In addition to these legal arguments presented in court, Angovi "changed her religion and turned papist, the better to entitle her to the benefit of this law." Angovi lost the case but appealed directly to D. João V, who because of her conversion ruled in her favor, whereupon she renewed her case in the Lisbon courts.[195]

Others like the Irish woman Helena Mahony returned to their previous Catholic faith after making their way to Lisbon. Mahony presented herself to the Inquisition voluntarily and declared, "After having arrived in this land and being illuminated by the Holy Spirit that pricked [my] heart with great remorse of conscience and terrible dreams on the matter, [I] resolved to embrace again the Roman Catholic religion."[196] Foreign sailors often saw conversion (real or feigned) in Lisbon as a means to escape their naval obligations or receive better pay in foreign service. This became a recurrent problem for English officials in port. Henry Worsley bemoaned the desertion of sailors, protesting that he was never able to recover English seamen from "the convents in this city, which daily give protection to his majesty's sailors who have a mind to quit their ships."[197]

In 1682 consul Maynard derided various English sailors whom he caught using conversion to escape the harsh punishment of desertion from the Virginia-bound *Golden Fortune*. The vessel was forced into Lisbon by bad weather whereupon about twenty men fled to Portuguese service. Maynard had the sailors arrested but then freed them when they promised to return to their ship. Maynard arrested them once again when they went back to the Portuguese ships instead. Some of the crew then "declared they would turn Roman Catholics" and notice was sent to the Inquisition, which then refused to turn the men over to the consul. The whole affair created a problem in port as the *Golden Fortune* lacked adequate hands to resume the journey to Virginia.[198] The ship was able to depart only after other English vessels agreed to spare some of their crew.[199]

The Portuguese defended the friars who aided these deserters and claimed that they were acting appropriately, given that the men were already Catholic or were willing to become such. Moreover, the sailors were in mortal danger considering that "Protestant officials and captains [were] accustomed to seizing and hanging [deserters]" without respecting the orders of the Portuguese magistrates.[200] The English were not the only ones to suffer the recruitment, and subsequent prison conversions, of their seamen in Lisbon. The English envoy Francis Parry noted in 1670 that a Dutch resident was having a particularly difficult time with a man whom he arrested for fleeing to Pernambuco on a small vessel before returning to Lisbon. The Dutch resident threw the man into jail where he was to await his transfer to Holland. But, as Parry noted, "the fellow knowing what would befall him when he came thither resolved to do anything to keep him thence, and therefore turned papist."[201] Lord Tyrawly decried the practice, noting that the English could ill afford to lose their sailors every year at such a rate, all because they were being harbored in an "Irish wine house, or rowdy house, or by getting into an Irish convent, and with a pair of beads in their hands, say they are Roman Catholics, and for this reason not returned to us."[202] He went on to describe the Irish friars in Lisbon as "the vilest set of fellows who ever breathed."[203]

Envoy-extraordinaire Charles Fanshaw witnessed firsthand the tenacious efforts of Catholic priests and friars in the city. In August 1684, he petitioned Pedro II for the return of his seventeen-year-old page, George Kingsley, who was "induced to run away from his house . . . by the flatteries and artifices of some persons upon pretense of religion."[204] The boy was eventually returned to Fanshaw, after which he related that it was the English seminarians that had encouraged him to leave.[205] Besides active proselytism, foreign friars also developed a method of attempted deathbed conversions among Protestants in the city. The envoy Thomas Lumley described the practice:

The wife of one William Fisher, an Englishman who keeps a public house in this place, being sick and thought in danger, was at her own request visited the 18th instant by Mr. Sims, chaplain to the factory. While this gentleman was there in the discharge of his duty, a band of Irish friars entered the room, accompanied by an officer belonging to the patriarch, and by force obliged him to retire out of it, pretending that she had sent for them and was desirous to change her religion . . . and after the woman had publicly declared herself a Protestant, and that she had been educated in that church, and was determined to die a member of it, they thought fit to leave the house, and have not since given her any further trouble. . . . But in a country so full of bigotry and superstition as this is, the ecclesiastics will grow audacious, and now and then go beyond the bounds of their authority in spite of the civil power, or any precautions taken by it.[206]

In a similar occurrence, the Englishman Dr. Cox Macro related that after entering the bedroom of a sick Englishman, the Catholic priest would "thrust a candle into his hand and if there were other people that could witness they saw the sick man with the candle in his hand, this would be enough in case he should offer to be a Protestant afterwards for the Inquisition to lay hold on him."[207] Protestants did at times convert at the end of their lives, as demonstrated by the case of the Calvinist merchant John Hacksaw, who after living in Lisbon for thirty years converted eight days prior to his death.[208] On the other hand, few if any Portuguese converted to Protestantism in the capital during the period.[209]

Other means were employed to convert Protestants. A particularly bizarre practice developed in the city during the beginning of the eighteenth century when some members of the Portuguese nobility began kidnapping English children and forcefully converting them. John Milner reported in 1706 that the Countess of Calheta and her mother had taken between twelve and fifteen English children alone![210] Milner further exclaimed that "so many great families [were] engaged in the carrying it on" that something had to be done about it.[211] Even the Count of Castelo-Melhor admitted that "twenty of the best families in Portugal were engaged in the same thing."[212] The practice became so widespread that João V issued a decree in August 1708 stating that "no one of any class or condition whatsoever can take minors from their parents, neither have them against the will of their parents, whether they be Catholic or Protestant."[213] Despite the decree, the trend continued. Milner mentioned the matter again in 1710 when his own child was taken along with many others.[214] He blamed the continuation of the custom on the very decree supposedly outlawing it, the consequences of which would be that "as there are many married families now in Portugal [it] exposes them to the hazard of losing their children forever."[215] The rest of João V's edict stated that the practice could continue in cases "in which the said children are of such an age [of seven or older] and have an understanding with which they can choose their religion."[216]

The habit persisted throughout the first half of the eighteenth century despite repeated protests from the English. Consul Thomas Burnett reported the extraordinary case of the naturalized Huguenot merchant James Belangé, whose daughter was taken by the Marquis of Marialva and his wife after the family had spent time on his estate.[217] Belangé and his wife were allowed to see their child on one occasion in Lisbon, and, as mother and daughter embraced, the girl said she wanted to come home. Belangé begged his daughter to tell the marquis, "but at that instant the Marquis on one side and the Marchioness on the other tore the child from her mother's arms and a [servant] that attended carried her away into another room." When Belangé told the marquis that his daughter had desired to return with him, he responded that the child had told him the contrary. When Belangé begged the marquis to take him and his wife as well, he replied that he would do so only if they converted, or if they converted, their daughter would be restored to them.[218] Despite his repeated pleas, his daughter was never returned. The envoy Henry Worsley noted almost two years later that the marquis justified his actions by claiming that the child was "resolved to be a Roman Catholic, and if she had said she would return to her parents it was out of fear of them, and that as she was above eight-years-old, by the laws of Portugal, she might choose her religion." Worsley quipped, "So little reason is required from a proselyte to the Portuguese Catholic religion."[219]

While Thomas Burnett reported that kidnappings were frequent, not every case was legitimate.[220] Truthfully, as ambassador John Methuen said on an earlier occasion, in most instances, the children were sold to the Portuguese for "a good deal of money" by their own parents, adding, "If any person from hence doth give you a different account it may proceed from great zeal, but it is without knowledge and contrary to the truth."[221] Altogether, given the difficulties they faced, many foreign Protestants living in Lisbon decided to convert, or at least live outwardly as Catholics until they departed.[222]

While the daily interactions with Lisbon's populace were often complicated and fraught, there was some degree of social commingling. English merchants often invited the Portuguese aristocracy to their parties and social gatherings. This was not the norm, given that the nobility often eschewed commercial participation, deeming it below their station.[223] Lord Tyrawly complained of the lack of social interaction with the Portuguese nobility in 1734, which he blamed on the "the dark and recluse manner of these people."[224] Over time, the parties thrown in celebration by foreigners slowly began to change the social attitudes among the Portuguese upper classes, and more of the aristocracy began to attend.[225] As Abraham Castres put it, "Little by little this country is becoming less uncivilized, but it will be a long time before social life achieves the same progress as it has in our northern countries."[226]

While the upper classes slowly expanded their social circles to include foreign diplomats and merchants, such congeniality was not viewed particularly favorably at times by the Portuguese masses. When the English in the city invited some of the aristocracy to a party celebrating the defeat of the Catholic pretender Bonnie Prince Charlie, the people were infuriated "that the heretics celebrated an action against a Christian prince" and "wanted to insult them with demonstrations of vengeance." They began by throwing stones at the torches lighting the wooden edifice constructed for the evening spectacle in hopes of starting a fire. The attempts were frustrated when a regiment of Portuguese cavalry was deployed and successfully dispersed the crowd.[227] The Portuguese in attendance were soon ridiculed in verse, with one poet declaring them, "Catholics in name but heretics concealed."[228] An English account published in the *Gentleman's Magazine* was careful to omit any such altercation.[229]

In general, the overt hostility toward the English came mostly from the common people rather than the king and government.[230] Yet even the popular classes showed restraint at times. Dr. Macro respected the fact that the Portuguese "generously forgive in foreigner what no thing but life shall atone for in a native."[231] In 1724, Thomas Sanderson noted, "Everything here is very quiet, and this court in a very friendly disposition with respect to us."[232] After visiting Lisbon in the 1730s, the Englishman Augustus Hervey wrote in his journal that he "left Lisbon with some regret from the great attentions that had been shown me there, and my intimacy with several Portuguese families, which are not easy for strangers to obtain."[233] Even the abrasive Lord Tyrawly grew to favor the Portuguese over time and established a close friendship with João V. The diplomat spent his later years often contending with English captains over their illegal exportation of gold before returning to England in 1741, taking with him "three wives and fourteen children; [of which] one of the former [was] a Portuguese with long black hair plaited

THE ENGLISH IN ATLANTIC LISBON

down to the bottom of her back." The women were most likely Tyrawly's concubines, considering his known penchant for promiscuity.[234]

The English became prominent in Lisbon precisely because the Atlantic increased in importance for the Portuguese. The period from 1668 to 1750 therefore has been aptly described as the golden age of English trade in Portugal as England rose to commercial dominance in the Portuguese capital through its Atlantic interests.[235] Clearly Lisbon was a vital piece to both imperial projects, and its history should be more fully integrated into future studies concerning Anglo-Portuguese relations and empire.

For the Portuguese, the price of alliance in Lisbon was high as English merchants and citizens often enjoyed social and commercial privileges in the city well beyond their own. Successful attempts to limit these privileges, along with the actions of the English, created a mercurial atmosphere in which commerce and collaboration often devolved into conflict. It was this combination of internal developments and Atlanticization that produced the remarkable tensions in the Portuguese capital during the period. While it would be an exaggeration to argue that the relationship was entirely one of strife, it is equally wrong to reduce the elevated discord to the occasional arrest or dustup. The truth is that studying the topic through an Atlantic lens reveals that the period did experience an uptick in contention, which at times became serious, as the English poured into the capital city especially after the discovery of gold and the signing of the Methuen Treaty.

Unlike the preceding centuries in which foreign trade in the city was shared predominantly with the Catholic nations of Spain, Italy, and France, the end of the seventeenth and beginning of the eighteenth centuries in Lisbon were characterized by the presence of large, conspicuous, groups of English Protestants who dominated certain aspects of daily life. The era after the restoration in Lisbon, therefore, marked a departure from previous periods in post-Tridentine Lisbon. The Portuguese perceived as a genuine threat the possibility of heretical contamination as the result of commercial dominance of the Protestant North Atlantic nations. Plainly stated, of the European port capitals examined during the period, only in Lisbon did a single nation of a different faith come to control so much commercial trade—and it did so precisely at the time of the revival of Lisbon's Inquisition, a theme discussed in the next chapter.

In essence, Lisbon became a contentious crossroads between the overlapping commercial, imperial, and religious networks of the North and South Atlantic. Thus, if diversity is one of the hallmarks of Atlanticization, so too is pushback, at least in the case of the Portuguese capital. Considering all this, it is likely that many foreign Protestants shared the sentiments of the bombastic Lord Tyrawly, who exclaimed in 1732, "This damned place is calculated in every respect to make a man mad, as fully as if it had been contrived so on purpose."[236] A weighty criticism, considering that Tyrawly, by the time of his departure from Lisbon in 1741, was accused by his own countrymen of being "almost naturalized amongst [the Portuguese and] trusted and beloved there."[237]

3

KEEPING LISBON CATHOLIC

Fifteen gold coins, worth 4,800 *réis* each, was the price of religious freedom in Lisbon. Or so it seemed to the twenty-eight-year-old Manuel Lopes Pinheiro, who sought to flee the terror of a resurgent Inquisition in 1702 aboard an English warship docked in port. Originally from the village of Freixo de Numão some four hundred kilometers northeast of Lisbon, near the Spanish border, Manuel emigrated to Lisbon, where he made his wealth in the rebounding sugar trade. His contacts extended well beyond the city and reached as far afield as Madrid. Clearly, they also included England, given his attempted flight to that country. While aboard the naval vessel, he encountered other New Christian merchants and their families who resided in Lisbon and were fleeing for the same reasons. Manuel, like so many of his peers during the period, was eventually apprehended by the Holy Office, which confiscated all his goods and forced him to participate in an *auto-da-fé* during which he was publicly humiliated for his sins.[1]

The limited details from this episode could never fully portray the varied experiences of the disparate groups targeted by the Inquisition during the period. Yet the story does help illustrate some of the broader points discussed in this chapter. These include a resurgence of the Inquisition and an explosion in the persecution of Lisbon's New Christian population (many of whom were successful merchants engaged in Atlantic trades) as shifting Atlantic commerce merged with internal developments. The chapter further highlights the growing connection between New Christians and the increasing number of English in the city who themselves at times became targets of the Holy Office through various means, including the confiscation of their enslaved Africans. The discussion also emphasizes inquisitorial concern over growing Afro-Brazilian impacts on religious culture among the popular classes. Altogether, the various religious influences coming out of both the North and South Atlantic and their overlap with events in Lisbon unleashed the Inquisition. In many ways, then, this chapter follows up on the theme of pushback against Atlantic currents by analyzing religious responses to those same stimuli.

While scholars have analyzed Atlantic influences on Portuguese inquisitorial activity to varying degrees during the previous restoration period under João IV or even the Brazilian focus of the Inquisition under João V in the first decades of the eighteenth century, the conversation remains piecemeal. This chapter brings together those historiographical voices and grounds them in everyday life in Lisbon to show in new detail the religious consequences of Lisbon's Atlanticization. Existing and new archival research gives voice to New Christians, Afro-Brazilians, and English Protestants who embodied the religious impact of the Atlantic on Lisbon. Lisbon became a religious crossroads of sorts as increasing dependence on Protestant foreigners and the growing religious influences of Afro-Brazilians combined with widespread resentment of New Christians enriched by the Brazil trade to produce the last assertion of inquisitorial authority before the beginning of its demise in 1769 under the Marquis of Pombal.[2]

New Christians in Lisbon

The majority of Lisbon's Portuguese merchants during the second half of the seventeenth century were New Christians.[3] "New Christian" was a social and ethnic designation for people of Jewish descent. Many New Christians possessed valuable financial skills and had originally emigrated from Spain after their expulsion in 1492. In Portugal, they were faced with the decision of forced conversion or exile in 1497 after King Manuel sought the favor of the Spanish monarchs in order to wed their daughter.[4] Portuguese Old Christians were generally suspicious of those who converted. They worried that these converts were still practicing Judaism secretly and posed a spiritual danger to Catholic society at large. They also despised New Christians for their wealth and commercial ability, which elevated them above the popular classes and threatened the nobility.

Overall, New Christian merchants in Lisbon excelled in commerce, and their capital was sought for investment in a new monopoly company designed to bolster Brazilian trade. Having lost much of the eastern empire, the Portuguese during the restoration conflict against Spain (1640–68) were utterly dependent on Brazilian sugar to finance the costly war.[5] Fear of attack on the Brazilian fleets led João IV (1640–56) to accept a proposal by the Jesuit António Vieira to establish a monopoly trading company. The Companhia Geral do Comércio do Brasil (Brazil Company) was established in 1649 and tasked with providing armed escorts for the vulnerable Brazil fleets in exchange for monopoly rights on Brazilian sugar and the exportation of olive oil, codfish, salt, wine, and wheat flour to the colony.[6] These enticements alone made the Brazil Company an attractive investment for many New Christian merchants.

João IV further incentivized New Christian participation in the new enterprise with a royal decree suspending inquisitorial confiscation. The exemption on confiscation was part of a larger plan to cripple the Inquisition (which ardently opposed the restoration and Portuguese independence) by eliminating its financial resources.[7] Lisbon's New Christian merchants were not the only investors in the Brazil Company, but they did provide a large portion of the needed capital for the company.[8] The Brazil Company ultimately paid off for João IV when it played a vital role in taking back the sugar regions of northeastern Brazil from the Dutch in 1654 by supplying needed men and ships.[9] The monarch himself declared that the company "reconquered Pernambuco without costing me a penny ['vintém'] something that the king of Spain desired so ardently and [for which] he spent so much without any result, and for which I would have given the Dutch nearly six-million [cruzados]."[10] The company proved equally beneficial for its investors in Lisbon as it opened up avenues for social and political ascension.[11]

The Inquisition, angered at the royal protection of New Christians, came roaring back after João IV's death as the queen regent, Luisa de Gusmão, reinstituted confiscations in 1657.[12] The result was a period of extensive confiscations and elevated arrests among New Christians that continued into the 1668 meeting of the *côrtes* that gave Pedro II the throne of his deposed brother Afonso VI. Furthermore, new taxes coming out of the *côrtes* to pay outstanding war debts to contractors—many of whom were wealthy New Christians—combined with an economic dependence on Brazil in the midst of European market closures to aggravate the already heightened anti–New Christian sentiment in the city.[13] As the famed economic historian Vitorino Magalhães Godinho put it, "Was not the increasing pressure of the Inquisition fed by an anti-mercantile feeling itself stimulated by the commercial depression? From 1668 to about 1693, the imperial economy had undergone a prolonged depression dominated by a crisis in the sugar, tobacco, silver and slave trades."[14] An English visitor in the early 1670s summed up the general feeling in Lisbon during the economic downturn by observing that the New Christians "engrossed the best part of the wealth of this kingdom, and by terror of the Inquisition, convey it away to the great impoverishment thereof."[15]

Tensions exploded in May 1671 after the theft, and destruction, of religious objects in a parish church on the outskirts of the city at Odivelas.[16] News that a group of New Christians had fled the capital on a French ship the morning after was proof enough for the masses that these were to blame.[17] English consul Thomas Maynard described the outrage and demands that "the crime be expiated with the blood of some of the Jews (or at least by banishing those that in the Inquisition have made themselves guilty of Judaism by their own confessions)" lest God's judgments fall on them.[18] The people of Lisbon flooded the city with leaflets denouncing New Christians in the wake of the sacrilege, and another round of imprisonment for wealthy merchants and their families began.[19]

The New Christians António Mogadouro and Diogo de Chaves, both revenue collectors for the Crown, were among this unfortunate group. Denunciations came from everyone and everywhere. Some of the earliest to denounce Mogadouro were the enslaved Africans who belonged to a family member.[20] Francisco Carlos, who bore the title of *fidalgo da casa real* and was the treasurer and a deputy on the board of the Brazil Company, was also arrested by the resurgent Inquisition.[21] His confiscations included a house on the central Rossio square worth 10,000 *cruzados* along with its rich furnishings and various enslaved individuals. The confiscation of his furnishings alone amounted to more than 5,000 *cruzados*.[22] An inventory clearly demonstrated that Francisco Carlos's wealth was derived primarily from his trade with Brazil.[23] Fernão Rodrigues Penso had properties of similar value seized as he awaited trial, the grand total of which easily outstripped the annual expenses of the entire city council.[24] Considering the widespread furor, it is no wonder some sought to escape the city by any means possible.

Those New Christians apprehended during the fervor rotted in the Inquisition's dungeons for years.[25] A poem composed by a survivor of the ordeal compares his eleven years of ruin and imprisonment to the fallen leaves and fruit of the plum tree, lamenting, "But you will regain what you have lost, while I will never again be what I was before."[26] Maynard wrote that the Inquisition was so full of New Christian prisoners after the events of Odivelas that an *auto-da-fé* "as great as hath been in this age" was being prepared.[27] The brutality of the crackdown against New Christian merchants was such that of the ninety merchants in the period 1620–1690 studied by David Grant Smith, seven died in the dungeons of the Inquisition in Lisbon—six of whom were arrested after the events at Odivelas in 1671.[28]

Public outrage forced Pedro II to act. He sent a *consulta* to the *Desembargo do Paço* concerning the legality of enacting an expulsion along the lines proposed previously during the 1668 *côrtes*. The judges responded that the decree was sound and should be issued, considering that João IV's earlier exemption served only to multiply the numbers of New Christians at home and foster infamy abroad. Truthfully, the Portuguese had become synonymous with Jews in various parts of Europe during the period due to the flight of so many New Christians out of Portugal.[29] Considering that among the Portuguese mercantile class New Christians were the majority, Maynard argued that an expulsion would be catastrophic and would lead to "the ruin of [Portuguese] commerce," which would adversely affect the English whose economic control in Lisbon was already substantial.[30] One of Pedro II's secretaries, Roque Monteiro Paim, boldly countered such arguments with the publication of a tract entitled *Perfídia Judaica* in which he contended that Old Christians could easily make up for any losses and manage commercial affairs.[31]

Pedro II issued a decree on 22 June 1671 expelling any New Christian who had confessed since the last general pardon of 1604. The decree encompassed not only those who had abjured since the last pardon but also their children and grandchildren and all who had ever abjured *de vehementi* along with their children.[32] Subsequent edicts modeled after the suggestions from the 1668 *côrtes* forbade intermarriage between Old and New Christians, barred New Christians from holding public offices, and prohibited penitents from practicing medicine or law—all this before the culprit in the desecration of Odivelas had even been discovered![33] The malefactor was arrested soon thereafter while committing another robbery in the vicinity of Odivelas in October 1671. The accused, António Ferreira, was discovered to be a New Christian before being tried, tortured, and hanged.[34] The people in Lisbon lauded Pedro II's bold actions as they posted lampoons against the New Christians and composed poems praising the prince regent's defense of the faith.[35]

The 1671 expulsion decree had a profoundly negative effect on trade in the capital. The English envoy Francis Parry worried that the decree put English commerce in an impossible position as they had become wary of doing business with the New Christians. Branching out to other traders would only worsen the situation by demonstrating "distrust" and would inevitably lead to the New Christians refusing "to pay anything for what goods they have already received." To make matters worse, the envoy stated, "the generality of [New Christians] are not able to satisfy their old debts but by new sales."[36] Parry informed Pedro II in a personal letter that, under the circumstances, the English merchants had put a stop to further importations, which prejudiced the monarch's customs and led to higher prices in the city during already difficult times.[37] Maynard echoed these sentiments and noted that "all strangers are fearful to sell their goods to such as come within the compass of the act."[38] Even the Inquisition opposed the strict enforcement of the decree, as they stood to lose their livelihood.[39] So, in the end, the expulsion decree was never enforced out of fear of the economic consequences that would inevitably follow. As one Portuguese declared, "It was necessary to conceal the tares so as to not uproot the wheat."[40]

There were additional attacks on New Christians in the capital after the inquisitor general published an edict in May 1672 forbidding those tried by the Holy Office from riding in coaches, on litters, or on horseback. They were also prohibited from wearing costly apparel.[41] The decree satisfied the old complaint in the city that these heretics flaunted their wealth in the face of Old Christians.[42] New Christians were further undercut as the Brazil Company (under complete Crown control since 1664) received a new charter in 1672 that expanded the board of directors from three individuals to five— the presidency and two of the seats being reserved for the aristocracy.[43] The reform represented a major blow to the political power of the mercantile community as a whole and for New Christians in particular, who, despite the resurgent Inquisition after D. João IV's death, managed to gain control of two of the three seats on the previous board. Furthermore, those two deputies on the board (Francisco Carlos and António Correia Bravo) had either been severely harassed or imprisoned by the Inquisition in the wake of the events at Odivelas.[44]

Hope for relief took hold as word spread in 1673 that António Vieira, who had been in Rome since 1669, was lobbying for the pope to grant a general pardon and reform of the Portuguese Inquisition in exchange for investment in an India company.[45] Three wealthy New Christians in Lisbon disturbed by the persecution (Manuel de Gama de Pádua, Pedro Álvares Caldas, and António Correia Bravo) picked up the idea and officially proposed an East Indies company in 1673 with Jesuit aid to Pedro II.[46] The company was to be patterned after the previous Brazil Company and funded by New Christian capital with a promise to send 5,000 troops to reconquer the Estado da Índia, along with an additional 1,200 troops each year thereafter and annual support of 20,000 *cruzados*. Missionaries and bishops sent to those conquests were to be supported by the company as well as the viceroy and governors. To top it all off, a stipend of 200,000 *réis* a month was promised to the Portuguese ambassador in Rome.[47] For the New Christians, the most important aspect of the general pardon was the reform of the Portuguese Inquisition in order to bring it in line with the Roman model by abolishing singular testimony and secret denunciations.[48]

António Vieira contended earlier that such a proposal would only help Portugal. He wrote:

> What is better? Declared Jews or hidden Jews? . . . Jews that enrich Italy, France, England, and Holland, or Jews that enrich Portugal? Jews who with their capital help heretics conquer territories and impede the faith by spreading heresy, or Jews that with that same capital help the armies of the most Catholic prince recover those same territories and divulge the faith throughout the world? . . . Of course, if Portugal in Lisbon, and in all the cities of the kingdom, permits English, Dutch, French, and Germans to enjoy freedom of conscience, mixing all the while with Catholics without markings or distinctions simply for the benefit of commerce . . . for what reason, by the same utility of commerce, are Portuguese Jews not permitted?[49]

He further argued that a company would be a vital step in confronting Portugal's reliance on foreign allies overseas who were simultaneously imperial rivals.[50] Padre Manuel Fernandes, the prince regent's Jesuit confessor, encouraged the monarch to accept the proposal by arguing that "there is not another prince in the world who has such a tribute," and that a donation from the New Christians was far better than "extortion through violence."[51]

Pedro II sent the details of the proposal to the Inquisition, which rejected it by arguing that the advantages of an East Indies company would fall short, considering some of the failures of the previous Brazil example.[52] It was also argued that a general pardon would attract thousands of Portuguese Jews living abroad to the capital where they would practice their religion openly without fear of punishment.[53] Further contentions included the idea that succumbing to pressure to conform to Roman standards would cede royal prerogative.[54] The inquisitorial refusal concluded by asking, "What does it matter if we send [missionaries] to convert the gentile nations of India [if] New Christians are allowed to live Judaism openly in Portugal?"[55]

Pedro II sent these complaints along with the opinion of those in support of the cause to various ministers, canons, and theologians seeking their assessment of the matter.[56] Research in the Jesuit files of Portugal's *Torre do Tombo* national archive reveals that over forty individuals responded that the prince regent could not only allow the proposal but that he should indeed favor it.[57] Among those who voiced their support was Francisco de Abreu Godinho, who argued, "These men who make poor the Catholic kingdoms being in the midst of the unfaithful will make poor the kingdoms of the unfaithful being in the midst of Catholics. . . . [and] if they all were in the kingdom the money of those that live in Portugal would not leave the kingdom."[58] Another proponent argued that all of Portugal was being ruined from lack of money, which was a direct result of the lack of "men of commerce" who were suffering imprisonment and confiscation. He further contended that with the weakening of the country and growing numbers of foreigners, Portugal would soon be overrun by English and Dutch heretics. He concluded by arguing that "if the Brazil Company restored Brazil, delivering it from the hands of the heretical Dutch, the same would occur in India if there were to be an India Company."[59]

During it all, fury gripped Lisbon when a rumor began to circulate that the prince regent had actually signed the pardon before he withdrew to Caldas da Rainha. In reality, Pedro II had only sent the proposal to the pontiff in Rome for review.[60] The popular tumult was fomented by the Inquisition, who could always count on anti-Semitic prejudices among the people to outweigh any concern for distant and decaying imperial outposts.[61] Leaflets and broadsides soon covered the city denouncing those individuals that supported the pardon, with the Jesuits and the prince being the main targets.[62] The Inquisition stirred up more commotion as bands went about the city at night yelling "Long live the Christian faith, death to Judaism!"[63] A group known as the twelve apostles threatened to burn Padre Manuel Fernandes alive as they hung a picture on his door of Christ crucified with two Jesuits hanged on either side.[64] Francis Parry described the tense scene that recurred night after night as many assembled in the streets, going about "well armed." The Englishman further declared that "the people's words and actions looked so much towards a mutiny . . . that many left the city for fear."[65]

Those few enlightened individuals among the nobility who had favored the cause of the New Christians were equally lambasted. A poster on the door of a butcher shop read:

> To the Marquis of Fronteira, I counsel you as your friend to not let yourself be deceived by the crookedness of António Correia Bravo because he is a cunning Jew, neither trust his proposals of sweet polished words that have a different meaning than they sound as well as those of the proxies and guarantors of this general pardon, because all they guarantee will be lacking and the money they promise will come from the blood in the veins of the Old Christians . . . and God grant that they do not also make you a Jew.[66]

The outrage spread while the Inquisition circulated letters encouraging the clergy to protest.[67] The Bishop of Leiria tried to dissuade Pedro II, reminding him, "[Even though] they promise your highness 500,000 *cruzados*, from them who are today imprisoned in the dungeons of the Holy Office . . . your highness has by just and holy laws given by God much larger sums."[68] The pressure only worsened as those supporting the deposed King Afonso VI saw their opportunity.[69] Speaking of the dangers facing the prince regent on all sides, António Vieira remarked that Pedro II's flight from the city only encouraged the people's riotousness. He further highlighted the pasquinades that followed, which declared that "[the] natural king was exiled and imprisoned and his honor lost, [while] the kingdom was impoverished [by a] tyrannical government, which above all, wanted to sell the faith and crucify Christ again."[70]

Pedro II ultimately decided to resolve the matter by calling a meeting of the *côrtes* in 1674. After deliberating, all three estates were unanimous in their decision that under no circumstances were the New Christians to be granted pardon.[71] The people were particularly vitriolic in their denunciation, going so far as to demand that the prince immediately cease his "unjust and scandalous" protection of the group.[72] Those who supported the pardon continued to be popular targets. The Marquis of Minas suffered the indignation of the people who suggested that the stroke that left his tongue hanging out of his mouth was God's punishment for his "having prayed many times in favor of the Jews."[73] D. Rodrigo de Meneses suffered a loss of speech for the same reason, and the Marquis of Fronteira's death was blamed on his support for the cause.[74] In short, while religious tolerance certainly existed at times among some Portuguese, the possibility of Atlantic influences threatening religious conformity during the period was treated quite seriously.[75]

After the rejection of the general pardon and the East India company, the New Christians and their Jesuit supporters focused solely on obtaining a papal reform of the Portuguese Inquisition's proceedings. As in the earlier pamphlets and broadsides, the debate played out in an extensive literary battle as António Vieira published a tract in favor of the changes under the title *Desengano católico sobre a causa da gente da nação hebreia,* to which the secretary of state Mendo de Fóios Pereira responded with *Engano judaico contra o dezengano católico de um réu enganoso e enganado.*[76] The desired reform was dealt a favorable hand around the same time when an ex-notary of the Lisbon Inquisition composed his insider's account of that tribunal's excesses.[77] The account created support for the New Christians outside of Portugal and influenced Pope Clement X to issue a brief in October 1674 suspending the Inquisition in Portugal as the tribunal came under papal review.[78] Francis Parry described the reaction of the populace at Coimbra, which was no doubt shared in Lisbon, noting, "Tis said that the people there threaten to fetch out the [New Christians] by force and burn them."[79] A string of ardent preachers further whipped up emotions in Lisbon, and Francis Parry recorded that many hoped that a decision in favor of the New Christians would again "make the people mutiny against the present government and restore the king."[80] The fear of popular action against Pedro II became even more real when, in the wake of the earlier plot, the prince regent transferred Afonso VI from the Azorean island of Terceira to the royal palace in Sintra outside of Lisbon in September 1674.[81] Cries of "Long-live D. Afonso! Death to the Jews!" soon rang out in the city streets.[82]

Pedro II, already angry at Rome for suspending the Holy Office without his consent, was shaken by the threat of revolt, which strengthened his resolve to side with the Inquisition.[83] The monarch's determination in the matter increased as Innocent XI (elected pontiff in 1676) demanded that five original trial records of Judaizers be delivered to Rome for procedural examination, to which the inquisitors offered only to send copies. The back-and-forth continued until December 1678, when Innocent XI ordered that the original records be sent within ten days or the inquisitors would lose their offices and jurisdiction to the secular bishops.[84] The prince regent forbade the inquisitors from sending the records under pain of exile and seized the keys to the Inquisition archives.[85] Pedro II then declared to Innocent XI that while the pope could "extinguish the Inquisition in these kingdoms . . . he would not allow its alteration in any form."[86]

The blowback against Rome grew as the *côrtes* met in 1679–80 and all three estates expressed their desire to see the Inquisition restored.[87] The gridlock was broken as Innocent XI decided to settle for two records (which were selected so as to portray the tribunal in a more positive light) before allowing the Holy Office to resume its work in August 1681.[88] The city rejoiced after receiving the news with days of celebrations.[89] Additionally, two *autos-da-fé* were planned and held within the same month of May 1682.[90] Michael Geddes, chaplain to the English factory, recorded these gruesome scenes and public delight, which included burning the faces of the accused before lighting the pyre. Even more disturbing was the fact that the victims were chained so high above the flames that they were "really roasted, and not burnt to death" and that the whole spectacle was "beheld by people of both sexes, and of all ages, with such transports of joy and satisfaction as are not on any other occasion to be met with."[91]

In the ten years following, there were a total of fourteen *autos-da-fé* involving 322 New Christian penitents in the capital, spelling ruin for the New Christian merchants that remained. Pedro II issued another decree in 1683 exiling those tried by the Holy Office. However, much like the 1671 version, this too was largely a dead letter.[92] Thomas Maynard was befuddled by such actions and noted the destructive effects on Atlantic commerce. He commented that these developments had placed the Portuguese on a "direct course to destroy the little trade and navigation which they [had] left," especially at a time when attempts to establish a program of domestic manufacturing were underway (discussed in chapter 4).[93] The economic price imposed by the Inquisition for desired religious conformity in Lisbon was undoubtedly high.

In the wake of the restoration of the Holy Office, hundreds of New Christians fled the capital on foreign ships.[94] Michael Geddes declared that the only option out of Lisbon was by sea on an English or Dutch vessel, as they dared not go by land into Spain. Yet even when safely aboard, if they heard Portuguese spoken, they immediately began to "tremble hand and foot" with worry that somehow they would be apprehended. Geddes concluded, "By the terrors which these poor fugitives are under, we may judge of the terrors they are under in the prisons of the Inquisition."[95] António Vieira noted that the resentment among the commoners against the English for these and similar actions was such that they threatened that if discovered, "no Englishman would remain alive."[96] One reason the English and other traders were more than willing to aid New Christians in their flight was the reality that if captured, these would be unable to repay their debts to foreign creditors.[97]

Persecution of the New Christians at the end of the seventeenth century only exaggerated the deepening dependency in the city as foreign firms opted to send their own factors to the capital rather than risk assets by trading through vulnerable New Christians.[98] The effects of Pedro II's actions were felt well into the reign of his son João V. An eighteenth-century petition of businessmen declared that the economy continued to suffer due to "the extermination of the Hebrews during the reign of king D. Pedro" and that "the commerce and money that remained now pertains totally to foreigners that were in the kingdom whom over the last seventy years have multiplied in such a manner that there must be 30,000 of them."[99]

The persecution further transformed society as the number of successful petitions to become familiars and commissaries of the Inquisition (which required extensive genealogical inquiry) exploded.[100] The whole process contributed to the rising obsession with blood purity that defined the era.[101] The arrival of gold in the capital by the beginning of the eighteenth century and the expansion of Brazilian trade only quickened the transformation as wealthy merchants became some of the most active petitioners eager to serve the Holy Office.[102]

Brazilian New Christians in Lisbon

The heightened inquisitorial persecution during the last quarter of the seventeenth century carried into the reign of João V, as the monarch continued the tradition initiated by his father of transferring captives from the other two Portuguese tribunals at Évora and Coimbra (which held prisoners from Porto) to Lisbon in order to aggrandize the spectacle and satisfy his growing absolutism and religiosity.[103] The overall impact was that from 1686 until 1756, no public executions occurred in Évora. Between 1701 and 1708 only twelve occurred in Coimbra, after which time there were none.[104]

To be fair, not every Portuguese agreed with the developments and saw clearly the destructive and retarding influence of a resurgent Inquisition. In 1703, the French Baron de Lahontan visited Lisbon and recorded an interesting conversation he had with a "sensible" and "wise" Portuguese man who had spent several years in both Brazil and Angola. After hearing of Lahontan's time among the "savages" of Canada and his description of the Iroquois who broiled their prisoners of war, the man exclaimed that the Iroquois of Portugal, by which he surely meant the Inquisition, "were yet more cruel than those of America, in burning without mercy their relations and friends." This was particularly true considering that the Native people of the New World "inflicted that punishment only upon the cruel enemies of their nation."[105] For his part, the famed Portuguese diplomat D. Luís da Cunha also argued (like Thomas Maynard) that the explosive persecution wreaked havoc on the nascent manufacturing program as entire regions were almost entirely depopulated by the Holy Office, which was surely hyperbole.[106]

Nevertheless, the assertion embodies the continued inquisitorial pushback against New Christians.

The combination of failing domestic manufactures and growing reliance on English merchants in the Portugal and Brazil trades naturally led to an increase in the number of English vessels in port. These developments only strengthened Lisbon's role as the premier gateway to Northern Europe for fleeing New Christians across Portugal. Gaspar Lopes da Costa admitted in 1726 to aiding multiple individuals in escaping from various parts of the kingdom on English vessels. On one occasion, he helped a certain José de Gamboa (who initially had a mind to flee to Brazil) secure passage on an English ship bound for London for the price of 24,000 *réis*.[107] On another occasion, he aided the New Christian Luís da Sylva Bahia in his plans to flee Lisbon after the man admitted that the Inquisition in Coimbra had imprisoned his mother and many others. Lopes da Costa put Bahia in contact with an English captain living in the city, who then agreed to take the poor fellow onboard for the price of ten gold coins.[108] Thus, Lisbon in a way became an underground railroad of sorts for fleeing New Christians during the period. The Portuguese ambassador in London and later Marquis of Pombal, Sebastião José de Carvalho e Melo, wrote in 1741, "I am very well informed that it is rare among us a man of the *nação* who does not have his eyes on the path for these parts."[109]

Portuguese New Christians were not the only ones fleeing Lisbon during the period. A sizable number of Spanish New Christians also used the city as a point of embarkation.[110] The Spaniard Francisco Mendes was arrested by the Lisbon Inquisition in 1727. Mendes was born in Málaga and lived in the neighborhood of Triana in Seville before moving to Lisbon with Manoel de Peralta, whom he served as an apprentice chocolatier. In his deposition, Mendes confessed to the inquisitors that he and others "came to this kingdom of Portugal and court of Lisbon where [they] wanted to flee to England."[111]

Those who were unable to pay for passage relied on the members of the synagogues in London or Amsterdam in exchange for their promise to fully convert to Judaism upon arrival.[112] The swell of New Christians fleeing Lisbon placed a significant strain on the Jewish community in London (and other European capitals, no doubt) as the leaders of that city's synagogue composed a letter to their associates in Jerusalem in 1705 complaining of their poverty as a result of "the many people which this *Kahal Kados* has welcomed from Spain and Portugal whom one must succor as they come fleeing the tyrannies of the Inquisition."[113] Others were aided by family members throughout the Portuguese Atlantic. The Marquis of Pombal remarked,

"There are no rich people from this *nação* in Portugal or Brazil who do not have money here [in England] . . . and even those who have little always succor their poor relatives that are found here."[114] Although the risks involved with flight from the city were often elevated, the threatening nature of a society fueled by a resurgent Inquisition made that choice preferable to many.

Despite the monarch's repeated petitions, English ships continued to harbor New Christians just as they did runaway slaves.[115] According to Lord Tyrawly, the practice would continue as long as New Christians were offering "a purse of gold" to English captains.[116] The envoy Henry Worsley justified English actions, noting, "[I could] with juster reason complain of the convents in this city, which daily give protection to his majesty's sailors who have a mind to quit their ships . . . besides [the] continual robbing his majesty's subjects of their children."[117]

Many New Christians returned to their trades in the capitals of Northern Europe. Those who fled to London often established themselves as some of the most influential merchants as they traded through English agents in Lisbon who were in turn dependent on Portuguese merchants for access to the Brazil and Lisbon trades.[118] Lord Tyrawly admitted that English trade to Lisbon was in part dependent on the New Christians in England, who were "the greatest dealers to Portugal in our woolen goods."[119] The same occurred in Holland, France, and the West Indies.[120] In Bordeaux alone, thirty-six Portuguese New Christian families were recorded in 1636. By 1675, there were so many that local commerce depended on them. In 1718, one hundred additional families arrived, and by 1749, half of the city's commerce was in the hands of the three hundred Portuguese New Christian commercial firms.[121]

Flight from the city during the first half of the eighteenth century largely coincided with bouts of renewed inquisitorial vigor and increasing royal absolutism despite an overall decline as previous decades of persecution took their toll on the New Christian community.[122] These intervals were the subject of the English consul Thomas Burnett's remarks, who observed in 1725, "Many rich Jews have been lately seized by the Inquisition in several parts of this kingdom, others who are missing are thought to have made their escape to Great Britain or Holland. So universal a seizure of those people has not been known these thirty years past."[123] In fact, during the period from 1720 to 1733, the London Sephardi community reached its highest immigration levels with roughly 1,500 arrivals, mostly from Portugal.[124]

D. Luís da Cunha contended that many of those apprehended were not practicing Jews but merely made into such. He lambasted the Inquisition in Lisbon by arguing, "Just as there is a house in [this city] that mints coins, so there is one in Rossio that mints Jews or New Christians."[125] The reality was more complex. While a large number of New Christians had fully accepted Catholicism over the centuries, there were also those who maintained tenets of Judaism. The fear of crypto-Judaizers meant that even the smallest gestures saw genuine Catholics arrested by the Holy Office.[126] In a 1683 letter to the inquisitors written while he was aboard the ship that was to take him to Brazil for banishment, the twenty-five-year-old Fernando de Morales Penso described the awful anguish of the falsely accused by declaring he had never strayed from his Christian faith and that in order to clear his conscience he needed to declare that his confessions concerning himself and others were entirely false and were offered only as a means to save his life.[127]

Other minds that had been exposed to Enlightenment principles abroad began to question the utility of the Inquisition during the period. Ribeiro Sanches, a Portuguese New Christian who converted to Judaism and fled to England in 1726–27 before later returning to Catholicism, was an ardent critic who penned a stinging tract entitled *Origem da denominação de Christão-Velho e Christão Novo em Portugal*.[128] In the piece, Sanches decried the common accusation of Judaizer against New Christians who had lived their whole lives as good Catholics. Such things, he argued, only encouraged many to "seek other kingdoms where they [could] live in liberty" without the constant danger of "being burned."[129] The famed Portuguese writer Francisco Xavier de Oliveira, better known as "O Cavaleiro de Oliveira," composed a similar denunciation in the 1750s, titled *A Pathetic Discourse on the Present Calamities of Portugal*, while living in England as a convert to Protestantism. In it, he lamented Portugal's lost economic opportunities as a result of the intense persecution under that tribunal that "obliged the most wealthy and powerful families of that nation to quit the kingdom and establish themselves elsewhere!"[130]

Sustained persecution under João V effected a complete transformation of the mercantile community in Lisbon as New Christian merchants began to disappear from the capital. In his landmark study concerning merchants in Lisbon during the second half of the eighteenth century, Jorge Miguel Pedreira found only twelve New Christians.[131] Their near disappearance represented an enormous change; previously, New Christians made up between two-thirds and three-quarters of the mercantile class in Lisbon. As a result, New Christians targeted by the Inquisition during João V's reign increasingly consisted of artisans from the interior or traders in Brazil rather than the few remaining wealthy merchants of the capital.[132] The broadening of focus toward Brazil during the period was driven in part by the fact that the Holy Office in Lisbon, maintained by confiscations, was notoriously short on funds and perceived an opportunity after the discovery of gold and diamonds. Yet even this new reserve proved too little considering João V granted the Inquisition a subsidy of 12,000 *cruzados* from the Junta da Administração do Tabaco (Tobacco Administration Council) near the end of his reign.[133]

In contrast to the Spanish empire with its various inquisitorial tribunals in the New World, Portugal never established an Inquisition in Brazil. Anyone unfortunate enough to be apprehended there was subsequently shipped to Lisbon for examination and João V's reign saw the highest number of confiscations in the history of the New World colony. The uptick in confiscations and imprisonments was a direct result of the discovery of gold and diamonds as many of these New Christian merchants traded in the mining region.[134] Among those apprehended and later tried in Lisbon were many merchants who had previously emigrated from Portugal.[135] This circulation was no doubt the result of both push and pull factors in Lisbon. Like other emigrants, the discovery of gold and burgeoning commercial opportunities in the colony were a strong attractor for Portuguese New Christian merchants, but the earlier resurgence of the Inquisition under Pedro II should not be overlooked as merchants sought to maintain their direct participation in Luso-Brazilian trade networks. The persecution was so economically heavy that D. Luís da Cunha went so far as to declare that the Inquisition had "discovered in Rio de Janeiro the mine of the Jews." With many New Christians also tied up in the rebounding sugar industry at the time, João V halted inquisitorial confiscations of mills due to the adverse effects on the commerce of that product.[136] Henry Worsley recounted that during that time, the Brazil fleets returned over one hundred New Christians but poor sugar cargos because a "great part of the sugar plantations [were] ruined by the Inquisition's taking up the Jews, who are the only planters and traders in the Brazils."[137]

Among the unfortunate individuals swept up in the fury were the family members of the famous Luso-Brazilian playwright António José da Silva, known more commonly as "O Judeu" (the Jew). The Silva family settled in Lisbon after being tried in the city subsequent to their seizure in Brazil. The Holy Office first apprehended António in 1726. He was finally reconciled after denouncing various relatives. António then devoted himself to composing theatrical and opera pieces, some of which were critical of the Inquisition. He was arrested again in 1737 only days after informing the inquisitors that he was likely to be denounced by an enslaved female whom he refused to manumit. António was ultimately condemned to death after spies in the dungeons reported to the inquisitors that they regularly witnessed him observe Jewish fasts.[138]

Afro-Brazilians in Lisbon

While New Christians continued to be the main focus throughout the period, the Lisbon Inquisition broadened its scope in other ways to combat unwanted consequences of the Portuguese capital becoming increasingly Atlanticized. African religious practices novel to the age became a target as the small uptick in Afro-Brazilians arriving in the capital (discussed previously) occurred during the period. Much of the inquisitorial focus was on talismans known as *bolsas de mandinga*, which became particularly popular in Lisbon. These artifacts consisted of a small pouch containing a syncretic mix of religious elements worn around the arm or neck for a variety of purposes, the most common being protection from physical harm. *Mandingas* trace their origins to Islamic influence among the Malinke people in the kingdom of Mali, who often wore religious amulets.[139]

The first recorded mention of *mandingas* in Lisbon (and outside of Africa) occurred in 1672 with the denunciation of an enslaved African named Manuel by a fellow servant. The servant reported to the Inquisition that Manuel taunted a soldier in the city and argued that he could not be harmed because of the *mandinga* he carried. The servant also divulged that Manuel had experimented with the *mandinga* previously by placing a sword in the ground and throwing himself on it without receiving harm.[140] Overall, *mandingas* were most commonly associated with Africans from the Guinea and Mina coasts.[141] It is no coincidence that they began to appear in Lisbon precisely during the period in which planters and traders in Brazil began to favor these individuals over captives from Angola.

Archival research among the documents of the Lisbon Inquisition reveals that *mandingas* in the city developed into Atlantic transmitters among the popular classes as they often contained African, Brazilian, and Portuguese elements. While the exact composition of each *mandinga* varied, the most common articles were sheets of paper containing Catholic prayers and various other symbols. Other ingredients such as blood, seeds, roots, stones, coins, and even the bones of unbaptized children were at times included.[142] The 1730 Inquisition case of the enslaved African named José Francisco Pedroso demonstrates that in addition to the syncretic nature of the compositional elements, the production of *mandingas* itself reflected a growing Atlantic influence. Pedroso was imprisoned by the Inquisition in July 1730 after being denounced by a priest. The cleric stated in his denunciation that he saw Pedroso place "some papers under the altar stone . . . with the characters he [brought] and [offered] to this board." The priest added that the papers were positioned under the altar so that masses could be said over them. Pedroso himself related that the papers did not belong to him but were "given to him by another black who was the slave of his master's brother."[143]

Pedroso declared in his examination that he was from Ouidah on the Mina coast of Africa and was baptized in Rio de Janeiro.[144] He further admitted that he worked with another enslaved African from Mina in Lisbon named José Francisco Pereira, who instructed him to place the papers under the altar stone, because "a lot of blacks wanted those papers."[145]

Further questioning revealed an elaborate network as Pedroso confessed that on various occasions he and other enslaved individuals, including some from Brazil and another owned by an Englishman in the city, would often accompany Pereira or others to a crossroads where they would bury the amulets at midnight before returning the next night to retrieve them.[146] The practice of leaving *mandingas* or other religious items at a crossroads stems from the African belief that these were places to leave bad influences behind.[147] Pedroso informed the inquisitors that it was during these moments that Pereira made pacts with demons who helped him prepare *mandingas*, which contained a special root for the purpose of turning away a master's anger. He could not recollect which root was used but did remember that it "smelled a lot and came from Brazil."[148] Pedroso further testified that Pereira's *mandingas* were popular among Africans in Lisbon due to his recent arrival from Rio de Janeiro and that, in addition to wearing them for protection, many wore them to ensure success with women. In contrast, other enslaved people sought out Pereira's services in preparation for their departure to Brazil.[149]

Pereira was also apprehended by the Inquisition. The subsequent examination revealed that he was from Mina, baptized in Recife, and christened in the mining region of Brazil.[150] Pereira's testimony corroborates much of the information provided earlier by Pedroso, albeit with interesting additions. Pereira noted that besides burying *mandingas* at crossroads, it was also common practice to inter them in churchyards.[151] He also added that he used other ingredients to make *mandingas*. According to him, on another occasion an enslaved individual named Francisco, while walking near the river, "found a dead baby . . . cut off one of the hands" and brought it to José "who used the said hand in the *bolsas*."[152]

When pressed about why he did such things, Pereira replied that "a lot of blacks sought him out to obtain *mandingas* that they believed he brought from Brazil."[153] Furthermore, he declared that some of the papers contained copies of Catholic prayers that were given to him in Brazil.[154] Pereira also revealed that he relied on an enslaved African named António, who was literate and had arrived with his master from Angola, to copy the characters and prayers for him.[155] At other times he employed the services of a white servant named António Guedes.[156]

Close contact among Africans and the lower classes facilitated the use of *mandingas* among white people in Lisbon, who by the eighteenth century were just as likely to buy *mandingas* as Black people.[157] Fifty-three-year-old José Ribeiro appeared before the Holy Office in July 1698 to declare that eighteen days prior he was passing the time in conversation with a group of men when a certain Francisco Tavares began to boast that there was nothing better for one's courage "than a *bolça* and that he knew well who sold them." Tavares then told the group that they could purchase *mandingas* from an African who lived in the parish of Santa Justa near the city center. When questioned by the inquisitors, Tavares revealed that he had spoken with the man on a previous occasion while fetching water when the two began talking of avoiding harm. According to Tavares, the African then proceeded to try to persuade him to purchase a *mandinga* by tying it to his dog and stabbing the poor creature repeatedly without causing any harm. Tavares swore that he had nothing to do with the *mandinga* but did confess to having related the episode to others while at a tavern.[158]

The African António was denounced in July 1702 for attempting to sell *mandingas* to two white men named Manoel Gomes and João da Matta. According to the document, the three men were together in Lisbon when António "took out a *bolçinha* and offered it to them for purchase," declaring that "whosoever possessed it would not be harmed."[159] The two men decided to put the amulet to the test, and Manoel Gomes "closed it in his hand . . . and with a sharp needle could not harm [his hand]." Amazed (and not a little bewildered), the two decided that the *mandinga* had to be from the devil.[160]

While *mandingas* were actively hawked to white people in Lisbon's public spaces, the case of the freed Black Patrício Andrade demonstrates that Africans at times peddled amulets to white people in their own homes and even to those of considerable social standing.[161] Patrício was apprehended in March 1690 with a *mandinga* containing various stones and a paper with curious writing.[162] He was denounced by Dona Mariana Bernarda Serafina de Castelo Branco and her nephew Manuel Garcia de Castelo Branco, who testified that Patrício attempted to demonstrate the virtues of his *mandingas* in their home by having Manuel try ramming a sword through Patrício's bare chest various times. Dona Mariana testified that each attempt left Patrício unharmed. Her nephew confirmed the story, adding that the *mandinga* was so effective that the blade of the sword bent during the experiment.[163] Ignácio Gomes divulged

KEEPING LISBON CATHOLIC

that Patrício also "sold to blacks and whites" and that "all were people of little consideration."[164] Patrício Andrade confessed to the inquisitors that after arriving from Cape Verde with his master, he heard about the necessity of *mandingas* from "many black lackeys and other persons of ordinary standing."[165] The Inquisition despaired at the widespread nature of the practice in the city "as many from the inferior class [used] similar *bolças*."[166]

Superstitious amulets were common in Portugal before the appearance of Afro-Brazilian *mandingas* at the end of the seventeenth century.[167] Yet it was Afro-Brazilians who transformed the practice into an Atlantic exotic in Lisbon as their services were consistently sought out by both Black and white people.[168] Despite the widespread use of the amulets among white people, Africans (as social outsiders) were far more likely to be tried by the Inquisition for such practices during the period.[169] More importantly, the Afro-Brazilian amulets demonstrate just how vibrant and influential Lisbon's African community was as it exercised a profound impact on the cultural and religious practices of the capital at the time. All this made Africans the more suspect as the metropole grappled with increasing cultural and religious diversity as a result of Atlanticization.

Protestants in Lisbon

Inquisitorial concern over growing foreign influence was not limited solely to the Afro-Brazilians and their religious objects making their way throughout the South Atlantic. Foreign Protestants, the English in particular, became another target as they began to arrive in greater numbers during the second half of the seventeenth century. Shackled by international treaties with England, the Inquisition in Lisbon developed various means of circumventing English religious privileges. The ascension of the Catholic James II to the English throne in 1685 created considerable difficulties for the English nation in Lisbon, as the inquisitors decided there was no longer a need to enforce treaty articles concerning religious practice.[170] In the absence of an English diplomat, consul Thomas Maynard was summoned by the Inquisition and told to end all religious meetings in his home and that the privilege was guaranteed only in the residence of the ambassador or envoy.[171] When Maynard complained that the practice had been allowed during his thirty years of service, the inquisitor general responded, "This cannot be granted you, for tis too great a scandal to the people."[172] The merchants of the factory petitioned London for diplomatic aid in the dispute and complained that the Dutch were allowed to worship in their consul's home.[173] Anglican services in Lisbon were, therefore, suspended until the arrival of the envoy Charles Scarburgh in 1686. After Scarburgh's recall in 1689, services ceased once again.[174] Put plainly, the Inquisition contributed in no small way to the widespread religious tensions among Protestants and Catholics discussed previously.

The English chaplain at the time, James Smallwood, highlighted popular resentment against Protestant worship after Scarburgh's departure, noting, "[The] Inquisition silenced our church, and forbade us meeting again in public under severe penalties, which orders we are forced at present to submit to, not thinking it safe either to oppose so uncontrollable a court, or to provoke the rabble."[175] Public worship for the English finally resumed in 1693 with the arrival of John Methuen.[176] Despite the restoration of services, the Inquisition continued to rile up the masses on occasion. In 1700, an Englishman noted that the inquisitors "took an occasion to publish an edict in all churches, which is to be seen at this day on most of the church doors . . . wherein the English in general are stigmatized, not only for heretics, but for usurpers likewise."[177]

As the English began arriving in greater numbers, they brought with them enslaved Africans from their Atlantic colonies—the Carolinas in particular, given the demand for rice and indigo that developed in Lisbon.[178] Enslaved Africans who spoke English were also highly desired among the English factory in Porto.[179] The influx of enslaved Africans owned by the English in Lisbon drew the attention of the Inquisition. In 1670, Maynard relayed a message to the factory that the Inquisition would no longer "suffer any blacks or negros to go out of this port in English ships notwithstanding they belong to his majesty's subjects as many times commanders of ships have boys to serve them and now and then here comes a seaman that is black." Maynard further added, "The negros which usually come in English ships, are born in his majesty's plantations, and initiated to the Church of England and consequently they are the king's subjects and therefore not subject to the Inquisition, which they will not understand, but claim a jurisdiction over all blacks."[180]

Consequently, the Inquisition seized various enslaved Africans owned by the English in the city with the justification that they would "have none of the prince of Portugal's subjects transported into England to be turned from the Roman Catholic religion."[181] English ships thereafter were regularly docked at great cost downriver at Belém to avoid the seizures.[182] Maynard complained that the practice was prohibited by the treaty articles and despaired, knowing that no ministers at the Portuguese court would concern themselves with anything regarding the Inquisition.[183] In his call for a new treaty, Francis Parry suggested that a clause be introduced that guaranteed English vessels the right to keep Black people without threat of seizure.[184]

Similar to the desertion of seamen discussed in the previous chapter, the religious conversion of enslaved Africans owned by the English only complicated matters. At times, enslaved Africans owned by the English converted and were protected by the Inquisition as they worked alongside the Portuguese in the city. Such was the case of Charles Compton's enslaved African named Carlos. Born somewhere in Guinea in the early eighteenth century, Carlos was enslaved at a young age near the port of Cacheu and eventually purchased in Lisbon by the English consul turned envoy. Carlos was put to work on Compton's estate where he was instructed in the English language and the rites of Anglicanism by an English teacher, eventually receiving baptism. Carlos worked inside the home alongside other English servants who were Anglicans, the lone exception being a Galician cook who was Catholic. The servants who worked outside were all Portuguese Catholics.

Carlos's daily interactions with the outside servants taught him the Portuguese language and the basic precepts of Catholicism. He eventually became convinced and began waking extra early to attend mass secretly. He was soon discovered by an English servant who saw his rosary. Compton asked Carlos who had given him the rosary and threatened to sell him to Brazil if he converted. Refusing to confess, Carlos was whipped and locked away with little food. The Galician cook subsequently informed one of the Portuguese servants of Carlos's captivity, who then informed the cowherd, who in turn told a Catholic teacher who had been sending Carlos catechism materials. The cleric then petitioned Jorge Fonseca de Melo, a knight in the Military Order of Christ and bailiff of the Inquisition in Lisbon, for help. Fonseca de Melo passed the word to a Portuguese official, who related the tale to the inquisitor general, who finally ruled in 1734 that, according to both civil and canonical law, Carlos as a Catholic could not be enslaved by a heretic. Meanwhile Carlos had escaped with the help of the other servants. Compton was ultimately informed by the inquisitors that if he desired Carlos's return, he himself must convert.[185]

The Inquisition targeted English Protestants in other ways as the Holy Office ramped up the persecution of New Christians, many tied to English commercial firms. Thus, as Carla Vieira has asserted, the persecution of New Christians was in many ways also an attack on rising foreign influence in the capital.[186] Those arrested in 1681 after the restoration of the Holy Office alone were indebted to English merchants by at least 45,000 crowns.[187] In the face of indirect attacks, it is not surprising that the English aided New Christians in their flight.

New Christians were not the only ones to take refuge aboard English vessels in Lisbon. Ambassador John Methuen sent an English youth, William Brereton, on a Swedish ship bound for England to help him escape the Inquisition.[188] Henry Worsley harbored a Catholic Englishwoman in his house while trying to secure her escape on one of the packet boats in 1717, to the great consternation of the inquisitors.[189] Not everyone was successful. In 1733, Lord Tyrawly reported that an Irish woman who had converted was among those paraded through the city in the latest *auto-da-fé* before being banished for two years. This was not the first instance—Tyrawly decried, "Subjects of England, Roman Catholics, have frequently been punished by the Inquisition and brought out at the public autos."[190]

The zeal of the Inquisition made coexistence between Protestants and Catholics difficult at times. A Portuguese source from 1732 mentions the arrest by the Inquisition of a Castilian woman in the city for concubinage to an Englishman named Samuel Granier.[191] The weekly *Mercúrio de Lisboa* recorded another instance in February 1746 in which a French woman was apprehended for being a concubine to an English Protestant. In an interesting twist, the Englishman renounced his "heresy" so as to be able to marry her.[192] The widow Catherine Col, a Roman Catholic, was denounced after her petition to the patriarch to marry a Protestant Englishman was denied. Catherine went ahead anyway and married the man in the envoy's residence.[193] Even the reverend John Colbatch made enemies among the merchants of the English factory for refusing to marry one of their number to a Catholic girl, he himself having been warned against it by the Inquisition.[194]

The English (and others) were also targeted for their participation in Freemasonry, which they had introduced into the capital during the first half of the eighteenth century. William Dugood, a Catholic, founded Lisbon's first Masonic lodge in 1728 and many members of the factory joined over the years. By the 1730s, the lodge had a Protestant Grand Master and was almost exclusively Protestant—its nickname being "Loja dos Hereges Mercantes" (the Heretical Merchants' Lodge). Irish Catholics formed their own lodge in 1733, which later disbanded due to inquisitorial threats after a papal bull was issued in 1738 condemning Freemasonry.[195]

Jean Coustos (of Swiss origin but a naturalized Englishman) came to Lisbon in the 1740s with hopes of making his way to Brazil to ply his trade as a jeweler.[196] While in the city, he founded another lodge composed mostly of Frenchmen and some English and Portuguese. Most were artisans by trade and Catholic by religion.[197] Coustos was eventually apprehended by the Inquisition after being betrayed by a Portuguese friend. He was held in the Inquisition dungeons in Rossio for just over a year, where he was repeatedly tortured before being marched out in the *auto-da-fé* of 21 June 1744 and condemned to four years as a galley slave. He was eventually released after diplomatic intervention and fled to London.[198] After his *auto-da-fé*, however, a host of foreigners presented themselves to the Inquisition and confessed to being Freemasons.[199]

Considering the persecution of English men and women during the period by the Inquisition and the people in Lisbon, it is not surprising that the contemporary Charles Brockwell exclaimed that "the Roman Catholic is the established religion of Portugal, to which some are, and all seem prodigiously bigoted."[200] According to D. Luís da Cunha, the inquisitors justified their newfound zeal by arguing that "it is better that many Catholics and good Christians should perish than to allow one heretic or Jew to escape."[201]

Atlanticization deeply affected religious society in Lisbon during the period following the Portuguese restoration. And New Christians at home and arriving from Brazil certainly kept the Inquisition busy in its efforts to maintain Lisbon's Catholic identity. To be sure, the importance of Brazil for Portugal's survival coupled with the Inquisition's restraint under João IV to create a favorable economic atmosphere for many New Christian merchants. Indeed, many such New Christians enjoyed marked social elevation and wealth accumulation. Yet this brought increased attention during the reign of Pedro II, and—as the thief in Odivelas found out—New Christians soon became the single most important target for the Holy Office. Paradoxically, then, Atlanticization brought both riches and ruin to many of Lisbon's New Christians.

The New Christian response to the blowback was multifaceted, ranging from a proposal for an East India company along the lines of the previous Brazil example and a general pardon to the petition for a papal review of inquisitorial practices and widespread flight aboard English vessels. The persecution had profound consequences as the mercantile class for the first time in centuries became predominantly Old Christian. In addition, there was an overwhelmingly negative effect on the newly established industries (discussed in the next chapter) as New Christian contractors and investors were rounded up.

With the decimation of Lisbon's New Christians who had been made wealthy through Atlantic trade, the Inquisition itself developed an Atlantic

Fig. 2. Characters and designs from the *bolsa de mandinga* contained in the Inquisition papers of José Francisco Pedroso. ANTT, Tribunal do Santo Ofício, Inquisição de Lisboa, processo 11774. Photo provided by ANTT.

scope as its focus shifted to Brazil after the discovery of gold and diamonds. The accused brought to the city for trial on suspicion of Judaism joined others from across the Atlantic world. Enslaved Afro-Brazilians introduced new religious ideas and practices among the popular classes during the period in the form of *bolsas de mandinga*. The widespread use of these objects among both Black and white people was a cause of concern for the Inquisition, which believed them to be the result of demonic pacts. While the use of superstitious amulets existed previously in the capital, the manufacture and distribution of *mandingas* in Lisbon reveals the impact of Atlanticization in the metropole as the objects took on Portuguese, African, and Brazilian elements. The Inquisition also began to fear the introduction of heretical ideas from the North Atlantic as English Protestants arrived in greater numbers and dominated commerce in the wake of New Christian flight. Hamstrung by international treaties, the Holy Office developed other means of circumventing the issue as Anglican services were suspended, enslaved Africans confiscated, marriages thwarted, and debts unpaid.

Overall, it was the revival of the Lisbon Inquisition that set the Portuguese capital apart from other Atlantic entrepôts of the day. This is particularly true when considering that the Holy Office was limiting its focus in Seville during the period (which also covered Cádiz), was never established in London, and existed in the Netherlands for only about twenty years in the sixteenth century.[202] Local developments alone cannot explain this resurgence. By tracing the link between shifting economic fortunes and the socio-religious consequences as a result of various Atlantic influences during the period and their combination with internal developments in Lisbon, it becomes clear that the Inquisition underwent a reawakening as it expanded its scope to battle a changing society as a result of Atlanticization. When viewed as such, there is no doubt that the period became one of the worst for inquisitorial persecution in the city's history. No wonder the contemporary diplomat José da Cunha Brochado declared, "It is certain that in Portugal everything is Inquisition."[203]

4

ECONOMIC CHANGE IN ATLANTICIZED LISBON

In 1678, the English ambassador in Lisbon, Francis Parry, wrote to the secretary of state, Sir Joseph Williamson, that he had observed two Englishmen in Lisbon's streets who he soon discovered were cloth dyers and were staying in the Count of Ericeira's house. The men would not give the ambassador their names or any other details besides the fact that they were Protestants. It was then that Francis Parry declared that he knew what business they were about and that it was very prejudicial to their country since they had "sold themselves for slaves to another Prince." One of the men took offense to this and stated that the two were not slaves but free to go anywhere they wished, to which Parry responded that they would suffer the same fate as the English clothworkers who came before them on the same errand, that is, they would "be sent to the frontiers of this kingdom, where they were to be kept to their work with the same severity as slaves, without any communication with their countrymen or hopes of ever returning thence; and which was worst of all, they would be forced to renounce the true religion they were bred in and become Papists."[1]

These men were part of an elaborate scheme devised by the Count of Ericeira to import foreign specialists as a means of revitalizing manufacturing and industry in and around Lisbon. The ultimate goal of the program was to counteract the deepening economic reliance on the English. While Ericeira's effort can in many ways be considered the high-water mark of reform during the period, it was merely one of many attempts to combat the negative economic impacts of increasing Atlanticization in Lisbon.

The fact that Portugal was consistently more dependent on its empire than other European powers of the day meant that Lisbon was particularly affected by any changes to its imperial economic sphere. Thus, and in a similar vein to the religious consequences analyzed in the previous chapter, this chapter traces the economic challenges and responses to Atlanticization in Lisbon. In sum, it presents a deeper dive into the unique commercial development of Lisbon during the period as novel programs were implemented and later altered or abandoned due to the shifting interplay between North and South Atlantic interests in the Portuguese capital. While some works on Portugal's economic development during the period exist, these generally favor a broad scope that targets Portugal as a whole. In contrast, this chapter highlights the unique economic effects of Atlanticization in Lisbon.

Between Sugar and Gold

Atlantic dependence beginning in the second half of the seventeenth century left Lisbon in a difficult situation when sugar prices plummeted due to Caribbean competition. However, the flight of New Christian merchants and a growing reliance on foreign capital further compounded the economic woes. It was against this backdrop that Pedro II and his ministers were forced to rethink the empire's commercial direction and that rigorous Crown intervention into economic affairs began.[2]

One of the most notable insertions into economic life was the creation of the Junta da Administração do Tabaco (Tobacco Administration Council) in 1674 as the decline in Brazilian sugar prices stimulated an increase in tobacco production in the colony.[3] The junta was established to increase profits from the royal monopoly on tobacco through tighter regulation and to provide necessary funds for the Crown after the restoration conflict.[4] The Italian Jesuit Giovanni Antonio Andreoni (writing under the pseudonym André João Antonil) described Brazilian tobacco's growing popularity at the time by declaring that all sorts of people—from enslaved individuals and soldiers to nobility and clergy—"cannot live without this 'fifth element,' puffing away at all hours at home and on the streets, chewing its leaves, using snuff wicks, and filling their noses with this powder" and that "all defend tobacco's excessive use."[5]

While taken in various forms, snuff was used most commonly in Lisbon. The junta itself declared in 1701 that snuff had become "a principal provision, so much so that even the most miserable people of the kingdom, who are poor beggars prefer it to the nourishment of bread."[6] The Englishman

Dr. Cox Macro noted that in Lisbon, "all sorts of people from the King to the beggar take snuff" and that "indeed this keeps the smell of the streets out, but it may be one reason of [the Portuguese] speaking so much in the nose."[7] Previous to the establishment of the junta, tobacco was transformed into snuff at various locales in Lisbon. By 1675, the junta established a factory near the customhouse on the riverfront (moving in 1678 to the parish of Santo Estevão de Alfama), which had the sole privilege of producing snuff in the city.[8]

Of course, illegal production skyrocketed in the capital as snuff became increasingly popular and profitable.[9] The junta ruthlessly targeted these operations, which led Dr. Macro to declare that "[in Lisbon,] tis safer to murder a man than for one to make snuff."[10] The clergy were among the worst offenders, and Lisbon's convents, monasteries, and churches became regular sites of contraband and confiscation.[11] Tobacco supplies for these enterprises were secured through cultivation within the monasteries themselves or from illegal purchase aboard ships arriving from Brazil.[12] They relied as well on tobacco from Spanish, English, and Dutch sources.[13] In 1704, the junta reported that the city was flooded with "Virginia tobacco, and in one warehouse alone . . . there was collected by order of the guarda-mor [head guard] of this body, almost four-hundred sacks . . . and there have been various additional seizures."[14] The English excused their actions by declaring that the tobacco was part of their sailors' daily rations. Lord Tyrawly complained, "This poor traffic is so inconsiderable that all that is landed from the king's ships in fifty years' time is not worth taking notice of."[15] Another Englishman admitted, however, that the ships often contained "a much larger quantity of tobacco on board than the company [could] consume in years."[16]

The junta generated significant results and tobacco became among the most profitable sources of revenue for the Crown.[17] Friar Raphael Bluteau declared that in Lisbon, "snuff and smoke become gold and silver."[18] Brazilian tobacco was profitable for the Crown well beyond the addictive habits of Lisbon's populace. Not only was it heavily traded for enslaved Africans from Mina in West Africa (as discussed previously), but it was also shipped to Goa via Lisbon, where it helped in some form to revitalize trade throughout the decaying Estado da Índia.[19] Antonil declared, "If Brazilian sugar has become known in all the kingdoms and provinces of Europe, its tobacco has become much more acclaimed throughout the four corners of the earth. Today it is highly desired, and people expend great effort to obtain it by any means."[20] Clearly, Atlanticization elevated tobacco's importance in Lisbon.

Other efforts attempted to combat economic decline. Among these was a Crown-sponsored program of transplanting Asian spices to Brazil with the overall goal of avoiding the costs associated with transport, defense, and production in the crumbling Estado da Índia. Thus, to some degree, the Portuguese court in Lisbon, which refused to accept the New Christian proposal to revive India based on the previous Brazil Company model, now looked to the declining global empire as a means of reinvigorating imperial commerce throughout the Atlantic. The influential Jesuit friar António Vieira, having previously failed in his efforts to persuade the Crown to establish an East Indies company, played a vital role in convincing Pedro II to begin the program, which eventually included a short-lived monopoly company designed to export products from Maranhão while also importing enslaved Africans to that region of northern Brazil. A similar program was later revived under the Marquis of Pombal.[21]

Duarte Ribeiro de Macedo, the Portuguese envoy in Paris and Vieira's close friend, had a hand in the transplantation program. Macedo published a tract in 1675 contending that if Brazil produced a variety of oriental spices, the riches generated would be "more useful and less costly than the mines of Peru or Sofalá." More importantly, he argued, product would arrive in the capital after a short two-month journey "and all the nations of Europe [would flock] to Lisbon because of the prices."[22]

These advantages appealed to Pedro II, especially when considering complaints that the city had been reduced to a "miserable state" from its former opulence.[23] Repeated dispatches were sent to the viceroy of the Portuguese state of India ordering him to "send in every monsoon [season], plants, cuttings, and seeds of all those types" as well as "a native of the land that understands their cultivation" and with particular instructions regarding in which climate the plants produce.[24] Pedro II required that the experiments be carried out all over the Atlantic empire, including Lisbon, and he ordered the governor general of Brazil to only "take part of the plants" and send the rest "to this kingdom so that here we can attempt the same."[25] Despite some success, the program largely failed due to a lack of technical skill and competing economic interests. Efforts continued haphazardly into the reign of João V but suffered from a lack of royal support after the discovery of Brazilian gold.[26]

As opposed to its continued focus on colonial commercial reform in Brazil, the Crown did little to combat the growing dependence on imported foodstuffs in the city. Having lost control of the Atlantic cod fisheries during the period of political union with Spain, Lisbon (like other Iberian cities) grew increasingly beholden to English vessels for fish.[27] During the restoration it was estimated that between fifty and sixty English ships delivered cod to Portugal each year.[28] Thomas Cox recorded at the beginning of the eighteenth century that the city consumed twenty thousand *quintais* (Portuguese hundredweights) of fish annually.[29] In 1707, the English cod trade to Portugal and Spain was estimated to be worth 130,000 pounds sterling each year.[30]

Grain was constantly in short supply, giving rise to a lively trade among English and other foreign merchants in the city. Dependence on foreign suppliers made Lisbon into a veritable crossroads where cereals were concerned. Wheat and rice often arrived on English vessels from the Mediterranean, other areas of Europe, or the various colonies in the New World.[31] By the 1730s, multiple North American cities were sending regular shipments to Lisbon. One American merchant declared in 1740, "I can well observe that Philadelphia is as much or more obliged to Lisbon than any port whatsoever, London excepted."[32] Put another way, Portugal as a whole was so dependent on foreign grain that in any given year, it imported as much as one-fifth of its total supply.[33] The reliance was such that the Portuguese diplomat José da Cunha Brochado lamented that the Portuguese could not subsist without the help of English "heretics" who gave them their "daily bread."[34] For his part, the English chaplain John Colbatch remarked, "We furnish them with necessaries of life, in exchange for supplies to our luxury."[35] In short, Lisbon was heavily dependent on the Atlantic world.

The Beginnings of Portuguese Manufacturing

Against this backdrop of economic decline at the end of the seventeenth century, the growing influx of foreign manufactures only compounded Lisbon's difficulties.[36] The Count of Vilar Maior, and others, repeatedly complained that foreign merchants took little in exchange and, as a result, precious money was leaving the kingdom.[37] The outlook became bleak as supplies of New World silver from Spanish America steadily declined after the break with Spain. In a mercantilist era, these factors combined to spur the beginnings of a royally sponsored program of manufacturing in the metropole—a program that the Marquis of Pombal later resumed during the subsequent period.[38] Increased agricultural production required large investments of land and threated the established social order, not to mention the fact that it faced stern opposition from powerful aristocratic interests invested in viniculture.[39] Thus, domestic manufacturing was the only feasible option to combat the outflow of precious monetary resources.

The new policy in Portugal, based largely on the economic ideas of the French minister Jean-Baptiste Colbert, was instituted around 1670 and driven largely by the Count of Ericeira, who was eventually named *vedor de fazenda*, or head of the treasury.[40] Ericeira was largely influenced by Colbertian principles through the writings of the previously mentioned Duarte Ribeiro de Macedo.[41] In his tract entitled *Sobre a introdução das artes*, Macedo claimed that the exportation of money by foreign merchants in exchange for manufactures was a major problem facing Portugal.[42] In the piece, he poignantly asked, "Who among us wears anything made in Portugal?"[43]

Ericeira's first step was to establish factories in and around Lisbon with the help of foreign artisans. The goal was to diversify and jump-start a Portuguese economy otherwise reliant on the declining value of Atlantic exports. News of the program worried foreign traders and diplomats in Lisbon. The French ambassador, Saint-Romain, warned his countrymen that the Portuguese were upset at French taxes on sugar and were actively seeking to establish industries by having Macedo send them "as many workers as he [could] for every kind of manufacture."[44] In a concerned letter to Lord Arlington, English consul Thomas Maynard wrote that the Portuguese were drawing up a new economic model to compete more effectively with foreigners, the English in particular, and had already begun producing both English and French manufactures after the arrival of various technicians from both countries. He further related that English clothworkers were being recruited by the English Catholic bishop Russell in Portugal and a certain Francis Holbech who was married to a Portuguese woman.[45] Besides these, masters were recruited from Venice to establish a glass furnace in the city and to teach the Portuguese how to produce crystal.[46]

In 1672, four Parisian hatters arrived in Lisbon and began producing beaver hats.[47] The endeavor ultimately failed as the dye proved poor in quality, beaver pelts were difficult to secure, and the French consul in Lisbon managed to convince two of the men to return home—one in exchange for a pardon and a pension of 200,000 *réis*.[48] Macedo bemoaned the downfall of the enterprise and declared that Portuguese "hats are already despised" and that there is not a "decent man who does not wear a French hat."[49] By 1681, the hatmakers in Lisbon petitioned Pedro II for relief, arguing that for years foreign hats of every style flooded the city and caused the office of hatter to become "largely extinct . . . [seeing as] the major part of those masters who had stores have left these and the trade due to such great misery and poverty [and] with their women and children have begun to go door to door begging in order to sustain themselves."[50]

Other efforts were attempted to combat the growing reliance on foreign manufactures. A series of sumptuary laws targeting the use of imported items proved a vital step in the development of domestic manufacturing. The first of these laws, issued in 1668, was largely ineffective due to a lack of domestic production to meet growing demand.[51] Moreover, the legislation proved futile in terms of regulating the worst offenders. One observer complained that when it came to the aristocracy, the pragmatic laws were like "spiders' webs where flies are caught but never birds."[52]

The bulk of foreign manufactures sold in Lisbon consisted of cloth that, according to Macedo, made up the "the greatest expense and waste of this kingdom."[53] A subsequent decree in 1677 outlawed the use of foreign cloth altogether.[54] Due to treaty obligations, Pedro II was able to outlaw only the use of foreign fabrics, not their importation.[55] The 1677 decree enjoyed greater success as the Count of Ericeira implemented a program of luxury silk production designed to divert aristocratic spending toward domestic goods.[56] The English were not seriously affected by the pragmatic, considering that the bulk of their trade was in woolen draperies like baize used by commoners, which was not technically considered cloth.[57]

Efforts to revive a moribund silk industry that had been neglected during sixty years of Habsburg rule began soon after the 1677 pragmatic.[58] At that time, Lisbon imported roughly eighty thousand pairs of silk stockings a year from England worth about 320,000 *cruzados*, not to mention other articles from France.[59] Revival began as Pedro II mandated that the city council have mulberry trees planted "in the greatest quantity possible in the fields, gardens, fallow lands, and other regions that [were] suitable."[60] Advocates argued that the program would decrease the drain of bullion as foreign merchants began to accept silk as payment for their imported goods and that the poor would benefit as they cared for the worms or spun in their homes.[61] That same year a Frenchman named Roland Duclos was awarded rights to establish a factory in the city that eventually boasted fifty English looms, a large spinning-mill, and employed not only foreigners, but also three hundred Portuguese women who spooled at home.[62] The fabric produced was then sold in a retail shop by two Portuguese merchants.[63]

The French, whose trade consisted largely of luxury fabrics, were the hardest hit by the 1677 pragmatic and early manufacturing push. The English worried that these developments would come at the expense of their lucrative woolen trade, which represented the largest drain on Portuguese currency since the widespread adoption of these fabrics in Portuguese urban centers.[64] English fears proved correct as Ericeira then began to focus on producing popular woolens.[65] A state contract was soon secured in 1677 with three New Christian weavers in Covilhã in the province of Beira to produce serge and baize. Various reasons underwrote Ericeira's focus on Covilhã and other interior towns for the new venture. First, these were existing centers of woolen production, which made reorganizing along monopolistic and proto-industrial lines easier than starting anew in Lisbon. Second, raw materials were close given the region's long pastoral history. Last, having an operation in the interior insulated the program from foreign meddling.[66] Distance, however, did not hamstring the English merchants in their attempts to impede the new factories. Early on, they offered to pay Pedro II a large sum to abandon the endeavor as Ericeira continued to recruit technicians from England.[67]

In 1677, consul Maynard reported that the Portuguese ambassador in London, at Lisbon's request, had recruited various English men and women to teach the Portuguese how to spin in the "English way." Such efforts, according to the consul, proved that "the ministers of this court have long endeavored to circumvent us in all our commerce with this kingdom; and now they have given us a deadly blow to the expense of all English manufactories."[68] When the men arrived in port, Maynard went so far as to board the ship and attempt to dissuade them from their design, noting that while they were contracted for about two shillings a day, he would pay them three until they returned to England and that he would also pay for their passage. The men expressed some inclination to accept the offer, but as soon as Maynard left, soldiers took them ashore and transported them beyond the Tagus River.[69] In 1678, the ambassador Francis Parry worried that unless something were done to stop the recruitment of Englishmen the entirety of English trade in manufactures to Portugal would be "utterly lost."[70] The English merchants in Lisbon made other attempts to dissuade their countrymen, going so far as to send an operative to the factory at Covilhã to discourage the new technicians. The design appeared to have worked for a time, as one group abandoned their work and headed for Lisbon in protest but was soon rounded up and coerced into staying on to finish the job.[71]

Improvements continued in the production of woolens as Ericeira recruited skilled dyers and weavers after Lisbon's tailors rejected the first bolts of cloth. The effectiveness of the changes was alarming. By 1680, the seventeen looms established at Covilhã produced three thousand bolts amounting to roughly half the baize and serge consumed in the kingdom. With such promising advancements in woolens, Ericeira envisioned branching out even further to cottons, which would then help revitalize trade in the Estado da Índia.[72] Despite the progress, in 1685, manufactured goods from other European countries still accounted for 79.7 percent of all imports to Lisbon.[73]

Establishing a retail store in the city played a vital role in Ericeira's project; he boasted that its purpose was for the people to "see with their own seasoned eyes the fruits of so much diligence."[74] Each bolt of woolens sold for between 21,000 and 22,000 *réis*, while English cloth commanded a price of 27,000 *réis*.[75] The English merchants attempted to undercut the store by dropping their prices, but the tactic ultimately failed as Lisbon's residents continued to purchase Portuguese products, some arguing that the cloths "were in quality so perfect that it was condemned as heretical reasoning to consider any difference between the baize of England and Portugal."[76] Price disparities were not always straightforward, however, as Portuguese products regularly incurred significant transportation costs as they made their way from the interior on terrible roads.[77]

In 1680, Francis Parry suggested that the overarching goal of Ericeira's program was eventually to deprive the English of their privileges through "indirect prohibitions [on] the sale of English goods [and] to discourage and by degrees destroy our trade."[78] By 1683, it had become clear to the envoy Charles Fanshaw that the establishment of Portuguese factories with imported workers had placed the English merchants in Lisbon in a difficult situation.[79] After the successful manufacture of baize and serge, Ericeira began to target the production of inexpensive druggets (coarse woolens used for clothing or coverings) that were imported in large quantities.[80] The pressure began to mount, and consul Maynard excoriated the Portuguese by reminding them that the English import "cheap and necessary commodities . . . whereas the French bring them dear and superfluous goods as cloth of gold, silks, ribbons, poins, bands, periwigs, and such like as the poverty of this nation cannot afford, and they carry from them very little."[81]

Pedro II issued another pragmatic in 1686 with the purpose of supporting the newly established factories by prohibiting Lisbon's customs house from dispatching types of foreign cloth while also prohibiting their sale in Lisbon's streets.[82] The decree, however, did not take full effect until 1688, due to the continued inability of the nascent industry to meet demand. An additional law was passed in 1698 outlawing the use of druggets, which were increasingly imported by the English to circumvent the 1686 pragmatic.[83] Despite the laws, both the English and the Dutch continued to import contraband product by passing it off as Portuguese.[84] After the passage of the 1677 pragmatic, for example, Padre António Vieira observed that "everything that was forbidden has increased."[85]

The pragmatics never fully closed the English woolen trade in Lisbon, as treaty privileges combined with loopholes and contraband to ensure a continuing market.[86] However, they were effective in limiting the trade, which suffered from constant assaults. By the 1690s, the English factory consisted of only eleven or twelve merchant firms of any significance—a marked decline from the initial heyday that followed the signing of the 1654 and 1661 treaties.[87] From 1698 until the signing of the Methuen Treaty in 1703, only a few hundred pieces of English woolens arrived in the capital.[88] The repeated proscriptions on imported fabrics and luxury items carried collateral consequences, as Portuguese dress in Lisbon became notoriously uniform and drab during the last decades of the seventeenth century.[89]

Other manufactures were promoted in and around the capital, most notably the production of leather goods. In June 1679 the city council petitioned Pedro II to outlaw the use of foreign leathers to conserve the trade from Brazil and suggested that the monarch should also "have some masters brought from England to teach those of this city how to make use of these leathers, just as your highness has done with the introduction of other factories."[90] Pedro II agreed and outlawed the use of foreign leather in the capital in 1680.[91] Maynard later complained but to no avail.[92] While designed to limit the outflow of monetary resources, the ban ultimately backfired as the cobblers of the city realized that there were not enough Brazilian hides to meet demand for shoes, which were "such a necessary thing."[93] The ban was lifted in 1693, but the shoemakers suffered considerably thereafter as foreigners began to flood the city with their own finished leather products.[94] Clearly, Lisbon struggled to combat the unforeseen economic consequences of Atlanticization.

Monetary Policy, Trade Imbalance, and the End of an Era

Despite the Count of Ericeira's and Pedro II's best efforts at providing and promoting domestic alternatives, they could not meet demand, and the trade imbalance continued.[95] Lisbon hemorrhaged money as Portuguese merchants had little choice but to pay for goods in precious coin and bullion in order to balance their accounts and receive further credit. Duarte Ribeiro de Macedo noted that under these circumstances, "no English ship leaves the port of Lisbon without taking a great sum of money."[96] Ericeira moved to curtail the practice by targeting English merchants as a result of their growing dominance in trade. Having seized over 15,000 pounds sterling aboard

English vessels on one occasion alone, he declared, "The country [is] almost undone by the carrying money out of it."[97]

Citing the same seizure, English consul Thomas Maynard worried, "If these ministers proceed as they have began, the [English] trade of this kingdom will be lost, and many of his majesty's subjects will be undone."[98] The merchant Willoughby Swift protested Ericeira's actions, noting that at the time of the confiscation, "a French ship [was] seized on with about 50 bags of money, but when the court had notice of it, the ship was sent out immediately with the money, the court not caring to make any of that nation an example."[99] Charles Scarburgh echoed this sentiment in 1688 when he complained exaggeratedly that the Portuguese in the city acted as if the English were "the only men that will ruin Portugal," adding, "This opinion has increased since they were taken in shipping of money" even though "they cannot be ignorant that all strangers do it in a greater proportion."[100]

The exportation of money created other problems as coin clipping and falsification became constant. Ericeira attempted to curtail this abuse in 1678 by introducing a coin press that produced specie with a stamped and milled edge, but the issues persisted.[101] In his effort to secure the remaining portion of Catarina's dowry promised to the English in the 1661 treaty, the envoy Charles Fanshaw lamented in 1684, "The current money, both [Spanish] pieces of eight and the coin of the country, [are] so generally clipped . . . that there is none weighty left amongst us, so that I hardly know how to make the returns when I shall receive [them]."[102] The lack of a stable currency made the economic situation in Lisbon all the more difficult. Serious efforts to confront the issue began in 1685–86 when Pedro II outlawed the circulation of underweight and altered coins.[103] Problems continued and at Ericeira's urging, a forced devaluation was finally decreed in 1688, which entailed collecting, milling, and stamping coins. The measure resulted in considerable losses as the amount of coinage in circulation halved.[104] Altogether, devaluation reduced the value of Portuguese currency by 20 percent as the nominal value was simply increased. Although difficult to bear, devaluation endowed the country with a reliable currency that would endure through the next decades. Additional resources poured in as foreign merchants, realizing they could purchase more for their money, began a rush on Brazilian products that had piled up in the city's warehouses.[105]

Other efforts helped in the economic recovery—namely, the revitalization of the Portuguese slave trade that had suffered from repeated Dutch attacks and the loss during the restoration war of the lucrative *asiento* contract, which allowed the Portuguese to provide the Spanish colonies with enslaved

Africans. The Cacheu company, supported by a string of forts along the Guinea coast, was founded in 1676 amid these difficult circumstances. The goal of the company was to further expand the slave market and better furnish slave labor to Brazil in an era of increasing prices and elevated demand due to foreign competition. Lisbon's economic fortunes directly improved as a result—particularly after the company secured the *asiento* from Spain in 1696, which brought much needed silver from Spanish America.[106]

Altogether, the policies and reforms implemented under Pedro II and the Count of Ericeira stabilized the economy during a period of general decline. Yet, despite their few successes, external forces combined with internal pushback to nullify many of the achievements. The *asiento* was lost with Portugal's entrance into the War of the Spanish Succession, monetary issues remained as imports continued to swell, and the manufacturing policy encountered opposition as ministers in Lisbon believed that it would damage colonial commerce.[107] According to Ericeira, these ministers claimed that the development of manufacturers would only deter foreigners from trading their own finished goods for Portuguese drugs and spices, which would lead to the loss of the overseas territories considering that "it is only through their exploitation that the royal treasury and customshouses are maintained." Ericeira concluded, "And this opinion is so respected that the introduction of manufacturing arts is looked down upon in the eyes of some and seen as dangerous in the eyes of many."[108]

The prevailing thought among critics was that by importing foreign manufactures, Lisbon would incentivize foreign nations to buy the more expensive Brazilian sugar in the city as opposed to the cheaper Caribbean variety.[109] One factor that contributed to the downfall of the program was the meddling of the Inquisition, as various New Christian merchants and artisans involved in the project were arrested or fled. An English visitor to Covilhã and Fundão in 1704 blamed the sorry state of the two manufacturing townships on the Holy Office.[110] The program was further hamstrung by a lack of investment and interest among Portuguese merchants who were otherwise focused on overseas commerce.[111] Critics among the landed nobility were expressly concerned with preserving the old economic order and developing viniculture rather than a manufacturing program.[112]

Other Atlantic interests shifted royal attention away from the program—namely, the establishment of the new Brazilian colony at Sacramento on the Río de La Plata in 1680. The purpose of the outpost was to obtain Spanish silver through contraband trade with Buenos Aires.[113] Expansion into the southern reaches of Brazil was in some ways also a direct result of emigration from Portugal during the era of economic decline after the restoration. One eyewitness in the 1690s recorded that every year nearly two thousand men from Viana, Porto, and Lisbon emigrated to Brazil.[114] Repeated decrees outlawing emigration were useless as economic necessity and hardship affected fortunes in the capital.[115] The demographic explosion in Brazil created a growing market for cheap manufactures in the colony. The fact that Ericeira's program had failed to meet the demands of the metropole, let alone those of Brazil, led many to call for the readmission of English manufactures on favorable terms. Southern expansion into Brazil also encouraged private prospecting for mines and an expanded search for precious metals, which were discovered in the last decade of the seventeenth century and led to even greater rates of emigration from Portugal.[116]

Attempts to limit foreign dependency and to stabilize an economy in decline through monetary reform and import-substitution policies therefore fell short due to political opposition, Atlantic developments, and the untimely death of the Count of Ericeira, who committed suicide in his Lisbon palace in 1690.[117] The disappointing progress of the manufacturing program and growing criticisms likely played a role in the count's final action.[118] The official death knell to what remained of the program was twofold, with the signing of the Methuen commercial treaty in 1703, which lifted all restrictions on the use of imported English cloth, and the influx of Brazilian gold.[119]

The Methuen Treaty: A New Look

The Methuen Treaty is often portrayed as the reason for Portuguese reliance on the English, when in reality it simply codified the existing commercial relationship of dependence that had developed by the end of the seventeenth century.[120] Diplomatic correspondence from the 1690s reveals that half of the cargos on the Brazil fleets at that time were English. By 1700, that share had grown to 70 percent.[121] The upward trend only continued in the wake of the treaty. In a letter to the Count of Viana in 1710, José da Cunha Brochado wrote, "Whoever sees us from afar will say that we have a booming trade, it being all from England and Holland." He further decried, "Lisbon is their colony and the Portuguese their cashiers."[122]

The previous limitations on imports through a program of domestic manufacturing and protective legislation, however, did combine with external factors to boost Portuguese trade at the end of the seventeenth century. The Portuguese position vis-à-vis the English by the 1690s had improved to such a point that ministers in Lisbon repeatedly refused any English attempts at a new commercial treaty, preferring instead to whittle away at the advantages issued in 1654 and 1661.[123] While the English sought a greater share of the Lisbon market with the arrival of Brazilian gold at the end of the century, the years leading up to the Methuen Treaty saw Portuguese wine production increase. Viniculture expanded, especially during the Nine Years' War (1688–97), as Portuguese wines found a market in England with the banning of French varieties. The effects of the growing wine trade on Portugal even before the Methuen Treaty were described by an Englishman in 1699, who noted, "It's plain that during the [recent] war the planters and vineyard dressers in Portugal finding greater request of their wine, sedulously multiplied the planting of vines, and employed far greater numbers of people in it than formerly: by which means there hath been a far greater exportation of our English manufactures."[124] Wine, therefore, became a balancing factor in trade and a bargaining chip for the Portuguese at the end of the century, as it was favored under the Methuen Treaty on the English market in exchange for a strict enforcement of the previously mentioned preferential tax rate of 23 percent on English woolens in Lisbon.[125]

The Methuen Treaty was a turning point for English fortunes in Lisbon as it reestablished commercial dominance vis-à-vis other trading nations. Portugal initially benefited in the immediate aftermath of the signing, as exports rose.[126] However, the English cloth trade eventually quadrupled, and Portugal's trade deficit ballooned by 235 percent.[127] The Portugal trade became so advantageous that a member of the English House of Commons stated that it "brought to England in times of war double the wealth of the trade of Spain in times of peace."[128]

The booming trade effectively reshaped Lisbon as the number of English merchants grew. By 1717 the English factory in Lisbon consisted of around 90 individuals. By 1755, there were over 150.[129] By way of comparison, it was estimated that 32 English mercantile families had established themselves in Porto in 1756.[130] While the trajectory for Portugal's second city was below that of the capital, it was still impressive considering that in 1668–69 there were only nine merchant houses.[131] The increasing amount of Brazilian gold helped fuel this expansion as Lisbon's import capacity exploded at the beginning of the eighteenth century.[132] Seeing the advantages, the Dutch pushed for a similar commercial treaty (which they achieved in 1705), but little came of it as a result of production problems in their own textile industry.[133]

While the Methuen Treaty did not cause the growing reliance on the English, it most certainly exaggerated that trend as wine production took hold and domestic manufacturing was largely abandoned.[134] As Charles Boxer demonstrated, it was the "sweet wines of Lisbon rather than the harsher Douro wines of the north which benefited immediately from that treaty."[135] However, over time the wines from Lisbon were increasingly reserved for internal consumption in Portugal and Brazil, while those of northern Portugal began to make up the bulk of exports in the wake of the treaty.[136] Moreover, Englishmen began to invest in vineyards. One French visitor in 1766 observed that by that time, the English owned all the best grape-producing land in Lisbon, Porto, and other regions of the country.[137] The overwhelming focus on wine production in Porto in the aftermath of the Methuen Treaty created a similar situation in that city that would play out in subsequent eras of increasing economic subversion to the capriciousness of English traders.[138]

While some scholars have recognized the inaccuracy of solely blaming the Methuen Treaty for Portuguese dependence on England, the myth seems to persist due to the heavy economic consequences that followed in Portugal. Yet an analysis of various Atlantic factors uncovers only a continuation of an already developing dependency. As reinforced here, English dependence was clearly growing in Lisbon before the treaty. Authorities recognized this, and when colonial reexports began to face stiff competition in the capital, they turned to developing domestic manufactures as a means to ameliorate the imbalance. Despite its eventual failure, the program did produce some results as the measures taken slowly began to mitigate Portugal's trade deficit. Yet the sumptuary laws designed to protect fledgling industry did more to limit English and French trade than they did to establish manufactures at home.[139]

Failure to meet demand, not only in Lisbon but also in Brazil, was another factor behind the program's demise. In that sense, Lisbon's domestic manufacturing push clearly demonstrates the depth of economic Atlanticization in the metropole that included a growing reliance not only on foreign products but also on fluctuating Brazilian markets. Maybe even more importantly, the program affirms that the Portuguese were aware and actively attempting to combat a pattern of deepening dependency.

Vitorino Magalhães Godinho argued that "The rise of a manufacturing industry had proved only an interlude between two clearly defined periods in Portugal's economic and social history: the 'cycle' of sugar and tobacco from Brazil, of Setúbal salt and Cádiz silver, and the 'cycle' of port, madeira and Brazilian gold."[140] Yet Lisbon's manufacturing program represents more than a distinctive economic interlude between different Brazilian reexports. It also further reinforces Lisbon's unique economic development vis-à-vis the whole of Portugal due to Atlanticization. In other words, while Lisbon and Porto both benefited economically from the development of agricultural exports throughout the period, only in the capital was a rigorous manufacturing program explored.

With the failure of Lisbon's manufacturing by the end of the seventeenth century, the city's only option to lessen trade imbalances and stem the outpouring of bullion was to expand the increasingly profitable wine industry. Unlike Brazilian sugar, Portuguese wine was a complementary element in the English imperial economy that produced its own colonial products. Facing this harsh reality, the Methuen Treaty was seen in some ways by both sides as a reinforcement of the developing economic specialties of each nation.[141] More importantly, when considering the serious threats posed by the War of the Spanish Succession to Brazil at a time when riches first began to pour into Lisbon, it makes sense that the Portuguese willingly shelved much of their fledgling manufacturing program and focused on growing wine exports if it meant imperial security through English protection. Thus, analyzing the Methuen Treaty of 1703 through the lens of Atlantic dependency over a longer period of time uncovers not a new departure in relations but a reinforcement of the same patterns exhibited throughout the previous century as Portugal consistently traded economic benefits for imperial security.[142] Simply stated, we cannot really understand the Methuen Treaty and its consequences in Lisbon nor the establishment and failure of domestic manufacturing without understanding Portugal's Atlantic dependency.

Brazilian Gold: Lisbon's Blessing and Curse

After the discovery of Brazilian gold in the 1690s, the amount of bullion reaching the capital continued to increase during the first half of the eighteenth century under the reign of João V. At that time, the city experienced a new golden age as commerce boomed, art and architecture flourished, and innovation abounded. Increased spending power brought about by Brazilian riches made it easier to import manufactured goods and foodstuffs rather than produce them in the capital, which (as previously mentioned) all but killed the initiatives implemented during the last quarter of the seventeenth century.[143]

While generations of historians have gone back and forth about the exact amount of wealth shipped to Lisbon during the first half of the eighteenth century, suffice it to say that according to the Genoese consul Pietro

Francesco Viganego, João V should have been "one of the most wealthy princes of Europe."[144] Brazil's three fleets brought on average a total of three billion *réis* (83,300 pounds sterling) to roughly 2,300 recipients annually.[145] While the Crown drew significant receipts, about 78 percent of legal remittances went to particular individuals or parties.[146] Over two-thirds of private remittances came through commercial dealings. The rest was the result of emigrants sending money home.[147] The Count of Povolide recorded that in 1723 alone, the arrival of the Brazil fleet brought four or five men possessing between 400,000 and 500,000 *cruzados*.[148] Another dimension to the wealth pouring into the capital appeared after 1729 with the discovery of diamonds in the Brazilian interior. These discoveries reached such quantities in Lisbon that one chronicler declared that "there is no more speaking in carats, but in pounds."[149] The vast number of diamonds that entered the Portuguese capital during the 1730s forced the European market price to drop by one-third. Draconian measures were soon adopted in Minas Gerais in order to stop production and raise prices. In effect, the area was closed by the Crown, and anyone found in the region was summarily arrested, fined, and expelled. Enslaved individuals apprehended in the territory were to be flogged and sold. The policy worked, as diamond prices soon began to rise.[150]

Whatever the true figures, it is certain that large-scale contraband in both gold and diamonds was a constant concern.[151] This would naturally be the case, considering that many Portuguese merchants and officials participated in the practice.[152] Viganego declared in 1714, "I do not believe that the king of Portugal receives a quarter of his income."[153] Even the king's personal secretary, Alexandre de Gusmão, questioned, "Is it to be expected that anyone would voluntarily deprive himself of a fifth part of his capital, when he can conceal it with a little risk and trouble?"[154] Compounding the problem, the Crown paid only 1,200 *réis* per *oitavo* of gold while the open market yielded between 1,350 and 1,500.[155] Contraband was so widespread that even the returning ships from the Estado da Índia routinely stopped over in Brazil instead of proceeding directly to Lisbon as commanded.[156]

The influx of Brazilian wealth yielded economic benefits for many in Lisbon as the city became one of the wealthiest in Europe.[157] Extant records indicate that as the gold trade expanded, the church and clergy were among the most active Portuguese participants (one of the largest groups being foreign traders).[158] D. Luís da Cunha lamented the excesses of the age that had developed among Lisbon's churches as a result of the influx of Brazilian wealth. The Portuguese statesman took particular issue with the wastefulness of using Brazilian bullion in gilt work that was, in his estimation, a product of the infectious ostentation that had taken over among the various classes in the capital city as religious brotherhoods often argued over whose chapel was "more magnificent and golden."[159] Lisbon's churches benefited in other ways as the period witnessed an uptick in petitions to the Crown for the right to beg alms in the mining region of Brazil.[160] The people in the neighborhood of Benfica just outside the city asked João V for this privilege in order to fund the expansion of their church with the justification that "in Rio de Janeiro, São Paulo, and Minas Gerais, the wealth is greater and there are many charitable people."[161]

Much like tobacco, gold and diamonds often made their way into the hands of the clergy illegally. In January 1732, a Lisbon gazette recorded the confiscation in the city's Carmelite convent of three *arrobas* of gold alongside another seizure of 80,000 *cruzados*, as well as diamonds that amounted to over 25 million (currency unspecified, but likely *cruzados*).[162] Minting houses were established in Brazil to reduce the contraband trade in gold dust, and as a result, large quantities of coins minted in the colony began circulating alongside those produced in the city. While increasing gold remittances led to the establishment of various mints in the colony, the result in Portugal was the opposite, as the Casa da Moeda in Lisbon became the only operating mint in the metropole after 1714.[163]

Further monetary changes occurred in Lisbon as a continual lack of small coinage for daily commerce led the king to mint a new golden currency bearing his image.[164] The coins were to be a symbol of the monarch's wealth and power and were the first Portuguese specie with the image of the monarch.[165] The English consul Thomas Burnett recorded that the pieces were all of a standard 22-karat gold and bore the phrase *In hoc signo vinces*, or "In this sign thou shalt conquer."[166]

Brazilian wealth led to inflation in Lisbon as gold became common. One contemporary noted, "In this court there is an abundance of bread, wine, olive oil, and other goods, although increasingly at higher prices."[167] Lisbon's populace experienced collateral effects as the influx of wealth arriving on the yearly Brazil fleets led to increased piracy in the waters off the coast of Portugal. The *Mercúrio de Lisboa* recorded in 1746 that officials were frantically trying to outfit four warships to go after five Moorish vessels in the company of French corsairs who were awaiting the arrival of the Brazilian fleets. Brazil ships were not allowed to leave and fishing vessels dared not take the risk. Lisbon, as a result, suffered "a great lack of fish, due to the fear of the Algerians."[168]

Remittances in gold and diamonds further affected supplies in the capital. The export of agricultural products from Brazil began to decline as Brazilian planters joined Portuguese emigrants in the mines. The Portuguese diplomat D. Luís da Cunha affirmed that "after the discovery of the mines, the cultivation of sugar and tobacco has diminished, and as a consequence, so have the ships that bring those products."[169] There were further negative effects on Portuguese shipping as gold became the common remittance in the city preferred by merchants rather than tropical products. The decrease in the shipping of Brazilian products dampened convoy revenues for the Junta do Comércio do Brasil—heir to the monopoly company established by João IV.[170] João V abolished the body in 1720 due to its financial hardships and transferred responsibilities over the Brazil fleets to the Conselho da Fazenda.[171]

As the volume of tropical products crossing the Atlantic began to decrease during the first half of the eighteenth century, the discovery of gold stirred up what must have seemed like a mass exodus from the metropole as hordes of Portuguese men left the country.[172] Fears about the lack of agricultural workers and the impact on the supply of foodstuffs in the city soon developed. An anonymous French visitor in 1730 noted that the country "does not produce more than half of its consumption needs [in wheat]" due to the emigration to Brazil, which "considerably depopulates the kingdom."[173]

João V repeatedly outlawed unlicensed emigration—issuing laws in 1709 and 1711 to little avail. In 1720 the monarch forbade government officials and other *fidalgos* from "taking more servants than necessary in keeping with their status and office" to the colony.[174] As the main port for the departing Brazil fleets, Lisbon invariably felt the effects of rural flight as migrants from the interior attempted to board outgoing vessels illegally. Those found were fined and exiled to Africa. All this, João V argued, was necessary to "avoid the frequency with which the kingdom is becoming depopulated."[175] The Jesuit Antonil described the social makeup of those headed to the mines as a mixture of "all sorts of people: men and women, young boys and old men, rich and poor, nobles and peasants, as well as secular and clerical figures."[176] The Crown adopted a passport system in 1720 in an attempt to limit the number of emigrants to Brazil, which in the rush years numbered between five and six thousand. Thereafter, the annual number of emigrants was likely around two thousand.[177] In spite of the laws, fines, and punishments, many (including foreigners) found ways of circumventing the need for government passports as they enlisted as sailors, soldiers, or servants and then deserted on arrival.[178]

The discovery of Brazilian wealth stimulated other transatlantic movements as wealthy Brazilians, aspiring to social prestige, began sending their children to Lisbon's monasteries and convents in greater numbers. D. Luís da Cunha detailed the pervasiveness of the trend, recounting that one rich Brazilian from Bahia placed no less than six of his daughters in the convent of Esperança in Lisbon with dowries of 6,000 *cruzados* each simply "because he had heard that only people of the highest condition entered the said convent."[179] The issue became such a problem that Portuguese women were often lacking in the colony. In response, João V issued a decree in 1732 specifically forbidding women from making their way to the capital in order to enter religious orders without his explicit consent.[180] The weekly *Mercúrio de Lisboa* of 13 March 1745 records that over one hundred women on the Rio de Janeiro fleet disembarked in the city to enter Lisbon's monasteries. Whether they had the king's permission to do so or not, it does not say.[181]

Despite the great wealth produced during his reign, João V experienced periods of financial strain. This was particularly true even after the War of the Spanish Succession and major threats to Brazil had subsided. Financial difficulties at the time combined with increasing imports of foreign goods to encourage João V to promote the establishment of manufactures (although not to the same extent as Pedro II previously).[182] In addition to concentrating on the usual silk, wool, glass, and iron, João V also focused on leather goods and paper production.[183] He established a military forge and a bell foundry in the city in 1726 and 1732, respectively, and kept what remained of the woolen manufactures in Covilhã alive by granting an exclusive monopoly for military uniforms and servant liveries.[184]

João V's main economic project got underway in 1734 when he approved the establishment of another silk factory under the aegis of the French Huguenot Robert Godin. Godin, like other artisans, left France after Louis XIV's previous Edict of Fontainebleau was renewed, which revoked religious toleration of Protestants in that country.[185] Like Roland Duclos before, Godin relied on the expertise of roughly two hundred artisans and over one thousand Portuguese women who spun silk in their homes.[186] Still, the old prejudices continued. The king's adviser, Cardinal da Mota, who personally believed that establishing silk manufactures was beneficial to the kingdom, warned that these manufactures could also prove injurious to royal coffers if taxable finished imports seriously declined.[187] Even so, the endeavor never quite got off the ground. The French consul Jacques Montagnac wrote, "According to all appearances they cannot sustain it, as such I believe that expenses to stimulate Mr. Godin and Sibert to cease and leave the country will not be necessary."[188] Production could not keep up with the growing demand for luxury items during João V's reign due to a lack of raw silk, so the factory was forced to import material from Spain and Macau.[189] The operation was ultimately taken over by the Crown in 1750 just before João V's death.[190]

A leather operation developed in the city's hinterland at Povos with some royal support during João V's reign. An advertisement in the weekly *Gazeta de Lisboa Occidental* in March 1731 broadcast the quality of the products, which were made "with the same perfection as those that come from England" and sold for 10 percent less. Interested buyers could find them in a certain Lisbon storehouse located in the neighborhood of São Nicolau.[191] To support these efforts, João V issued a decree outlawing the use of foreign hides competing with those from Brazil.[192] These successes, as in the previous period, led to sabotage by the English merchants in Lisbon who not only aided one Moorish technician from North Africa in his flight to England but also continuously threatened the others if they did not do the same. English merchants also bribed factory workers to let hides rot as they established an illegal operation in the interior of the country.[193]

A rich Portuguese merchant made a proposal to João V early in his reign to establish a cloth factory that would augment the limited production that had continued from the previous period in exchange for various privileges and a title of nobility. According to the French consul at the time, "The English were informed and immediately found the man, and without even mentioning this business, they proposed to establish him here as the commissioner of all wool embarked for England."[194] Such behavior led the visitor Charles Frédéric de Merveilleux to declare that the English watched over their commercial dealings "even in the least important trades, and they do not desist until they cause all these initiatives to fail . . . and they obstinately annoy the ministers and all those involved until they achieve their ends."[195]

While foreign competition and interference deterred domestic manufacturing under João V, the distraction of Brazilian wealth and an increased colonial focus ensured that the program never became a major priority, as it had been under the previous monarch.[196] João V himself declared, "God gave to some industry, and to others precious metals."[197] According to Merveilleux, the Marquis of Fronteira admitted that various foreigners presented schemes to the king that would have enriched the country through agricultural and manufacturing developments, but "God made [them] masters of the gold . . . from Brazil almost without having to dig for it." He continued:

If this gold had been in Portugal we would have had all the manufactures that exist in France and England because our riches would permit it, and more than any other nation we could build strong fortresses with numerous garrisons. However, our gold is in Brazil over two hundred leagues inland, and foreigners arriving in our ports can easily deprive us of the benefits of such treasures. We have [nothing to] fear, while the English use our country as an outlet for the products of their lands and the industry of the natives of their kingdoms. Under these conditions they will protect [Portugal] and shed their blood to the last drop to defend us from anyone who dares attack.[198]

For the Marquis of Fronteira and so many others of the time, the defense of Brazil and its vast reserves of wealth clearly outweighed any serious attempt at combating foreign dependency through manufactures.

The lack of a viable manufacturing program during the first half of the eighteenth century and the increasing arrival of gold adversely affected many of the city's artisans as entire trades became dependent on foreign suppliers or were overrun by the arrival of foreign masters. In 1712 the city council complained that foreigners were not only bringing raw materials but also "finished works" and practicing their trades, which had reduced the artisans "to penury never before seen." The council further argued that in Lisbon alone, there were "entire trades without a single vassal of your majesty."[199]

Others benefited as gold shipments began to increase during the eighteenth century. In 1705, the city council suggested that merchants, due to growing wealth, were importing more luxury items than the nobility.[200] Luxury artisans rose socially during the period as the demand for ornate items grew. The gold- and silversmiths even petitioned the city council to be reclassified separately from other simple artisans known as *mecânicos*.[201] The number of goldsmiths expanded to such a degree that by 1718 the city council was forced to enlarge the designated areas of six other guilds to accommodate the growth.[202] The influx of foreigners who were experts in the trade helped fuel the expansion.[203] Other artisans associated with luxury trades established themselves or increased their production as wealth poured in. These included coach-makers and painters, sculptors, marble artists, decorators, gilders, weavers, lace and button makers, and ceramicists.[204] The growing numbers of artisans led to disputes and divisions among the twenty-four representatives of their political body (the Casa dos Vinte e Quatro), which resulted in the addition of three more representatives. After reviewing the matter, João V decreed a return to the original number.[205]

The expanding Brazil trade after the discovery of gold transformed the city's mercantile class. By the first decades of the eighteenth century, even those with rudimentary experience began to engage in commerce.[206] The English merchant Thomas Cox, disgusted at this trend, remarked, "All shopkeepers in general send something to the Brazils and therefore they called themselves merchants."[207] In his *Universal Dictionary of Trade and Commerce*, published around the middle of the eighteenth century, the English commercial expert Malachy Postlethwayt commented on Portugal's economic growth, writing, "Since their discovery of the gold mines . . . they have advanced their commerce to more than twenty times. . . . This increase of their trade adds a very great increase to the wealth, and consequently to the strength of their government, as well as to that of their private merchants."[208]

Many of these newly minted merchants, like the wildly successful Francisco Pinheiro, came from rural and artisan backgrounds.[209] João de Castro Guimarães made his way to Lisbon and began shipping goods to Brazil. Guimarães's business became so successful that it propelled his son into the upper echelons of the mercantile community during the second half of the eighteenth century.[210]

Capital accumulation among the mercantile class in Lisbon developed a transatlantic character during the period as merchants routinely spent years in Brazil as factors before returning to the metropole wealthy enough to climb the social ladder.[211] A return to Lisbon was the goal of the majority of agents in Brazil and other regions of the Portuguese Atlantic. One of Francisco Pinheiro's factors complained bitterly, "I remain here purging myself of my sins in this city [Salvador] or rather in this place of banishment."[212] In many ways, successful merchants embodied the Atlanticization of Lisbon as their activities further strengthened the intensifying ties between metropole and colony that recast the Portuguese capital in economic and cultural ways. Social ascension transformed the upper crust of the group, and they soon had more in common with the lesser nobility than with their fellow traders.[213] Thomas Cox related that as soon as Portuguese shopkeepers achieved a level of comfort in life due to their commerce, they became gentlemen and left their shops to their sons. Yet he declared they believe "it is beneath the son of a gentleman to keep a shop" and that such popular attitudes "contributed in a great measure to the rendering them so poor as they are at present."[214]

The perception in Iberian society that commerce was below the station of the aristocracy further deepened the reliance on foreign traders, as nationals repeatedly abandoned the practice to gain or maintain social standing.[215] Even those who continued their trade were largely beholden to foreign credit and manufactures.[216] Francisco Pinheiro left a tantalizing trace of this in his correspondence, noting in 1719 that he had nothing to send to his factors in Brazil due to the lack of English goods in the city.[217] However, as discussed in the previous chapter, the influx of gold to some extent contributed to the reorganization of the mercantile class that had been decimated by the Inquisition at the end of the seventeenth century.[218] The reliance on the English, however, impeded the formation of a strong bourgeoisie, which hampered Lisbon in developing an economic system based on merchant capitalism and hollowed out the developing royal absolutism.[219]

Altogether, Atlantic wealth papered over the lopsided trade deficit that exploded during João V's reign. The prosperity of Lisbon's new golden age began to diminish during the last decade of the monarch's life as financial obligations from grandiose projects mounted and gold supplies declined.[220] In 1742, the king's Spanish daughter-in-law described the downturn in a letter to her mother, commenting in particular that "everything is ending."[221] Things only worsened when João V suffered a series of health conditions beginning in 1742, after which he became increasingly religious and the government fell largely into the hands of his trusted advisers.[222] Alexandre de Gusmão recognized the economic difficulties and published a tract condemning the "passive commerce" of the Portuguese who consistently paid for manufactured goods rather than produce them. Gusmão further lamented the massive emigration from the country at a time when industry was in decay, imports were on the rise, and "each time less gold [came] from the mines." Among his many recommendations, including the reestablishment of manufactures, he suggested that another pragmatic was desperately needed.[223] Others began looking to a revival of Asian commerce in the Estado da Índia as a means to augment royal coffers.[224] The future Marquis of Pombal went so far as to craft a proposal for an East India company based on the successful English model. The scheme was blocked by his political enemies in Lisbon and the company never came to fruition.[225] It was in this state of affairs, and on the advice of his councillors, that the aging monarch attempted to shore up a decaying economy by issuing his final pragmatic in 1749.[226] Like those that preceded it, the law proved ineffective in the face of economic dependency firmly tied to the Atlantic world.[227] In essence, Lisbon had let the Atlantic cat out of the bag and was helpless to put it back.

Lisbon had become too Atlanticized for domestic production to flourish. Indeed, dependence on Atlantic commerce left the city in a difficult situation as sugar prices plummeted due to foreign competition during the second half of the seventeenth century. The decline led to various endeavors at economic diversification at home and abroad as new programs and policies were enacted alongside the establishment and reform of regulatory bodies. More broadly, these efforts represent not only an attempt to revitalize Lisbon's economy by limiting foreign dependency, but also a realignment of Lisbon's economic policy with the most powerful monarchies of Europe.[228] Alongside the greater regulation of tobacco and the transplantation of Asian spices in the capital, the breakout of Portuguese manufacturing before the discovery of Brazilian gold and diamonds represents a unique development in Lisbon's economic history and a step toward economic modernization—albeit short-lived. Stated plainly, Lisbon's economy developed an internal modernizing aspect alongside its traditional overseas focus during the period as a result of increasing Atlantic influences.

While the efforts of the Count of Ericeira and others seemed to pay dividends, the discovery of Brazilian gold worked alongside the signing of the Methuen Treaty to shift the economic focus back to the Atlantic and undercut the need for manufacturing or domestic agricultural production. The neglect and eventual downfall of the program meant that Lisbon under João V would import manufactures, luxuries, and other necessities on an even larger scale as the city embarked on a sort of "consumer evolution" as opposed to the "industrious revolution" of Northern Europe.[229] In the end, an awareness of the Atlantic stimuli for, and impediments to, Lisbon's manufacturing program allows for a better understanding of the deepening dependency that developed in Lisbon and the need to address the imbalance long before the Methuen Treaty—something to which the Marquis of Pombal later devoted his political career.

Furthermore, employing an Atlantic scope to analyze economic transformations in Lisbon clearly debunks any remaining argument for Portuguese economic passivity. Rather, the Portuguese were keenly aware of the instability of their situation and actively sought greater balance before ultimately choosing to favor their Atlantic economic networks over domestic development. Overall, we cannot truly understand English dependency, the Methuen Treaty, or the unique nature of Lisbon's economy during the period without studying the difficult balance between North and South Atlantic influences in the capital.

The lives of Lisbon's residents were deeply affected by the economic changes of the time. Many from rural and mechanical backgrounds entered the ranks of the mercantile class with the influx of gold and in some ways filled the vacuum left by the persecuted New Christian merchants. Wealth brought social elevation to some as they penetrated the lower levels of Lisbon's aristocracy. Others were not as fortunate, as their trade and livelihoods were increasingly dominated by foreign competitors, inevitably contributing to the social tension characteristic of the city at the time.[230] Many chose to emigrate to Brazil hoping to ply their trade or strike it rich in one of the new gold fields. These migrants were overwhelmingly male, which had profound effects on both colony and capital. Some returned to Lisbon after making their fortunes. Thus, constant movement to and away from Lisbon became a hallmark of Atlanticization and economic change during the period.

Altogether, Lisbon's economy evolved and adapted to new pressures as a result of increasing Atlantic ties. The growing reliance on foreign merchants and the shift toward ostentation at the expense of manufacturing placed the city in a unique position, as it was largely unable to take advantage of Brazil's newly discovered wealth to promote greater economic strength and independence. It was against this paradoxical background that a particular brand of royal absolutism developed in the Portuguese capital as João V became one of Europe's wealthiest but most dependent monarchs—the topic of the next chapter.

5

ATLANTIC OPULENCE AND THE LOCAL MANIFESTATIONS OF A DEVELOPING ROYAL ABSOLUTISM

"He possesses a good figure, a long face, and tawny complexion like the majority of the Portuguese. He uses a large black powdered wig and habitually dresses with great magnificence." This was how the Swiss-born traveler César de Saussure described the forty-one-year-old João V in early 1730. He continued, "The king is considered a witty and clever person, but [he is] completely deprived of culture" and is "extremely scathing and rash," especially with ministers and those who "do not treat him like a prince and much less a king." Saussure's description concludes with mention of João V's love for all things magnificent and opulent, especially monuments that "cost fabulous quantities" and foreign luxuries, the parting line declaring, "[He] has such a great quantity of clothes that he could never wear them all."[1]

In many ways, this terse portrait perfectly describes the wider effects in Lisbon of a developing royal absolutism backed by Atlanticization—the focus of this last chapter. The particulars of João's character and actions are a harbinger of themes discussed throughout the chapter: his treatment of royal ministers foreshadows the taming of the court nobility in the city and the acceleration of political modification through wealth, his love for opulent monuments heralds the urban transformation of the capital, and his extravagant wardrobe presages the cultural changes that ran throughout Lisbon society. The dichotomy between João V's passion for all things foreign despite a supposed cultural backwardness highlights the monarch's (and the era's) seemingly paradoxical mixture of advancement and intransigence that made Lisbon unique during the period. In short, that paradox and its consequences for Lisbon were in many ways the result of a monarch who was growing more absolute but increasingly dependent due to intensifying Atlantic influences. While many of the features and consequences of João V's reign—including his obsessive imitation of Louis XIV—have been well documented, his intense devotion to his capital city and his particular brand of absolutism and its local manifestations that developed as a result of Lisbon's Atlanticization remain understudied.

João V's Absolutism

Many of the changes Lisbon experienced were in response to the royal policies of João V (1706–50) as internal developments combined with Atlantic stimuli to develop a progressively absolutist regime. Internally, the previous actions of Pedro II helped in part to pave the way for João V, but it was Portugal's involvement in the War of the Spanish Succession that amplified the developing royal absolutism. The Portuguese diplomat José da Cunha Brochado remarked during the heat of that conflict that the Portuguese court in Lisbon was purely consultative and that "no one knows how to do his duty." He further lamented that "we do not know how to command, nor do we know how to obey."[2] It was against this background that expanding Atlantic revenues sufficiently freed João V to implement the necessary reforms.

It must be stated that throughout the early modern period, the overseas empire repeatedly supplied over half of the Portuguese Crown's revenue.[3] Thus, as colonial returns increased with the expansion of Brazilian tobacco and the discovery of Brazilian wealth, so too did the political power of the monarch. One Englishman described the Brazilian impact on the Portuguese monarchy by declaring, "Their gold and diamond mines have enabled their monarchs, of late, to figure among the great potentates of Europe."[4] Effectively, it was Atlantic prosperity that accelerated existing currents toward political centralization and executive control—both of which would have lasting impacts on Lisbon.

Some of the first attempts at political centralization occurred previously under Pedro II and included the reorganization of various governmental councils and the creation of others.[5] These included the reform of the Brazil Company, the creation of the Junta da Administração do Tabaco, and the reorganization of the city council.[6] While showing glimpses of absolutism, Pedro II was still very much beholden to the nobility.[7] Speaking of the

124 ATLANTIC CROSSROADS

monarch's reliance on the Council of State (the administrative council with the most responsibility), an English visitor commented that Pedro II referred all matters to this body, "seldom, or never, resolving upon anything before the affair had been considered and debated among them," and that the reason for such deference was that these "had a great hand in advancing him to his brother's throne."[8] That sentiment was equally shared by a visiting Frenchman at the time.[9]

An independent Inquisition also hampered Pedro's effective political control. After the Inquisition's pushback against Pedro II and the general pardon discussed earlier, António Vieira declared, "In Portugal it is better to be the inquisitor than the king."[10] The medieval assembly of the *côrtes* was another limitation on his royal power. Revived under João IV as a means of legitimizing and funding his independence bid against the Spanish Hapsburgs, this semiparliamentary body suffered a constant decline thereafter as Pedro II grew emboldened with the death of Afonso VI in 1683 and the discovery of Brazilian gold.[11] The prince regent turned monarch summoned the body for the last time in 1697–98 simply as a matter of protocol to declare João V the rightful heir to the throne—the three estates proclaiming "in their agony that they were the very source of all power."[12]

Yet things changed under João V. João himself never convened the assembly despite mentioning the possibility early in his reign.[13] In a further blow to that body, the monarch used the War of the Spanish Succession as an excuse to issue new taxes and prolong other tributes without the consent of the *côrtes* despite their historical role in the process.[14] The overall effect of these changes was a notable weakness of intermediary political bodies in Lisbon as opposed to the political configurations of other eighteenth-century monarchies such as in France and Spain.[15]

While largely unique from his neighbors in this regard, João V did follow the Bourbon example of abandoning governing councils in favor of personal ministers and secretaries.[16] Still, even here the Portuguese monarch stood apart. In contrast to Bourbon Spain and its sudden implementation of new governmental structures in the wake of the War of the Spanish Succession, João V's masterstroke consisted of maintaining older governmental forms after the war while incrementally instituting broader changes. The move effectively eliminated serious political pushback and radicalism.[17] However, those with the means to potentially oppose the Portuguese monarch were effectively cowered into submission through either force or favor. It is telling that the only real opposition (discussed later) that João V received from the nobility centered around perceived slights in matters of privilege or precedent.

ATLANTIC OPULENCE

The political sway of the nobility was further curtailed by João V as the Council of State almost ceased to function, meeting for the last time in 1725. In its place the king came to prefer the input of handpicked juntas and councillors who met with him privately.[18] Other government councils were at times without a sitting president appointed by the king.[19] Any appeal through the printed word was out of the question as the monarch actively censored political content in Lisbon's gazette. The Englishman Abraham Castres later exclaimed that in Portugal nothing "that relates to a political matter or in the least concerns the administration, can appear in print, but what has passed in strict examination before one of the secretaries of state."[20] As a result the formation of a politically active populace in Lisbon was seriously impeded.[21] No one, it seemed, stood in the way of a deepening absolutism emboldened by burgeoning Atlantic wealth.

Alexandre de Gusmão (the king's Brazilian-born secretary and private counselor), described the consequences of João V's iron grip on power as he worked under royal supervision for many years without interruption, often "confusing night and day, and never knowing what amusement was."[22] The king's intense personal involvement in all matters of government led to massive amounts of paperwork. The overseas council complained in 1724 that such developments led to longer working hours.[23] Whether they liked it or not, the nobility gradually became resigned to their new consultative role as the Portuguese monarch tightened control of governmental affairs.[24] The opposite occurred in Spain under Philip V as the old aristocracy continued to direct much of the political system despite reform efforts.[25] In many ways, then, João V and his government had more in common with Louis XIV than the French monarch had with his own grandson in Spain.[26]

In a trend later magnified by the Marquis of Pombal, João V further undermined the political grip of the old nobility at home with the appointment of wealthy merchants and university-trained officials to various administrative positions. Conversely, the nobility of the court increasingly came to play an important role as Crown administrators overseas after the discovery of mineral wealth.[27] These postings had distinct advantages as noblemen often returned at the end of their service having amassed considerable fortunes. D. Brás da Silveira made his way to Lisbon as a wealthy man after having served as governor of Minas Gerais; the same was true for the Count of Assumar who later occupied that same role.[28]

For the most part, however, the nobility became utterly dependent on royal favor. Reflecting on the situation that developed, the Italian Giuseppe Gorani wrote after the middle of the eighteenth century that the aristocracy in Lisbon could no longer be considered rich. Worse yet, he contended, if the monarch were to withdraw his support, the group would be left in a sorry state.[29] The Portuguese sovereign himself summed up the transformation in high politics on the back of swelling Atlantic revenues when he asserted, "My grandfather owed and feared, my father owed, and I neither owe nor fear."[30] The nod to a deepening absolutism is obvious in the monarch's assertion, but what really stands out is the recognition of an amplification of existing political changes through growing Atlantic wealth.

The nobles in Lisbon at times pushed back against the dissolution of their political power. On one occasion, João V exiled almost thirty *fidalgos* from Lisbon after they banded together to disobey a local magistrate. The Swiss naturalist Charles Frédéric de Merveilleux, who was living in the city at the time, described the episode as "the last blow that D. João gave to the nobility."[31] The whole affair marked a clear departure from the previous reign, as a significant portion of the nobility was absent from court for a year and a half.[32] It's little wonder the Englishman Arthur Stert remarked at the time of the confrontation, "[João V] now thinks himself wiser than anybody and is pretty violent and ungovernable."[33] The repeated exercise of royal power against the historically unruly aristocracy led another visitor to declare in 1730, "The king is just as feared as he is loved by the people, [but] the nobles fear him more than they love him."[34] This fear had a novel effect in Lisbon, as the monarch's absolute power and wealth impeded the formation of threatening political factions that had plagued the Bragança monarchs since the initial days of the restoration.[35]

Having politically subdued the nobility, João V moved to control the group further by codifying their long-standing privileges, which served to transform them from a social class into a social caste.[36] João created twenty-four new noble titles over the course of his reign, but he also eliminated twenty-two. To be clear, many of the new titles were merely honorary grants to court widows with no possibility of transmission.[37] The high-water mark of the recasting was a 1739 decree mandating specific titles in speech and writing according to status as a result of the debasement of distinction and "confusion" of rank that had become pervasive.[38] The decree also reiterated the requirement of royal approval for marriages contracted by the titled nobility. Yet with growing social concerns in Lisbon regarding blood purity, as discussed previously, João V merely ratified marriage decisions already made by this increasingly solidified caste of Old Christians who proudly labeled themselves *puritanos* (puritans).[39]

The growing ossification of the nobility led to infighting and division within João V's court as older members contended with the newly developing

ATLANTIC OPULENCE

aristocracy of governmental bureaucrats. While both parties were divided on a host of issues, including blood purity and the role of the Inquisition, each supported (and was dependent on) the absolute monarch. A particularly divisive subject was the role of foreign ideas in Lisbon. Many of the older nobility wholly supported traditional structures and fought against all foreign pressures, especially those emanating from England and France, while the new aristocrats began to question established institutions considered sacrosanct and welcomed foreign ideas.[40]

Some of the nobility sided with the latter group, having cut their teeth during the War of the Spanish Succession, which intensified Portuguese involvement in the high politics of Europe.[41] These individuals, who often spent years on assignment or in study in the various European capitals, were deeply affected by their time abroad. Exposed to new currents and manners, several were known as *estrangeirados*, or the foreignized, as they became increasingly critical of what they perceived as Portuguese backwardness.[42] Despite these criticisms, many *estrangeirados* saw royal absolutism along French lines as a useful tool, particularly in interventionist and mercantilist terms. Most subscribed to a host of foreign ideas, including those put forth previously by Louis XIV's influential minister Jean-Baptiste Colbert.[43] While favorable toward foreign intellectual trends and cultural advancements, the intense focus on internal development of the metropole made many *estrangeirados* anti-British in their economic attitudes.[44]

The most notable critic of João V's absolutism from this group was the diplomat D. Luís da Cunha. Having served as ambassador in the major royal courts of Europe, he came to internalize a host of Enlightenment ideas, which caused the Portuguese monarch to accuse him of being too French in his thinking.[45] At one point in a letter to a fellow Portuguese diplomat, Cunha decried João V's government as despotic owing to the lack of his meetings with the Council of State.[46] To be clear, while Cunha and other *estrangeirados* could be quite critical of João V personally, they were not necessarily opposed to the establishment of royal absolutism itself.[47] Yet while Cunha was at times disappointed in João V, particularly concerning his defense of the Inquisition and negligence toward England and the production of domestic manufactures, even he recognized the monarch's qualities and admitted that the king was in fact "a lord whose genius and clear understanding, and whose holy and righteous intentions are more than enough to make even less experienced ministers capable."[48] He further suggested that João V could easily make the changes needed to combat the dependence on England, considering the "people have formed such an exalted opinion of the most prudent and religious resolutions of His Majesty, and of the firmness with which he knows how to sustain them."[49]

João V remained wary, yet receptive, to many of these new currents. Some of the *estrangeirados*, Alexandre de Gusmão in particular, even served as his closest advisers or occupied significant government positions. Nevertheless, the fact remained that others in João V's circle were very much beholden to the political and economic status quo. As such, the monarch was faced with a precarious choice between continuing traditional models and deepening their reliance on England or shifting courses entirely. The former equaled a continual check, to some extent, on his growing absolutism but also on the guaranteed security of the Atlantic realm that in many ways propelled such political developments. The latter meant potentially risking all this for internal development and greater independence. In other words, the overall nature of João V's Atlantic-backed absolutism was complex as he simultaneously became politically independent at home and diplomatically dependent abroad.

A Frenchman visiting the country later highlighted the conflict. He noted that João V was "a prince of superior understanding, great in all his designs, magnificent, gallant, and proud . . . [but] he was much attached to his alliance with England, and did not sufficiently reflect on the empire that greedy nation usurped over his country."[50] While the description holds true, it does not fully represent João V's unique absolutism or his efforts to combat English dependency. In reality, there were times when the monarch lost patience with his English allies as they repeatedly disrespected his laws in blatant fashion. Lord Tyrawly experienced João V's absolutist wrath after an English captain seized a gang of English and Irish Catholic crimps who lived in the city and worked to debauch sailors through drunkenness and other revelries into the naval service of Portugal and other nations. The envoy complained after João V ordered the forts on the Tagus to stop the guilty ship from leaving if the men were not set at liberty.[51] When Tyrawly argued that what was done was in no way different from the actions of other nations in times past, João V responded defiantly that "the Tagus was his river, as much as Lisbon was his town, and that people could no more be forced out of his country afloat than ashore." The monarch concluded the matter by warning Tyrawly that he would not "suffer his authority to be violated," especially "in sight of the windows of his palace."[52]

João V exercised his absolute power over the English at other times. When the HMS *Lowestoft* was struck by an outgoing Portuguese vessel in 1729 as it docked in Lisbon, the English crew caused significant damage as they cut both mast and rigging of the Portuguese ship in order to free themselves. João V demanded restitution despite evidence that the Portuguese craft was at fault, and ordered all the forts along the Tagus to impede the departure of the *Lowestoft* until his terms were met.[53] Lord Tyrawly, writing a month later with the *Lowestoft* still detained, described the treatment that he and the English factory experienced in the wake of the event as the Portuguese "mob, and even some of a better rank," became "as cold and even unpolite as possible."[54] Worse yet, he reported that the Portuguese "court seems as if they intended to support what they have done in relation to the Man-of-War, having repaired all their batteries upon the river of Lisbon, mounted guns where they were wanted, and doubled the guards in all their forts to the sea."[55] Tyrawly grew increasingly tired of Portuguese intransigence, suggesting to his superiors in London that the only option left was to send a squadron, which would frighten the Portuguese "out of the small stock of wits God has given them."[56] The issue was finally resolved when England agreed to pay a sum of just over 1,400 pounds sterling.[57] The show of strength paid off for João V and proved to be one of the few diplomatic victories in an era otherwise marked by an increasing reliance on England.

In sum, João V could only push back so hard against the English in Lisbon considering that he was largely an absolute monarch only so far as the relationship with his most important ally, which proved integral to protecting one of the major foundations of his absolutist regime, remained intact. Little wonder he remained aloof, unlike other absolutist monarchs, from the major European conflicts of his day. Constrained as he was, João V developed a brand of absolutism particularly focused on the elevation of his image through the transformation of his imperial capital.

Lisbon's Urban Transformation

Having cleared away any real internal opposition, João V was free to use his growing Brazilian wealth to recast his city as a physical reflection of his developing political prestige and power.[58] One of the first steps he took was transforming the royal chapel into a patriarchal church. The move was the result of a November 1716 papal bull that elevated the royal chaplain to the office of patriarch (along the lines of what was earlier granted to the Spanish monarchs) independent of Lisbon's archbishop.[59] The bull effectively split the city spiritually and was issued as thanks to João V for sending the Portuguese navy to aid Venice against the Turks.[60] More importantly, it opened the door for João V, in true absolute fashion, to exercise more control over the church.

All felt the ramifications of such developments, as João V lost no time in capitalizing on the honor and, in a show of absolute power, decreed the physical division of the city in 1717 along the same lines outlined in the edict from Rome.[61] The portion of the city subject to the ecclesiastical jurisdiction of the new patriarch was to be known as Lisboa Occidental, while the older part of the city under the archbishop became Lisboa Oriental. The decree further solidified the separation, as the monarch created a new independent city council for Lisboa Occidental and mandated that all official correspondence reflect the divide, which lasted until August 1741. After that, both the pope and João V saw fit to abolish the cumbersome innovation.[62]

Invigorated by the honors flowing from Rome and growing Atlantic revenues, João V began plans for a new grandiose palace and patriarchal basilica worthy of his name along the lines of Louis XIV's Versailles. Two plans were proposed for the project and drawn up by the Italian architect Filippo Juvarra.[63] The first entailed a complete remodeling and expansion of the existing royal palace on the Terreiro do Paço. The second proposed the construction of a new palace complex modeled after Saint Peter's, complete with a zoo, just west of the city.[64] Although the king favored the latter, nothing came of the project. Charles Frédéric de Merveilleux claimed that the dream of a new palace with all the trappings of royal largesse and power never materialized after the secretary of state, Diogo de Mendonça Corte-Real, urged the king to first endow the city with desperately needed fountains, stating, "[By so doing] the people seeing the care with which your majesty satisfied common needs, would later view the expenses favorably of constructing a palace, [and] patriarchal church, along with other buildings that are not needed." Merveilleux added that the enormous sums then being spent on the construction of another immense palace-convent near the Atlantic coast at Mafra (which itself took fourteen years to complete) also weighed in the decision.[65]

According to Lord Tyrawly in April 1730, such monarchial whims threw not only the city but the entire country into disorder. He wrote that João V had sent enormous numbers of workers to Mafra on top of seizing all the oxen and mules from the surrounding countryside. Agriculture was particularly affected as fields lay fallow for want of workers and livestock. The Englishman further remarked that Lisbon was devoid of "all most any tradesmen you can think of" as a result and that all construction materials had been seized for the king's use. His frustration boiled over as he had to send no less than ten messages to the secretary of state for permission simply "to buy half a moeda's worth of lime to whitewash some part of my house, and I must have an order signed by the king before I can have one shovel full."[66]

The drain on Lisbon's resources to satisfy the monarch only continued. A mere five months later, Tyrawly added that most of the horses and mules from the royal family, nobility, and cavalry were sent to draw materials at Mafra. Men were being pressed to work on the site and the families of those who fled were imprisoned until they returned and surrendered their labor. The need for workers on the project reached such levels that on one occasion in 1731, João V had all the convicts bound for India unloaded and marked with an *M* on their foreheads before being sent to work on the mammoth palace.[67]

Foreigners were no exemption to the impressment as many had their servants, horses, and carts confiscated. While Tyrawly was able to restore those items taken from the English, he despaired that "the whole kingdom is in a confusion next to a rebellion upon account of this building."[68] It is no surprise then that Merveilleux, who visited the Mafra site, declared, "Three quarters of the king's treasure and the gold brought by the fleets from Brazil have been metamorphosed into stone."[69] Speaking of the expenses of interior decoration at Mafra alone, one official asserted, "It cannot even be dreamed what things there are here."[70] It was reported that when João V received an exorbitant estimate from the foundry at Liège for a new carillon (which even the Belgians did not believe he would accept), he paid double in new gold coins.[71]

In addition to these monetary concerns at Mafra, others claimed the monarch was disheartened that a new palace on the Tagus was too large an undertaking to be completed in his lifetime.[72] Work, therefore, began on reforming the royal palace in Lisbon and its adjacent patriarchal church. There were various phases of construction and alterations to the church and the project lasted almost the entirety of João V's reign. During one phase of expansion the monarch purchased and demolished no less than six hundred residences near the structure in order to make room for improvements.[73] The *Folheto de Lisboa* records that during another phase of development, the purchase price for many of the properties was as much as one-third above their appraised value.[74] The scale of the undertaking was such that João V threw various private construction projects in the city into disarray when on one occasion he had many of Lisbon's stone masons put to work on a new staircase.[75] In 1732 João V spent 300,000 *cruzados*, or about 33,750 pounds sterling, on a cross and candlesticks for the church.[76] He later spent 10,000 *cruzados* on new bells and installed six confessionals built from Brazilian hardwood to the tune of 875 *cruzados* each.[77] To put these expenditures into perspective, a month's wages for an unskilled laborer in the city amounted to only 16 *cruzados*.[78]

João V justified the project by stating, seeing as "Our Lord God [has] augmented my revenues with the gold taken from Minas Gerais, [it is] just to take some portion from the royal fifth and apply it to the church in recognition of that great blessing."[79] Merveilleux asserted that the furnishing and function of the church alone "absorbed the riches of many of the Brazil fleets."[80] Yet the exorbitance only increased, to the point that the monarch's Spanish daughter-in-law declared in a letter to her family in Madrid that "nobody speaks at present of anything but the loans which he [the king] has raised for the patriarchate." She further confessed that she did not believe João V would have funds enough, considering "it is said that he needs two million [*cruzados*]."[81]

While vast amounts of time and money went to Mafra and other royal expenditures, it is important to recognize that the patriarchal church was João V's earliest undertaking and longest lasting project, attesting to its importance to the monarch. Altogether it was to be the centerpiece of monarchial power where divine cult and royal absolutism met in full display. In essence, the appointment of a patriarch and the expansion and renovation of the royal chapel into a patriarchal church along baroque lines represented João V's rising absolute power over his city. It also curtailed ecclesiastical power in the capital as the patriarch (completely favored by the king) superseded the old archbishop, whose position eventually ceased to exist.[82]

However, the expansion of the royal palace and chapel in Lisbon were not João V's only major construction projects in the capital. The monarch decreed that work begin on the Águas Livres Aqueduct in 1731 to solve the age-old problem of water supply to his subjects.[83] Although a royally supervised project, the monumental aqueduct was funded almost entirely by taxation on the city's populace—including an otherwise exempt clergy. João V flexed his absolute will as he ordered the clergy to pay their fair share for the project. His reasoning was simply that they too would drink the water.[84] When the patriarch threatened in protest to stop churches from celebrating sacred rites, the king responded equally emphatically that if necessary, he would use his "sovereign powers that God had given him to free his vassals from these and other similar oppressions."[85]

With the matter resolved, the king himself contributed 10,000 *cruzados* to the project, a small sum considering the city council imposed taxes on seven major commodities in Lisbon in order to raise the 1.2 million *cruzados* needed to fund the project.[86] Yet, according to the *Folheto de Lisboa*, the aqueduct provided work for many in the city and a new pastime as crowds watched the construction of the towering arches across the Alcântara valley.[87] While the aqueduct eventually brought huge benefits to Lisbon, João V's control angered many as he opted for higher (and more expensive) arches.[88]

There were other local manifestations of João V's growing absolutism. In a first attempt at what might be termed modern urban planning, João decreed on 13 April 1745 that future streets throughout the entire city must maintain a certain width to accommodate the populace. The reason given was that these widened arteries would add "symmetry and adornment to the city" rather than continue the "deformity" of existing streets and neighborhoods.[89] The regulation accompanied constant efforts to mend city streets, which had fallen into such disrepair that during the period there were even accidents among sedan chairs.[90]

In addition to beautification and order, one of the main stimuli for widening Lisbon's future streets was the increasingly fashionable use of carriages among the well-to-do.[91] In the same vein, even balconies were regulated by the monarch after 1745 to allow for the passage of carriages.[92] The city council was always responsible for funding the improvements. On one occasion, when they lacked the necessary funds due to the demands of creditors, João V suspended their debts for a year.[93] Other arteries were constructed or repaired, including a new highway to Mafra.[94] The monarch also planned and built portions of a road leading westward toward Belém along the banks of the Tagus. The purpose of the project was to link Lisbon to the royal residences outside of the city (considering the fastest means of travel along the river was by boat). It was also to be a beautiful promenade full of exquisite gardens and spectacular views. Unfortunately, the sections constructed were lost during the 1755 earthquake.[95]

Other projects also reflected the king's vision of urban functionality. In the waning years of João V's reign, the city council urged the monarch to repair the decrepit stone wharf used by the tobacco customs house. The arguments provided included avoiding possible damage to that edifice if the wharf continued in its current state and that such a work would prove beneficial to the public interest. Discussions on the topic began in 1742 and lasted four years. The project was finally begun by the Crown only after the council complained that they lacked the necessary funds.[96]

On top of all this, João V concerned himself with the overall cleanliness of his recently divided city. He chastised both city councils via his secretary of state after the outbreak of yellow fever (which most likely originated from

Brazil) in 1723 for their lack of attention to removing trash and other debris, which he thought contributed to the swift spread of the disease.[97] Efforts to keep roadways uncluttered were also instituted during the monarch's reign. Indeed, it was João V's personal interest in the functioning of his imperial capital that led to an increase in surveys and proposed solutions to the city's multitude of problems. All this made João V the first Portuguese monarch to attempt a serious program of urban renewal and regulation.[98] While efforts at beautification and greater urban order were typical of all Bourbon-era monarchs, for João V, these were vital elements for an aspiring absolutist eager to assert his place among the powers of Europe who otherwise paid him little heed.

The urban and architectural transformation of Lisbon during the period was also the result of other novelties previous to the discovery of Brazilian riches. Yet even these were heavily influenced by the influx of wealth. For example, the vast majority of the nobility, previously drawn to Madrid during the union with Spain, flocked to Lisbon in the aftermath of the restoration where they purchased or constructed palaces of no particular quality in order to be near the new monarch and royal privilege.[99] The move was so complete by the end of the seventeenth century that the few holdouts who remained in their provincial courts were viewed as outliers; the nobility of Lisbon jokingly referred to the Count of Unhão as "the prince of the hills" for residing at his palace near Santarém.[100] The opposite occurred, to some degree, as João V came to the throne. As the monarch increasingly moved to curtail the privileges of the nobility in Lisbon, some members, resigned to the political change, decided it was better to retire for good to their country estates rather than compete with upstarts favored by the king.[101] Nevertheless, when taken as a whole, the aristocracy in Lisbon became among the most physically and figuratively contained in Europe as they came progressively under royal patronage.[102]

While baroque style reached Lisbon during the last quarter of the seventeenth century and was reflected in some of the noble palaces, it was a growing Atlanticization during the first half of the eighteenth century that accelerated that process. In fact, the influx of Brazilian wealth led to the transformation and expansion of noble residences in the city by the second decade of João V's reign.[103] César de Saussure, who visited in 1730, commented, "Lisbon possesses a great number of magnificent palaces that belong to the *fidalgos* or aristocracy of Portugal . . . each has a balcony, some of them gilded, which produces an optimal effect. The architecture of a great number of these palaces is of the highest taste."[104] Another visitor echoed these sentiments while adding that the structures did much to contribute to the "beautification of the city."[105]

Art historian Hellmut Wohl provided a tantalizing glimpse of Lisbon and its Atlantic-inspired transformation by describing in detail the parameters of Portuguese baroque architecture with its gilded woodwork interiors and cut stone exteriors—all with an eye toward "rich ornamentation . . . characterized by vigor, opulence, and exuberance and charged with sculptural energy."[106] No wonder Robert C. Smith, another famed art historian, declared that "in the Joanine era Portuguese architecture was again brought up to date with that of Italy."[107] Interestingly enough, the gilded woodwork carving that made the Portuguese baroque of Porto and northern Portugal famous to this day initially spread from Lisbon as it developed under the patronage of João V.[108]

Individual churches and monasteries also began to reflect the change. João V personally endowed various churches with rich works of art and patronized a variety of architectural improvements. The most famous of these was the royal chapel dedicated to St. John the Baptist in the Jesuit São Roque church. The chapel, replete with gold and lapis lazuli stone, was constructed in Rome and blessed by the pope before being shipped to Lisbon and reassembled.[109] Other royal projects included the erection of the baroque *Menino Deus* church.[110] Altogether, the urban transformation of Lisbon became an intrinsic manifestation of João V's growing absolutism. While the end of the restoration war allowed Pedro II to focus on the modernization of the city by addressing pressing issues, the monumentalization of Lisbon began under João V as the monarch sought to use his growing Atlantic wealth to transform the city into a respectable and functioning imperial capital.[111]

Religious Impacts

João V's developing absolutism, fueled by Brazilian wealth, affected not just the material church but the spiritual church as well. The independence movement begun by João IV in 1640 against Spain placed Portugal in a difficult situation with regard to papal relations as a succession of pontiffs, pressured by powerful Spanish diplomats, refused to recognize Portuguese independence until the war's end. By the beginning of João V's reign, the power balance began to shift in Portugal's favor as Brazilian riches were placed on the scale. As with the transformation of his city, João V saw the elevation of the Portuguese church as a reflection of his own status and a means of restoring

Portugal's image among European powers. The series of honors bestowed on the church and clergy in Lisbon largely began with the previously discussed advancement of the royal chaplain to the rank of patriarch. Almost immediately after the awarding of this honor, the Portuguese monarch began petitioning Rome to grant a cardinal's hat to the patriarch and his successors. The request was finally fulfilled in 1737.[112]

Rank and honor from Rome, while generous, paled in comparison to the wealth and social prestige the monarch lavished on the new patriarch and the canons of the patriarchal church. The Count of Povolide was amazed that João V added 1,200 *cruzados* of salary to each of the canons, who numbered over twenty and already enjoyed a yearly sum of 400 *cruzados*. The king also granted the patriarch and his successors a perpetual annual gift of three *arrobas* of gold along with other rents and favors, the yearly cost of which was estimated at roughly 50,000 *cruzados*.[113] To top it off, João V personally supported singers, musicians, and other individuals who, combined with the canons and clergy associated with the patriarchal church, numbered 444 by 1747.[114]

The goal of João V was to make the patriarch and the canons as much like the pontiff and his sacred college of cardinals as possible. For such an end, he spared no amount or effort.[115] One observer noted that in Lisbon, the patriarch even outshone the pope at times.[116] The patriarch was further honored with the right to anoint the Portuguese kings in 1720 after João V successfully petitioned the pontiff to transfer the responsibility from the archbishop of Braga.[117]

The privileges bestowed on the patriarch and canons shook up the traditional hierarchies of the Lisbon court as some among the nobility resented their elevation to an equal, or even higher, footing.[118] Many were upset that João V made the patriarch a member of the Council of State. Jealousies also infected the ecclesiastical hierarchy. The papal nuncio considered the patriarch's unofficial elevation to cardinal by João V to be an act of royal convenience rather than actual position and refused to visit the patriarchal church. Even the dukes and marquises resented the superior station conferred on the patriarch and murmured among themselves that "the patriarch was not a cardinal, which would out-rank them, and even though the king, our lord, had granted him the honors of a cardinal, he was not a cardinal."[119]

In 1717, the counts sent a petition to João V complaining of the social rank and precedence granted to the canons.[120] The Count of Povolide recorded that the petition came after the counts discovered that the canons were to precede them not only at ecclesiastical but at secular and civil functions in order and hierarchy.[121] Worst of all, according to the petition, the move ensured that the younger brothers and sons of the nobility would outrank their natural superiors, considering these usually entered the priesthood. The petition never questioned the king's power, just its despotic application.[122] Coolly, João V waited until 1723 to respond, which he did in favor of the canons.[123] With the matter so settled, it was reported that the dean of the patriarchal church was finally participating in the Junta dos Três Estados—the majority of whose members were counts.[124]

The social and political elevation of those clerics associated with the new patriarchal church literally carried over into Lisbon's streets as some among the titled nobility refused to yield their own coaches at intersections to that of the new patriarch in a show of disrespect. The Count of Prado was imprisoned for the offense after responding defiantly to the secretary of state that he would yield only if the king "issued a law that everyone should yield to the patriarch." The nobleman spent over three years detained in the citadel of Cascais before he managed to flee to France.[125] After the incident, the Count of Povolide emphasized that all the nobility stopped their coaches for the patriarch.[126] While the Count of Prado's treatment may seem harsh, it was certainly better than the 1686 decree of Pedro II requiring a fine and a period of exile to Brazil for those who refused to yield at congested intersections of the city.[127]

João V's constant efforts to elevate his own image through the Catholic Church at times created conflict with Rome. The most notorious example was the years-long debate over the elevation of the papal nuncio Vincenzo Bichi in Lisbon to the rank of cardinal. The issue was important for the monarch, who correctly perceived the privilege as a matter of honor and prestige, considering that the nuncios at the courts of Madrid, Paris, and Vienna were all awarded such laurels.[128] The honor was of such magnitude to João V that he began efforts to sway the papacy as early as 1707.[129] Years of influence appeared to pay off when Benedict XIII responded favorably in 1725. However, the college of cardinals pressured the new pontiff to reconsider as it outlined Bichi's terrible record of service.[130] The Genoese consul in Lisbon, Pietro Francesco Viganego, recorded similar sentiments among the Portuguese, who continually complained that in his capacity as nuncio, Bichi "auctioned justice and everything could be obtained with money."[131] When news reached João V in 1728 that Benedict XIII granted a cardinal's hat to another candidate, the monarch became livid and recalled his ambassador from Rome.[132] Like Louis XIV (1643–1715) and Philip V of Spain (1700–1746) before him, João V did not hesitate to confront Rome head-on as he severed all relations and rumors of a Portuguese schism swelled.[133] These were taken seriously as

João V began to evince curiosity concerning all things relating to patriarchs and Oriental Christianity.[134]

The situation only worsened when Monsignor Firrao (appointed as Bichi's replacement) refused to vacate the city after relations were severed. The extent of the diplomatic rift was such that João V even ordered Bichi out of the city.[135] Firrao responded defiantly to João V's demands that he depart by stating, "I am not at liberty to leave this kingdom without license of His Holiness."[136] The stance was seen as an attack on royal jurisdiction, to which João V's ministers responded, "His majesty is lord absolute without dependence on anyone and he can expel from his kingdom all the ecclesiastical prelates that he sees fit."[137] After more back-and-forth with the secretary of state Diogo de Mendonça Corte-Real, Firrao finally left Lisbon on 1 April 1728. In July, João V declared the expulsion of all subjects of the papal states from his dominions and forbade any communication or commerce between the two courts. Relations were restored in September 1731 when the new pope, Clement XII, fearing a break with the church in Portugal, finally relented and granted the cardinal's hat to nuncios serving in the Portuguese capital.[138] The loss of Brazilian gold flowing to the eternal city no doubt played a decisive role in the capitulation.[139]

The granting of the cardinal's hat did not deter João V from seeking additional privileges from Rome. The crowning validation of his reign came near its end in 1748 as the aging ruler and his successors received the perpetual title of *Fidelíssimo*, or most faithful. The honorific title placed João V and all subsequent Portuguese monarchs alongside the *Católico* kings of Spain and the *Cristianíssimo* kings of France.[140] Yet, unlike these monarchies who effectively earned their titles, it can be argued that João V used his impressive Atlantic wealth to buy such honors.

João V's obsessive desire to elevate himself and his city through religion separated him from Europe's other absolute monarchs at the time. His entire reign, it seemed, was devoted to emulating every aspect of the papal court, so much so that some referred to Lisbon as a New Rome.[141] João V's ardent religiosity and developing absolutism had profound consequences for popular Catholicism in Lisbon. Some of the most important religious festivals and processions were completely transformed as he eliminated pagan influences and profane displays that accompanied these celebrations.[142] In a letter to the Count of Viana in 1709, José da Cunha Brochado noted the irreverence that had developed as he declared, "These processions, which are not from the first centuries of the church, should not be, neither repeated, nor so multiplied because . . . that Catholic gathering today is nothing more than a profane spectacle."[143] The Portuguese diplomat went further, worrying that unless something changed, God was certain to allow the loss of Rio de Janeiro and the rich mines of Brazil—an event that occurred only two years later, when the French seized that city during the War of the Spanish Succession.[144] Ultimately, João V sought to regulate and reform the festivities as he increasingly tied his own image to that of popular religion.[145] In effect, no other European sovereign of the period was as invested in this process as the Portuguese monarch.[146] José da Cunha Brochado lauded the king's efforts, commenting, "To see Lisbon I once went to the Corpo de Deus procession, where my eyes had the pleasure of seeing the majesty of the king, our lord, who with his joyous and cheerful countenance showed his authority and devotion."[147]

No other religious pageant in the Portuguese capital underwent a greater transformation than the annual Corpo de Deus procession. In preparation for the 1717 celebration, Diogo de Mendonça Corte-Real, under João V's direction, sent a letter to the city council declaring that during the proceedings there should be no "giants, serpents, dragons . . . and similar [decorations] that are regularly given to officials, nor any dancing or Moors that usually attend with St. George."[148] In a subsequent letter, the monarch barred the "black horn players" from all processions put on by the city council.[149] All brotherhoods, including Black brotherhoods, however, were required to participate in the Corpo de Deus procession.[150] At times, the city itself was the focus of the changes as João V proposed on one occasion the demolition of every residence between the Madalena church and the Rossio square in order to improve the spectacle.[151] The transformation successfully recast religious observance as the procession became inextricably linked to the monarch and the vehicle by which the public simultaneously became witnesses to, and actors in, João V's absolute power.[152]

The growing demands of an absolute monarch on religious observance were felt in other ways as the city council constantly bore the expenses imposed. At the apogee of the Corpo de Deus procession in 1719, its costs reached 124,000 *cruzados*. The money was used to clean the city streets along the route and to pay a host of decorative artisans.[153] The procession under João V became a spectacular show of imperial grandeur. A later visitor described the lavish scene with silk-lined streets covered in foliage and flowers and intricate triumphal arcades as one "with a pomp and solemnity that exceeds, as I believe, everything that is practiced in all the other places of Christendom . . . [and] the scene is superb."[154] Put simply, it was here where a city transformed by Atlantic influence put on one of its most vibrant cultural displays.

Absolutism and Cultural Change

Cultural change and innovation flooded Lisbon as João V cut an increasingly absolutist figure, foreigners arrived in greater numbers, and Atlantic wealth poured in. The French consul Mornay noted in 1715, "It can be assured that the commerce of Portugal is not what it was fifteen years ago." At that time, he continued, the Portuguese were "less wealthy and as a consequence they spent less." Now, he contended that there "was introduced among them a luxuriousness previously unknown."[155]

The change occurred as Brazilian gold shipments began to steadily arrive in the capital, which in turn reinvigorated commerce.[156] Put another way, almost one-fourth of a skilled worker's wage in Lisbon was the result of colonial trade during the first half of the eighteenth century.[157] The larger effect was that by 1750, only the populations of cities like Antwerp, Amsterdam, and London had higher patterns of consumption in western Europe.[158]

As was true for many European capitals of the time, one of the most visible innovations in consumption was an alteration in clothing styles as the Portuguese court developed a taste for all things French in opposition to the previously popular Spanish style.[159] This trend, as well as the impact of Italian and English influences, only accelerated under João V.[160] In fact, beards were abandoned and everyone wore French wigs.[161] A Portuguese observer at the turn of the century lamented the changes, noting that "everyone says that shaving is healthy and clean, I say it is craziness" and that "there are wigs for home, for strolling, for the court, for military dress, and I am wondering when they will begin buying wigs for sleeping or for their deathbeds."[162] The account further lambasts the fetish for all things foreign, especially among women who dressed after the French manner, "supposing it a defect to dress like the Portuguese." The disgruntled patriot closes his criticism of the wanton ostentation among Portuguese women in Lisbon by declaring that it was rare to find one who does not "use more cloth on their sleeves than a tall ship does for its sails" and whose heads were wrapped with so much ribbon they look "like flags on a Dutch ship."[163]

In a letter at the end of the seventeenth century, the Portuguese diplomat José da Cunha Brochado lamented the changing trends and asked, "Who would have believed that in our land, where even the natives for reasons of bad habit and education, [would] make it a point of nobility and erudition to idolize everything that covers them with the sacred name of foreign?"[164] D. Luís da Cunha, having spent considerable time in Paris, likened the changes to a drug exported from the French capital and decried the fact that "the Portuguese only desire and love what comes to them from abroad, following crazily the variety of fashions and spending on them what they do not have."[165] Foreign influences were clearly a part of Lisbon's development as an Atlantic crossroads.

Damião António de Lemos Faria e Castro bemoaned the spreading trend among the aristocracy and warned, "After luxury takes hold . . . many times a family will not have wherewith to eat, or pay the pensions from their entails, as they comply with the obligations of style and the precepts of vanity."[166] The changing tastes of the time were not limited to ostentatious aristocrats. Lisbon's clergy were also heavily influenced by the new trends as their vestments grew quite sumptuous.[167] Even the nuns in the city followed suit as they regularly donned silk stockings, makeup, and other luxury styles.[168] One French visitor remarked that the nuns of the age wore not only makeup but also corsets "which show their assets to the best advantage."[169]

Surprising pastimes arose as wealth and ostentation took hold in the city. As the upper classes became more closed and socially suitable partners for second and third daughters more difficult to find, many aristocratic women were placed in convents throughout Lisbon. The elevated number of noble and other well-off ladies in the city's convents made these into locales of diversion for *fidalgos* who thought of themselves as déclassé if they were not *freiráticos*.[170] The term *freirático* itself derives from the Portuguese for nun. Being a *freirático* meant maintaining a relationship that was often (but not always) platonic in nature. Many a nobleman fathered illegitimate children from such encounters as the convent grates proved quite pervious.[171] According to the *Folheto de Lisboa Occidental*, the pastime was also practiced among the English in the capital.[172] The Englishman Augustus Hervey described such meetings in detail, noting that on one occasion he was introduced by a Portuguese noblewoman to "all the handsome women that could be brought to the grate." After being invited to visit the convent again, he "stayed late, making love in the *frereatica* [*sic*] way."[173]

While definitely not novel to the age, the custom exploded in popularity under João V, largely due to his own participation.[174] Ironically, and in true absolutist fashion, João V became a voracious legislator against the practice but to little avail.[175] Lisbon's gazettes from the period are full of examples of *fidalgos* and others being apprehended for the same social infraction. Those among the Portuguese nobility who were repeat offenders were exiled. One unfortunate individual was sent to the island of Madeira, while the *fidalgo* António de Miranda was banished to the North African outpost of Mazagão.[176]

The example set by the king in this regard proved an expensive one, as the monarch enjoyed multiple partners during various periods of his reign. His most famous exploit was with a certain nun named Paula in the Odivelas convent. João V gave Paula an annual income of 4,270 *cruzados* and had a special house built near the convent for their amorous encounters. The structure was a wonder to behold with gilded ceilings, floors made of Brazilian hardwoods, and various panels of intricate tilework. Nine servants attended to Paula there.[177] The aesthetics of the structure were such that it became a prototype for townhouses throughout the country during the eighteenth century.[178] The lavish expenses for João's partners would not stop there. The prodigal monarch ordered a golden bathtub from London weighing one hundred kilos for another lover in a different convent. The tub remained in the royal palace after a storm destroyed part of the convent roof, and the nun, taking it as a sign from God, cloistered herself.[179] Altogether, João V fathered three illegitimate sons with various nuns, all of whom were generously supported by a monarch enriched and emboldened by Brazilian wealth.[180]

The love of ostentation spread from the Crown and nobility to the bourgeoisie and even reached working people.[181] A Portuguese contemporary from the end of the seventeenth century noted that even "the shoe-maker wants to appear as the nobleman, the tailor like the merchant, and everyone like *fidalgos*."[182] Foreigners also noticed the changes in consumption among the people as a result of increasing Atlantic wealth and foreign influence. Well into João V's reign, a Frenchman observed that the fishwives "distinguish themselves by their cleanliness and rich adornments [of] bracelets, necklaces, rings, crucifixes, earrings, and some jewels worth more than a mark of gold."[183] In 1730, an English reverend noted that even the "meanest mechanics" dressed in velvet complete with diamond buttons from Brazil.[184] César de Saussure, whose description of João V opened the chapter, concurred, noting:

> [In the city,] it is frequent to find here simple artisans dressed like great lords. Here is an example: on the morning following my arrival to Lisbon, I being in need of a shave . . . sent for a barber. I waited and walked the salon. After a quarter of an hour I saw a subject enter who I immediately thought was a *fidalgo* or gentleman. He wore a very decent black coat and a cap of silk of the same color; a long black wig . . . a large Portuguese sword . . . large bordered cuffs, albeit somewhat coarse, excellent black silk stockings, and the rest

after this quality of style. What most impacted me, however, was the large and excellent pair of glasses he had on his nose, even though he did not appear to be more than thirty-years of age . . . I turned around and called the owner of the house who was in his office, telling him that some important person was there to see him. He hurried to see who it was, and I was surprised when I heard him say: "Ah! It's the barber."[185]

These descriptions, by Portuguese and foreigner alike, were confirmed by the king's adviser Cardinal da Mota. He noted that in Lisbon even "the poorest official dresses in silk equal to the civilized man and there is no difference here between *fidalgo* and mechanic."[186]

The pervasive luxury in the city was a direct result of Atlanticization and the influx of Brazilian wealth, as well as a reflection of the pattern set by an ostentatious monarch eager to elevate himself in the eyes of Europe.[187] However, none could shine as bright as the monarch and absolutism by its nature required hierarchy. Thus, João V, like his father before him, further regulated the social classes by passing pragmatic laws against ostentation. These laws specifically targeted the "confusion" that crept in among the various classes with the "relaxation of dress."[188] Of course, the simple fact that various laws were issued signals widespread noncompliance in the city during the period.

Other cultural changes beyond pageantry and fashion occurred as João V and his court sought out all things foreign. Artistic expression and other diversions also bore witness to the deeper cultural transformation precipitated by growing Atlantic wealth and foreign influence. In imitation of Louis XIV, the monarch recruited foreign artisans to the capital in order to showcase himself and his city while sending Portuguese pupils to Rome.[189] The efforts of the monarch paid off as baroque styles flooded Lisbon and certain artistic expressions, such as stone and metal work, reached new heights under his patronage.[190] The arts in Portugal also benefited from gold remittances during the period as individuals and institutions in Brazil commissioned baroque works in the metropole destined for the colony.[191] Yet the influence of Brazilian wealth was not all positive as the windfall of riches allowed for the importation of large amounts of Chinese porcelain to the detriment of Portuguese ceramics.[192]

Foreign music masters were also recruited to practice and teach their trade in Lisbon. New comedies, plays, and a host of other diversions were the result.[193] Italian melodramas and French tragedies soon replaced Castilian theater in popularity, and the knowledge of these two languages became increasingly common—at times rivaling Castilian in printed works.[194] The arrival of Italian opera in the city was a direct result of João V's contracting Italian musicians and singers to provide sacred music for his new patriarchal church.[195] Italian opera first opened to the public in 1735, and João V had a royal opera house built in 1737.[196]

Additional forms of entertainment became popular as noble men and women transformed gardens and other spaces into locales of social recreation.[197] Masquerades were prevalent, with the monarch himself often in attendance early in his reign. These were attended by Portuguese and foreigner alike. Efforts to stop the illicit cavorting between the sexes that occurred at these events, however, led the patriarch to decree excommunication in 1721 for those who attended. Interestingly enough, the decree apparently targeted only those dances that charged admission. The masquerades continued for a time but eventually disappeared—due in part, no doubt, to João V's own withdrawal.[198] However, when taken as a whole, the influx of wealth and foreign influence completely transformed the Lisbon court during the first half of the eighteenth century from its previous austere and provincial nature.[199]

João V set an extremely high bar for ceremony and comportment in his imperial capital, and his court quickly became one of the most brilliant in Europe.[200] The Genoese consul Viganego noted that while everything was "more magnificent than before; the expenses [were] also infinitely greater."[201] Lord Tyrawly wrote in concern to London in 1728 complaining at "the expenses the king's minister is obliged to be at in this court," which he continued, "I can take upon me to affirm (from having been at most other courts) is much greater than in any other court in Europe. . . . Provisions, servant's wages, and all other articles are so exorbitantly risen, that I am confident five hundred pounds in London will go further than near a thousand here."[202] When the Portuguese nobility complained of their neglect at court, the king's advisers suggested they "retire and live frugally upon their own estates, and not splendidly at Lisbon."[203] Adding to the costs was the fact that in contrast to the other capitals of Europe, the Portuguese court remained in Lisbon year-round.[204]

Even the prodigiously spendthrift monarch encountered financial constraints during his reign as he became increasingly beholden to Brazilian revenues in his ambition to become a sort of Portuguese *roi soleil*. With an ardent desire to showcase his wealth and prestige beyond Portugal, João V made plans for an incognito trip along the lines of Tsar Peter the Great's Grand Embassy through Europe's various capitals.[205] The design was ultimately stymied in 1716 due to a lack of funds. One of the leading men at court, the Duke of Cadaval, wrote to João V when he got wind of the design and begged the monarch to remain, given the financial constraints that resulted from the War of the Spanish Succession and the possible perils that could occur from such a journey. He further argued that the imposition of new taxes, combined with the king's absence, could lead to the loss of Brazil.[206] Merveilleux contended that additional opposition at court came from the "fear that the king, with his wasteful habits, would spend more than the state could support and that he might become accustomed to foreign practices and principles."[207] The trip would have been expensive, considering João V insisted on taking a retinue of retainers along with forty self-portraits and other gifts of gold and silver to distribute along the way.[208]

In an effort to circumvent some of these difficulties before the plan was abandoned, João V sought out personal loans. Henry Worsley reported that the Portuguese monarch had reached out to one Tempest Milner of the English factory in Lisbon for a sum of two million *cruzados* for the journey.[209] Such loans were not out of the ordinary. César de Saussure claimed that one of the greatest businesses of the English merchants in the city was lending money to João V, which was then paid back in Brazilian bullion.[210]

João V was able to bypass his inability to travel through the astute use of his diplomatic corps. The monarch endowed his diplomats throughout the courts of Europe and beyond with copious amounts of wealth to accomplish his ostentatious objectives. In 1715, João V instructed the Count of Ribeira Grande to throw out thousands of gold and silver coins cast with the monarch's image to the masses of Paris during his official entry in order to "proclaim the glory of your king and the Portuguese nation."[211] In 1726, João V sent Alexandre de Metelo de Sousa e Meneses as ambassador to Beijing to reassert João's responsibility vis-à-vis Rome over the *padroado real*, or papal grant, allowing the Portuguese monarch alone the right to appoint missionaries to the Orient. Meneses, accompanied by an imposing baggage train of 326 people, threw an impressive amount of silver coins to those he encountered along the entire route to and from his meeting with the Chinese emperor.[212] The entourage was a splendid response to the emperor's own ambassadorial mission to Lisbon in 1722, during which his representative presented João V with a gift of exquisite pearls.[213] The Marquis of Fontes made his entry into Rome in 1716 with four golden coaches depicting in allegorical form the overseas conquests of Portugal.[214] The Count of Galveias's official entrance in that city in 1718 was so spectacular that foreign nations ceased the practice for a time in despair of achieving such splendor.[215] In what perhaps amounts to one of his most vain endeavors to elevate his own image abroad, João V instructed Cardinal da Cunha while in Rome in 1721 to give out plenty of gold, and if there was no one there, to throw it in the Tiber.[216]

The only thing more impressive than the amount of Brazilian wealth arriving in the Portuguese capital was João V's ability to spend it. The wastefulness was felt in Lisbon. José da Cunha Brochado observed in September 1708 that as a result of the mounting expenses from the War of the Spanish Succession and various royal projects, the monarch's kitchen had been buying supplies on credit for over a month. Under the circumstances, Brochado argued, "the arrival of these [Brazil] ships has never been more important or necessary for the common welfare, and for the king."[217] Padre Carbone, echoing some of these same sentiments in the last decade of the monarch's reign, wrote that João V had a very skewed idea of the wealth of the royal treasury.[218] Still the spending continued. In 1730, Merveilleux reported, "His majesty must have more clothes in his closet than all of Lisbon's merchants have in their stores combined. Surely it is the richest closet in the universe."[219] Yet even the monarch worried at times that he had stretched himself too thin. In a letter to the patriarch in 1738, he confessed that he had become beholden to the yearly Brazil fleets and that serious repercussions could result if "one or more fleets do not arrive, or one or another mine plays out."[220]

Absolutism and Intellectual Reform

João V's contemporaries, as well as modern scholars, have at times rightfully criticized the monarch for his indulgent spending. However, to truly understand the period and its Atlantic transformations, the benefits of such habits must also be highlighted. In addition to the cultural renovation previously discussed (as expensive as it was), João V employed his Atlantic wealth to help propel Lisbon out of its previous intellectual isolation in the eyes of Europe. Improvements to both the mechanical arts and education were made, and the rate of progress led Padre Raphael Bluteau to exclaim, "Every day there are new inventions for the use and convenience of humankind."[221]

As was the case with Lisbon's cultural evolution, intellectual reform was largely the result of Atlantic wealth and foreign influence. For example, João V established a medical academy in Lisbon where he supported foreign surgeons and doctors, two of whom gave classes on anatomy and surgical technique at the hospital.[222] Foreigners filled other vital roles. João V relied on foreign shipbuilders to introduce the latest methods in naval construction. The Marquis of Fronteira complained to João V that improvements were badly needed, as most of the Portuguese shipmasters were men of little mathematical comprehension or skill and wholly ignorant of current developments.[223] On another occasion he argued that such advancements were crucial, because without them, the Portuguese could neither "conserve nor enjoy the treasures of America."[224] Rebuilding the Portuguese navy was, therefore, vital to reducing the reliance on English and Dutch cruisers to protect the rich Brazil fleets.[225] While progress was definitely made, there were multiple confrontations with the foreign masters. One Frenchman was consistently undercut by the Portuguese builders and eventually ended up in jail, while an English shipwright offered his services to Spain after deeming the one hundred gold coins he received too small a recompense for the valuable technology he introduced.[226] No wonder the Genoese consul Viganego bluntly stated, "The Portuguese cannot accept that a foreigner has come to teach them."[227]

Ships aside, Lisbon was devoid of able seamen. D. Luís da Cunha poignantly remarked, "Even though [João V] can buy ships, these . . . will serve him nothing if they do not have sailors."[228] The lack of trained navigators was evident as early as Pedro II's reign. In 1692, the French ambassador in Lisbon, Abbe Jean d'Estrées, remarked that if it were not for foreign masters and crew, the Portuguese would have much difficulty in going to Brazil.[229] Once famous throughout Europe for their seafaring abilities, the Portuguese had become reliant on foreigners at a time when they were most dependent on their overseas empire. João V attempted to remedy the situation by purchasing instructional manuals abroad and establishing a navigation school.[230]

The monarch was himself a passionate consumer of the sciences, seeing its value on both a personal and political level. He often sent long orders to his diplomats for texts, instruments, and other luxuries from across Europe.[231] The number of books in the capital grew as a result.[232] The price of new technology could be high; João V spent over 6,000 *cruzados* on a single sextant.[233] He had two astronomical observatories built, one in the royal palace and the other in the neighborhood of Santo Antão, the findings of which were subsequently published in London's *Philosophical Transactions of the Royal Society*.[234] He even protected and assisted the aviation experiments of the Brazilian padre Bartolomeu de Gusmão, brother to his adviser Alexandre de Gusmão.[235] João invested heavily in his own personal library at the royal palace and transformed it into one of the largest in Europe with over seventy thousand volumes.[236] His ultimate goal for the collection was to make it public, but the plan never came to fruition.[237]

There were additional changes in research and education as João V began construction on another convent-palace on the western limits of the city known as Nossa Senhora das Necessidades after his miraculous recovery from a paralytic attack in 1742. The convent became a center of learning and innovation as the secular order of Oratorians in charge received various privileges that elevated them in educational terms to the level of the traditionally favored Jesuit institutions.[238] Other religious orders, like the Theatines, pioneered further developments.[239] In a major change along Enlightenment principles, João V decreed in 1745 that the Oratorians at Nossa Senhora das Necessidades open their educational courses to all those who wished to participate.[240] The Crown supported the institution financially, provided it with one of the largest libraries in Portugal, and continuously ordered foreign instruments needed for teaching a scientific curriculum.[241] João V even had the Oratorian Luís António Verney study teaching methods throughout Europe in order to improve Portuguese education. He later published his findings under the title *Verdadeiro método de estudar.*[242]

The increasing arrival of foreigners as a result of growing Atlantic commerce meant that more ideas and books entered Lisbon to the benefit of the populace as the period witnessed an increase in the number of translated volumes. Under João V, Lisbon became aware of European affairs on a regular basis as the royally backed *Gazeta de Lisboa* first appeared in 1715. The monarch even commissioned the Swiss-born Merveilleux in 1723 to establish a natural history museum and requested that specimens be sent from all over his empire.[243] As discussed previously in the chapter, foreign ideas and influence also reached Lisbon via the *estrangeirados* as diplomatic demands necessitated greater contacts beyond the Iberian Peninsula.

Various philosophical academies developed during the period, helping expose Portugal to modern ideas as members maintained close correspondence with foreign thinkers.[244] The intellectual ferment was so profound in the capital that roughly eighteen private academies came into existence or were revived between 1721 and 1755 alone.[245] Other social spaces of intellectual exchange began to appear as both Portuguese and foreigners opened cafés—including one established in 1740 by an Englishwoman.[246] Lisbon, it appears, entered a new period of intellectual dynamism under João V.

The monarch himself was directly involved in the fervor. In 1720, he founded and funded the Academia Real da História Portuguesa for the purpose of writing "the ecclesiastical history of these kingdoms, and afterward everything that pertains to all their history and conquests."[247] Beyond merely being the patron, João V often attended the academy's meetings alongside other members of the royal family.[248] While founded on previous French and Italian models, the academy stood apart with its sole focus on historical study, and it excited considerable interest throughout the rest of Europe.[249] The members, much like the diplomats, were approved by João V and became an extension of the monarch's image in their efforts to elevate the glory of Portugal at home and abroad. For their part, many members saw the academy as a means to escape traditional research controls imposed by the church-dominated university system and eagerly joined.[250]

On a deeper level, the establishment of a royal academy signified the absolute monarchy's institutionalization of scientific study and a means of further projecting its interventionist power and control. For João V personally, the academy served to further fortify his carefully manicured image of a forward-thinking and all-powerful monarch who subsumed traditional and outdated hierarchies to restore the prestige of his nation and capital city throughout Europe. With the king as their financial patron and frequent guest, the members and their work soon reflected this vision of absolute monarchy. At the opening of one of the meetings, Francisco Xavier de Meneses went so far as to proclaim that João V superseded even the best Portuguese kings in his virtues. A month later, the Marquis of Abrantes went even further and labeled João V as God's gift to the Portuguese.[251]

Concurrent with Enlightenment thinking, the academy opened the way for the eventual transformation of historical study in Lisbon beyond the ecclesiastical works composed by clerics as a royal decree opened all archives and repositories to members of the academy.[252] Research efforts were further supported by João V, who ruled in 1721 that all structures and artifacts prior to the end of the reign of D. Sebastião (1557–78) were to be protected from demolition or defacement.[253] The greatest intellectual privilege, however, was exemption from any outside censorship or inquisitorial approval and licensing for their published work.[254] This academic milieu fostered the publication of important contributions to Portuguese history, including the *Bibliotheca lusitana*, the first Portuguese bibliography, and the *História genealógica da casa real portugueza*.[255] The academy also published the first catalog of Portuguese material contained at the Archive of Simancas in Spain.[256]

Efforts to reform historical study did not stop there as João V paid exorbitant amounts of money to fund the collection and compilation of Portuguese documents in the papal archives. The project alone consisted of 237 volumes and has been estimated to have cost the king as much as 500,000 *cruzados*.[257] The monarch did much for intellectual life in Lisbon beyond these efforts as he sponsored the publication of numerous authors, encouraged the study of mathematics, brought foreign professors into the country, incentivized the natural sciences, reformed medical instruction, and made plans to completely transform higher education, all of which paved the way for the intellectual reception of the Enlightenment in Portugal.[258]

The Inquisition was not spared from these developments as intellectuals and others influenced by Enlightenment thinking began to question its purpose and discuss its reform. The sentiment soon spread among ecclesiastics, most notably the bishop of Lamego, D. Nuno Álvares Pereira de Melo, who stated openly, "The inquisitors are all brutes."[259] By contrast, João V was an avid supporter of the Inquisition, so much so that he brought the tribunal increasingly under royal influence and control. Furthermore, much of the broadening of inquisitorial scope discussed previously to combat invading Atlantic influences was a direct reflection of his own royal priorities. The alterations were a logical outgrowth of the time considering the Inquisition's increasing reliance on the monarch and his wealth.[260] Thus, while Pedro II had repeatedly cowered before the Lisbon Inquisition, João V and his Brazilian wealth effectively subdued it.[261] The transformation was such that one contemporary declared that the Inquisition "is in a very different position today from what it previously enjoyed, nothing being done without the license of the king."[262]

Lisbon's intellectual ambient developed an interesting trajectory under João V as the mechanical arts, scientific study, and philosophical discussion all flourished under royal patronage during a period concurrently marked by inquisitorial expansion and aggressiveness. Both developments were a reflection of monarchical priority as João V sought simultaneously to consolidate his power at home and elevate his image abroad. Lisbon bore witness to the overlap as the establishment of academies and other institutions of philosophical and scientific learning joined the construction of elaborate baroque churches and the expansion of Catholic pageantry as hallmarks of the age. Stated plainly, Lisbon was becoming a unique crossroads in an intellectual sense as a result of a particular vision of royal absolutism.

A Particular Brand of Absolutism

João V wielded a powerful, yet intimate, brand of absolutism replete with a strong sense of paternalism that distinguished him from many of the other crowned heads of Europe. Additionally, he clearly understood Lisbon's simultaneous role as the center of a burgeoning Atlantic empire and the stage for developing his absolutist image. As such, he was more firmly wedded to his capital city and its advancement than probably any other absolute monarch of the day. By comparison, Louis XIV hated life in Paris and despised the poor, while foreign ambassadors complained of having to constantly follow Philip V from palace to palace beyond Madrid.[263]

João V was completely devoted to his city and, therefore, more visible in his capital than other contemporary rulers.[264] He held public audience several times a week where he heard the concerns of individuals from every social station and distributed gold to those with whom he sympathized.[265] Nothing seemed to escape his attention as all concerns were posted publicly in the royal palace chamber of halberdiers for everyone to observe how they were resolved.[266] A French witness noticed that João V went so far as to keep a locked box where the public could deposit written complaints.[267]

João V often went throughout Lisbon without his guards or servants and was quite familiar with his people.[268] When yellow fever struck the capital in 1723, the monarch disregarded the recommendations of his advisers and doctors and stayed in the city to help take care of the sick and afflicted, declaring, "It was not befitting of a pious king to forsake his vassals on such an occasion."[269] His example set a high standard as he demanded the nobility do the same.[270] English consul Thomas Burnett recorded that João V gave "above two thousand pounds sterling to be divided amongst the poor in this city; and for such of them as are sick, there is a physician, a surgeon, and an apothecary appointed to treat them at his majesty's expense."[271] João V even distributed money to the victims' families. He was also present on more than one occasion to help combat the house fires that were all too frequent in the capital.[272] It was a mixture of ardent religiosity and growing Atlantic wealth that encouraged the monarch to do such things. Little wonder his cognomen was "The Magnanimous." Thus, the lived experience of many Lisboans with royal absolutism was at times intimate and responsive.

Yet the monarch's exorbitant spending and growing absolutism in the face of widespread squalor fostered significant discontent at times. The Genoese consul Viganego was astounded at the openness with which many in the city criticized their king.[273] Not everyone shared in the gold-fueled extravagance, as many parts of Lisbon remained underdeveloped and basic needs went unmet.[274] During the War of the Spanish Succession, Viganego recorded that desertions among Portuguese soldiers became widespread due to lack of payment from the monarch.[275] Yet, he continued, "it is said that the king is obsessed with more than one thing and there are many complaints of his vast expenditures in a time where everyone suffers for lack of money."[276] Like the soldiers before them, the laborers at Mafra went on strike in 1731–32 when they failed to receive their wages from the king.[277] In 1730, a recorded forty-five thousand workers on site were drawn from all over Portugal, not counting the seven thousand soldiers who served as guards.[278] In 1729, laborers at the royal shipyard walked out and marched to the palace after they failed to receive their wages for eighty weeks.[279] A similar episode occurred at the beginning of João's reign when in 1709, the fishwives in the city came close to rioting as wheat supplies dwindled.[280] Even the coachmen and servants of the royal palace went on strike after not being paid.[281] During it all, the Portuguese memorialist José Soares da Silva complained of the palace banquets costing 1,000 *cruzados* a day "that the king is sustaining" while the whole kingdom was in a "miserable state."[282] Emigration from the capital became a popular avenue at times for escaping the crushing waste and negligence of the monarch. In 1709, hunger became so widespread in the city that José Cunha Brochado wrote, "The Brazil fleet is leaving and the whole kingdom wants to embark, believing that in that state there is less hunger."[283]

Certainly, Brazilian wealth allowed João V to emulate the Bourbon theory of absolute monarchy in many respects.[284] Yet the Portuguese ruler exhibited unique characteristics beyond an intense tie to his capital city and its people. While war was a tool of Bourbon absolutism, João V's reign was relatively peaceful, at least in Europe. Given his dependence on Brazil and the English, João could ill afford to cultivate the warlike mentality of Louis XIV or to upset traditional alliances, both of which would threaten his Atlantic empire and disrupt the economic foundations of his reign.

There were consequences to João V's neutrality in European affairs as growing dependence on England to protect Portugal's Atlantic interests impeded the development of a full-fledged style of Bourbon absolutism in Lisbon.[285] The king's secretary, Alexandre de Gusmão, summarized João V's precarious balance between royal absolutism and dependence when he attended a meeting of counselors where the discussion ended with the ridiculous adage of "War with the whole world and peace with England."[286] No doubt João had these considerations in mind when he declared that his rule consisted of "contenting myself with what is mine without desiring that which belongs to others."[287]

While largely hamstrung in the European theater, João V employed these doctrines alongside his Brazilian wealth to flex his absolute might overseas and revitalize Portuguese imperial claims to some degree in both South

America and Asia. It was Brazilian riches that enabled João V to recruit cartographers and astronomers to determine the limits of Brazil and build new fortifications, both of which helped the monarch successfully press these expanded claims against Spain through the 1750 Treaty of Madrid.[288] The monarch also used Brazilian wealth to dispatch from Lisbon one of the largest military expeditions to India in 1740 after the shocking loss of the Province of the North to the Marathas a year earlier.[289]

There were limits to what Brazilian wealth could buy as only a few years later the ships sent to strengthen Goa were filled with forced recruits. Lisbon was directly affected by the renewed focus on India as those impressed into Crown service were gathered indiscriminately throughout the city at gaming houses and other public places.[290] D. Luís da Cunha likened such annual levies to a blood-letting that weakened the body, and argued that the king was uselessly emptying his coffers by sending ships and soldiers without reforming the government or commerce of that state.[291] Yet these developments constituted a renewal of Crown interest in India and the beginning of the New Conquests continued later by the Marquis of Pombal.[292]

More profoundly, João V's actions represented a challenge to the long-held notion that the Portuguese maintained a "shoestring empire" in Asia during the period simply as a matter of honor.[293] Rather, this was in a sense the reversal of Pedro II's previous scheme of utilizing the resources of one area of empire to revitalize another. João V was personally invested in the resurrection of his Asian holdings and with tears in his eyes declared to the departing viceroy in 1744 that the restoration of that state was of "upmost importance."[294] João V's overall goal was to use his Atlantic resources to resurrect a productive global empire that would to some degree restore Portuguese prestige.

While distinct on many levels, João V's overall obsession with patterning his reign after that of Louis XIV—mirroring French culture, constructing monumental palaces, and bypassing traditional channels of power—had unforeseen consequences in Lisbon as the baroque became fashionable at a time when it was in decline throughout much of Europe.[295] Furthermore, the Portuguese royal court was unique in the sense that it never left the city, and thus its members maintained contact with the general populace rather than becoming mere courtiers like those at Versailles. The same was true of João V personally, who was far more accessible than the French king he emulated.[296] While largely a French imitation in political matters, João V's Catholic obsession also made him look to Rome for artistic and religious influence.[297] The mix was best represented by the construction (and dream) of multiple palace-convents in and around the city with all the trappings of sanctity and largesse. While absolutist thought tied the monarch to the church in order to reinforce his power and place, João V took this element to the extreme. One historian declared, "In matters of the faith no more prodigal monarch has sat upon a European throne than Dom João V of Portugal."[298]

Contemporary descriptions of João V's character and his vision reflect his unique nature. These often ranged from disdain and mockery to praise and adulation. While many focused solely on his hyper religiosity, others saw a more rounded character and lauded his competence. Voltaire derided the Portuguese sovereign as a religious fanatic, stating that "when he wanted a festival, he ordered a religious parade. When he wanted a new building, he built a convent, when he wanted a mistress, he took a nun."[299] The description was not far off—yet the French ambassador Chavigny declared, "No other prince has more talent, more spirit, or even possibly more knowledge of affairs than him."[300] Lord Tyrawly initially painted João V as despotic as he petitioned for a transfer, fearing "the temper of His Portuguese Majesty."[301] After becoming acquainted with the monarch over a period of years, an unlikely friendship developed between them.[302] He wrote to the Duke of Newcastle in 1735, "I hope it will be no crime to say that I have certainly the utmost regard and high esteem for his person, not only for the treatment I meet with from him, but for his great qualities, for nobody had ever better parts, better sense, more wit, more quickness, and if one may use so familiar a term to so great a man, there never was one more thoroughly agreeable than the king of Portugal."[303] Simply stated, João V was the perfect embodiment of his capital city's unique nature during the period. He was a progressive monarch that loved science and learning but was wholly devoted to religion and tradition. He was a king who was almost entirely absolute at home while completely dependent abroad. In sum, he was a unique monarch who used his Atlantic wealth to develop a distinctive form of royal absolutism that ultimately transformed his city and his image in the eyes of Europe.

The justification for, and the basis of, João V's royal absolutism rested largely in the emerging empire of the South Atlantic.[304] D. Luís da Cunha recognized as much as he suggested that João V leave Lisbon and European affairs in the hands of a viceroy to establish himself as the head of a powerful empire of the West in Rio de Janeiro. There, Cunha argued, João V would be better situated to support the Estado da Índia and resurrect the global empire.[305] Obsessed with his image among his European counterparts, the

Fig. 3. Filippo Juvarra, *Projeto de Juvarra para o Palácio Real de Lisboa* (Juvarra's project for the Royal Palace of Lisbon), 1717. Musei Civici di Torino. Photo: Wikimedia Commons / Cristiano Tomás.

monarch chose instead to reform the seat of his empire as Brazilian wealth combined with foreign influence to remake Lisbon into a true imperial capital complete with all the pomp and circumstance of the baroque. Lisbon's transformation was, therefore, inextricably linked with the development of a distinct form of royal absolutism backed by Atlantic wealth and influence.

The consequences of Lisbon's Atlanticization were widespread. Atlantic riches did more than simply invigorate royal absolutism, politically speaking; they also allowed João V the means to transform the sociocultural milieu along with the urban space itself. The Portuguese monarch was deeply entrenched in the cultural and intellectual developments of his day and wholly devoted to his capital city. As such, he spent fabulous sums recruiting foreign artisans and other effects to Lisbon where they transformed science, education, and the mechanical arts. Prodigious amounts were equally dedicated to ornate churches, palace-convents, and other religious projects and processions of a grandiose nature. Each element was expertly wielded by João V as a means of solidifying his power and aggrandizing his capital with the ultimate goal of elevating his image abroad. In effect, everyone and everything seemingly felt the consequences of Atlantic-backed absolutism as the city bore witness to the deep and lasting political, urban, and cultural reforms. Lisbon, therefore, became a unique stage where João V fully displayed his distinctive form of absolutism by mixing his intense focus on religion and renewed imperial grandeur of the Portuguese past with European innovation to produce a unique baroque masterpiece.

While seemingly straightforward, the reign of João V was simultaneously marked by a dichotomy of absolutism and dependency, by traditional orthodoxy and progress, by fanaticism and free-thinking, by advancement and intransigence. This struggle was never more apparent than in the character of the monarch himself. At times wasteful and wanton, João V did bring benefits to Lisbon as he pushed back against England, confronted Rome, and constructed the desperately needed aqueduct. While these and other efforts were beneficial, one must consider them with a critical eye as the English increasingly brought Portugal under their influence, Rome siphoned off large quantities of Brazilian wealth for meaningless privileges, and new taxes almost completely funded the aqueduct. The use of Brazilian wealth, however, ushered Lisbon into a new golden age as João V elevated Portugal's image abroad and transformed society at home. The Duke of Cadaval put it another way when he declared, "Today much of the conservation of Portugal absolutely depends on Brazil."[306]

CONCLUSION

A City Lost

Of that global emporium,
Where Neptune raised his trident,
And all the Orient, America, and the most distant provinces
Bestowed their treasures in continuous fleets,
There is nothing more, except a pitiable memory.
　　—Francisco de Pina e de Mello, 1756

On 1 November 1755, at around ten o'clock in the morning, a massive earthquake struck Lisbon. Survivors recorded that the magnitude was enough to make "the surface of the earth to resemble the waves of the sea" and that buildings reeled "to and fro like ships in a gale of wind" before they collapsed.[1] It being All Saints' Day, the churches were brimming with worshippers and filled with lighted candles. Many of those trapped in the rubble burned to death as fires spread throughout the city.[2] Others drowned as three monstrous tsunamis arrived in succession.[3] Those fortunate enough to have escaped to higher ground watched helplessly as they heard the agonizing screams. Contemporary estimates of the dead ranged widely, with some claiming that the city lost almost eighty thousand souls.[4] While there is no way to know for sure, fifteen thousand has been proposed as a more realistic figure.[5] The devastation was such that it took twenty-five years for the city's population to recover from the disaster.[6]

One English witness wrote that the earthquake "seemed to be immediately under the city, for the damage either above or below Lisbon [on the river was] not so considerable."[7] João V's royal palace with its wealth of treasures and his magnificent patriarchal church were destroyed.[8] Thirty-five parish churches collapsed, and only about three thousand of the city's twenty thousand residences remained habitable.[9] In what must have seemed like a miracle, the great aqueduct survived and continued to provide water to the living.[10] Altogether, in a matter of minutes, much of João V's opulent city lay in ruins.[11]

Paralyzed by shock, José I (João V's son and ruling heir) turned to his adviser Sebastião José de Carvalho e Melo (known later as the Marquis of Pombal) for direction. The earthquake effectively propelled Pombal to power as the minister rose to the occasion and took control amid the ensuing chaos.[12] Pombal ultimately oversaw the rebuilding of the city over roughly two decades, but it would not be the same as the baroque splendor of João V's "New Rome" gave way to a city based on functionality.[13] While the capital itself changed greatly in the aftermath of that fateful day, much of what took hold in Lisbon as a result of growing Atlantic pressure would continue in some form or fashion under Pombal.

Lisbon was a very different place in 1668 compared to 1750, and the years between provide fertile ground for analysis of the changes resulting from increasing Atlanticization. Lisbon was altered along racial and cultural lines as the growing focus on Brazil and the consequent evolution of the slave trade meant that for the first time in the city's history, enslaved Africans were most likely born in the metropole or arrived from Brazil rather than Africa. This interplay between Atlanticization and Iberianization allowed Afro-Lisboans and their influences to become increasingly integrated among the popular classes, which became one of Lisbon's most distinguishing features during the period. However, men and women of African descent were themselves profoundly affected by these same processes as enslaved individuals were routinely sent to Brazil with rising labor demands, and baroque obsessions combined with increased intermixing to expand racial exclusion.

There were additional consequences of Lisbon's Atlanticization as the alliance with England became vital to the survival of the Portuguese empire in the South Atlantic. The cost of the alliance in Lisbon was high as extraordinary social and economic concessions repeatedly placed English men and women in a privileged position. Thus, as the Atlantic grew in importance to the Portuguese, so too did Lisbon's importance for the English. In short, for the first time in Lisbon's history, Protestants from the North

Atlantic rather than the Catholic nations of the Mediterranean overwhelmingly dominated its commerce. Considerable tension and strife were often the result.

Perhaps the most devastating effect of Lisbon's Atlanticization was the resurgence of the Inquisition. As in previous periods, Lisbon's New Christians and their accumulated wealth were the primary target when an economic downturn produced by increasing Atlantic competition began. Events in Lisbon became the spark for the powder keg of brewing social tension, and the result was one of the worst periods of inquisitorial persecution in the city's history. With Lisbon's New Christians decimated, the city's Inquisition began to develop an Atlantic scope as wealthy New Christians in Brazil (many of whom had fled Portugal previously), Afro-Lisboans, and Englishmen all became targets. Thus, if toleration and diversity were often the effect of Atlantic influence on a given locale, so too were persecution and pushback.

Lisbon's economic fortunes underwent profound changes as the result of the growing Atlantic connection. The utter reliance on Brazil and the associated slave trade left the city dangerously vulnerable to economic changes in the broader Atlantic world. Yet a steep economic decline and growing foreign dependency by the last decades of the seventeenth century proved the catalyst for a unique period of economic diversification in and around the city. While novel, these programs were eventually neglected, if not abandoned altogether, as a result of changing Atlantic influences.

In many ways, the most lasting effect of Lisbon's Atlanticization was the development of royal absolutism. Ironically, the reliance on the Atlantic simultaneously propelled João V toward greater power at home while deepening his dependence abroad. Put simply, because João V became so reliant on his Brazilian wealth there was little leverage to combat the deepening English dependency in Lisbon. While this paradox made João V distinct among absolute monarchs of the day, his intense devotion to Lisbon and his ardent religiosity further set him apart. The city itself bore witness to this fact as monumental palace churches and elaborate religious processions joined a seemingly contradictory program of cultural renovation and intellectual reform. In essence, Atlanticization made Lisbon into a unique baroque canvas designed to elevate João V's idealistic image as a powerful monarch of a burgeoning empire. Clearly Lisbon's Atlanticization in some way affected almost everyone and everything.

In spite of the continuing popularity of all things Atlantic, the study of its effects on major European capitals are limited. Atlantic history, rather, is overwhelmingly concerned with the colonial New World. No wonder critics argue

Fig. 4. Jacques Philippe le Bas, *Praça da Patriarchal* (The Patriarchal Square), 1757. Museu de Lisboa (MC.GRA.0441). Coleção do Museu de Lisboa / EGEAC / Câmara Municipal de Lisboa.

that it is merely imperial history repackaged.[14] This work helps to fill that gap by demonstrating that Lisbon underwent a profound transformation after the restoration in large part due to a greater dependence on the Atlantic sphere.

Global history has begun to challenge the apparent hegemony of an Atlantic lens as of late. Lisbon, it is true, was still very much the product of a global overseas empire during the period. However, that empire had been severely reduced to the Atlantic sphere with an overwhelming focus on Brazil. Moreover, it was the Atlantic that produced fabulous wealth and fueled monarchal aspirations of restoring the global empire. Thus, while there are definite limitations to an Atlantic approach in general, it nevertheless proves useful and enlightening in the case of Lisbon. The overarching argument of this work, then, is that in order to fully comprehend Lisbon and its transformation between the restoration and the earthquake, scholars and students alike must also understand the broader Atlantic world.

The intersection of the North Atlantic with the Luso-Afro-Brazilian South Atlantic separated Lisbon from the other European port capitals. This convergence forced individuals and institutions to negotiate increasing diversity and change on a number of levels. That diversity, while a hallmark of the city since the early days of Portuguese expansion, grew during the period—particularly after the discovery of Brazilian wealth.[15] Enslaved Afro-Brazilians brought novel cultural practices, significant tensions resulted from English commercial dominance, the Inquisition raged at new religious influences, innovative industries were established, and royal absolutism transformed the urban space and introduced new ideas. In the end, Lisbon was a major epicenter of the Atlantic world and a distinct crossroads where a considerable amount of encounter and exchange occurred. It was where the North and South Atlantic met, where European and African Atlantics converged, and where Atlantic influence was both accepted and rejected. The city was, therefore, unique among Atlantic spaces and convincingly demonstrates, as Bernard Bailyn argues, that Atlantic history "is more than the sum of its parts."[16]

Visitors to Lisbon today will find few physical remnants of João V's Atlantic capital beyond the enormous aqueduct. Rare is the person who ventures beyond the famous medieval quarter and Pombal's grid-patterned streets downtown to tour its mammoth arcades. Most know nothing about its construction. As such, the aqueduct serves as the perfect symbol of understudied processes during a largely overlooked period in Lisbon's history. Yet, as we have seen, the effects of Lisbon's Atlanticization are far-reaching and worthy of increased attention but seldom appreciated.

CONCLUSION

163

Notes

Abbreviations

ACL	Academia das Ciências de Lisboa
AHPL	Arquivo Histórico do Patriarcado de Lisboa
AHU	Arquivo Histórico Ultramarino
ANTT	Arquivo Nacional da Torre do Tombo
BA	Biblioteca da Ajuda
BL	The British Library
BNP	Biblioteca Nacional de Portugal
BPE	Biblioteca Pública de Évora
BPMP	Biblioteca Pública Municipal de Porto
TNA SP	The National Archives of the United Kingdom—State Papers

Introduction

Epigraph from Cervantes, *Los trabajos de Persiles y Sigismunda*, 234. The work was first published posthumously in 1617.

1. Elliott, "Afterword," 239.
2. Games, "Atlantic History," 744, 750.
3. Pedreira et al., "Great Escape?," 8–9.
4. Burnard and Vidal, "Location," 146; Burnard, *Atlantic in World History*, 4.
5. Griffin, "Plea for a New Atlantic History," 236.
6. Greene and Morgan, *Atlantic History*, 3–5.
7. Games, "Atlantic History," 741–42.
8. Rothschild, "Late Atlantic History," 634.
9. Castelo-Branco, *Lisboa seiscentista*; Murteira, *Lisboa da restauração às luzes*; Augusto-França, *Lisboa*.
10. Armitage, "Three Concepts of Atlantic History," 15, 21–27.
11. Hatfield, *Atlantic Virginia*; Fuente, *Havana and the Atlantic*.
12. Burnard and Vidal, "Location," 147.
13. Cañizares-Esguerra and Seeman, *Atlantic in Global History*, xxvi; Coclanis, "Atlantic World or Atlantic/World?," 726.
14. Coclanis, "Drang Nach Osten," 171.
15. Bailyn, *Atlantic History*, 16.
16. Montgon, "Do Caia ao paço da ribeira," 112.

17. "Descrição da cidade de Lisboa (1730)," 38. For the conversion to miles, Humboldt, *Views of the Cordilleras*, 395.

18. Stevens, *Ancient and Present State of Portugal*, 178.

19. Stevens, *Ancient and Present State of Portugal*, 181.

20. Chantal, *A vida quotidiana em Portugal*, 243.

21. BL, Manuscripts, Add. 23726, *Account of Portugal. Diary of Thomas Cox*, fol. 10r. See also Cox and Macro, *Relação do reino de Portugal*, 55.

22. E. Oliveira, *Elementos*, 11:263–64.

23. E. Oliveira, *Elementos*, 14:430.

24. BA, 44-XIV-1, fols. 161r–162r.

25. "Descrição da cidade de Lisboa (1730)," 38; BL, Manuscripts, Add. 23726, *Account of Portugal. Diary of Thomas Cox*, fol. 12r; Cox and Macro, *Relação do reino de Portugal*, 61.

26. Stevens, *Ancient and Present State of Portugal*, 182.

27. E. Oliveira, *Elementos*, 11:431. Matos, "Lisboa na restauração," 483.

28. Matos, "Lisboa na restauração," 473.

29. BL, Manuscripts, Add. 23726, *Account of Portugal. Diary of Thomas Cox*, fol. 10r; Cox and Macro, *Relação do reino de Portugal*, 55.

30. Tours, "Travels Through Portugal and Spain," 101.

31. Villiers, "Portuguese Society," 62.

32. Castelo-Branco, *Lisboa seiscentista*, 47, 49.

33. Matos, "Lisboa na restauração," 471.

34. Olival, "Os lugares e espaços do privados," 251, 255.

35. Olival, "Os lugares e espaços do privados," 245.

36. Olival, "Os lugares e espaços do privados," 247–48; Rijo, "Os escravos na Lisboa joanina," 117.

37. Olival, "Os lugares e espaços do privados," 271.

38. "Descrição da cidade de Lisboa (1730)," 38; Murteira, *Lisboa da restauração às luzes*, 49–50.

39. José Serrão, "O quadro humano," 62–64; Donovan, "Crime, Policing, and the Absolutist State," 54.

40. Bairoch, Batou, and Chèvre, *La population des villes Européennes*, 278.

41. Lisbon's population continued to grow into the eighteenth century, but due to massive emigration to Brazil as a result of the gold rush and the War of the Spanish Succession, it entered a phase of decline until about 1730. From then on it grew at a steady rate of roughly 1.25 percent per year until the 1755 earthquake. See José Serrão, "O quadro humano," 63–64; Costa, Lains, and Miranda, *Economic History of Portugal*, 166.

42. Costa, Lains, and Miranda, *Economic History of Portugal*, 131, 168–69.

43. Ferrão, "Lisboa barroca," 246.

44. Murteira, *Lisboa da restauração às luzes*, 51–52.

45. Rodrigues, *Cinco séculos*, 57.

46. Rodrigues, *Cinco séculos*, 35.

47. Castelo-Branco, *Lisboa seiscentista*, 26–28.

48. Matos, "Lisboa na restauração," 483.

49. Castelo-Branco, *Lisboa seiscentista*, 30–31.

50. Matos, "Lisboa na restauração," 478.

51. F. Melo, *Apólogos dialogais*, 80.

52. P. Braga, "Alemães na Lisboa seiscentista," 423.

53. Dellon, "De Goa a Lisboa," 34.

54. Alessandrini, "Italianos em bairros de Lisboa," 118.

55. Ferrão, "Lisboa barroca," 248.

56. Sweet, "Hidden Histories of African Lisbon," 237.

57. H. Monteiro, "A população Portuguesa por 1700," 137–38, 191.

58. Almeida and Peres, *História da igreja em Portugal*, 2:203–4.

59. Stevens, *Ancient and Present State of Portugal*, 190.

60. Boxer, *Portuguese Seaborne Empire*, 189.

61. F. Melo, *Auto do fidalgo aprendiz*, 37.

62. Villiers, "Portuguese Society," 58.

63. Tours, "Travels Through Portugal and Spain," 101.

64. Matos, "Lisboa na restauração," 475.
65. Colbatch, *Account of the Court of Portugal*, 1:11–12.
66. Donovan, "Crime, Policing, and the Absolutist State," 59–60.
67. Castelo-Branco, *Lisboa seiscentista*, 12.
68. Villiers, "Portuguese Society," 47.
69. C. Antunes, "Population Growth," 124, 130.
70. Chantal, *A vida quotidiana em Portugal*, 225–26, 235.
71. Hanson, *Economy and Society*, 202, 205–6.
72. Madahil, "Viagem de Cosme de Médici a Lisboa," 52.
73. Mauro, "La bourgeoisie portugaise," 241; O'Flanagan, *Port Cities of Atlantic Iberia*, 131, 153; Polónia, "Dinâmicas comerciais," 258–61.
74. Costa, Lains, and Miranda, *Economic History of Portugal*, 126.
75. Fisher, *Portugal Trade*, 54–55; Gash-Tomás and Miranda, "Imperial Economies," 440–41.
76. Costa, Lains, and Miranda, *Economic History of Portugal*, 144.
77. Grafe and Pedreira, "New Imperial Economies," 586.
78. Rosário, *Frutas do Brasil*, 51.
79. C. Antunes, "Population Growth," 119–20; *Mercator's Letters on Portugal*, 9; O'Flanagan, *Port Cities of Atlantic Iberia*, 160.
80. Costa, Lains, and Miranda, *Economic History of Portugal*, 144, 162.
81. Costigan, *Sketches of Society and Manners*, 361–62.
82. Costa, Lains, and Miranda, *Economic History of Portugal*, 170.
83. Polónia, "Dinâmicas comerciais," 276.
84. See Bulut, "Rethinking the Dutch Economy," 391–424.
85. Beier and Finlay, *London, 1500–1700*, 115–18; Gauci, *Emporium of the World*, 2.
86. Bustos, *Historia de Cádiz*, 54; Ortiz, *Historia de Sevilla*, 24–25.
87. Pedreira et al., "Great Escape?," 8–9; Pedreira, "Costs and Financial Trends," 72.
88. O'Flanagan, *Port Cities of Atlantic Iberia*, 286.

Chapter 1

1. ANTT, Tribunal do Santo Ofício, Inquisição de Lisboa, processo 433, fols. 3r–7v.
2. P. Marques, *Portugal e a escravatura dos Africanos*, 58.
3. "Trans-Atlantic Slave Trade Database," SlaveVoyages, accessed April 2024, https://www.slavevoyages.org/assessment/estimates.
4. Alencastro, *Trade in the Living*, 20, 255.
5. Caldeira, *Escravos em Portugal*, 87.
6. Godinho, "Portugal and Her Empire," 509 10; Boxer, *Golden Age of Brazil*, 25; F. Silva, "O tráfico de escravos," 63.
7. Alencastro, *Trade in the Living*, 21.
8. "Cópia do papel que o senhor Dom Joam de Lancastro fez [. . .]," in Rau and Silva, *Os manuscritos do arquivo da casa de Cadaval*, 14–17; "Exposição de Simão Costa, alvitrando a maneira de, no Brasil, aumentar os rendimentos da coroa," in Rau and Silva, *Os manuscritos do arquivo da casa de Cadaval*, 370–75; Antonil, *Brazil*, xii; Schwartz, "Plantations and Peripheries," 97.
9. Boxer, *Golden Age of Brazil*, 45–46.
10. J. Fonseca, *Escravos no sul de Portugal*, 74.
11. Caldeira, *Escravos em Portugal*, 112.
12. A few examples of selling Africans in Brazil come from the letters of Francisco Pinheiro dated 2 June 1724 and 14 September 1748. Both are transcribed in Pinheiro, *Negócios coloniais*, 5:55–56, 357. Mention of enslaved Africans being kidnapped alongside freedmen for sale are found in Lahon, "Eles vão, eles vêm," 89.
13. "Consulta da câmara a el-rei em 16 de Fevereiro de 1672," in E. Oliveira, *Elementos*, 7:326.
14. Caldeira, *Escravos em Portugal*, 108.
15. Tellez, *Chronica da companhia de Jesu*, 223.
16. Reginaldo, "África em Portugal," 298.
17. Villiers, "Portuguese Society," 196–97. For earlier periods, see Saunders, *Social History of Black Slaves*, 62.

NOTES TO PAGES 9–18

18. Caldeira, *Escravos em Portugal*, 161; Rijo, Aragonez, and Francisco, "A freguesia de Santa Justa," 117.
19. Caldeira, *Escravos em Portugal*, 144–45.
20. Rijo, Aragonez, and Francisco, "A freguesia de Santa Justa," 117–19.
21. Caldeira, *Escravos em Portugal*, 138.
22. Neto, *A freguesia de Santa Catarina*, 88–89. According to economic historian V. M. Godinho, the first gold shipment of significance reached Lisbon in 1699. For details, see Godinho, "Portugal and Her Empire," 534–35.
23. Neto, *A freguesia de Santa Catarina*, 88–89; Neto, *A freguesia de Nossa Senhora das Mercês*, 46; Ascenso, "A freguesia da Sé," 62; F. Oliveira, "A freguesia de São Cristovão," 142. For a discussion on the overall declining number of enslaved people in Lisbon despite some parishes showing growth, see Caldeira, *Escravos em Portugal*, 138–39.
24. F. Silva, "O tráfico de escravos," 56.
25. Caldeira, *Escravos em Portugal*, 87.
26. *Gazeta de Lisboa Occidental*, no. 36, 4 September 1727.
27. *Gazeta de Lisboa Occidental*, no. 30, 29 July 1723. An additional reference to Portuguese slavers arriving in Lisbon is highlighted on 4 August 1740 but lacks exact detail of the number of captives delivered.
28. Lisboa, Olival, and Miranda, *Gazetas manuscritas*, 1:157.
29. Caldeira, *Escravos em Portugal*, 88.
30. Alencastro, *Trade in the Living*, 25; Caldeira, *Escravos em Portugal*, 87–88.
31. Lahon, *O negro no coração do império*, 36.
32. Lahon, "O escravo Africano na vida económica," 74–75.
33. ANTT, Tribunal do Santo Ofício, Inquisição de Lisboa, processo 10034, fols. 3v–4v. Apparently the man was baptized in Guinea by the Portuguese before being captured by the Moors at sea. He then lived a number of years in Algiers before being captured once again at sea by an English vessel and sold in Lisbon to Pedro II.

34. Letter of Francisco Pinheiro to Senhor Manoel Pinto Madeira em Pernambuco, 15 July 1734, transcribed in Pinheiro, *Negócios coloniais*, 4:629; Letter of Francisco Pinheiro to Senhor João Francisco Mussi em Rio de Janeiro, 13 April 1728, transcribed in Pinheiro, *Negócios coloniais*, 5:158.
35. BL, Manuscripts, Add. 23726, *Account of Portugal. Diary of Thomas Cox*, fol. 61r. See also Cox and Macro, *Relação do reino de Portugal*, 159.
36. *Gazeta de Lisboa Occidental*, no. 5, 6 February 1720; *Gazeta de Lisboa Occidental*, no. 45, 9 November 1741; Lisboa, Olival, and Miranda, *Gazetas manuscritas*, 2:224.
37. Rijo, "Os escravos na Lisboa joanina," 114; Neto, *A freguesia de Santa Catarina*, 88.
38. Baretti, *Journey from London to Genoa*, 273.
39. Caldeira, *Escravos em Portugal*, 138; J. Fonseca, *Escravos no sul de Portugal*, 28; J. Fonseca, *Escravos e senhores*, 90–100.
40. Henriques, *Os Africanos em Portugal*, 20.
41. Sweet, "Hidden Histories of African Lisbon," 236–37. See also Henriques, *Os Africanos em Portugal*, 20.
42. Stella, *Histoires d'esclaves*, 51–52, 57. In contrast to Lisbon, the background of enslaved people in Cádiz was varied during the second half of the seventeenth century. It was only during the 1670s that Cádiz began to move away from Mediterranean slavery and into the African slavery of the Atlantic world. See García, *Una metrópoli esclavista*, 134. Furthermore, it was only during the first half of the eighteenth century that the Spanish port city came to rely almost entirely on enslaved Africans. See García, "Los caminos de la esclavitud," 4–6.
43. Gerzina, *Black England*, 5; Large and Miranda, "British Slaves," 166; Hondius, "Black Africans in Seventeenth-Century Amsterdam," 89; Ponte, "Black in Amsterdam," 45, 55.

44. Lahon, "Esclavage et confréries noires," 1:53–54. For a more detailed discussion of the Mina ethnic grouping, see Law, "Ethnicities of Enslaved Africans," 247–67.

45. Boxer, *Golden Age of Brazil*, 46.

46. Lahon, "Esclavage et confréries noires," 1:53.

47. "Descrição da cidade de Lisboa (1730)," 81; Boxer, *Golden Age of Brazil*, 175.

48. Lahon, "Da redução da alteridade," 54.

49. Neto, *A freguesia de Santa Catarina*, 98; Neto, *A freguesia de Nossa Senhora das Mercês*, 48; Ascenso, "A freguesia da Sé," 73.

50. Rijo, "Os escravos na Lisboa joanina," 114.

51. P. Marques, *Portugal e a escravatura dos Africanos*, 61, 68–69; Schwartz, *Sugar Plantations*, 239–40.

52. Lahon, "Eles vão, eles vêm," 80.

53. Lahon, "O escravo Africano na vida económica," 74.

54. Rijo, "Os escravos na Lisboa joanina," 114; Rijo, "Escravos e libertos," 282.

55. Caldeira, *Escravos em Portugal*, 144; Rijo, "Os escravos na Lisboa joanina," 118. For the earlier periods, see Saunders, *Social History of Black Slaves*, 63–64.

56. Donovan, "Commercial Enterprise," 107; D. Smith, "Mercantile Class of Portugal," 181.

57. Large and Miranda, "British Slaves," 163, 166.

58. Caldeira, *Escravos em Portugal*, 166.

59. Merveilleux, "Memórias instrutivas," 215.

60. "Descrição da cidade de Lisboa (1730)," 60–61.

61. António Rodovalho Duro first mentions an African participating in a bullfight during D. Sebastião's reign (1557–78). No other major mentions of Africans in bullfighting are listed until the examples provided. See Duro, *História do toureiro em Portugal*, 194.

62. BNP, códice 309, fols. 12v–13r.

63. BNP, códice 510, *Archivo e novelario de várias curiosidades de 1696*, fol. 261r.

64. Carvalho, "Cartas de José da Cunha Brochado," *O Instituto* 70, 570–71.

65. Tinhorão, *Os negros em Portugal*, 222–24.

66. BL, Manuscripts, Add. 23726, *Account of Portugal. Diary of Thomas Cox*, fol. 58r. See also Cox and Macro, *Relação do reino de Portugal*, 153.

67. Sequeira and Macedo, *A nossa Lisboa*, 201–2.

68. Menezes, *Nova história de Portugal*, 439; ANTT, Tribunal do Santo Ofício, Inquisição de Lisboa, processo 11767, fols. 74r–74v.

69. "Descrição da cidade de Lisboa (1730)," 61.

70. "Consulta da câmara a el-rei em 19 Novembro 1706," E. Oliveira, *Elementos*, 10:330–32.

71. Chantal, *A vida quotidiana em Portugal*, 242.

72. *Gazeta de Lisboa Occidental*, no. 9, 2 March 1719; *Gazeta de Lisboa Occidental*, no. 1, 4 January 1720; *Gazeta de Lisboa*, supplement to no. 3, 17 January 1743.

73. Lahon, "Eles vão, eles vêm," 77; F. Silva, "O tráfico de escravos," 64.

74. Magalotti, *Viaje de Cosme*, 369.

75. "Descrição da cidade de Lisboa (1730)," 61.

76. Stevens, *Ancient and Present State of Portugal*, 182.

77. BPMP, M-FA-15, Salvador António Ferreira, *Várias notícias de cazos acontecidos em Portugal*, fols. 150v–151r.

78. For more details of this event, see Farnsworth and Cardim, "Mulheres negras protestam em Lisboa em 1717."

79. BNP, códice 554, *Mercúrio de Lisboa*, fol. 178v.

80. BNP, códice 8065, *Folheto de Lisboa*, 30 July 1740.

81. "Consulta da câmara a el-rei em 6 de Julho de 1689," in E. Oliveira, *Elementos*, 9:133.

82. "Consulta da câmara a el-rei em 13 de Março de 1703," in E. Oliveira, *Elementos*, 10:169–70.

83. Caldeira, *Escravos em Portugal*, 198–99.

84. Tours, "Travels Through Portugal and Spain," 102.

85. Donovan, "Crime, Policing, and the Absolutist State," 63.

86. BNP, códice 674, "Sentença pelo conselho de guerra contra Luiz Alvarez de Andrade e Cunha [. . .]," fols. 168v–169r; A. Oliveira, "As execuções capitais," 115.

87. BPE, CIV/1–9d, Folheto de Lisboa Occidental, Saturday, 12 August 1741.

88. BPE, CIV/1–9d, Folheto de Lisboa Occidental, Saturday, 19 August 1741; BNP, códice 554, fol. 380r.

89. Castelo-Branco, Lisboa seiscentista, 130–31.

90. BPE, CIV/1–17d, Mercúrio de Lisboa, 21 January 1747.

91. Hanson, Economy and Society, 16. See also Lourenço, D. Pedro II, 150.

92. "Consulta da câmara a el-rei em 24 de Setembro 1687," in E. Oliveira, Elementos, 9:18–19.

93. As quoted in Guimarães, Summario de varia história, 3:121–22.

94. Constituições sinodais, 137; BL, Manuscripts, Add. 23726, Account of Portugal. Diary of Thomas Cox, fol. 61r. See also Cox and Macro, Relação do reino de Portugal, 159.

95. Caldeira, Escravos em Portugal, 341–43.

96. Caldeira, Escravos em Portugal, 142, 191.

97. Sweet, "Hidden Histories of African Lisbon," 237.

98. Lahon, "Esclavage et confréries noires," 1:178.

99. For increasing marriages among the enslaved, see Rijo, "Os escravos na Lisboa joanina," 122; Lahon, "Esclavage et confréries noires," 1:160. For marriage percentages among enslaved couples, see Neto, A freguesia de Santa Catarina, 124; Rijo, "Os escravos na Lisboa joanina," 121; Neto et al., "A freguesia do Santíssimo Sacramento," 112.

100. Neto, A freguesia de Santa Catarina, 81; Neto et al., "A freguesia do Santíssimo Sacramento," 102.

101. Caldeira, Escravos em Portugal, 346.

102. Neto, A freguesia de Santa Catarina, 88.

103. Lahon, "Esclavage et confréries noires," 1:160.

104. The term denotes illicit sexual relations. Rijo, "Escravos na Lisboa joanina," 119.

105. AHPL, Livro dos termos da devassa da visita a Alfama 1707 (cota 28), fol. 15r.

106. AHPL, Livro dos termos da devassa da visita a Alfama 1707 (cota 28), fol. 25r.

107. Lourenço, D. Pedro II, 150; Serrão, Uma relação do reino de Portugal, 21. The account was written by the Marquis of Torcy, French envoy in Lisbon. Chantal, A vida quotidiana em Portugal, 114–15.

108. Ataíde, Portugal, Lisboa, e a corte, 188; Lourenço, D. Pedro II, 239.

109. Caldeira, Escravos em Portugal, 352.

110. Baretti, Journey from London to Genoa, 273–74.

111. Baretti, Journey from London to Genoa, 275.

112. Lahon, "Da redução da alteridade," 75; Sweet, "Hidden Histories of African Lisbon," 239.

113. Rhys, Account of the Most Remarkable Places, 237; Lahontan, New Voyages to North America, 640.

114. I. Braga, "A mulatice como impedimento," 5–7; Lahon, "Exclusion, integration et métissage," 281; E. Oliveira, Elementos, 7:291–93n3. For the development of the same concept in Spain and Spanish America, see Martínez, Genealogical Fictions.

115. Raminelli, "Los límites del honor," 58.

116. Raminelli, "Impedimentos da cor," 720.

117. Lahon, "Esclavage et confréries noires," 2:602.

118. Decree of 16 August 1671, in Justino Silva, Collecção chronologica da legislação, 8:191–92.

119. Raminelli, Nobrezas do novo mundo, 235, 238.

120. Raminelli, "Impedimentos da cor," 716; Raminelli, Nobrezas do novo mundo, 238.

121. Dutra, "Ser mulato," 109–10.

122. Lahon, "Da redução da alteridade," 65.

123. J. Fonseca, Religião e liberdade, 10. Brotherhoods and Confraternities were not technically the same, but they performed much the same functions. Brotherhoods enjoyed all the privileges among equal brothers, including the operation of the organization.

Confraternities were made up of members who had common principles. For the purposes of the discussion, I use both terms interchangeably due to the fact that most of the organizations in Lisbon employed aspects from both. See J. Fonseca, *Religião e liberdade*, 17–19.

124. Lahon, "Esclavage et confréries noires," 2:471, 617; Lahon, "Da redução da alteridade," 67.

125. J. Fonseca, *Religião e liberdade*, 65–67. Fonseca lists a second Black brotherhood in the city but never clarifies when the organization began during the eighteenth century.

126. Moreno, *La antigua hermandad*, 73–74, 76.

127. Phillips, *Slavery*, 95–96.

128. Russell-Wood, "Black and Mulatto Brotherhoods," 576. For Black confraternities in Mexico City, see Nicole Von Germeten's *Black Blood Brothers*, 83–84.

129. Lahon, "Esclavage et confréries noires," 2:617. While Didier Lahon argues that importation of enslaved Africans increased during the last quarter of the seventeenth century, this chapter has provided evidence that it was not until the first decades of the eighteenth century that this actually occurred and thus was one of the causes for the expansion of Black confraternities in Lisbon.

130. J. Fonseca, *Religião e liberdade*, 11–12.

131. Lahon, *O negro no coração do império*, 69.

132. Lahon, "Esclavage et confréries noires," 1:193.

133. Tinhorão, *Os negros em Portugal*, 125–26.

134. Scarano, "Black Brotherhoods," 5.

135. "Descrição da cidade de Lisboa (1730)," 69.

136. J. Fonseca, *Religião e liberdade*, 20.

137. Lahon, "Esclavage et confréries noires," 2:380.

138. J. Fonseca, *Religião e liberdade*, 21–22; Lahon, "Esclavage et confréries noires," 2:380.

139. J. Fonseca, *Religião e liberdade*, 24, 30; Lahon, "Esclavage et confréries noires," 2:391.

140. Lahon, "Da redução da alteridade," 74.

141. Lahon, "Exclusion, integration et métissage," 291; J. Fonseca, *Religião e liberdade*, 36.

142. Lahon, "Exclusion, integration et métissage," 293.

143. J. Fonseca, *Religião e liberdade*, 27. Didier Lahon argues that there were no mulatto brotherhoods in Lisbon until the end of the eighteenth century. See Lahon, "Esclavage, confréries noires, sainteté noire," 145–46.

144. J. Fonseca, *Religião e liberdade*, 65–67; Lahon, "Esclavage, confréries noires, sainteté noire," 161.

145. García, *Una metrópoli esclavista*, 272.

146. Vianna, *O idioma da mestiçagem*, 144.

147. J. Fonseca, *Religião e liberdade*, 17–19, 73.

148. BNP, códice illuminado 151, fols. 4r–4v.

149. Lahon, *O negro no coração do império*, 69.

150. Caldeira, *Escravos em Portugal*, 307. An example was the early eighteenth-century confraternity of Nossa Senhora do Rosário e Adoração dos Santos Reis Magos, which eventually allowed six white brothers and also white women to join. See J. Fonseca, *Religião e Liberdade*, 77.

151. Scarano, "Black Brotherhoods," 5.

152. J. Fonseca, *Religião e liberdade*, 81.

153. ANTT, Chancelaria Régia, João V, livro 40, fol. 63v (1714).

154. Lahon, *O negro no coração do império*, 68.

155. J. Fonseca, *Religião e liberdade*, 106; Lahon, *O negro no coração do império*, 73.

156. Soares and Metz, *People of Faith*, 114.

157. Lahon, "Da redução da alteridade," 54, 68.

158. Soares and Metz, *People of Faith*, 121.

159. Lahon, "Esclavage et confréries noires," 2:446.

160. BNP, códice iluminado 151, fol. 2r.

161. Lahon, "Da redução da alteridade," 56. See also Rijo, "Os escravos na Lisboa joanina," 115–16.

162. Lahon, "Exclusion, integration et métissage," 291.

NOTES TO PAGES 29–31

163. J. Fonseca, *Religião e liberdade*, 97.

164. Lahon, "Esclavage, confréries noires, sainteté noire," 136.

165. F. Almeida, *História de Portugal*, 153.

166. ANTT, Chancelaria Régia, Pedro II, livro 18, fols. 173r–173v (1688); livro 44, fols. 287v–288r (1702); J. Fonseca, *Religião e liberdade*, 97.

167. Lahon, "Esclavage, confréries noires, sainteté noire," 137; ANTT, Chancelaria Régia, João V, livro 40, fol. 63v (1714); livro 42, fol. 71v (1714).

168. Lahon, "Esclavage et confréries noires," 2:518–19; Lahon, *O negro no coração do império*, 67.

169. Lahon, *O negro no coração do império*, 67.

170. Lahon, "Esclavage, confréries noires, sainteté noire," 136. This was also the case for enslaved Africans in the Portuguese slave port of Luanda in Angola. See Alencastro, *Trade in the Living*, 145–46.

171. Lahon, "Esclavage et confréries noires," 2:548.

172. ANTT, Chancelaria Régia, Joao V, livro 106, fol. 24v (1742); Caldeira, *Escravos em Portugal*, 311.

173. Lahon, "Esclavage et confréries noires," 2:454–59.

174. J. Fonseca, *Religião e liberdade*, 89.

175. Godinho, "Portugal and the Making of the Atlantic World," 319.

176. BPE, CIV/1–19d, *Mecúrio de Lisboa*, 31 May 1749.

177. Santana, *Chronica dos Carmelitas*, 679. João V also donated the generous sum of 96,000 *réis* to the Black Rosary brotherhood of Porto in 1739 for their altar. See J. Fonseca, *Religião e liberdade*, 65.

178. Santana, *Chronica dos Carmelitas*, 679.

179. Lahon, "Esclavage et confréries noires," 2:536; Santana, *Chronica dos Carmelitas*, 678.

180. Russell-Wood, "God and Mammon," 207–8.

181. J. Fonseca, *Religião e liberdade*, 99.

182. Decree of 18 March 1684, in Justino Silva, *Collecção chronologica da legislação*, 10:8–11.

183. BPE, CXII/1–21d, "Vida del Rey D. Pedro II de Portugal escrita pelo seu confessor o P. Sebastiam de Magallaens," fol. 34r.

184. Villiers, "Portuguese Society," 198.

185. Lahon, "Exclusion, integration et métissage," 290.

186. Lahon, "Esclavage, confréries noires, sainteté noire," 139.

187. ANTT, Desembargo do Paço, Maço 1006, doc. 30 (1757), transcribed in Lahon, "Esclavage, confréries noires, sainteté noire," 138.

188. Letter of Francisco Pinheiro to João Francisco Mussi em Rio de Janeiro, 28 March 1723 and Letter of Francisco Pinheiro to Luiz Alz. Prettoem Rio de Janeiro, 9 April 1723, transcribed in Pinheiro, *Negócios coloniais*, 5:27–28, 32.

189. Tinhorão, *Os negros em Portugal*, 265.

190. Tinhorão, *As origens da canção urbana*, 107–8.

191. Letter of Francisco Pinheiro to Luís Alz. Pretto em Rio de Janeiro, 8 September 1725, transcribed in Pinheiro, *Negócios coloniais*, 5:105.

192. Merveilleux, "Memórias instrutivas," 208.

193. BL, Manuscripts, Add. 23726, *Account of Portugal. Diary of Thomas Cox*, fol. 80r. See also Cox and Macro, *Relação do reino de Portugal*, 197.

194. BNP, códice reservados 113v, *Folheto de Ambas Lisboas*, no. 7, 6 October 1730, fol. 32r.

195. BL, Manuscripts, Add. 23726, *Account of Portugal. Diary of Thomas Cox*, fol. 78v. See also Cox and Macro, *Relação do reino de Portugal*, 194.

196. Tinhorão, *Os negros em Portugal*, 327–30.

197. Henriques, *A herança Africana*, 161.

198. Merveilleux, "Memórias instrutivas," 184; Lahontan, *New Voyages to North America*, 640.

199. Tinhorão, *As origens da canção urbana*, 121–22.

200. Budasz, "Black Guitar-Players," 9, 11.

201. Santa Catarina and Zeferino, *Anatomico jocoso*, 209. English translation in Budasz, "Black Guitar-Players," 5.

202. Tinhorão, *O rasga*, 12.
203. Henriques, *A herança Africana*, 159.
204. Merveilleux, "Memórias instrutivas," 209.
205. Tinhorão, *As origens da canção urbana*, 125–26. Mention of the musical styles coming from Cabo Verde and Bahia is found in Chantal, *A vida quotidiana em Portugal*, 271.
206. Chantal, *A vida quotidiana em Portugal*, 271.
207. BNP, reservados 113v, *Folheto de Ambas Lisboas*, no. 7, 6 October 1730. fol. 32v.
208. Sweet, "Hidden Histories of African Lisbon," 243–46.
209. Tinhorão, *As origens da canção urbana*, 130.

Chapter 2

1. TNA SP 89/47, 13 June 1749, fols. 31r–31v, Duke of Bedford to Abraham Castres. For a list of English diplomats and consuls during the period, see Shaw, *Anglo-Portuguese Alliance*, 213–14.
2. Lodge, "The English Factory at Lisbon," 227–28. For more details of the Stepney affair, see Lodge, *Private Correspondence*, 130n1.
3. A similar incident occurred later in June 1749 as an enslaved African sought refuge on an English vessel in port after murdering his Portuguese master as he slept. See BNP, códice 480, *Notícias Annuaes*, 1740–1749, 17 June 1749, fol. 128v. These actions had been occurring for years in Lisbon despite Portuguese complaint. In 1725 the Portuguese secretary of state Diogo de Mendonça Corte-Real complained that English ships were harboring enslaved Moors, including one of his majesty's servants. See TNA SP 89/31, 1 December, 1725, fols. 351r–351v, Diogo de Mendonça Corte-Real to James Dormer.
4. Santa Maria, *Santuario mariano*, 33.
5. Rau, *Subsídios para o estudo*, 239–40; Abreu-Ferreira, "Reluctant Hosts," 20. A similar situation occurred in Porto where English and Dutch merchants came to control commerce during the eighteenth century while French participation declined. See Polónia, "Dinâmicas comerciais," 279.

6. Costa, Lains, and Miranda, *Economic History of Portugal*, 198.
7. Menezes, *Nova história de Portugal*, 168.
8. Costa and Cunha, *D. João IV*, 199.
9. Macaulay, *They Went to Portugal*, 54–55.
10. Boxer, "Vicissitudes of Anglo-Portuguese Relations," 28.
11. Boxer, "Second Thoughts," 22.
12. Cardoso, "Leitura e interpretação do tratado de Methuen," 21–22; Costa and Rocha, "Merchant Networks and Brazilian Gold," 160–61. The Dutch and French claimed many of the same privileges but did not always receive them. See Francis, *Methuens and Portugal*, 20.
13. Lydon, *Fish and Flour*, 9.
14. Lahontan, *New Voyages to North America*, 631.
15. Boxer, "Second Thoughts," 24.
16. Boxer, "Vicissitudes of Anglo-Portuguese Relations," 29; Sideri, *Trade and Power*, 22.
17. Sideri, *Trade and Power*, 23; Prestage, *Chapters in Anglo-Portuguese Relations*, 150.
18. Sideri, *Trade and Power*, 21–22.
19. Boxer, *Salvador de Sá*, 339; Prestage, *Chapters in Anglo-Portuguese Relations*, 149.
20. Boxer, "Vicissitudes of Anglo-Portuguese Relations," 29.
21. Labourdette, *La nation française*, 12; José Castro, *Collecção dos tratados*, 339–41.
22. Labourdette, *La nation française*, 12.
23. TNA SP 89/8, 24 November 1667, fol. 246r, Pedro II to Charles II; Prestage, *Royal Power*, 28–29.
24. Prestage, *Chapters in Anglo-Portuguese Relations*, 155; Labourdette, *La nation française*, 13.
25. Labourdette, *La nation française*, 13.
26. Labourdette, *La nation française*, 37–38.
27. Labourdette, *La nation française*, 28–30. For a list for French diplomats and consuls during the period, see

NOTES TO PAGES 35–44

Menezes, *Nova história de Portugal*, 188; Labourdette, *La nation française*, 274–88.

28. José Castro, *Collecção dos tratados*, 261, 265, 269; Pedreira, "Costs and Financial Trends," 63.

29. Joaquim Serrão, *História de Portugal*, 70.

30. Mendes, "Comunidade Flamenga e Holandesa em Lisboa," 68.

31. Shillington and Chapman, *Commercial Relations*, 227.

32. Saussure, "Cartas escritas de Lisboa," 276.

33. Lodge, "The English Factory at Lisbon," 223.

34. Arenas, "La situación de los comerciantes españoles," 102–3.

35. Shillington and Chapman, *Commercial Relations*, 204.

36. TNA SP 89/44, 20 January 1744, fol. 8r, Abraham Castres to Andrew Stone.

37. As quoted in Shaw, *Anglo-Portuguese Alliance*, 100.

38. Littleton, *Groans of the Plantations*, 33.

39. Godinho, "Portugal and the Making of the Atlantic World," 319.

40. Godinho, "Portugal and the Making of the Atlantic World," 319.

41. Costa, Lains, and Miranda, *Economic History of Portugal*, 150.

42. TNA SP 89/15, 26 October 1682, fol. 12r, Charles Fanshaw to Sir Leoline Jenkins.

43. Francis, *Portugal 1715–1808*, 5.

44. Prestage, *Chapters in Anglo-Portuguese Relations*, 157n1.

45. Ataíde, *Portugal, Lisboa, e a corte*, 147.

46. TNA SP 89/18, 24 September 1701, fol. 18v, Paul Methuen to James Vernon.

47. TNA SP 89/18, 4 October 1701, fol. 26r, Paul Methuen to James Vernon.

48. Francis, "Anglo-Portuguese Alliance in the 18th Century," 31.

49. TNA SP 89/18, 7 February 1702, fol. 55r, Paul Methuen to James Vernon.

50. TNA SP 89/18, 6 September 1701, fols. 3r–5r, Paul Methuen to James Vernon.

51. Lodge, "English Factory at Lisbon," 218, 218n1.

52. Prestage, *Chapters in Anglo-Portuguese Relations*, 159–60.

53. Pinto, *O ouro brasileiro*, 18.

54. Lourenço, *D. Pedro II*, 261.

55. Lodge, "Historical Revision," 35.

56. Costa, Lains, and Miranda, *Economic History of Portugal*, 155–56.

57. For a discussion on the later effects of English dominance of the Portuguese wine trade, see Hancock, *Oceans of Wine*.

58. Fisher, *Portugal Trade*, 35–36. In direct contradiction to what other historians cited throughout the chapter have stated, H. E. S. Fisher suggests the treaties between England and Portugal did not have as much of an influence on English ascendancy in Portugal during the period. Rather, he argues the international relations played a much larger role. My argument is that the two factors went hand in hand.

59. TNA SP 89/17, 8/18 April 1693, fol. 21r, John Methuen to the Earl of Nottingham.

60. Letter to Abade Le Grande, 25 August 1711, transcribed in Viganego, *Ao serviço secreto*, 66.

61. TNA SP 89/23, 31 July 1715, fol. 247r, Lisbon Factory to James Stanhope.

62. TNA SP 89/21, 1/12 May 1711, fol. 138r, Thomas Leffever to Lord Dartmouth.

63. Law of 8 February 1711, transcribed in *Collecção da legislação antiga*, 376–78. An additional law was promulgated in 1715. See *Gazeta de Lisboa*, no. 11, 19 October 1715.

64. Boxer, *The English and the Portuguese Brazil Trade*, 2.

65. Pijning, "Passive Resistance," 180–82.

66. Couto, "D. João V," 256; Claro, *A Aliança inglesa*, 116.

67. Pijning, "Passive Resistance," 185.

68. Sideri, *Trade and Power*, 21. The same situation would develop in Porto during the eighteenth century. See Schneider, *O marquês de Pombal*, 134.

69. Cunha, *Instruções políticas*, 343.

70. Costa, Lains, and Miranda, *Economic History of Portugal*, 150.

71. Pinto, *O ouro brasileiro*, 268. Pinto erroneously states that Mornay was the consul.

72. Magalotti, *Viaje de Cosme*, 368.

73. Donovan, "Commercial Enterprise," 210.

74. Pijning, "Passive Resistance," 185.

75. Labourdette, "L'ambassade de Monsieur de Chavigny," 49.

76. "Cópia do papel que o senhor Dom Joam de Lancastre fez [. . .] ," in Rau and Silva, *Os manuscritos do arquivo da casa de Cadaval*, 14–15.

77. TNA SP 89/21, 19 October 1711, fols. 348r–348v, John Milner to the Lord High Treasurer.

78. TNA SP 89/21, 19 October 1711, fol. 348v, John Milner to the Lord High Treasurer.

79. Labourdette, *La nation française*, 171.

80. Shillington and Chapman, *Commercial Relations*, 239.

81. TNA SP 89/24, 18 February 1716, fol. 22r, Consul Poyntz and English Factory to Henry Worsely; for further reading on English interactions with pirates, see Colley, *Captives*.

82. Labourdette, *La nation française*, 447–48.

83. TNA SP 89/37, 29 September 1734, fols. 303r–303v, Lord Tyrawly to Duke of Newcastle.

84. Pijning, "Passive Resistance," 188.

85. TNA SP 89/40, 30 December 1741, fol. 282v, Charles Compton to Duke of Newcastle.

86. TNA SP 89/29, 25 January 1720, fol. 13r, Thomas Burnett to James Craggs. A *moeda* was a Portuguese coin worth 27 shillings and 6 pence, according to Boxer, "Lord Tyrawly in Lisbon," 796.

87. TNA SP 89/35, 30 May 1728, fol. 41r, Lord Tyrawly to Duke of Newcastle.

88. TNA SP 89/37, 2 May 1732, fol. 167v, Lord Tyrawly to the Duke of Newcastle.

89. Boxer, "Brazilian Gold and British Traders," 469.

90. Paice, *Wrath of God*, 31–32.

91. Boxer, "Brazilian Gold and British Traders," 471.

92. Pinto, *O ouro brasileiro*, 271.

93. Lisboa, Olival, and Miranda, *Gazetas manuscritas*, 3:314, 373–82.

94. Boxer, "Brazilian Gold and British Traders," 470.

95. Paice, *Wrath of God*, 32–33; Fisher, *Portugal Trade*, 136.

96. TNA SP 89/35, 30 May 1728, fol. 40v, Lord Tyrawly to Duke of Newcastle.

97. "Sátira geral a todo o reyno, e governo de Portugal," as quoted in Hansen, Moreira, and Souza, "Nota sobre a 'sátira geral,'" 186.

98. Costa and Rocha, "Merchant Networks and Brazilian Gold," 155.

99. TNA SP 89/20, 13/24 October 1710, fol. 215r, Thomas Leffever to Lord Dartmouth.

100. TNA SP 89/37, 29 September 1734, fols. 303r–303v, Lord Tyrawly to Duke of Newcastle.

101. TNA SP 89/37, 17 April 1734, fols. 279v–280r, Lord Tyrawly to Duke of Newcastle.

102. TNA SP 89/24, 10 March 1716, fol. 53r, William Poyntz to Steven Poyntz.

103. TNA SP 89/40, 22 August 1738, fol. 22r, Lord Tyrawly to Duke of Newcastle; TNA SP 89/47, 28 September 1749, fol. 42r, Mr. Consul Russell to R. N. Aldworth.

104. Boxer, *The English and the Portuguese Brazil Trade*, 5.

105. Sandwich, *Voyage Performed*, 522.

106. Costa, Lains, and Miranda, *Economic History of Portugal*, 195.

107. Sideri, *Trade and Power*, 53.

108. Pijning, "Passive Resistance," 188–89.

109. Pinto, *O ouro brasileiro*, 277.

110. Chavigny to Amelot, 14 September 1740, as quoted in Labourdette, "L'ambassade de Monsieur de Chavigny," 35–36.

111. Pinto, *O ouro brasileiro*, 277.

112. Gabriel Paquette discussed the deepening dependency upon the English that developed during the period and the efforts of the Marquis of Pombal to reverse the decline afterward. See Paquette, *European Seaborne Empires*, 92; Paquette, *Imperial Portugal in the Age of Revolutions*, 25.

113. Even amidst the height of Catholic persecution in the Netherlands during the 1650s Amsterdam was the exception. See Kooi, *Calvinists and Catholics*, 121, 123–25; Gelderblom, *Cities of Commerce*, 16, 60, 162–63; Gauci, *Emporium of the World*, 90–92; Israel, *Empires and Entrepots*, 425.

114. O'Flanagan, *Port Cities of Atlantic Iberia*, 102.

115. TNA SP 89/12, 7/17 May 1672, fol. 72r, Thomas Maynard to Lord Arlington.

116. E. Oliveira, *Elementos*, 7:352.

117. TNA SP 89/24, 4 December 1716, fol. 139v, William Poyntz to Paul Methuen.

118. TNA SP 89/24, 14 November 1716, fols. 132r–132v, Henry Worsley to Paul Methuen.

119. TNA SP 89/30, 10 May 1723, fols. 196r–196v, Thomas Lumley to Lord Carteret.

120. TNA SP 89/21, 26 October 1711, fol. 356v, Anthony Corbiere to Erasmus Lewis.

121. For an example, see TNA SP 89/17, 9 June 1699, fol. 352r, Paul Methuen to James Vernon.

122. As quoted in Shaw, *Trade, Inquisition, and the English Nation*, 124.

123. TNA SP 89/35, 14 August 1728, fol. 96r, Lord Tyrawly to Duke of Newcastle.

124. Pijning, "Passive Resistance," 185.

125. Labourdette, *La nation française*, 37–38.

126. TNA SP 89/22, 8 November 1712, fol. 174r, George Delaval to Lord Dartmouth.

127. TNA SP 89/22, 17 June 1713, fol. 268r, George Delaval to Antony Corbiere.

128. TNA SP 89/37, 11 February 1730, fol. 10v, Charles Compton to Duke of Newcastle.

129. TNA SP 89/12, 5/15 March 1672, fols. 33r–34v; TNA SP 89/15, 2/12 February 1683, fol. 76r, Thomas Maynard to Sir Leoline Jenkins.

130. A. Marques, *História da Maçonaria*, 22.

131. McLachlan, *Trade and Peace with Old Spain*, 24–25.

132. Boxer, *Some Contemporary Reactions*, 6.

133. Chantal, *A vida quotidiana em Portugal*, 201–2.

134. BL, Manuscripts, Add. 23726, *Account of Portugal. Diary of Thomas Cox*, fol. 28v. See also Cox and Macro, *Relação do reino de Portugal*, 94; Francis, *Methuens and Portugal*, 14.

135. TNA SP 89/10, 4 February 1670, fols. 173v–174r, Thomas Maynard to Lord Arlington.

136. José Silva, *Gazeta em forma de carta*, 1:92.

137. Carvalho, "Cartas de José da Cunha Brochado," *O Instituto* 69, 442.

138. TNA SP 89/18, 13 September 1701, fol. 6r, Paul Methuen to William Blathwayt.

139. TNA SP 89/22, 13 September 1712, fol. 144r, Diogo de Mendonça Corte-Real to George Delaval.

140. TNA SP 89/37, 14 June 1731, fol. 83v, Charles Compton to Duke of Newcastle.

141. Lisboa, Olival, and Miranda, *Gazetas manuscritas*, 1:133.

142. TNA SP 89/37, 20 June 1731, fols. 94r–94v, Affidavit of the crew of the HMS *Rose*.

143. TNA SP 89/37, 20 June 1731, fols. 90r–91r, Charles Compton to Duke of Newcastle.

144. TNA SP 89/37, 3 August 1731, fol. 104v, Lord Tyrawly to Duke of Newcastle.

145. Francis, *Portugal 1715–1808*, 33.

146. TNA SP 89/37, 14 July 1731, fol. 100v, Charles Compton to Duke of Newcastle.

147. TNA SP 89/37, 23 June 1731, fols. 102r–102v, Representation of the Factory at Lisbon to Consul Compton.

148. TNA SP 89/37, 3 August 1731, fol. 108r, Lord Tyrawly to Duke of Newcastle.

149. TNA SP 89/37, 3 August 1731, fol. 105r, Lord Tyrawly to Duke of Newcastle.

150. TNA SP 89/37, 3 August 1731, fol. 108v, Lord Tyrawly to Duke of Newcastle.

151. TNA SP 89/40, 17 October 1741, fol. 261v, Charles Compton to Lord Harrington and Duke of Newcastle.

152. TNA SP 89/42, 22 October 1742, fol. 81r, Charles Compton to Duke of Newcastle.

153. TNA SP 89/9, 31 October/10 November 1668, fols. 138r–138v, Sir Robert Southwell to Lord Arlington.

154. Jenefer, *Saudades Journal*, 26.

155. Hervey, *Augustus Hervey's Journal*, 121.

156. TNA SP 89/35, 25 February 1729, fol. 141r, Lord Tyrawly to Charles Delafaye.

157. BNP, códice 10745, *Novidades de Lisboa 1732–1733*, 18–28 February 1733, fols. 111v–112r.

158. BPE, CIV/1–9d, *Folheto de Lisboa 1741*, 3 June 1741.

159. Overall, issues regarding Protestantism in Portugal during earlier periods largely surround French and Dutch foreigners in the country and not necessarily the English. Thus, a matter of scale and intensity must be considered in comparison to the period under study. See I. Braga, "Ecos dos problemas religiosos," 233–37.

160. For more on the closure of Portuguese society after the Council of Trent, see Xavier, *A invenção de Goa*, 40–41; Shaw, *Anglo-Portuguese Alliance*, 4; Disney, *History of Portugal and the Portuguese Empire*, 1:172.

161. Abreu-Ferreira, "Reluctant Hosts," 29–30; TNA SP 89/28, January 1720, fol. 19r, Consul Burnett and the British Factory at Lisbon to King George I.

162. TNA SP 89/11, 8/18 May 1671, fol. 128r, Consul Thomas Maynard to Lord Arlington.

163. Almeida and Peres, *História da igreja em Portugal*, 489.

164. TNA SP 89/21, 13 May 1711, fol. 146r, George Delaval to Erasmus Lewis.

165. TNA SP 89/20, July 1710, fols. 121r–121v, Consul Milner and the British Factory to Queen Anne.

166. TNA SP 89/35, 7 November 1728, fols. 117r–117v, Lord Tyrawly to Duke of Newcastle.

167. Francis, *Portugal 1715–1808*, 46; Shaw, *Anglo-Portuguese Alliance*, 54.

168. Saussure, "Cartas escritas de Lisboa," 266.

169. BA, 49-IV-20, doc. 84, "Cópia da consulta que fez a junta que sua magestade mandou formar para este negócio," 4 July 1654, fol. 211r.

170. BL, Manuscripts, Add. 23726, *Account of Portugal. Diary of Thomas Cox*, fol. 25r. See also Cox and Macro, *Relação do reino de Portugal*, 89.

171. Francis, *Methuens and Portugal*, 21; Francis, *Portugal 1715–1808*, 42.

172. Black, "Portugal in 1730," 86.

173. Shaw, *Trade, Inquisition, and the English Nation*, 127. For further details, see Matos and Neto, "Cemitério Inglês," 252.

174. BNP, códice 512, *Gazeta em forma de carta*, 15 January 1710, fols. 150v–151r.

175. TNA, SP 89/15, 15 February 1683, fol. 101v, Charles Fanshaw to Sir Leoline Jenkins.

176. Shaw, *Trade, Inquisition, and the English Nation*, 29.

177. Saussure, "Cartas escritas de Lisboa," 264–65.

178. Merveilleux, "Memórias instrutivas," 178.

179. Merveilleux, "Memórias instrutivas," 178.

180. TNA SP 89/14, 11/21 March 1678, fol. 59v, Francis Parry to Secretary Coventry.

181. Shaw, *Anglo-Portuguese Alliance*, 85.

182. TNA SP 89/35, 17 July 1729, fol. 191v, Lord Tyrawly to Duke of Newcastle.

183. Shaw, *Anglo-Portuguese Alliance*, 85.

184. Colbatch, *Account of the Court of Portugal*, 2:171.

185. Colbatch, *Account of the Court of Portugal*, 2:171. While visiting Lisbon in the 1720s, Charles Frédéric de Merveilleux wrote that no foreigner was to be seized upon by the Inquisition without João V's license. The effect of which was that there were "many hundreds of English" and other foreign Protestants established in the city who publicly professed their religion "and no one dares harass them." See Merveilleux, "Memórias instrutivas," 172.

186. Saussure, "Cartas escritas de Lisboa," 272.

187. Schneider, *O marquês de Pombal*, 161.

188. Shaw, *Trade, Inquisition, and the English Nation*, 112, 148. For discussions on funding, see Brockwell, *Natural and Political History*, 184.

189. Jenefer, *Saudades Journal*, 24.

190. *Gazeta de Lisboa Occidental*, no. 25, 18 June 1733.

191. *Gazeta de Lisboa Occidental*, no. 3, 15 January 1722.

192. P. Braga, *Portugueses no estrangeiro*, 283. Other examples of large conversion can be found in the *Gazeta de Lisboa Occidental*. Among various examples are those of the supplemental issue to no. 52, 29 December 1746, which records the conversion of twenty-three people in a single instance in the convent of São Domingos, as well as the *Gazeta de Lisboa Occidental* no. 9, 3 March 1729, describing the efforts of the German nuns of a Carmelite convent established by Maria Anna of Austria and who had converted over 120 souls to Catholicism from various northern countries.

193. *Gazeta de Lisboa Occidental*, no 5, 30 January 1738.

194. Macaulay, *They Went to Portugal Too*, 41, 46–47.

195. TNA SP 89/30, September 1722, fols. 61r–61v, Mr. Whinnyat's Case.

196. ANTT, Tribunal do Santo Ofício, Inquisição de Lisboa, processo 8175, fol. 4v.

197. TNA SP 89/28, 11 November 1720, fols. 140v–141r, Henry Worsley to James Craggs.

198. TNA SP 89/14, 2/12 May 1682, fols. 201r–201v, Charles Maynard to Sir Leoline Jenkins.

199. TNA SP 89/14, 9 June 1682, fol. 216r, Charles Maynard to Sir Leoline Jenkins.

200. BNP, códice PBA 650, *Secretária de Estado: Vários objectos realtivos à secretária do estado dos negócios de reino* [. . .], fols. 65v–66r.

201. TNA SP 89/10, 28 March/ 7 April 1670, fol. 195v, Francis Parry to Joseph Williamson.

202. TNA SP 89/40, 7 January 1741, fol. 212r, Lord Tyrawly to Duke of Newcastle.

203. Boxer, "Lord Tyrawly in Lisbon," 793.

204. TNA, SP 89/16, 14/15 August 1684, fols. 111r–111v, Charles Fanshaw to D. Pedro II.

205. TNA, SP 89/16, 28 August 1684, fols. 114r–114v, Charles Fanshaw to Earl of Sunderland.

206. TNA, SP 89/30, 31 May 1723, fols. 215r–216r, Thomas Lumley to Lord Carteret.

207. BL, Manuscripts, Add. 23726, *Account of Portugal. Diary of Thomas Cox*, fols. 95v–96r. See also Cox and Macro, *Relação do reino de Portugal*, 228–29.

208. *Gazeta de Lisboa Occidental*, no. 48, 1 December 1718.

209. Guichard, "Le protestantisme au Portugal," 463. According to the Genoese consul Viganego, Lord Galway often joked with various nobility in the city about changing their religion. See the letter of Viganego to the Marquis of Torcy, 23 January 1714, transcribed in Viganego, *Ao serviço secreto*, 150.

210. Shaw, *Anglo-Portuguese Alliance*, 179.

211. TNA SP 89/19, 16 January 1706, fol. 7r, John Milner to Sir Charles Hedges.

212. TNA SP 89/19, 16 January 1706, fols. 6v–7r, John Milner to Sir Charles Hedges.

213. Law of 3 August 1708, transcribed in *Collecção da legislação antiga*, 362–63.

214. TNA SP 89/20, 18 November 1710, fol. 247v, John Milner to George Delaval.

215. TNA SP 89/20, 18 November 1710, fol. 247v, John Milner to George Delaval.

216. Law of 3 August 1708, transcribed in *Collecção da legislação antiga*, 362–63.

217. Shaw, *Anglo-Portuguese Alliance*, 179.

218. TNA SP 89/28, 30 December 1719, fol. 16r, Certificate of Consul Burnett Concerning the Child of Mr. James Belangé.

219. TNA SP 89/29, 13 September 1721, fol. 139v, Henry Worsley to Lord Carteret.

220. TNA SP 89/28, January 1720, fol. 19r, Consul Burnett and the British Factory at Lisbon to King George I.

221. TNA SP 89/19, 19 February 1706, fol. 15r, John Methuen to Sir Charles Hedges.

222. Shaw, *Trade, Inquisition, and the English Nation*, 30.

223. TNA SP 89/31, 21 November 1724, fol. 157r, Thomas Burnett to Duke of Newcastle; TNA SP 89/33, 15 June 1726, fols. 129r–129v, Thomas Burnett to Duke of Newcastle. For examples of French parties, see BNP, códice 10746, *Novidades de Lisboa 1735–1749*, 3 February 1746, fols. 118r–120v. For nobility and trade, see Francis, *Methuens and Portugal*, 20.

224. Boxer, *The English and the Portuguese Brazil Trade*, 8.

225. Villiers, "Portuguese Society," 184. A gazette from 14 February 1730 recorded that the Marquis of Távora and various other Portuguese *fidalgos* had an exquisite dinner with the English captain Bings. Lisboa, Olival, and Miranda, *Gazetas manuscritas*, 1:79. There were repeated mentions of dances attended by illustrious individuals. See Lisboa, Olival, and Miranda, *Gazetas manuscritas*, 3:303.

226. Boxer, *The English and the Portuguese Brazil Trade*, 8.

227. BNP, códice 480, *Notícias annuaes 1740–1749*, August 1746, fol. 64r.; BNP, códice 10746, *Novidades de Lisboa 1735–1749*, September 1746, fols. 120v–122r.

228. BNP, códice 480, *Notícias annuaes 1740–1749*, August 1746, fol. 63v, "A estes nada noteis, que os sacrifícios occultas são da moda, e os indultos a ley de Deos lhe consome, são Catholicos no nome porém hereges occultos."

229. Urban, "Account of the Magnificent Feast," 473–74.

230. Shillington and Chapman, *Commercial Relations*, 228.

231. BL, Manuscripts, Add. 23726, *Account of Portugal. Diary of Thomas Cox*, fols. 40r–40v. See also Cox and Macro, *Relação do reino de Portugal*, 117–18.

232. TNA SP 89/31, 14 December 1724, fol. 167r, Thomas Sanderson to Duke of Newcastle.

233. Hervey, *Augustus Hervey's Journal*, 127.

234. Walpole, *Horace Walpole's Correspondence*, 18:104; Boxer, "Lord Tyrawly in Lisbon," 798.

235. Lodge, "The English Factory at Lisbon," 223.

236. TNA SP 89/37, 18 July 1732, fol. 203r, Lord Tyrawly to Duke of Newcastle.

237. Walpole, *Horace Walpole's Correspondence*, 22: 48.

Chapter 3

1. ANTT, Tribunal do Santo Ofício, Inquisição de Lisboa, processo 2378, fols. 12r, 17r–31v, 45r–46r, 52r–53r.

2. Maxwell, *Pombal*, 91.

3. D. Smith, "Mercantile Class of Portugal," 19.

4. Costa, Lains, and Miranda, *Economic History of Portugal*, 33; Disney, *History of Portugal and the Portuguese Empire*, 1:153.

5. D. Smith, "Old Christian Merchants," 236–37. For a deeper analysis of the background of the imperial shift toward the Atlantic, see the Costa, *Império e grupos mercantis*.

6. D. Smith, "Old Christian Merchants," 236–37, 253.

7. D. Smith, "Old Christian Merchants," 237–38, 254.

8. Boxer, *Portuguese Seaborne Empire*, 222–23; D. Smith, "Old Christian Merchants," 239.

9. Costa and Cunha, *D. João IV*, 285.

10. As quoted in D. Smith, "Mercantile Class of Portugal," 173. Brackets in translated original.

11. Costa and Cunha, *D. João IV*, 273.

12. D. Smith, "Mercantile Class of Portugal," 173.

13. Hanson, *Economy and Society*, 146; Olival, *As ordens militares*, 305–6.

14. Godinho, "Portugal and Her Empire," 511.

15. Jenefer, *Saudades Journal*, 24.

16. J. Azevedo, *História dos cristãos-novos Portugueses*, 290.

NOTES TO PAGES 66–74

17. Paixão, *Monstruosidades do tempo*, 2:121–22.
18. TNA SP 89/11, 7 July 1671, fol. 156r, Thomas Maynard to Lord Arlington.
19. Hanson, *Economy and Society*, 106; Remedios, "Depois da restauração," 88.
20. ANTT, Tribunal do Santo Ofício, Inquisição de Lisboa, processo 5412, fols. 14, 16v; ANTT, Tribunal do Santo Ofício, Inquisição de Lisboa, Cadernos do Promotor 46, livro 243, fol. 213v.
21. J. Azevedo, *História de António Vieira*, 2:109–10; D. Smith, "Mercantile Class of Portugal," 56–58.
22. D. Smith, "Mercantile Class of Portugal," 57–58. The unit of currency was 2 *contos de réis*, which is equal to 2 million *réis*. With 1 *cruzado* being equal to 400 *réis*, the total is 5,000 *cruzados*. For currency values, see Donovan, "Commercial Enterprise," xiii.
23. D. Smith, "Mercantile Class of Portugal," 59.
24. Hanson, *Economy and Society*, 80.
25. D. Smith, "Mercantile Class of Portugal," 232.
26. Crasto and Branco, *Os Ratos da Inquisição*, 161.
27. TNA SP 89/11, 1/11 June 1671, fol. 140r, Thomas Maynard to Lord Arlington.
28. See D. Smith, "Mercantile Class of Portugal," 239–40.
29. J. Azevedo, *História dos cristãos-novos Portugueses*, 290–92; BNP, códice 8702, "Cópia da consulta que se fez no Desembargo do Paço sobre os meios que pareçem convenientes para se extinguir o judaismo em Portugal, 2 de Junho 1671," fols. 123r–124r; Hamm, "Between the Foreign and the Familiar."
30. TNA SP 89/11, 1/11 June 1671, fol. 140r, Thomas Maynard to Lord Arlington.
31. J. Azevedo, *História dos cristãos-novos Portugueses*, 296.
32. J. Azevedo, *História dos cristãos-novos Portugueses*, 293. There were two types of confession, *de vehemeti* and *de leve*, the former being for serious offenses. Hanson, *Economy and Society*, 91.

33. BA, 44-XIII-43, fols. 117v–118r; BNP, códice 8702, "Cópia da consulta que se fez no Desembargo do Paço sobre os meios que pareçem convenientes para se extinguir o judaismo em Portugal, 2 de Junho 1671," fol. 112r; Decree of 16 August 1671, in Justino Silva, *Collecção chronologica da legislação*, 8:191–92; J. Azevedo, *História dos cristãos-novos Portugueses*, 289, 293.
34. Hanson, *Economy and Society*, 92.
35. Paixão, *Monstruosidades do tempo*, 2:123–25.
36. TNA SP 89/11, 11/21 September 1671, fols. 200r–200v, Francis Parry to Lord Arlington.
37. TNA SP 89/11, 2 October 1671, fols. 207r–207v, Francis Parry to Prince-Regent of Portugal D. Pedro II.
38. TNA SP 89/11, 15/25 October 1671, fol. 227r, Thomas Maynard to Lord Arlington.
39. J. Azevedo, *História dos cristãos-novos Portugueses*, 293.
40. Hanson, *Economy and Society*, 91; Paixão, *Monstruosidades do tempo*, 3:5–6.
41. Paixão, *Monstruosidades do tempo*, 3:36.
42. J. Azevedo, *História dos cristãos-novos Portugueses*, 293.
43. D. Smith, "Mercantile Class of Portugal," 175; Decree of 19 September 1672, in Justino Silva, *Collecção chronologica da legislação*, 8:208–9.
44. D. Smith, "Mercantile Class of Portugal," 175.
45. Remedios, "Depois da restauração," 87; J. Azevedo, *História de António Vieira*, 2:114.
46. Hanson, *Economy and Society*, 94. The Jesuits were vital to the proposal and aided in the entire process of negotiation over the general pardon and Inquisition reform. See Chakravarti, *Empire of Apostles*, 301–2.
47. ANTT, Armário Jesuítico, Maço 29, no. 20, "Segundo projecto que ofereceram os Cristãos novos ao principe . . . 1673," fols. 5v–6r.
48. I. Braga, *Bens de hereges*, 42.

49. Vieira, *Cartas do Padre António Vieira*, 2:368–69.
50. Chakravarti, *Empire of Apostles*, 302.
51. ANTT, Armário Jesuítico, Maço 29, doc. 32, fols. 20v–21r, "Carta do confessor Manuel Fernandes dando conta ao rei da conferência que tivera com os cristãos-novos . . . 15 de Junho de 1673."
52. J. Azevedo, *História dos cristãos-novos Portugueses*, 296; Costa, *O transporte no Atlântico*, 559–71.
53. ANTT, Armário Jesuítico, Maço 29, doc. 23.
54. Chakravarti, *Empire of Apostles*, 303.
55. ANTT, Armário Jesuítico, Maço 29, doc. 21, fol. 150r, "Primeira consulta feita pela inquisição ao príncipe sobre as propostas dos Crisãos-Novos [. . .]."
56. Remedios, "Depois da restauração," 92–93; ANTT, Armário Jesuítico, Maço 29, doc. 23.
57. ANTT, Armário Jesuítico, Maço 29, doc. 23, fols. 7v–8r.
58. ANTT, Armário Jesuítico, Maço 29, doc. 38, fols. 15r–15v, "Pareçeres de Francisco de Almada, Francisco de Abreu Godinho e de outros doutores [. . .]."
59. ANTT, Armário Jesuítico, Maço 29, doc. 38, fols. 28v, 32r.
60. Paixão, *Monstruosidades do tempo*, 3:60; ANTT, Armário Jesuítico, Maço 29, doc. 45, "Primeira carta que o príncipe D. Pedro escreveu ao papa pedindo-lhe mande examinar o requerimento do perdão geral e reforma dos estilos da Inquisição"; J. Azevedo, *História de António Vieira*, 2:117.
61. Chakravarti, *Empire of Apostles*, 307.
62. Paixão, *Monstruosidades do tempo*, 3:61–63.
63. TNA SP 89/12, 5/15 August 1673, fols. 252r–252v, Francis Parry to Lord Arlington; Paixão, *Monstruosidades do tempo*, 3:62.
64. Paixão, *Monstruosidades do tempo*, 3:64.
65. TNA SP 89/12, 5/15 August 1673, fol. 253r, Francis Parry to Lord Arlington.
66. ANTT, Armário Jesuítico, Maço 29, doc. 40, fol. 1r, "Papel que se achou sobre a porta do açouge [. . .]."
67. J. Azevedo, *História dos cristãos-novos Portugueses*, 297; J. Azevedo, *História de António Vieira*, 2:118.
68. "Carta do Bispo de Leiria, D. Pedro Vieira, sobre o perdão geral, 6 August 1673," transcribed in Remedios, "Depois da restauração," 113.
69. Vieira, *Cartas do Padre António Vieira*, 2:658.
70. Vieira, *Cartas do Padre António Vieira*, 2:626–27.
71. J. Azevedo, *História dos cristãos-novos Portugueses*, 301.
72. As quoted in M. Araújo, "Um 'papel em defença,'" 126–27.
73. Paixão, *Monstruosidades do tempo*, 4:17.
74. J. Azevedo, *História de António Vieira*, 2:142.
75. Even Stuart Schwartz in his work on religious tolerance acknowledges its limited nature during the period. See Schwartz, *All Can Be Saved*.
76. J. Azevedo, *História de António Vieira*, 2:143–46.
77. J. Azevedo, *História dos cristãos-novos Portugueses*, 310; Saraiva, Salomon, and Sassoon, *Marrano Factory*, 66–67.
78. Hanson, *Economy and Society*, 97.
79. TNA SP 89/13, 24 November/4 December 1674, fol. 33r, Francis Parry to Sir Joseph Williamson.
80. J. Azevedo, *História de António Vieira*, 2:149; TNA SP 89/13, 30 March/9 April 1675, fol. 66v, Francis Parry to Sir Joseph Williamson.
81. Lourenço, *D. Pedro II*, 172–73. Afonso VI lived out the remainder of his days in Sintra under virtual house arrest. After his death in 1683, Pedro II became the king of Portugal and began using that title.
82. Remedios, "Depois da restauração," 97.
83. Azevedo, *História de António Vieira*, 2:147–48.
84. BPE, CV/2–9, fols. 86v–87r; J. Azevedo, *História dos cristãos-novos Portugueses*, 315.

85. J. Azevedo, *História dos cristãos-novos Portugueses*, 315–16.

86. Paixão, *Monstruosidades do tempo*, 4:65.

87. ANTT, Armário Jesuítico, Maço 30, no. 78, fols. 1r–1v, "Proposta do estado da nobreza ao estado dos povos para que juntamente recorressem ao papa para a restituição dos Santo Ofício [. . .] 29 de Novembro 1679."

88. J. Azevedo, *História dos cristãos-novos Portugueses*, 321. Other records were sent previously in 1679 to the ambassador in Rome, D. Luís da Sousa, who chose not to turn these over to the pope, remarking, "If I show the trial record that I received to the pope, it will serve more as an embarrassment than a remedy: those that I asked for I hope are on their way . . . and when they arrive I will choose the most useful." See Sanches, *Origem da denominação*, 23.

89. TNA SP 89/14, 29 September 1681, fol. 137v, Charles Fanshaw to Sir Leoline Jenkins.

90. In 1682 there were *autos-da-fé* in Coimbra and Évora as well. One-hundred and seventeen people were tried in Portugal that year, ninety of whom for Judaizing. See J. Azevedo, *História dos cristãos-novos Portugueses*, 323.

91. Geddes, "View of the Court of Inquisition in Portugal," 449–50.

92. Remedios, "Depois da restauração," 103–4.

93. TNA SP 89/15, 17/27 July 1683, fol. 200v, Thomas Maynard to Sir Leoline Jenkins; Shaw, *Trade, Inquisition, and the English Nation*, 165; Hanson, *Economy and Society*, 100.

94. TNA SP 89/15, 15/25 May 1683, fol. 191r, Thomas Maynard to Sir Leoline Jenkins.

95. Geddes, "View of the Court of Inquisition in Portugal," 518–19.

96. Vieira, *Cartas do Padre António Vieira*, 3:356.

97. Shaw, *Anglo-Portuguese Alliance*, 25.

98. Sanches, *Origem da denominação*, 21; Cunha, *Instruções políticas*, 256.

99. "Petição dos homens de negócio sobre o registo [. . .]," in Rau and Silva, *Os manuscritos do arquivo da casa de Cadaval*, 338–39.

100. Torres, "Da repressão religiosa," 123.

101. Torres, "Da repressão religiosa," 113; Olival, "Rigor e interesses,"159–60.

102. Torres, "Da repressão religiosa," 131.

103. J. Martins, *Portugal e os Judeus*, 1:206; Cunha, *Testamento político*, 117. The Holy Office of Coimbra covering Porto meant that in direct contrast to Lisbon, no captives were held or tried in that city during the period.

104. J. Azevedo, *História dos cristãos-novos Portugueses*, 336.

105. Lahontan, *New Voyages to North America*, 632.

106. Cunha, *Testamento político*, 107–8.

107. ANTT, Tribunal do Santo Ofício, Inquisição de Lisboa, processo 8766, fols. 110r–111r. *Milréis* is equal to 1,000 *réis*.

108. ANTT, Tribunal do Santo Ofício, Inquisição de Lisboa, processo 8766, fols. 111r–112r.

109. BNP códice PBA 656, fol. 11v, 2 January 1741, transcribed in Vieira, "Mercadores Ingleses em Lisboa," 119–20.

110. Vieira, "Mercadores Ingleses em Lisboa," 120.

111. ANTT, Tribunal do Santo Ofício, Inquisição de Lisboa, processo 849, fols. 4r–5v.

112. Barnett, "Diplomatic Aspects of the Sephardi Influx," 216.

113. As quoted in Barnett, "Diplomatic Aspects of the Sephardi Influx," 210.

114. As quoted in Vieira, "As 'Relações Judaicas,'" 277–78.

115. TNA SP 89/32, 16 August 1726, fols. 93v–94r, Charles Delafaye to Brigadier Dormer; TNA SP 89/32, 20 September 1726, fols. 97r–98r, Duke of Newcastle to Brigadier Dormer.

116. TNA SP 89/37, 26 September 1732, fol. 209r, Lord Tyrawly to Duke of Newcastle.

117. TNA SP 89/28, 11 November 1720, fols. 140v–141r, Henry Worsley to James Craggs.

118. Vieira, "Família, perseguição, e mobilidade," 52–53; Vieira, "Mercadores Ingleses em Lisboa," 123, 131.

119. TNA SP 89/37, 23 May 1732, fol. 151r, Lord Tyrawly to Duke of Newcastle.

120. Francis, *Methuens and Portugal*, 188.

121. J. Azevedo, *História dos cristãos-novos Portugueses*, 375–76.

122. M. Braga, *A inquisição em Portugal*, 65–66; Bethencourt, "Declínio e extinção do Santo Ofício," 78–79.

123. TNA SP 89/31, 21 July 1725, fol. 236v, Thomas Burnett to Duke of Newcastle.

124. Diamond, "Problems of the London Sephardi Community," 40.

125. Cunha, *Testamento político*, 114.

126. Pieroni, "Outcasts from the Kingdom," 245.

127. ANTT, Tribunal do Santo Ofício, Inquisição de Lisboa, processo 6307, fol. 178r; Pieroni, "Outcasts from the Kingdom," 248–49.

128. Boxer, "Ribeiro Sanches," 271–72.

129. Sanches, *Origem da denominação*, 5–6, 21.

130. F. Oliveira, *Pathetic Discourse*, 24.

131. Pedreira, "Os negociantes de Lisboa," 426; Vieira, "Família, perseguição, e mobilidade," 49.

132. D. Smith, "Mercantile Class of Portugal," 19; Pimentel, *Arquitectura e poder*, 59.

133. Novinsky, *Inquisição*, 14. The figure listed was 4.8 million *réis*.

134. Novinsky, *Inquisição*, 14, 17.

135. C. Fonseca, "Comércio e Inquisição no Brasil," 197, 200.

136. Cunha, *Testamento político*, 120.

137. TNA SP 89/23, 9 November 1714, fol. 98r, Henry Worsley to James Stanhope.

138. Saraiva, Salomon, and Sassoon, *Marrano Factory*, 95–98.

139. Calainho, *Metrópole das mandingas*, 96. Claudia Geremia examined this same topic in the Canary Islands in her dissertation "L'Inquisizione spagnola nelle Isole Canarie."

140. ANTT, Tribunal do Santo Ofício, Inquisição de Lisboa, Cadernos do Promotor, 51, livro 248, fols. 283r–285v; Sweet, "Slaves, Convicts, and Exiles," 197. Daniela Buono Calainho has produced an excellent book on the topic of Mandingas in Portugal entitled *Metrópole das Mandingas*.

141. Sweet, "Slaves, Convicts, and Exiles," 196.

142. Calainho, *Metrópole das mandingas*, 176–77.

143. ANTT, Tribunal do Santo Ofício, Inquisição de Lisboa, processo 11774, fols. 5r–8r. I have added the surname of his enslaver so as to distinguish him from his accomplice José Francisco Pereira.

144. ANTT, Tribunal do Santo Ofício, Inquisição de Lisboa, processo 11774, fols. 33r–33v.

145. ANTT, Tribunal do Santo Ofício, Inquisição de Lisboa, processo 11774, fols. 23r–23v.

146. ANTT, Tribunal do Santo Ofício, Inquisição de Lisboa, processo 11774, fols. 69r–69v, 92v–93r.

147. Calainho, "Magias de cozinha," 166–67.

148. ANTT, Tribunal do Santo Ofício, Inquisição de Lisboa, processo 11774, fol. 69v.

149. ANTT, Tribunal do Santo Ofício, Inquisição de Lisboa, processo 11774, fols. 23v–25v.

150. ANTT, Tribunal do Santo Ofício, Inquisição de Lisboa, processo 11767, fols. 11v–12r.

151. ANTT, Tribunal do Santo Ofício, Inquisição de Lisboa, processo 11767, fol. 19v.

152. ANTT, Tribunal do Santo Ofício, Inquisição de Lisboa, processo 11767, fol. 39r.

153. ANTT, Tribunal do Santo Ofício, Inquisição de Lisboa, processo 11767, fol. 27v. While the price of *mandingas* varied in Lisbon, they could be expensive. Historian Francisco Santana discovered that on one occasion an enslaved individual secured a *mandinga*

for the price of four gold *cruzado novo* coins, which was equal to twenty liters of olive oil or twenty kilos of rice at the time. Santana, "Processos de escravos e forros," 17–18.

154. ANTT, Tribunal do Santo Ofício, Inquisição de Lisboa, processo 11767, fols. 24v–25r. For further reading on the use of *mandingas* and Afro-Brazilian healers in the Portuguese Atlantic world during the period, see Sweet, *Domingos Álvares*.

155. ANTT, Tribunal do Santo Ofício, Inquisição de Lisboa, processo 11767, fol. 36r.

156. ANTT, Tribunal do Santo Ofício, Inquisição de Lisboa, processo 11767, fols. 73r–74v.

157. Sweet, "Slaves, Convicts, and Exiles," 197, 199.

158. ANTT, Tribunal do Santo Ofício, Inquisição de Lisboa, Cadernos do Promotor, 264, livro 70, fols. 254r–257r.

159. ANTT, Tribunal do Santo Ofício, Inquisição de Lisboa, Cadernos do Promotor, 267, livro 73, fol. 337r.

160. ANTT, Tribunal do Santo Ofício, Inquisição de Lisboa, Cadernos do Promotor, 267, livro 73, fol. 337r.

161. ANTT, Tribunal do Santo Ofício, Inquisição de Lisboa, processo 3670, fol. 22r.

162. ANTT, Tribunal do Santo Ofício, Inquisição de Lisboa, processo 3670, fol. 4r.

163. ANTT, Tribunal do Santo Ofício, Inquisição de Lisboa, processo 3670, fols. 7r–9v.

164. ANTT, Tribunal do Santo Ofício, Inquisição de Lisboa, processo 3670, fols. 13r–13v.

165. ANTT, Tribunal do Santo Ofício, Inquisição de Lisboa, processo 3670, fols. 22r–22v, 26r.

166. ANTT, Tribunal do Santo Ofício, Inquisição de Lisboa, processo 2355. Transcribed in Santana, *Bruxas e curandeiros*, 85.

167. Paiva, *Bruxaria e superstição*, 113–14.

168. Sweet, "Slaves, Convicts, and Exiles," 199–201. For the popularity of Afro-Brazilian healers, see Walker, "Sorcerers and Folkhealers," 89.

169. Walker, "Sorcerers and Folkhealers," 84.

170. Shaw, *Anglo-Portuguese Alliance*, 172.

171. Shaw, *Anglo-Portuguese Alliance*, 172–73.

172. TNA, SP 89/16, 7/17 September 1685, fols. 301r–301v, Thomas Maynard to Earl of Sunderland.

173. Shaw, *Trade, Inquisition, and the English Nation*, 130.

174. Shaw, *Anglo-Portuguese Alliance*, 174.

175. TNA, SP 89/16, 4/14 January 1690, fol. 377r, James Smallwood to Earl of Shrewsbury.

176. Shaw, *Anglo-Portuguese Alliance*, 174.

177. Colbatch, *Account of the Court of Portugal*, 2:172.

178. Large and Miranda, "British Slaves," 161–62.

179. Schneider, *O marquês de Pombal*, 161.

180. TNA SP 89/10, 13/23 April 1670, fols. 205v–206r, Thomas Maynard to Lord Arlington.

181. TNA SP 89/10, 13/23 April 1670, fol. 206r, Thomas Maynard to Lord Arlington; TNA SP 89/11, 5/15, October 1671, fol. 220r, Thomas Maynard to Lord Arlington; TNA SP 89/15, 1/11 August 1683, fols. 211v–212r, Thomas Maynard to Sir Leoline Jenkins.

182. Shaw, *Trade, Inquisition, and the English Nation*, 126.

183. TNA SP 89/11, 5/15 October 1671, fol. 227v, Thomas Maynard to Lord Arlington.

184. Shaw, *Trade, Inquisition, and the English Nation*, 126.

185. ANTT, Tribunal do Santo Ofício, Inquisição de Lisboa, processo 6600, summarized in Caldeira, *Escravos em Portugal*, 297–300.

186. Vieira, "Mercadores Ingleses em Lisboa," 119.

187. TNA SP 89/15, 15/25 May 1683, fol. 191r, Thomas Maynard to Sir Leoline Jenkins.

188. TNA SP 89/17, 5 September 1693, fol. 62v, John Methuen to Earl of Nottingham.

189. TNA SP 89/25, 8 January 1717, fols. 1r–2r, Henry Worsley to Paul Methuen.
190. TNA SP 89/37, 22 September 1733, fols. 264r–264v, Lord Tyrawly to Duke of Newcastle.
191. BNP, códice 10745, *Novidades de Lisboa 1732–1733*, 15 July 1732, fol. 35v.
192. BPE, CIV/1–16d, *Mercúrio de Lisboa*, 26 February 1746.
193. Baião, *Episódios dramáticos*, 42–43.
194. Macaulay, *They Went to Portugal*, 219.
195. A. Marques, *História da Maçonaria*, 23–25, 28–30.
196. Coustos, *Sufferings*, 6.
197. A. Marques, *História da Maçonaria*, 34.
198. Coustos, *Sufferings*, 16, 70–76; A. Marques, *História da Maçonaria*, 35.
199. Cortesão, *Alexandre de Gusmão*, 1:138.
200. Brockwell, *Natural and Political History*, 91.
201. Cunha, *Instruções políticas*, 250.
202. Kamen, *Spanish Inquisition*, 225; Ortiz, *Historia de Sevilla*, 194; Israel, *Dutch Republic*, 99, 144–46.
203. Carvalho, "Cartas de José da Cunha Brochado," *O Instituto* 70, 270.

Chapter 4
1. TNA SP 89/14, 6/16 August 1678, fols. 52r–52v, Francis Parry to Sir Joseph Williamson. The warning was apropos considering multiple Englishmen had converted at the mills. See the letters of Gonçalo Vilas Boas to the Conde de Ericeira dated 11 February 1678 and 31 March 1678, ACL Azul, códice 309, fols. 16r, 20v–21r; Dias, *Os lanifícios*, 51–52.
2. Ames, "Pedro II and the Estado da Índia," 3.
3. Hanson, *Economy and Society*, 160.
4. J. Azevedo, *Épocas de Portugal económico*, 291–92.
5. Antonil, *Brazil*, 134.
6. Caldeira, "O Tabaco Brasileiro," 574.
7. BL, Manuscripts, Add. 23726, *Account of Portugal. Diary of Thomas Cox*, fol. 64v. See also Cox and Macro, *Relação do reino de Portugal*, 166.

8. Gonçalves, "Usos e consumos de tabaco," 128.
9. Hanson, *Economy and Society*, 64.
10. BL, Manuscripts, Add. 23726, *Account of Portugal. Diary of Thomas Cox*, fol. 22v. See also Cox and Macro, *Relação do reino de Portugal*, 84.
11. ANTT, Junta da Administração do Tabaco, Consultas, Maço 2, Consulta de 30 April 1683, doc. 98.
12. ANTT, Junta da Administração do Tabaco, Consultas, Maço 4A, Consulta de 29 August 1698.
13. ANTT, Junta da Administração do Tabaco, Consultas, Maço 13, consulta 17 July 1732.
14. ANTT, Junta da Administração do Tabaco, Consultas, Maço 6, Consulta de 20 December 1704.
15. TNA SP 89/35, 14 September 1728, fols. 101v–102r, Lord Tyrawly to the Duke of Newcastle.
16. Lydon, *Fish and Flour*, 38.
17. Hanson, "Monopoly and Contraband," 155.
18. As quoted in Santos, *Os tabacos*, 25.
19. Disney, *History of Portugal and the Portuguese Empire*, 2:305.
20. Antonil, *Brazil*, 123. Brazilian tobacco became a valuable commodity among the Mina Africans along the slave coast who preferred this tobacco to all others. Gold dust from Minas Gerais was also illegally traded for enslaved Africans in the region. See Boxer, *Portuguese Seaborne Empire*, 170–71.
21. Boxer, "Great Luso-Brazilian Figure," 30; Vieira, *Cartas do Padre António Vieira*, 3:152–53; Alencastro, *Trade in the Living*, 140. For a discussion on Pombal's monopoly company focused on Maranhão, see Maxwell, *Conflicts and Conspiracies*, 18.
22. ANTT, Manuscritos de Brasil, livro 39, fol. 3v, Duarte Ribeiro de Macedo "Discurso sobre a transplantação das plantas de especiarias da Ásia para a América [. . .]."
23. "Consulta da câmara a el-rei em 1 de Abril de 1675," in E. Oliveira, *Elementos*, 8:101.

NOTES TO PAGES 93–100

24. Letter of Pedro II to D. Pedro de Almeida, Viceroy of India, 9 April 1677, transcribed in L. Almeida, *Aclimatação de plantas*, 423.

25. L. Almeida, *Páginas dispersas*, 96–97; BNP, códice 8538, fol. 29r, Pedro II to the Viceroy of India 21 March 1678; Letter of Pedro II to Roque da Costa Barreto, 30 March 1678, transcribed in *Documentos históricos*, 67:316.

26. L. Almeida, *Páginas dispersas*, 123–25.

27. Hanson, *Economy and Society*, 203; Costa, Lains, and Miranda, *Economic History of Portugal*, 145–46.

28. Shaw, *Trade, Inquisition, and the English Nation*, 85.

29. BL, Manuscripts, Add. 23726, *Account of Portugal. Diary of Thomas Cox*, fol. 19r. See also Cox and Macro, *Relação do reino de Portugal*, 77. The *quintal* was the Portuguese hundredweight. See Boxer, *Golden Age of Brazil*, 356.

30. Hanson, *Economy and Society*, 204.

31. Fisher, "Lisbon, Its English Merchant Community and the Mediterranean," 25.

32. As quoted in Lydon, *Fish and Flour*, 139.

33. Hanson, *Economy and Society*, 202.

34. Carvalho, "Cartas de José da Cunha Brochado," *O Instituto* 70, 268.

35. Colbatch, *Account of the Court of Portugal*, 2:169; Hanson, *Economy and Society*, 203.

36. Boxer, *Golden Age of Brazil*, 25.

37. BNP, códice 4493, fols. 50r–50v, "Carta de Conde de Vilar Maior [. . .]."

38. Lourenço, *D. Pedro II*, 303; Godinho, "Portugal and the Making of the Atlantic World," 320–21. For an analysis of the Pombal's renewed efforts at manufacturing in Portugal, see Maxwell, *Conflicts and Conspiracies*, 51–53.

39. Rossini, "As pragmáticas Portuguesas," 120.

40. Godinho, "Portugal and Her Empire," 512; Hanson, *Economy and Society*, 162–64.

41. Hanson, *Economy and Society*, 132, 162.

42. Macedo, "Sobre a introdução das artes," 167.

43. Macedo, "Sobre a introdução das artes," 174.

44. Godinho, "Portugal and Her Empire," 512.

45. TNA SP 89/11, 4 May 1671, fol. 113v, Thomas Maynard to Lord Arlington.

46. Godinho, "Portugal and Her Empire," 512.

47. Hanson, *Economy and Society*, 165.

48. Godinho, "Portugal and Her Empire," 512–13; Macedo, "Sobre a introdução das artes," 200.

49. Macedo, "Sobre a introdução das artes," 174.

50. "Consulta da câmara a el-rei em 18 de Junho de 1681," in E. Oliveira, *Elementos*, 8:422–23.

51. Hanson, *Economy and Society*, 166.

52. Paixão, *Monstruosidades do tempo*, 1:87–88.

53. Macedo, "Sobre a introdução das artes," 187–88.

54. Decree of 25 January 1677, in Justino Silva, *Collecção chronologica da legislação*, 9:26.

55. Rossini, "As pragmáticas Portuguesas," 126.

56. Hanson, *Economy and Society*, 166.

57. Boxer, "Vicissitudes of Anglo-Portuguese Relations," 22; Francis, *Methuens and Portugal*, 189; Hanson, *Economy and Society*, 166.

58. Hanson, *Economy and Society*, 166, 169. Hanson also demonstrates that the Portuguese wool industry suffered a similar fate during the Iberian union.

59. Macedo, "Sobre a introdução das artes," 172; Lourenço, *D. Pedro II*, 304.

60. "Decreto de 25 de Setembro de 1677," in E. Oliveira, *Elementos*, 8:232–36.

61. BNP, códice PBA 67, "Alvitre que se deo no anno de 1679 sobre três conveniências para o nosso reyno," fols. 143r, 147r.

62. Godinho, "Portugal and Her Empire," 513; Hanson, *Economy and Society*, 167. Owen Stanwood argues that many Huguenots often claimed an expertise in silk manufacture that they really did not possess. See Stanwood, *Global Refuge*, 72.

63. Macedo, *Problemas de história da indústria Portuguesa*, 32.

64. Costa, Lains, and Miranda, *Economic History of Portugal*, 137–38.

65. Hanson, *Economy and Society*, 168.

66. Costa, Lains, and Miranda, *Economic History of Portugal*, 138–40; Francis, *Methuens and Portugal*, 189.

67. "Discurso I de Gonçalo da Cunha Vilas Boas," transcribed in Dias, *Os lanifícios*, 89.

68. TNA SP 89/14, 2/12 August 1677, fol. 15r, Thomas Maynard to Secretary Coventry.

69. TNA SP 89/14, 2/12 August 1677, fol. 15r, Thomas Maynard to Secretary Coventry.

70. TNA SP 89/14, 23 July/2 August 1678, fol. 50r, Francis Parry to Sir Joseph Williamson.

71. "Discurso I de Gonçalo da Cunha Vilas Boas," transcribed in Dias, *Os lanifícios*, 91–92.

72. Costa, Lains, and Miranda, *Economic History of Portugal*, 140–41; Disney, *History of Portugal and the Portuguese Empire*, 2:307.

73. Costa, Lains, and Miranda, *Economic History of Portugal*, 144.

74. "Carta do Conde da Ericeira de 1 de Agosto de 1679," transcribed in Macedo, *Problemas de história da indústria Portuguesa*, 32.

75. Costa, Lains, and Miranda, *Economic History of Portugal*, 141.

76. "Discurso I de Gonçalo da Cunha Vilas Boas," transcribed in Dias, *Os lanifícios*, 100, 103.

77. Macedo, *Problemas de história da indústria Portuguesa*, 141.

78. TNA SP 89/14, 1/11 June 1680, fol. 74v, Francis Parry to Sir Leoline Jenkins.

79. Shaw, *Anglo-Portuguese Alliance*, 18.

80. Hanson, *Economy and Society*, 183.

81. TNA SP 89/15, 20/30 July 1683, fol. 209v, Consul Thomas Maynard to Mr. Trevanion.

82. Rossini, "As pragmáticas Portuguesas," 127; Law of 9 August 1686, in Justino Silva, *Collecção chronologica da legislação*, 10:65.

83. Dias, *Os lanifícios*, 22.

84. Rossini, "As pragmáticas Portuguesas," 127–28.

85. Letter to Duarte Ribeiro de Macedo, 13 September 1678, transcribed in Vieira, *Cartas do Padre António Vieira*, 3:320.

86. Rossini, "As pragmáticas Portuguesas," 128.

87. Francis, *Methuens and Portugal*, 20.

88. Sideri, *Trade and Power*, 27.

89. Francis, *Methuens and Portugal*, 192.

90. "Consulta da câmara a el-rei em 7 de Junho de 1679," in E. Oliveira, *Elementos*, 8:341–42.

91. "Consulta da câmara a el-rei em 7 de Junho de 1679," in E. Oliveira, *Elementos*, 8:344n1.

92. "Consulta da câmara a el-rei em 11 de Dezembro de 1682," in E. Oliveira, *Elementos*, 8:473–75.

93. "Consulta da câmara a el-rei em 8 de Outubro de 1692," in E. Oliveira, *Elementos*, 9:280–82.

94. "Consulta da câmara a el-rei em 8 de Outubro de 1692," in E. Oliveira, *Elementos*, 9:285n1; "Consulta da câmara a el-rei em 22 de Junho de 1699," in E. Oliveira, *Elementos*, 9:557.

95. Macedo, *Problemas de história da indústria Portuguesa*, 41; Fisher, *Portugal Trade*, 20.

96. Macedo, "Sobre a introdução das artes," 172.

97. TNA SP 89/15, 16 January 1683, fols. 54r–55r, Charles Fanshaw to Sir Leoline Jenkins; TNA SP 89/15, 11/21 January 1683, fols. 61r–61v, Thomas Maynard to Sir Leoline Jenkins.

98. TNA SP 89/15, 11/21 January 1683, fols. 61r–61v, Thomas Maynard to Sir Leoline Jenkins.

99. TNA SP 89/15, 23 January 1683, fol. 66r, Willoughby Swift to Messrs. A. Duncan and T. Goddard.

100. TNA SP 89/16, 8/18 May 1688, fol. 354r, Charles Scarburgh to Earl of Sunderland.

101. Hanson, *Economy and Society*, 156.

102. TNA SP 89/16, 12 May 1684, fol. 80v, Charles Fanshaw to Sir Leoline Jenkins.

103. Hanson, *Economy and Society*, 156–57.

104. BNP, códice 748, fols. 266r–267v, Conde de Ericeira to Pedro II 2 July 1688; Godinho, "Portugal and Her Empire," 514.

105. Godinho, "Portugal and Her Empire," 514; Hanson, *Economy and Society*, 159.

106. Godinho, "Portugal and Her Empire," 514–15.

107. Macedo, "Sobre a introdução das artes," 193.

108. Letter of the Conde de Ericeira, 6 September 1678, transcribed in Macedo, *Problemas de história da indústria Portuguesa*, 30n1.

109. Macedo, *Problemas de história da indústria Portuguesa*, 29.

110. Hanson, *Economy and Society*, 269. Apparently, those with interest in the woolen industry who were left out of the monopolistic contract granted to the three New Christian weavers were responsible for inquisitorial intervention. Costa, Lains, and Miranda, *Economic History of Portugal*, 142.

111. Pedreira, "Indústria e atraso económico," 15–16.

112. Sideri, *Trade and Power*, 41.

113. Costa, Lains, and Miranda, *Economic History of Portugal*, 143.

114. "Informação do estado do Brasil e de suas necessidades," 466. Charles Ralph Boxer dates the memorial to the 1680s. For more information about emigration to Brazil during the second half of the seventeenth century, see Boxer, *Golden Age of Brazil*, 10.

115. Joel Serrão, "Conspecto histórico da emigração Portuguesa," 601.

116. Costa, Lains, and Miranda, *Economic History of Portugal*, 150, 152–53.

117. BNP, códice 309, fol. 22r, *Annaes das couzas mais notaveis* [. . .].

118. Hanson, *Economy and Society*, 267–68.

119. Dias, *Os lanifícios*, 69; Macedo, *Problemas de história da indústria Portuguesa*, 42.

120. Godinho, "Portugal and the Making of the Atlantic World," 323–24.

121. Costa, Lains, and Miranda, *Economic History of Portugal*, 150.

122. Carvalho, "Cartas de José da Cunha Brochado," *O Instituto* 71, 595.

123. Francis, *Methuens and Portugal*, 191–92.

124. As quoted in Fisher, *Portugal Trade*, 29.

125. Costa, Lains, and Miranda, *Economic History of Portugal*, 156; Disney, *History of Portugal and the Portuguese Empire*, 1:248.

126. Francis, *Methuens and Portugal*, 201, 206.

127. Shillington and Chapman, *Commercial Relations*, 225; Sideri, *Trade and Power*, 44.

128. McLachlan, *Trade and Peace with Old Spain*, 19.

129. A. Marques, *História da Maçonaria*, 22.

130. Schneider, *O marquês de Pombal*, 133.

131. Magalotti, *Viaje de Cosme*, 369.

132. Pedreira, "Diplomacia, manufacturas e desenvolvimento económico," 152.

133. Costa, Lains, and Miranda, *Economic History of Portugal*, 157–58.

134. Sideri, *Trade and Power*, 41.

135. Boxer, *Portuguese Seaborne Empire*, 168.

136. Shaw, *Anglo-Portuguese Alliance*, 38–39. For internal consumption, see Lourenço, *D. Pedro II*, 311.

137. Lydon, *Fish and Flour*, 137.

138. O'Flanagan, *Port Cities of Atlantic Iberia*, 196–97.

139. Sideri, *Trade and Power*, 28.

140. Godinho, "Portugal and Her Empire," 523.

141. Costa, Lains, and Miranda, *Economic History of Portugal*, 157.

142. Sideri, *Trade and Power*, 42.

143. Maxwell, "Eighteenth-Century Portugal," 106, 128–29.

144. Letter to the Marquis of Torcy, 15 May 1714, transcribed in Viganego, *Ao serviço secreto*, 184. For a historiographical overview of the amount of gold arriving in Lisbon during João V's reign, see Costa, Rocha, and Sousa, "O ouro cruza o Atlântico"; Godinho, "Portugal and the Making of the Atlantic World," 329–30. These numbers do not reflect contraband.

145. Costa, Rocha, and Brito, "Alchemy of Gold," 1148.

146. Costa, Rocha, and Araújo, *O ouro do Brasil*, 72.

147. Costa, Rocha, and Araújo, *O ouro do Brasil*, 126–27.

148. Ataíde, *Portugal, Lisboa, e a corte*, 351.

149. Lisboa, Olival, and Miranda, *Gazetas manuscritas*, 1:142.

150. Boxer, *Golden Age of Brazil*, 209–11.

151. Jaime Cortesão argues that the total amount of contraband gold shipped was likely greater than declared quantities during the period. See Cortesão, *Alexandre de Gusmão*, 1:65.

152. João V's Brazilian-born secretary, Alexandre de Gusmão, fought diligently against contraband. In a letter to one of the high court judges, Gusmão informed the man that João V was aware of his participation in the widespread contraband that had developed in the city despite the monarch's efforts to eliminate abuse. See the letter of Alexandre de Gusmão to Pedro Mariz Sarmento, 3 May 1746, transcribed in *O investigador Português em Inglaterra*, 1:450.

153. Letter to the Marquis of Torcy, 15 May 1714, transcribed in Viganego, *Ao serviço secreto*, 185.

154. As quoted in Boxer, "Brazilian Gold and British Traders," 460.

155. Boxer, "Brazilian Gold and British Traders," 460. An *oitavo* was equal to 72 *grãos* (grains) during the period 1700–1750. For measurements, weights, and values, see Boxer, *Golden Age of Brazil*, 356.

156. Boxer, *Portuguese Seaborne Empire*, 219–20.

157. Fisher, *Portugal Trade*, 32.

158. Costa, Rocha, and Araújo, *O ouro do Brasil*, 129–30.

159. Cunha, *Instruções políticas*, 286.

160. AHU, Conselho Ultramarino, Reino, caixa 39, pasta 1; BPE, CIV/1–10d, *Folheto de Lisboa*, 14 April 1742.

161. AHU, Conselho Ultramarino, Reino, caixa 41, pasta 27, "1740 Requerimento ao rei D. João V, dos moradores da freguesia de Nossa Senhora do Amparo de Benfica, em Lisboa."

162. Lisboa, Olival, and Miranda, *Gazetas manuscritas*, 2:49. A Portuguese *arroba* is equivalent to about fifteen kilos.

163. Costa, Rocha, and Araújo, *O ouro do Brasil*, 65–66.

164. *Gazeta de Lisboa Occidental*, no. 44, 3 November 1718; *Gazeta de Lisboa Occidental*, no. 17, 23 April 1722,

165. Gallas and Gallas, *O barroco no reinado de D. João V*, 196.

166. TNA SP 89/30, 24 April 1722, fol. 12v, Thomas Burnett to Lord Carteret.

167. As quoted in Cortesão, *Alexandre de Gusmão*, 1:86.

168. BPE, CIV/1–16d, *Mercúrio de Lisboa 1746*, 10 December 1746.

169. Cunha, *Testamento político*, 114.

170. ACL, Azul, códice 127, "Consulta da Junta do Comércio Geral sobre o estado [. . .]," 22 May 1715, fols. 95r–95v. For repeated examples of merchants requesting remittances in gold over agricultural products, see the correspondence of the Lisbon merchant Francisco Pinheiro transcribed in the five volumes of Pinheiro, *Negócios coloniais*.

171. AHU, Conselho Ultramarino, Reino, caixa 22, pasta 1, "Alvará de 1 Fevereiro 1720 do rei [D. João V] suprimindo e extinguindo o Tribunal da Junta do Comércio Geral [. . .]."

172. Rijo, Aragonez, and Francisco, "A freguesia de Santa Justa," 104–5. Emigrants left mostly from the densely populated areas of the northern provinces. Yet some of the same effects were felt in Lisbon.

173. "Descrição da cidade de Lisboa (1730)," 44–45.

174. Law of 20 March 1720, transcribed in *Annaes da Bibliotheca Nacional do Rio de Janeiro*, 146.

175. Law of 20 March 1720, transcribed in *Annaes da Bibliotheca Nacional do Rio de Janeiro*, 146.

176. Antonil, *Brazil*, 152.

177. Boxer, *Golden Age of Brazil*, 49. Emigration numbers for the period vary widely. José Vicente Serrão, for example,

argues that the annual number was between eight and ten thousand a year. See José Serrão, "O quadro humano," 65–66.

178. M. B. Silva, *D. João V*, 173.

179. Cunha, *Instruções políticas*, 224.

180. Decree of 10 March 1732, in *Collecção da legislação antiga*, 431–32.

181. BNP 554, *Mercúrio de Lisboa*, 13 March 1745, fols. 318v–319r.

182. Godinho, "Portugal and Her Empire," 535. There was also other pragmatics and sumptuary legislation under João V's reign.

183. Macedo, *Problemas de história da indústria Portuguesa*, 64.

184. Couto, "D. João V," 257; Macedo, *Problemas de história da indústria Portuguesa*, 65.

185. L. Almeida, "A fábrica das sedas de Lisboa," 3; Macedo, *Problemas de história da indústria Portuguesa*, 70–71; L. Pereira, "Ourives franceses," 105–6; Stanwood, *Global Refuge*, 200.

186. Madureira, *Cidade*, 61; L. Almeida, "A fábrica das sedas de Lisboa," 21.

187. Falcon, *A época Pombalina*, 234, 238.

188. Letter of Consul Montagnac, 18 March 1732 as quoted in Pinto, *O ouro brasileiro*, 275.

189. Letter of Sebastião José de Carvalho e Melo to Marco António Azevedo Coutinho 24 September 1741, transcribed in S. Melo, *Escritos económicos de Londres*, 129; L. Almeida, "A fábrica das sedas de Lisboa," 14.

190. Macedo, *Problemas de história da indústria Portuguesa*, 71–72.

191. *Gazeta de Lisboa Occidental*, no. 11, 15 March 1731.

192. E. Oliveira, *Elementos*, 13:372.

193. Macedo, *Problemas de história da indústria Portuguesa*, 68–69.

194. Letter of Consul Duverger 25 September 1713 as quoted in Pinto, *O ouro brasileiro*, 274–75.

195. Merveilleux, "Memórias instrutivas," 221.

196. Chaves, *O Portugal visto por três forasteiros*, 22.

197. As quoted in Chantal, *A vida quotidiana em Portugal*, 27.

198. Merveilleux, "Memórias instrutivas," 197–98.

199. "Consulta da câmara a el-rei em 3 de Fevereiro de 1712," in E. Oliveira, *Elementos*, 10:588. John Villiers described the same transformation for various trades in Lisbon. See Villiers, "Portuguese Society," 187–89.

200. Villiers, "Portuguese Society," 183; E. Oliveira, *Elementos*, 10:286–89.

201. Villiers, "Portuguese Society," 193–94; "Consulta da câmara a el-rei reformada em 5 de Dezembro de 1743," in E. Oliveira, *Elementos*, 14:209–10n1.

202. "Assento de vereação de 14 de Outubro de 1718," E. Oliveira, *Elementos*, 11:287–88.

203. Villiers, "Portuguese Society," 195–96.

204. Cortesão, *Alexandre de Gusmão*, 1:86.

205. BNP, códice PBA 646, fols. 131r–133r.

206. Costa, Rocha, and Araújo, "Social Capital and Economic Performance," 7; Costa, Rocha, and Araújo, *O ouro do Brasil*, 128.

207. BL, Manuscripts, Add. 23726, *Account of Portugal. Diary of Thomas Cox*, fol. 23r. See also Cox and Macro, *Relação do reino de Portugal*, 85.

208. "Brazil," in Postlethwayt, *Universal Dictionary of Trade and Commerce*.

209. Donovan, "Commercial Enterprise," 58, 62. Jorge Pedreira lists various additional examples of the same process. See Pedreira, "Os homens de negócio," 215–22.

210. Like other merchants involved in the Brazil trade at the time, Guimarães most likely dealt predominantly in English manufactures. See the discussion about Francisco Pinheiro in this chapter. His dealings in the colony went through both established factors and traveling agents. See Costa, Rocha, and Araújo, "Social Capital and Economic Performance," 19.

211. Costa, Rocha, and Araújo, *O ouro do Brasil*, 147, 152; Pedreira, "To Have and to Have Not," 108.

212. Letter of Manoel de Almada Soares to Francisco Pinheiro, 10 August 1709, in Pinheiro, *Negócios coloniais*, 1:11. English translation found in Alden, "Vicissitudes of Trade," 289.

213. Olival, "Os lugares e espaços do privados," 244.

214. BL, Manuscripts, Add. 23726, *Account of Portugal. Diary of Thomas Cox*, fol. 43r. See also Cox and Macro, *Relação do reino de Portugal*, 123.

215. M. J. Silva, *Fidalgos-mercadores*, 20.

216. "Descrição da cidade de Lisboa (1730)," 85.

217. Letter of Francisco Pinheiro to factor in Bahia 14 August 1720 and to factor in Rio de Janeiro 31 January 1719 transcribed in Pinheiro, *Negócios coloniais*, 4:592–93, 736–39.

218. Pimentel, *Arquitectura e poder*, 46.

219. Cortesão, *Alexandre de Gusmão*, 1:54.

220. Both production and remittances to the capital began to wane around the middle of the eighteenth century. See Costa, Rocha, and Araújo, *O ouro do Brasil*, 57–58.

221. Letter of D. Mariana Vitória 15 February 1742, transcribed in Vitória, *Cartas da Rainha D. Mariana Vitória*, 182.

222. Nizza, *D. João V*, 204–5.

223. Gusmão, "Cálculo sobre a perda do dinheiro do reino," 221–25.

224. Lopes, *Goa setecentista*, 28; Sim, *Portuguese Enterprise*, 174–75.

225. Maxwell, *Pombal*, 7–8.

226. Beloff, *Age of Absolutism*, 100–101.

227. Pedreira, "Indústria e atraso económico em Portugal," 24–25.

228. Costa, Lains, and Miranda, *Economic History of Portugal*, 135–36.

229. Grafe and Pedreira, "New Imperial Economies," 584–85.

230. Villiers, "Portuguese Society," 188.

Chapter 5

1. Saussure, "Cartas escritas de Lisboa," 267.

2. N. Monteiro, "A secretaria de estado dos negócios do reino," 28.

3. Pedreira, "Costs and Financial Trends," 72. In the case of Spain, a maximum

of one-quarter of the royal revenue was derived from the empire. See A. Marques, *History of Portugal*, 392. While Marques rightfully argues that other sources of revenue, including increasing internal taxation, provided much more for the crown than Brazilian gold alone, he does note the vital importance of both gold and tobacco to the increasing crown finances.

4. *Mercator's Letters on Portugal*, 9.

5. N. Monteiro, "Identificação da política setecentista," 967.

6. "Decreto de 5 de Setembro de 1671," in E. Oliveira, *Elementos*, 7:307.

7. Prestage, *Mode of Government in Portugal*, 263. For discussion of the absolutism of the contemporaries Louis XIV of France and Felipe V, see Lough, "France Under Louis XIV"; Brading, "Bourbon Spain and Its American Empire."

8. Colbatch, *Account of the Court of Portugal*, 1:164.

9. Prestage, *Memórias sobre Portugal*, 17.

10. Vieira, *Cartas do Padre António Vieira*, 2:641–42.

11. Prestage, *Mode of Government in Portugal*, 270.

12. M. Almeida, "Portugal na época de D. João V," 257.

13. A. Marques, *History of Portugal*, 1:394.

14. L. Almeida, *Páginas dispersas*, 184–85.

15. N. Monteiro, "Identificação da política setecentista," 966; Kamen, *Philip V of Spain*, 220–22.

16. Bicalho, "Inflexões na política imperial," 38; Lough, "France Under Louis XIV," 234; Brading, "Bourbon Spain and Its American Empire," 391.

17. N. Monteiro, *D. José*, 42; Cardim and Monteiro, *Political Thought*, 38–39.

18. López-Cordón and Monteiro, "Enlightened Politics in Portugal and Spain," 476; L. Almeida, *Páginas dispersas*, 192. The council met weekly during Pedro II's reign. For more on this, see Hespanha, *As vésperas do leviathan*, 248.

19. Ataíde, *Portugal, Lisboa, e a corte*, 416.

20. Francis, *Portugal 1715–1808*, 11.

21. Cardim and Monteiro, *Political Thought*, 38–39.

22. As quoted in Carnaxide, *D. João V e o Brasil*, 50.

23. Sim, *Portuguese Enterprise*, 50.

24. R. Oliveira, "As metamorfoses do império," 128–29.

25. Kamen, *Philip V of Spain*, 221.

26. Kamen, *Philip V of Spain*, 221–23.

27. Macedo, "Nobreza," 392–93; López-Cordón and Monteiro, "Enlightened Politics in Portugal and Spain," 477. For the same pattern during the Pombaline era, see Maxwell, *Pombal*, 78.

28. Ataíde, *Portugal, Lisboa, e a corte*, 310, 340. An additional example from 1733 is mentioned in Lisboa, Olival, and Miranda, *Gazetas manuscritas*, 2:229.

29. As quoted in N. Monteiro, *O crepúsculo dos grandes*, 207.

30. As quoted in Matos, "Lisboa na restauração," 465.

31. Merveilleux, "Memórias instrutivas," 181–82.

32. Cunha and Monteiro, "Velhas formas," 419.

33. TNA SP 89/33, 28 July 1726, fol. 166v, Arthur Stert to Charles Delafaye.

34. "Descrição da de Lisboa (1730)," 69.

35. L. Almeida, *Páginas dispersas*, 199–200; N. Monteiro, *D. José*, 53–54.

36. Cortesão, *Alexandre de Gusmão*, 1:93.

37. A. Marques, *History of Portugal*, 1:396.

38. Decree of 29 de Janeiro de 1739, in *Collecção da legislação antiga*, 467.

39. N. Monteiro, *O crepúsculo dos grandes*, 127–28; Boxer, *Portuguese Seaborne Empire*, 356.

40. Cortesão, *Alexandre de Gusmão*, 1:112–14.

41. Cardim and Monteiro, *Political Thought*, 20–21.

42. Russell-Wood, "Portugal and the World," 19.

43. Cunha, *Testamento político*, 51–52; Boxer, *Portuguese Seaborne Empire*, 356.

44. Cardim and Monteiro, *Political Thought*, 21.

45. A. Martins, "Estrangeirados," 470.

46. Cunha, *Instruções políticas*, 206–7.

47. Macedo, "Absolutismo," 12–13.

48. Cunha, *Testamento político*, 42–43; Cunha, *Instruções políticas*, 192–93.

49. Cunha, *Instruções políticas*, 372. Translation quoted in Cardim and Monteiro, *Political Thought*, 220.

50. Dumouriez, *Account of Portugal*, 223–24.

51. TNA SP 89/40, 7 January 1741, fol. 210v, Lord Tyrawly to the Duke of Newcastle.

52. TNA SP 89/40, 7 January 1741, fols. 210v–211r, Lord Tyrawly to the Duke of Newcastle.

53. TNA SP 89/35, 19 May 1729, fol. 167r, Deposition of Captain Henry Lynslager; TNA SP 89/35, 2 June 1729, fols. 161r–162r, Lord Tyrawly to the Duke of Newcastle.

54. TNA SP 89/35, 26 June 1729, fol. 181r, Lord Tyrawly to the Duke of Newcastle.

55. TNA SP 89/35, 26 June 1729, fol. 181r, Lord Tyrawly to the Duke of Newcastle.

56. TNA SP 89/35, 7 August 1729, fol. 198r, Lord Tyrawly to Charles Delafaye.

57. Shaw, *Anglo-Portuguese Alliance*, 86.

58. Macedo, "Do poder absoluto ao absolutismo," 352.

59. A. Silva, "A Básilica patriarcal de D. João V," 28–30.

60. Brazão, *D. João V e a santa sé*, 185.

61. "Alvará régio de 15 de Janeiro de 1717," in E. Oliveira, *Elementos*, 11:167.

62. "Alvará régio de 31 de Agosto de 1741," in E. Oliveira, *Elementos*, 13:617.

63. Rossa, "Lisbon's Waterfront Image," 168–71.

64. Afonso et al., *Lisbon in the Age of Dom João V*, 14; Rossa, "Lisbon's Waterfront Image," 171–72.

65. Merveilleux, "Memórias instrutivas," 153; J. Azevedo, *Épocas de Portugal económico*, 386.

66. R. Smith, "Building of Mafra," 360–61.

67. R. Smith, "Building of Mafra," 364; Lisboa, Olival, and Miranda, *Gazetas manuscritas*, 1:122.

68. R. Smith, "Building of Mafra," 363–64.

69. As quoted in R. Smith, "Building of Mafra," 363.

70. Letter of Jozé Correa de Abreu, 17 December 1728, transcribed in Carvalho, *D. João V e a arte do seu tempo*, 2:399.

71. Boxer, *Some Contemporary Reactions*, 5.

72. Sylva, *Elogio funebre*, 90.

73. Delaforce, "Lisbon, 'This New Rome,'" 72–73.

74. BPE, CIV/1–9d, *Folheto de Lisboa Occidental*, 20 May 1741.

75. BNP, códice 10746, *Novidades de Lisboa 1735 a 1749*, fols. 102r–102v.

76. Villiers, "Portuguese Society," 152.

77. BNP, códice 554, *Folheto de Lisboa*, 10 August 1743, fol. 15v; BNP, códice 554, *Mercúrio de Lisboa*, 12 December 1744, fol. 271v. The figure listed is 350,000 *réis*, which converts to 875 *cruzados*.

78. Costa, Rocha, and Brito, "Alchemy of Gold," 1154. The monthly rate was 6,400 *réis*, which equals 16 *cruzados* considering that 400 *réis* equaled one *cruzado* at the time.

79. Sylva, *Elogio funebre*, 82–83.

80. Merveilleux, "Memórias instrutivas," 222.

81. As quoted in Villiers, "Portuguese Society," 152.

82. A. Silva, "A Básilica patriarcal de D. João V," 11, 31.

83. Rossa, *Beyond Baixa*, 71.

84. Rossa, *Beyond Baixa*, 72; Gusmão, *Collecção de vários escritos*, 18.

85. Gusmão, *Collecção de vários escritos*, 8.

86. Lisboa, Olival, and Miranda, *Gazetas manuscritas*, 1:136; M. B. Silva, *D. João V*, 185.

87. BNP, códice 8065, *Folheto de Lisboa*, 28 May 1740 and 16 July 1740.

88. Rossa, *Beyond Baixa*, 74–75.

89. "Decreto de 13 de Abril de 1745," in E. Oliveira, *Elementos*, 14:411–12.

90. BPE, CIV/1–8d, *Diário 1738–1740*, 9 December 1738; Villiers, "Portuguese Society," 50.

91. "Consulta da câmara a el-rei em 23 de Novembro de 1676," in E. Oliveira, *Elementos*, 8:173; Barreiros, "Urban Landscapes," 212.

92. Rossa, *Beyond Baixa*, 34.

93. "Carta do escrivão do senado da câmara ao secretário de estado Diogo Mendonça Corte-Real—19 de Novembro de 1735" and "Decreto de 28 de Novembro de 1735," in E. Oliveira, *Elementos*, 13:133–35.

94. Sylva, *Elogio funebre*, 234–35; Nizza, *D. Joao V*, 82.

95. Rossa, "Lisbon's Waterfront Image," 178.

96. Murteira, *Lisboa da restauração às luzes*, 106.

97. E. Oliveira, *Elementos*, 1:493–94; F. Pereira, "Lisboa barroca da restauração," 355.

98. Rossa, *Beyond Baixa*, 21–23.

99. Cunha and Monteiro, "Que casas são 'grandes casas'?," 207–8.

100. As quoted in N. Monteiro, *O crepúsculo dos grandes*, 426–27.

101. A. Marques, *History of Portugal*, 1:396–97.

102. Cunha and Monteiro, "Que casas são 'grandes casas'?," 208.

103. C. Azevedo, *Solares portugueses*, 65, 78.

104. Saussure, "Cartas escritas de Lisboa," 265–66.

105. Merveilleux, "Memórias instrutivas," 215.

106. Wohl, "Portuguese Baroque Architecture," 139.

107. R. Smith, *Art of Portugal*, 101.

108. Wohl, "Portuguese Baroque Architecture," 144.

109. Sylva, *Elogio funebre*, 103–4; Pimentel, "Les grandes enterprises du roi D. João V," 39.

110. Sylva, *Elogio funebre*, 108.

111. Murteira, "A cidade capital e o conceito moderno," 465, 468.

112. Brazão, *D. João V e a santa sé*, 183, 222, 280.

113. Ataíde, *Portugal, Lisboa, e a corte*, 282, 319. An *arroba* was equal to roughly 25–36 pounds depending on region. See Donovan, "Commercial Enterprise," xii.

114. Pimentel, *Arquitectura e poder*, 98.

115. Villiers, "Portuguese Society," 149–50.

116. Merveilleux, "Memórias instrutivas," 222.

117. Sylva, *Elogio funebre*, 95–96.

118. N. Monteiro, "Identificação da política setecentista," 981.

119. Ataíde, *Portugal, Lisboa, e a corte,* 295–96.

120. M. B. Silva, *D. João V,* 93.

121. Ataíde, *Portugal, Lisboa, e a corte,* 283–85.

122. A. Araújo, "Ritualidade e poder," 206–7.

123. N. Monteiro, "Identificação da política setecentista," 983.

124. Ataíde, *Portugal, Lisboa, e a corte,* 361.

125. Ataíde, *Portugal, Lisboa, e a corte,* 296–97.

126. Ataíde, *Portugal, Lisboa, e a corte,* 337–38.

127. Castelo-Branco, *Lisboa seiscentista,* 39.

128. Brazão, *D. João V e a santa sé,* 303.

129. Russell-Wood, "Portugal and the World," 21.

130. Brazão, *D. João V e a santa sé,* 305, 320.

131. Letter to the Marquis of Torcy, 26 September 1713, transcribed in Viganego, *Ao serviço secreto,* 105.

132. Brazão, *D. João V e a santa sé,* 321.

133. Whiteman, "Church and State," 138; Kamen, *Philip V of Spain,* 83; Brazão, *D. João V e a santa sé,* 327–28.

134. Pimentel, *Arquitectura e poder,* 98.

135. Brazão, *D. João V e a santa sé,* 344–45.

136. Letter of Monsenhor Firrao to Diogo de Mendonça Corte-Real 30 March 1728, transcribed in Biker, *Supplemento à collecção dos tratados,* 341.

137. Almeida and Peres, *História da igreja em Portugal,* 2:348n1.

138. Brazão, *D. João V e a santa sé,* 359–60.

139. Merveilleux, "Memórias instrutivas," 211–12.

140. Afonso et al., *Lisbon in the Age of Dom João V,* 11.

141. Delaforce, "This New Rome," 52; Rossa, "Lisbon's Waterfront Image," 167n19.

142. Bebiano, "D. João V, poder e espectáculo," 154–56.

143. Letter of José da Cunha Brochado, 17 August 1709, in Carvalho, "Cartas de José da Cunha Brochado," *O Instituto* 71, 483.

144. Letter of José da Cunha Brochado, 17 August 1709, in Carvalho, "Cartas de José da Cunha Brochado," *O Instituto* 71, 483.

145. Bebiano, "D. João V, poder e espectáculo," 150.

146. Augusto-França, *Lisboa,* 297.

147. Letter of José da Cunha Brochado, 1 June 1709, in Carvalho, "Cartas de José da Cunha Brochado," *O Instituto* 71, 375.

148. "Carta do secretário de estado Diogo de Mendonça Corte-Real ao presidente do senado da câmara occidental—12 de Maio de 1717," in E. Oliveira, *Elementos,* 11:192–93.

149. "Declaração sobre não irem nas procissões charamelas homens pretos . . . 25 de Agosto de 1717," in E. Oliveira, *Elementos,* 11:216.

150. Lahon, *O negro no coração do império,* 73.

151. Villiers, "Portuguese Society" 295–96.

152. Bebiano, "D. João V, poder e espectáculo," 139, 156–57.

153. Sequeira, "A cidade de D. João V," 53. An earlier example comes from 1717 in E. Oliveira, *Elementos,* 11:192–93.

154. "Descrição da cidade de Lisboa (1730)," 63.

155. Letter of consul Mornay, 12 November 1715 as quoted in Pinto, *O ouro brasileiro,* 268.

156. Palma and Reis, "From Convergence to Divergence," 31.

157. Grafe and Pedreira, "New Imperial Economies," 585–86. Jorge M. Pedreira provides more exact details of this breakdown in Pedreira et al., "Great Escape?," 1–22.

158. Palma and Reis, "From Convergence to Divergence," 23–24.

159. Villiers, "Portuguese Society," 5.

160. Letter of José da Cunha Brochado, 10 November 1708, in Carvalho, "Cartas de José da Cunha Brochado," *O Instituto* 70, 568.

161. Brockwell, *Natural and Political History,* 20; João Castro, *Mappa de Portugal,* 212.

162. Madahil, "Notícias de Lisboa no final do século XVII," 240.

163. Madahil, "Notícias de Lisboa no final do século XVII," 241–42.

164. Letter of 25 January 1699, in Brochado, *Cartas,* 76–77.

165. Cunha, *Testamento político*, 123; Cunha, *Instruções políticas*, 205.
166. D. Castro, *Política moral*, 204.
167. Sucena, "Corpo, moda e luxo," 186.
168. Sequeira, "História do trajo em Portugal," 51.
169. Paice, *Wrath of God*, 35.
170. Cortesão, *Alexandre de Gusmão*, 1:94–96.
171. Paice, *Wrath of God*, 35; A. Marques, *History of Portugal*, 1:420.
172. BPE, CIV/1–9d, *Folheto de Lisboa Occidental*, 19 August 1741.
173. Hervey, *Augustus Hervey's Journal*, 121–22.
174. Cardim, "A corte régia," 176.
175. Cortesão, *Alexandre de Gusmão*, 1:96.
176. "Descrição da cidade de Lisboa (1730)," 67; BPMP, M-FA-15, Salvador António Ferreira, *Várias notícias de cazos acontecidos em Portugal*, fol. 115r.
177. Lourenço, Pereira, and Troni, *Amantes dos reis*, 189. The number is 1,708,000 réis, which equals 4,270 *cruzados*.
178. Wohl, "Portuguese Baroque Architecture," 155.
179. Saussure, "Cartas escritas de Lisboa," 267–68; Lourenço, Pereira, and Troni, *Amantes dos reis*, 194.
180. Lourenço, Pereira, and Troni, *Amantes dos reis*, 187, 194; Letter to the Marquis of Torcy, 9 January 1714, transcribed in Viganego, *Ao serviço secreto*, 141.
181. Cortesão, *Alexandre de Gusmão*, 1:82, 96.
182. Madahil, "Notícias de Lisboa no final do século XVII," 241.
183. "Descrição da cidade de Lisboa (1730)," 46.
184. Black, "Portugal in 1730," 74–75.
185. Saussure, "Cartas escritas de Lisboa," 271. Spectacles did in fact become popular. The Englishman Charles Brockwell related that the Portuguese "never appear abroad without spectacles (especially friars and priests), which by a silk fastened to the rim, which contains the glass, are tied behind their ears." For this discussion, see Brockwell, *Natural and Political History*, 14.
186. Falcon, *A época Pombalina*, 236.

187. Sucena, "Corpo, moda e luxo," 3.
188. Pimentel, *Arquitectura e poder*, 46; Dias, "Luxo e pragmáticas no pensamento económico," 85.
189. Delaforce, "This New Rome," 52; Calado, "Academia de Portugal em Roma," 18; Pimentel, "Les grandes enterprises du roi D. João V," 35; Wittkower, "Art and Architecture," 156.
190. L. Almeida, *Páginas dispersas*, 6.
191. Russell-Wood, "God and Mammon," 208–9.
192. R. Smith, *Art of Portugal*, 262.
193. Russell-Wood, "Portugal and the World," 18; Ribeiro, "El-rei D. João, o quinto, e a música no seu tempo," 75; Cortesão, *Alexandre de Gusmão*, 1:96–97.
194. A. Martins, "Estrangeirados," 469.
195. Brito, "Da ópera ao divino," 315.
196. Brito, "A música profana," 112; Russell-Wood, "Portugal and the World," 18. After suffering his paralytic attack in 1742, João V became religiously fanatic and outlawed any theater in the city besides those put on by religious organizations. One Italian composer complained that it appeared the monarch was trying to make the people of Lisbon into saints by force. See Brito, "A música profana," 114.
197. I. Araújo, *Quintas de recreio*, 11–12.
198. Ataíde, *Portugal, Lisboa, e a corte*, 251, 339.
199. Cardim, "A corte régia," 166–67.
200. Levenson, *Age of the Baroque in Portugal*, 11.
201. Letter to Abade Le Grand, 1 April 1712, transcribed in Viganego, *Ao serviço secreto*, 76.
202. TNA SP 89/35, 10 July 1728, fols. 81r–81v, Lord Tyrawly to the Duke of Newcastle.
203. TNA SP 89/28, 27 January 1720, fol. 23v, Thomas Burnett to James Craggs.
204. Donovan, "Commercial Enterprise," 102.
205. Merveilleux, "Memórias instrutivas," 149.
206. As quoted in A. Antunes, "D. Nuno Álvares Pereira de Melo," 2:219–23. For Portugal's role in the War of the Spanish

Succession, see Joaquim Serrão, *História de Portugal*, 226–29, 237–42.

207. Merveilleux, "Memórias instrutivas," 151.

208. Villiers, "Portuguese Society," 95–96.

209. TNA SP 89/23, 14 December 1715, fols. 326v–327r, Henry Worsley to James Stanhope.

210. Saussure, "Cartas escritas de Lisboa," 277.

211. As quoted in Bebiano, "D. João V, rei sol," 117.

212. M. B. Silva, *D. João V*, 281–82; Biker, *Abreviada relação*, 46.

213. Disney, *History of Portugal and the Portuguese Empire*, 2:343.

214. Apolloni, "Wondrous Vehicles," 89–90, 97.

215. Sousa, *História genealógica*, 228.

216. As quoted in Bebiano, "Metamorfoses," 38. There were other examples such as the public entry of the Marquis of Abrantes to Madrid in 1727. For these, see Couto, "D. João V," 245.

217. Letter of 22 September 1708, in Carvalho, "Cartas de José da Cunha Brochado," *O Instituto 70*, 345–46.

218. BA, 51-X-32, fol. 136v, "Carta de João Baptista Carbone para Sampaio de 8 de Outubro de 1743."

219. Merveilleux, "Memórias instrutivas," 219.

220. As quoted in M. B. Silva, *D. João V*, 164.

221. As quoted in L. Almeida, *Páginas dispersas*, 7.

222. Augusto-França, *Lisboa*, 329; Lisboa, Olival, and Miranda, *Gazetas manuscritas*, 1:87, 122.

223. Rau and Silva, *Os manuscritos do arquivo da casa de Cadaval*, 120–21. Alongside the recruitment of foreign technicians, João V made improvements to the naval shipyard in the city. See L. Almeida, *Um constructor naval Francês*, 6.

224. "Proposta do Marquês de Fronteira [. . .]," in Rau and Silva, *Os manuscritos do arquivo da casa de Cadaval*, 108–10.

225. Francis, *Portugal 1715–1808*, 17.

226. Letter to Abade Le Grand, 15 October 1711, transcribed in Viganego, *Ao serviço*

secreto, 69. BNP, códice 512, *Gazeta composta em forma de carta* [. . .], fol. 188r; L. Almeida, *Páginas dispersas*, 160; L. Almeida, *Um constructor naval Inglês*, 9.

227. Letter to the Marquis of Torcy, 10 July 1714, transcribed in Viganego, *Ao serviço secreto*, 197–98.

228. Cunha, *Instruções políticas*, 299.

229. Abbe Jean d'Estrées to Pontchartrain 22 December 1692, as quoted in Labourdette, *La Nation française*, 250.

230. L. Almeida, *Um constructor naval Francês*, 7; Letter to the Marquis of Torcy, 12 December 1713, transcribed in Viganego, *Ao serviço secreto*, 130.

231. L. Almeida, *Páginas dispersas*, 3; Russell-Wood, "Portugal and the World," 16.

232. Menezes, *Nova história de Portugal*, 492.

233. Cortesão, *Alexandre de Gusmão*, 2:354.

234. F. Cunha, "Ensino e difusão das ciências," 411; N. Cunha, *Elites e académicos*, 70.

235. Augusto-França, *Lisboa*, 329.

236. L. Almeida, *Páginas dispersas*, 218; Pimentel, *Arquitectura e poder*, 43.

237. L. Almeida, *Páginas dispersas*, 220.

238. Afonso et al., *Lisbon in the Age of Dom João V*, 15–16.

239. See Ceia, "Os académicos teatinos."

240. Afonso et al., *Lisbon in the Age of Dom João V*, 15–16. A. Cobban argues that part of the Enlightenment included extending scientific knowledge to a broader group. Cobban, "Enlightenment," 88.

241. Afonso et al., *Lisbon in the Age of Dom João V*, 17.

242. Couto, "D. João V," 264.

243. Russell-Wood, "Portugal and the World," 16–18.

244. A. Martins, "Estrangeirados," 469; Maxwell, "Eighteenth-Century Portugal," 110–11.

245. Lousada, "Nova formas," 432–33. Elze Maria Henny Vonk Matias details which academies were founded during the period. See Matias, *Guia ilustrativo das academias*, 553–60.

246. Lousada, "Nova formas," 449–50.

247. Cortesão, *Alexandre de Gusmão*, 2:327; Sylva, *Elogio funebre*, 139–40.
248. Cortesão, *Alexandre de Gusmão*, 2:328.
249. A. Marques, *History of Portugal*, 1:410; Mota, *A academia real da história*, 350.
250. Mota, *A academia real da história*, 38, 211; Villarmayor, *Collecçam dos documentos*.
251. Mota, *A academia real da história*, 211–12, 300–303.
252. Cortesão, *Alexandre de Gusmão*, 2:328; Cobban, "Enlightenment," 95.
253. Delaforce, "This New Rome," 54.
254. Lousada, "Nova formas," 435; Boxer, *Portuguese Seaborne Empire*, 358.
255. Couto, "D. João V," 263–64.
256. Russell-Wood, "Portugal and the World," 16.
257. Brazão, *D. João V: Subsídios*, 39–40. The listed figure before conversion is 200 *contos de réis*, or 200 million *réis*. See Branco, *Portugal na epocha de D. João V*, 243.
258. Sylva, *Elogio funebre*, 141; Ameal, "D. João e a sua época," 16.
259. As quoted in Pimentel, *Arquitectura e poder*, 42.
260. Joaquim Serrão, *História de Portugal*, 368; Menezes, *Nova história de Portugal*, 210; Pimentel, *Arquitectura e poder*, 59.
261. C. Fonseca, "Comércio e Inquisição no Brasil," 197; Branco, *Portugal na epocha de D. João V*, 223.
262. Merveilleux, "Memórias instrutivas," 150.
263. Wilkinson, *Louis XIV*, 43; Kamen, *Philip V of Spain*, 138.
264. Sequeira, "A cidade de D. João V," 57.
265. Merveilleux, "Memórias instrutivas," 147;
266. Francis, *Portugal 1715–1808*, 28–29.
267. Montgon, "Do Caia ao paço da ribeira," 119.
268. Santarém, *Quadro elementar*, cclvi.
269. Sylva, *Elogio funebre*, 132.
270. Villiers, "Portuguese Society," 261.
271. TNA SP 89/30, 19 October 1723, fol. 304v, Thomas Burnett to Lord Carteret.
272. Ameal, "D. João e a sua época," 14, 18.
273. Letter to the Marquis of Torcy, 23 January 1714, transcribed in Viganego, *Ao serviço secreto*, 150.
274. Boxer, *Some Contemporary Reactions*, 6.
275. Letter to the Marquis of Torcy, 7 November 1713, transcribed in Viganego, *Ao serviço secreto*, 120.
276. Letter to the Marquis of Torcy, 19 December 1713, transcribed in Viganego, *Ao serviço secreto*, 133.
277. L. Almeida, *Páginas dispersas*, 138.
278. Pimentel, *Arquitectura e poder*, 143.
279. Lisboa, Olival, and Miranda, *Gazetas manuscritas*, 1:68.
280. BPMP, M FA 15, Salvador António Ferreira, *Várias notícias de cazos acontecidos em Portugal*, fol. 59r.
281. Couto, "D. João V," 257.
282. José Silva, *Gazeta em forma de carta*, 1:187.
283. As quoted in L. Almeida, *Páginas dispersas*, 142.
284. Villiers, "Portuguese Society," 97. For the French example, see chapter 2 in Mandrou, *L'Europe "absolutiste."*
285. Guedes, *História administrativa do Brasil*, 59.
286. Gusmão, *Cartas*, 132.
287. Mandrou, *L'Europe "absolutiste,"* 65, as quoted in Santarém, *Quadro elementar*, 312n392.
288. Cortesão, *Alexandre de Gusmão*, 1:76.
289. Lopes, *Goa setecentista*, 28; Cortesão, "Domínio Ultramarino," 671.
290. M. B. Silva, *D. João V*, 254. BNP, códice 10746, *Novidades de Lisboa 1735–1749*, fols. 76v–77r.
291. Cunha, *Testamento político*, 113; Cunha, *Instruções políticas*, 302.
292. Lobato, "A Guerra dos Maratas," 329; Disney, *History of Portugal and the Portuguese Empire*, 2:320–21.
293. Charles Boxer uses this phrase. See Boxer, *Portuguese Seaborne Empire*, 146–48.
294. M. B. Silva, *D. João V*, 254.
295. Bebiano, "D. João V, rei sol," 116; Russell-Wood, "Portugal and the World," 15.
296. Villiers, "Portuguese Society," 63.

NOTES TO PAGES 149–154

297. Menezes, *Nova história de Portugal*, 32; Bebiano, "D. João V, rei sol," 117.
298. Wohl, "Portuguese Baroque Architecture," 140.
299. As quoted in Maxwell, "Eighteenth-Century Portugal," 103.
300. As quoted in Santarém, *Quadro elementar*, note on ccxv.
301. TNA SP 89/37, 28 September 1731, fols. 122r–123r, Lord Tyrawly to the Duke of Newcastle.
302. Dumouriez, *Account of Portugal*, 224.
303. TNA SP 89/38, 26 August 1735, fol. 153r, Lord Tyrawly to the Duke of Newcastle.
304. Macedo, "Absolutismo," 12–13.
305. Cunha, *Instruções políticas*, 366, 369–71. The diplomat even suggested that in order to expand Brazil, a trade could be arranged with Castile for the kingdom of Chile in exchange for the Algarve.
306. As quoted in A. Antunes, "D. Nuno Álvares Pereira de Melo," 2:223.

Conclusion
Epigraph cited from Molesky, *This Gulf of Fire*, 21.
1. Farmer and Anonymous, *Two Very Circumstantial Accounts*, 8.
2. Farmer and Anonymous, *Two Very Circumstantial Accounts*, 5–6.
3. Molesky, *This Gulf of Fire*, 124.
4. Consul Edward Hay, as quoted in Boxer, "Pombal's Dictatorship," 732.
5. Maxwell, *Pombal*, 24.
6. José Serrão, "O quadro humano," 63.
7. Boxer, *Some Contemporary Reactions*, 7.
8. Boxer, "Pombal's Dictatorship," 732; Farmer and Anonymous, *Two Very Circumstantial Accounts*, 4–5.
9. Maxwell, *Pombal*, 24.
10. Farmer and Anonymous, *Two Very Circumstantial Accounts*, 5.
11. Maxwell, *Pombal*, 21.
12. Boxer, "Pombal's Dictatorship," 732.
13. França, *A reconstrução de Lisboa*, 47–50; Murteira, *Lisboa da restauração às luzes*, 45. The monuments constructed by João V served as a sort of hands-on technical school that prepared many of the able men with the skills necessary to rebuild Lisbon after the earthquake. See R. Smith, "Building of Mafra," 365.
14. Bassi, "Beyond Compartmentalized Atlantics," 704.
15. Gschwend and Lowe, *Global City*.
16. Bailyn, *Atlantic History*, 60.

Bibliography

Archives
Academia das Ciências de Lisboa (ACL)
Arquivo Histórico do Patriarcado de Lisboa (AHPL)
Arquivo Histórico Ultramarino (AHU)
Arquivo Nacional da Torre do Tombo (ANTT)
Biblioteca da Ajuda (BA)
The British Library (BL)
Biblioteca Nacional de Portugal (BNP)
Biblioteca Pública de Évora (BPE)
Biblioteca Pública Municipal de Porto (BPMP)
The National Archives of the United Kingdom—State Papers (TNA SP)

Published Primary Sources
Annaes da Bibliotheca Nacional do Rio de Janeiro. Vol. 28. Rio de Janeiro: Officinas de Artes Graphicas da Bibliotheca Nacional, 1908.
Antonil, André João. *Brazil at the Dawn of the Eighteenth Century*. Translated and edited by Timothy J. Coates, completing partial translation begun by Charles R. Boxer. Translated from *Cultura e opulência do Brasil por suas drogas e minas*, first published in Lisbon 1711. Dartmouth, MA: Tagus Press, 2012.

Ataíde, Tristão da Cunha de, Conde de Povolide. *Portugal, Lisboa, e a corte nos reinados de D. Pedro II e D. João V: Memórias históricas de Tristão da Cunha de Ataíde, 1 conde de Povolide*. Lisbon: Chaves Ferreira, 1990.
Baretti, Giuseppe Marco Antonio. *A Journey from London to Genoa, Through England, Portugal, Spain, and France*. Vol. 1. London: T. Davis and L. Davis, 1770.
Biker, Júlio Firminio Júdice. *Abreviada relação da embaixada que a sereníssima majestade do senhor D. João V, Rei de Portugal, mandou ao imperador da China [. . .]*. Lisbon: Imprensa Nacional, 1879.
———. *Supplemento à collecção dos tratados, convenções contratos, e actos públicos celebrados entre a côroa de Portugal e as mais potencias desde 1640*. Vol. 10. Lisbon: Imprensa Nacional, 1873.
Black, Jeremy. "Portugal in 1730 by the Reverend John Swinton." *British Historical Society of Portugal* 13 (1986): 65–87.
Brochado, José da Cunha. *Cartas*. Edited by António Álvaro Dória. Lisbon: Livraria Sá da Costa, 1944.

Brockwell, Charles. *The Natural and Political History of Portugal: From its First Erection into a Kingdom by Alphonso son of Henry* [. . .]. London: T. Warner, 1726.

Carvalho, Joaquim de. "Cartas de José da Cunha Brochado ao Conde de Viana, D. José de Meneses (1705–1710)." *O Instituto* 69–71 (1922–24).

Castro, Damião António de Lemos Faria e. *Política moral, e civil, aula da nobreza lusitana* [. . .]. Vol. 1. Lisbon: Na Officina de Francisco Luiz Ameno, 1749.

Castro, José Ferreira de Borges de. *Collecção dos tratados, convenções, contratos e actos publicos: Celebrados entre a côroa de Portugal e as mais potencias desde 1640 ate ao presente.* Vol. 1. Lisbon: Imprensa Nacional, 1856.

Castro, Padre João Bautista de. *Mappa de Portugal Antigo, e Moderno* [. . .]. Vol. 1. Part 1. Capítulo XIV. Lisbon: Officina Patriarcal de Francisco Luíz Ameno, 1762.

Cervantes, Miguel de. *Los trabajos de Persiles y Sigismunda.* Madrid: Real Academia Española, 2017.

Colbatch, John. *An Account of the Court of Portugal, Under the Reign of the Present King Dom Pedro II, With some Discourses on the Interests of Portugal with Regard to other Sovereigns* [. . .]. 2 parts. London: Thomas Bennet at the Half-Moon in St. Paul's Church Yard, 1700.

Collecção da legislação antiga e moderna do reino de Portugal. Vol. 2. Coimbra, Portugal: Real Imprensa da Universidade, 1819.

Constituições sinodais do arcebispado de Lisboa novamente feitas no sinodo diocesano que celebrou na sé metropolitana de Lisboa [. . .]. *1640.* Lisboa Oriental: Filippe de Sousa Villela, 1737.

Costigan, Arthur William. *Sketches of Society and Manners in Portugal in a Series of Letters from Arthur William Costigan* [. . .]. Vol. 1. London: T. Vernor, Birchin-Lane, Cornhill, 1787.

Coustos, John. *The Sufferings of John Coustos for Free-Masonry, and for Refusing to Turn Roman Catholic in the Inquisition at Lisbon* [. . .]. London: W. Strahan, 1746.

Cox, Thomas, and Cox Macro. *Relação do reino de Portugal.* Translated and edited by Isabel Lousadas, João Paulo A. Pereira da Silva, and Maria Leonor Machado de Sousa. Lisbon: Biblioteca Nacional, 2007.

Crasto, António Serrão de, and Camilo Castelo Branco. *Os Ratos da Inquisição.* Lisbon: Frenesi, 2004.

Cunha, D. Luís da. *Instruções políticas.* Edited by Abílio Diniz Silva. Lisbon: Comissão Nacional para as Comemorações dos Descobrimentos Portugueses, 2001.

———. *Testamento político ou carta de conselhos ao senhor D. José sendo príncipe.* Edited by Abílio Diniz Silva. Lisbon: Biblioteca Nacional de Portugal, 2013.

Dellon, Charles. "De Goa a Lisboa (1676–1677)." In *Portugal nos séculos XVII & XVIII: Quatro testemunhos,* edited by Castelo Branco Chaves, 21–43. Lisbon: Lisóptima Edições, 1989.

"Descrição da cidade de Lisboa (1730)." In *O Portugal visto por três forasteiros,* edited by Castelo Branco Chaves, 35–93. 2nd ed. Lisbon: Biblioteca Nacional de Lisboa, 1989.

Documentos históricos. Vol. 67. Rio de Janeiro: Ministério da Educação e Saúde, Biblioteca Nacional, 1945.

Dumouriez, Charles François Du Périer. *An Account of Portugal, as it appeared in 1766 to Dumouriez: Since a Celebrated General in the French Army.* London: Printed for C. Law, 1797.

Farmer, Mr., and Anonymous. *Two Very Circumstantial Accounts of the Late Dreadful Earthquake at Lisbon* [. . .]. Boston: D. Fowle and Z. Fowle, 1756.

Geddes, Michael. "A View of the Court of Inquisition in Portugal with a List of the Prisoners that Came Forth in the Act of Faith Celebrated at Lisbon, in the Year 1682." In *Miscellaneous Tracts in Three Volumes,* 2nd ed., 1:423–50. London: J. Churchill, 1714.

Gusmão, Alexandre de. "Cálculo sobre a perda do dinheiro do reino, oferecido à El Rei Dom João V no anno de 1748 por Alexandre de Gusmão." In *O investigador*

Portuguez em Inglaterra: Ou jornal literario, politico, &c., 12:221–31. London: T. C. Hansard, 1811–19.

———. *Collecção de vários escritos inéditos, politicos, e litterários de Alexandre de Gusmão* [. . .]. Edited by T. M. T. de C. Porto, Portugal: Typografia de Faria Guimarães, 1841.

———. "Letter to Pedro Mariz Sarmento 3 May 1746." In *O investigador Portuguez em Inglaterra: Ou jornal literário, politico, &c.*, 1:450–51. London: H. Bryer, 1811.

Gusmão, Alexandre de, and Andrée Rocha, eds. *Cartas*. Lisbon: Imprensa Nacional–Casa da Moeda, 1981.

Hervey, Augustus. *Augustus Hervey's Journal, Being the Intimate Account of the Life of a Captain in the Royal Navy Ashore and Afloat, 1746–1759*. Edited by David Erksine. London: William Kimber, 1953.

Humboldt, Alexander von. *Views of the Cordilleras and Monuments of the Indigenous Peoples of the Americas: A Critical Edition*. Edited by Vera M. Kutzinski and Ottmar Ette. Translated by J. Ryan Poynter. Chicago: University of Chicago Press, 2012.

"Informação do estado do Brasil e de suas necessidades." *Revista do instituto histórico e geográfico Brasileiro* 25 (1862): 465–78.

Jenefer, James. *Saudades Journal*. In *Fifteenth Report. Appendix. Part 1: The Manuscripts of the Earl of Dartmouth*, 3:23–27. Great Britain Royal Commission on Historical Manuscripts. London: Eyre and Spottiswoode, 1896.

Lahontan, Baron de. *New Voyages to North America: Reprinted from the English Ed. of 1703, with Facsimiles of Original Title Pages, Maps, and Illustrations, and the Addition of Introduction, Notes, and Index.* Vol. 2. Edited by Reuben Gold Thwaites. New York: Burt Franklin, 1970.

Lisboa, João Luís, Fernanda de Olival, and Tiago C. P. dos Reis Miranda. *Gazetas manuscritas da biblioteca pública de Évora*. 3 vols. Lisbon: Edições Colibri, 2002–11.

Littleton, Edward. *The Groans of the Plantations: Or a True Account of Their Grievous and Extreme Sufferings by the Heavy Impositions upon Sugar, and other Hardships Relating more Particularly to the Island of Barbados*. London: M. Clark, 1689.

Macedo, Duarte Ribeiro de. "Sobre a introdução das artes 1675." In *Antologia das economistas portugueses, século XVII*, edited by António Sergio, 166–262. Lisbon: Livraria Sá da Costa Editora, 1974.

Madahil, A. G. da Rocha. "Notícias de Lisboa no final do século XVII." *Feira da Ladra* 2 (1930): 228–43.

———, trans. "Viagem de Cosme de Médici a Lisboa, em 1669: Narrativa do Conde Lorenzo Magalotti." *Revista Municipal* 3, nos. 13–14 (1942): 45–58.

Magalotti, Lorenzo. *Viaje de Cosme III de Médici por España y Portugal, 1668–1669*. Translated by David Fermosel. Madrid: Miraguanos S. A. Ediciones, 2018.

Melo, D. Francisco Manuel de. *Apólogos dialogais*. Vol. 1. Edited by José Pereira Tavares. Lisbon: Livraria Sá da Costa, 1959.

———. *Auto do fidalgo aprendiz*. 2nd ed. Edited by Joaquim Mendes dos Remédios. Coimbra, Portugal: França Amado, 1915.

Melo, Sebastião José e Carvalho de. *Escritos económicos de Londres (1741–1742)*. Edited by José Barreto. Lisbon: Biblioteca Nacional, 1986.

Mercator's Letters on Portugal and Its Commerce. Containing also a Faithful Relation of the Disputes which have Arisen between our Merchants and that Court. London: C. Say, 1754.

Merveilleux, Charles Frédéric de. "Memórias instrutivas sobre Portugal, 1723–1726." In *O Portugal de D. João V visto por três forasteiros*, 2nd ed., edited by Castelo Branco Chaves, 131–230. Lisbon: Biblioteca Nacional, 1989.

Montgon, Charles Alexandre. "Do Caia ao paço da ribeira, 1729." In *Portugal nos séculos XVII & XVIII: Quatro testemunhos*, edited by Castelo Branco Chaves, 99–124. Lisbon: Lisóptima Edições, 1989.

Oliveira, Eduardo Freire de., ed. *Elementos para a história do município de Lisboa.* 17 vols. Lisbon: Typographia Universal, 1882–1943.

Oliveira, Francisco Xavier de. *Pathetic Discourse on the Present Calamities of Portugal Addressed to His Countrymen and, in Particular, to His Most Faithful Majesty, Joseph, King of Portugal.* 2nd ed. London: R. Baldwin, 1756.

Paixão, Alexandre de. *Monstruosidades do tempo e da fortuna.* 4 vols. Edited by Damião Peres. Barcelos: Companhia Editora do Minho, 1938–39.

Pinheiro, Francisco. *Negócios coloniais: Uma correspondência comercial do século XVIII.* 5 vols. Edited by Luís Lisanti. Brasília, Brazil: Ministério da Fazenda, 1973.

Prestage, Edgar. *Memórias sobre Portugal no reinado de D. Pedro II.* Lisbon: Bertrand, 1935.

Rau, Virgínia, and Maria Fernanda Gomes da Silva. *Os manuscritos do arquivo da casa de Cadaval respeitantes ao Brasil.* Vol. 2. Coimbra, Portugal: Universidade de Coimbra, 1958.

Rhys, Udal Ap. *An Account of the Most Remarkable Places and Curiosities in Spain and Portugal.* London: J. Osborn, 1749.

Rosário, António. *Frutas do Brasil numa nova, e asética monarchia consagrada à santíssima senhora do rosário [. . .].* Lisbon: António Pedrozo Galram, 1702.

Sanches, António Nunes Ribeiro. *Origem da denominação de christão-velho e christão novo em Portugal.* Edited by Raul Rêgo. Porto, Portugal: Sociedade de Papelaria, 1956.

Sandwich, Earl of (John Montagu), John Cooke, Joseph Collyer, and Thomas Gainsborough. *A Voyage Performed by the Late Earl of Sandwich round the Mediterranean in the Years 1738 and 1739.* London: T. Cadell and W. Davies, 1799.

Santa Catarina, Frei Lucas de, and Frei Francisco Rey de Abreu Matta Zeferino. *Anatomico jocoso, que em diversas operações manifesta a ruindade do corpo humano para emenda do viciososo [. . .].*

Vol. 3. Lisbon: Officina do Doutor Manoel Álvarez Solano, 1758.

Santa Maria, Frei Agostinho de. *Santuario mariano, e história das imagens milagrosas de Nossa Senhora [. . .].* Vol. 7. Lisboa Occidental: Officina António Pedrozo Galram, 1721.

Santana, Frei José Pereira de. *Chronica dos Carmelitas da antiga, e regular observância nestes reynos de Portugal, Algarves e seus dominios [. . .].* Vol. 1. Lisbon: Officina dos Herdeiros de António Pedrozo Galram, 1745.

Saussure, César de. "Cartas escritas de Lisboa no ano de 1730." In *O Portugal visto por três forasteiros,* edited by Castelo Branco Chaves, 261–79. 2nd ed. Lisbon: Biblioteca Nacional de Lisboa, 1989.

Serrão, Joaquim Veríssimo, ed. *Uma relação do reino de Portugal em 1684.* Coimbra, Portugal: Universidade de Coimbra, 1960.

Silva, José Soares da. *Gazeta em forma de carta por José Soares da Silva: Académico do número da academia real da história portuguesa anos de 1701–1716.* Vol. 1. Lisbon: Biblioteca Nacional, 1933.

Silva, Justino de Andrade e. *Collecção chronologica da legislação portugueza.* 11 vols. Lisbon: Imprensa Nacional, 1854–1859.

Sousa, António Caetano de. *História genealógica da casa real portugueza [. . .].* Vol. 8. Lisboa Occidental: Na Officina de Joseph António da Sylva, Impressor da Academia Real, 1741.

Stevens, John. *The Ancient and Present State of Portugal. Containing the Description of that Kingdom [. . .].* London: W. Bray, 1713.

Sylva, Francisco Xavier da. *Elogio funebre, e histórico do muito alto, poderoso, augusto, pio, e fidelíssimo rey de Portugal, e Senhor D. João V [. . .].* Lisbon: Regia Officina Sylviana e da Academia Real, 1750.

Tellez, Padre Balthazar. *Chronica da companhia de Jesu da provincia de Portugal [. . .].* Part 2. Lisbon: Paulo Craesbeeck, 1647.

Tours, François de. "Travels Through Portugal and Spain by Father François de Tours,

Capuchin Preacher, in 1699." In *Lisbon Before the 1755 Earthquake: Panoramic View of the City*, 98–109. Lisbon: Gótica, 2004.

Urban, Sylvanus. "Account of the Magnificent Feast, given by the English Factory at Lisbon, on their receiving the News of the decisive Victory of Culloden, gained by his Royal Highness the Duke of Cumberland over the Rebels." *Gentleman's Magazine* 16 (September 1746): 472–74. London: E. Cave.

Vieira, António. *Cartas do Padre António Vieira*. 3 vols. Edited by João Lúcio de Azevedo. Lisbon: Imprensa Nacional, 1971.

Viganego, Pietro Francesco. *Ao serviço secreto da França na corte de D. João V*. Translated by Fernando de Morais do Rosário. Lisbon: Lisóptima, Biblioteca Nacional, 1994.

Villarmayor, Conde de (Fernão Teles da Silva). *Collecçam dos documentos, estatutos, e memorias da academia real da historia portugueza, que neste anno de 1721 se compuzerão, e se imprimirão por ordem dos seus censores*. Lisbon: Pascoal da Sylva, 1721.

Vitória, D. Mariana. *Cartas da Rainha D. Mariana Vitória para a sua família de Espanha*. Edited by Caetano Beirão. Lisbon: Empresa Nacional de Publicidade, 1936.

Walpole, Horace. *Horace Walpole's Correspondence*. Vol. 18. Edited by W. S. Lewis, Warren Hunting Smith, and George L. Lam. New Haven: Yale University Press, 1954.

———. *Horace Walpole's Correspondence*. Vol. 22. Edited by W. S. Lewis, Warren Hunting Smith, and George L. Lam. New Haven: Yale University Press, 1960.

Secondary Sources

Abreu-Ferreira, Darlene. "Reluctant Hosts and Tenacious Guests: Lisbon's Response to the English Mercantile Community in the Seventeenth Century." *Portuguese Studies Review* 12, no. 1 (2004): 19–31.

Afonso, Simonetta, Luísa Arruda, Leonor Ferrão, and José Fernandes Pereira. *Lisbon in the Age of Dom João V (1689–1750)*. Lisbon: Instituto Português de Museus, 1994.

Alencastro, Luiz Felipe de. *The Trade in the Living: The Formation of Brazil in the South Atlantic, Sixteenth to Seventeenth Centuries*. Translated by Gavin Adams and Luiz Felipe de Alencastro. Albany: State University of New York Press, 2018.

Alessandrini, Nunziatella. "Italianos em bairros de Lisboa (século XVII)." *Cadernos do Arquivo Municipal* 2, no. 3 (January–June 2015): 109–25.

Alden, Dauril. "Vicissitudes of Trade in the Portuguese Atlantic Empire During the First Half of the Eighteenth Century: A Review Article." *Americas* 32, no. 2 (1975): 282–91.

Almeida, Fortunato de. *História de Portugal*. Vol. 5. Coimbra, Portugal: Fortunato de Almeida, 1928.

Almeida, Fortunato de, and Damião Peres. *História da igreja em Portugal*. Vol. 2. Porto, Portugal: Portucalense, 1967.

Almeida, Luís Ferrand de. *Aclimatação de plantas do Oriente no Brasil durante os séculos XVII e XVIII*. Coimbra, Portugal: Universidade de Coimbra, 1976.

———. *Um construtor naval Francês em Portugal e Espanha (1718–1721)*. Coimbra, Portugal: Universidade de Coimbra, 1964.

———. *Um construtor naval Inglês em Portugal (1721–1723)*. Coimbra, Portugal: Universidade de Coimbra, 1962.

———. "A fábrica das sedas de Lisboa no tempo de D. João V." *Revista Portuguesa de História* 25 (1990): 1–48.

———. *Páginas dispersas: Estudos de história moderna de Portugal*. Coimbra, Portugal: Universidade de Coimbra, 1995.

Almeida, M. Lopes de. "Portugal na época de D. João V: Esbôco de interpretação político-cultural da primeira metade do século XVIII." In *Atas do Colóquio Internacional de Estudos Luso-Brasileiros*, 253–59. Nashville: Vanderbilt University Press, 1953.

Almeida, Pedro Tavares de, and Paulo Silveira e Sousa, eds. *Do reino à administração interna: História de um ministério (1736–2012)*. Lisbon: Imprensa Nacional–Casa da Moeda, 2015.

Ameal, João. "D. João e a sua época." In *D. João V: Conferências e estudos comemorativos do segundo centenário da sua morte (1750–1950)*, 7–22. Lisbon: Publicações Culturais da Câmara Municipal de Lisboa, 1952.

Ames, Glenn J. "Pedro II and the Estado da India: Braganzan Absolutism and Overseas Empire, 1668–1683." *Luso-Brazilian Review* 34, no. 2 (1997): 1–13.

Antunes, Ana Maria Pessoa de Oliveira. "D. Nuno Álvares Pereira de Melo, 1 Duque de Cadaval (1638–1727)." 2 vols. Master's thesis, Universidade de Lisboa, 1997.

Antunes, Cátia. "Population Growth, Infrastructural Development and Economic Growth: Amsterdam and Lisbon in the 17th Century—A Comparison." In *European Seaport Systems in the Early Modern Age—A Comparative Approach, International Workshop, Proceedings*, edited by Amélia Polónia and Helena Osswald, 115–31. Porto, Portugal: Instituto de História Moderna, Universidade do Porto, 2007.

Apolloni, Marco Fabio. "Wondrous Vehicles: The Coaches of the Embassy of the Marquês de Fontes." In *The Age of the Baroque in Portugal*, edited by Jay A. Levenson, 89–100. Washington, DC: National Gallery of Art, 1993.

Araújo, Ana Cristina. "Ritualidade e poder na corte de D. João V: A génese simbólica do regalismo politico." *Revista de história das ideias* 22 (2001): 175–208.

Araújo, Ilídio de. *Quintas de recreio*. Braga, Portugal: Livraria Cruz, 1974.

Araújo, Maria Benedita. "Um 'papel em defença da gente de nasção' no tempo do regente D. Pedro." In *Carlos Alberto Ferreira de Almeida: In Memoriam*, edited by Mário Jorge Barroca, 1:125–37. Porto, Portugal: Faculdade de Letras da Universidade de Porto, 1999.

Arenas, Mar García. "La situación de los comerciantes españoles en Lisboa desde la perspectiva de los diplomáticos de la monarquía hispánica destinados en Portugal en el Setecientos." *Ammentu: Bollettino Storico e Archivistico del Mediterraneo e delle Americhe* 7 (July–December 2015): 91–113.

Armitage, David. "Three Concepts of Atlantic History." In *The British Atlantic World, 1500–1800*, edited by David Armitage and M. J. Braddick, 11–27. New York: Palgrave Macmillan, 2009.

Ascenso, María Eurídice da Costa Ramos. "A freguesia da Sé de Lisboa no primeiro quartel do século XVIII." Honors thesis, Universidade de Lisboa, 1960.

Azevedo, Carlos de. *Solares portugueses: Introdução ao estudo da casa nobre*. Mem Martins, Portugal: Livros Horizonte, 1988.

Azevedo, João Lúcio. *Épocas de Portugal económico: Esboços de história*. Lisbon: Livraria Clássica Editora, 1929.

———. *História de António Vieira*. 3rd ed. 2 vols. Lisbon: Clássica Editora, 1992.

———. *História dos cristãos-novos Portugueses*. 2nd ed. Lisbon: Livraria Clássica Editora, 1975.

Baião, António. *Episódios dramáticos da Inquisição portuguesa*. Vol. 3. Lisbon: Seara Nova, 1938.

Bailyn, Bernard. *Atlantic History: Concepts and Contours*. Cambridge: Harvard University Press, 2005.

Bairoch, Paul, Jean Batou, and Pierre Chèvre. *La population des villes Européennes, 800–1850: Banque de données et analyse sommaire des résultats*. Geneva: Librairie Droz, 1988.

Barnett, Richard D. "Diplomatic Aspects of the Sephardi Influx from Portugal in the Early Eighteenth Century." *Transactions of the Jewish Historical Society of England* 25 (1973): 210–21.

Barreiros, Maria Helena. "Urban Landscapes: Houses, Streets and Squares of 18th Century Lisbon." *Journal of Early Modern History* 12 (2008): 205–32.

Barreyre, Nicolas, Michael Heale, Stephen Tuck, and Cécile Vidal, eds. *Historians*

Across Borders: Writing American History in a Global Age. Berkeley: University of California Press, 2014.

Bassi, Ernesto. "Beyond Compartmentalized Atlantics: A Case for Embracing the Atlantic from Spanish American Shores." *History Compass* 12, no. 9 (2014): 704–16.

Bebiano, Rui. "D. João V, poder e espectáculo." In *Sociedade e cultura portuguesas*, edited by Maria José Ferro Tavares, António Camões Gouveia, and Manuel Filipe Cruz Canaveira, 2:138–63. Lisbon: Universidade Aberta, 1990.

———. "D. João V, rei sol." *Revista de História das Idéias* 8 (1986): 111–21.

———. "Metamorfoses do 'reinado do ouro.'" *Claro-Escuro* 2–3 (May–November 1989): 35–40.

Beier, Augustus Leon, and Roger Finlay. *London, 1500–1700: The Making of the Metropolis*. London: Longman, 1986.

Beloff, Max. *The Age of Absolutism, 1660–1815*. Watford, UK: Mayflower Press, 1954.

Bethencourt, Francisco. "Declínio e extinção do Santo Ofício." *Revista de História Económica e Social* 20 (1987): 77–85.

Bicalho, Maria Fernanda. "Inflexões na política imperial no reinado de D. João V." *Anais de História de Além-Mar* 8 (2007): 37–56.

Boxer, Charles Ralph. "Brazilian Gold and British Traders in the First Half of the Eighteenth Century." *Hispanic American Historical Review* 49, no. 3 (1969): 454–72.

———. *The English and the Portuguese Brazil Trade, 1660–1780: Some Problems and Personalities*. Bundoora, Australia: Institute of Latin American Studies, La Trobe University, 1981.

———. *The Golden Age of Brazil 1695–1750: Growing Pains of a Colonial Society*. Berkeley: University of California Press, 1962.

———. "A Great Luso-Brazilian Figure: Padre António Vieira, S.J., 1608–1697." The Canning House Annual Lecture, Februrary 6, 1957, Canning House, London. 4th Lecture. London: Hispanic and Luso-Brazilian Councils, 1963.

———. "Lord Tyrawly in Lisbon: An Anglo-Irish Protestant at the Portuguese Court, 1728–41." *History Today* 20, no. 11 (1970): 791–98.

———. "Pombal's Dictatorship and the Great Lisbon Earthquake, 1755." *History Today* 5, no. 11 (1955): 729–36.

———. *The Portuguese Seaborne Empire, 1415–1825*. New York: Alfred A. Knopf, 1969.

———. "Ribeiro Sanches: An Enlightened Portuguese." *History Today* 20, no. 4 (April 1970): 270–77.

———. *Salvador de Sá and the Struggle for Brazil and Angola, 1602–1686*. Westport, CT: Greenwood Press, 1975.

———. "Second Thoughts on the Anglo-Portuguese Alliance, 1661–1808." *History Today* 36, no. 6 (June 1986): 22–26.

———. *Some Contemporary Reactions to the Lisbon Earthquake of 1755*. Lisbon: Universidade de Lisboa, 1956.

———. "Vicissitudes of Anglo-Portuguese Relations in the 17th Century." In *600 Years of Anglo-Portuguese Alliance*, 27–30. London: BBC, Her Majesty's government, Canning House, [1960?].

Brading, David Anthony. "Bourbon Spain and Its American Empire." In *The Cambridge History of Latin America*, vol. 1, *Colonial Latin America*, edited by Leslie Bethell, 389–440. Cambridge: Cambridge University Press, 1984.

Braga, Isabel M. R. Mendes Drumond. *Bens de hereges: Inquisição e cultura material, Portugal e Brasil (séculos XVII–XVIII)*. Coimbra, Portugal: Universidade de Coimbra, 2012.

———. "Ecos dos problemas religiosos além Pirinéus no Portugal moderno." In *Estudos em homenagem a João Francisco Marques*, edited by Amélia Polónia, 1:231–49. Porto, Portugal: Faculdade de Letras da Universidade de Porto, 2001.

———. "A mulatice como impedimento de acesso ao 'Estado do Meio.'" In *Actas do Congresso Internacional—Espaço Atlântico de antigo regime: Poderes e sociedade*, 1–12. Lisbon: Instituto Camões, 2008.

Braga, Maria Luísa. *A Inquisição em Portugal: Primeira metade do século XVIII, O inquisidor geral D. Nuno da Cunha de Athayde e Mello*. Lisbon: Imprensa Nacional–Casa da Moeda, 1992.

Braga, Paulo Drumond de. "Alemães na Lisboa seiscentista: As conversões ao catolicismo." In *Portugal, Indien und Deutschland: Akten der V. Deutsch-Portugiesischen Arbeitsgespräche (Köln, 1998); Portugal, Índia e Alemanha: Actas do V Encontro Luso-Alemão*, edited by Helmut Siepmann, 421–34. Lisbon: Centro de Estudos Históricos, Universidade de Lisboa, 2000.

———. *Portugueses no estrangeiro, estrangeiros em Portugal*. Lisbon: Hugin Editores, 2005.

Branco, Manoel Bernardes. *Portugal na epocha de D. João V*. Lisbon: A. M. Pereira, 1886.

Brazão, Eduardo. *D. João V e a santa sé: As relações diplomáticas de Portugal com o govêrno pontifício de 1706 à 1750*. Coimbra, Portugal: Coimbra Editora, 1937.

———. *D. João V: Subsídios para a história do seu reinado*. Porto, Portugal: Portucalense Editora, 1945.

Brito, Manuel Carlos de. "Da ópera ao divino à ópera burguesa: A música e o teatro de D. João V a D. Maria I." In *Portugal no século XVIII de D. João V à revolução francesa—Congresso Internacional*, 314–18. Lisbon: Sociedade Portuguesa de Estudos do Século XVIII, Universitária Editora, 1991.

———. "A música profana e a ópera no tempo de D. João V: Vários factos e alguns argumentos." *Claro-Escuro* 2–3 (May–November 1989): 105–18.

Budasz, Rogério. "Black Guitar-Players and Early African-Iberian Music in Portugal and Brazil." *Early Music* 35, no. 1 (2007): 3–21.

Bulut, Mehmet. "Rethinking the Dutch Economy and Trade in the Early Modern Period, 1570–1680." *Journal of European Economic History* 32, no. 2 (2003): 391–424.

Burnard, Trevor. *The Atlantic in World History, 1490–1830*. London: Bloomsbury Academic, 2020.

Burnard, Trevor, and Cécile Vidal. "Location and the Conceptualization of Historical Frameworks: Early American History and Its Multiple Reconfigurations in the United States and Europe." In *Historians Across Borders: Writing American History in a Global Age*, edited by Nicolas Barreyre, Michael Heale, Stephen Tuck, and Cécile Vidal, 141–62. Berkeley: University of California Press, 2014.

Bustos, Manuel. *Historia de Cádiz: Los siglos decisivos*. Madrid: Silex, 1990.

Calado, Margarida. "Academia de Portugal em Roma." In *Dicionário da arte barroca em Portugal*, edited by José Fernandes Pereira and Paulo Pereira, 18. Lisbon: Editorial Presença, 1989.

Calainho, Daniela Buono. "Magias de cozinha: Escravas e feitiços em Portugal, séculos XVII e XVIII." *Cadernos Pagu* 39 (July–December 2012): 159–76.

———. *Metrópole das mandingas: Religiosidade negra e Inquisição Portuguesa no antigo regime*. Rio de Janeiro: Garamond, 2008.

Caldeira, Arlindo Manuel. *Escravos em Portugal, das origens ao século XIX*. Lisbon: A Esfera dos Livros, 2017.

———. "O Tabaco Brasileiro em Portugal: Divulgação e formas de consumo durante o antigo regime." In *Actas do Congresso Luso-Brasileiro*, edited by Maria Fernanda Correia, Eduardo Frutuoso, and Maria de Fátima Vasconcelos, 1:567–86. Lisbon, November 9–12, 1999. Lisbon: Grupo de Trabalho do Ministério da Educação, 2000.

Cañizares-Esguerra, Jorge, and Erik R. Seeman, eds. *The Atlantic in Global History, 1500–2000*. Upper Saddle River, NJ: Pearson Education, 2007.

Cardim, Pedro. "A corte régia e o alargamento da esfera privada." In *História da vida privada em Portugal: A idade moderna*, edited by José Mattoso and Nuno Gonçalo Monteiro, 160–201. Lisbon: Temas e Debates, 2011.

Cardim, Pedro, and Nuno Gonçalo Monteiro. *Political Thought in Portugal and Its Empire, c. 1500–1800*. Cambridge: Cambridge University Press, 2021.

Cardoso, José Luís. "Leitura e interpretação do tratado de Methuen: Balanço histórico e historiográfico." In *O tratado de Methuen (1703): Diplomacia, guerra, política e economia*, edited by João Vidigal, 11–29. Lisbon: Livros Horizonte, 2003.

Carnaxide, Visconde de (António de Sousa Pedroso). *D. João V e o Brasil: Ensaio sobre a política atlântica de Portugal na primeira metade do século XVIII*. Lisbon: Publicações Culturais da Câmara Municipal de Lisboa, 1952.

Carvalho, A. Ayres de. *D. João V e a arte do seu tempo*. 2 vols. Mafra, Portugal: Ayres de Carvalho, 1962.

Castelo-Branco, Fernando. *Lisboa seiscentista*. Lisbon: Livros Horizonte, 1990.

Ceia, Sara. "Os académicos teatinos no tempo de D. João V—Construir saberes enunciando poder." Master's thesis, Universidade Nova de Lisboa, 2010.

Chakravarti, Ananya. *Empire of Apostles: Religion, Accommodatio, and the Imagination of Empire in Early Modern Brazil and India*. Oxford: Oxford University Press, 2018.

Chantal, Suzanne. *A vida quotidiana em Portugal ao tempo do terramoto*. Translated by Álvaro Simões. Lisbon: Livro do Brasil, 1965.

Chaves, Castelo Branco. *O Portugal visto por três forasteiros*. 2nd ed. Lisbon: Biblioteca Nacional de Lisboa, 1989.

Claro, João V. *A Aliança inglesa: História e fim dum mito*. 2nd ed. Lausanne, Switzerland: Editorial Liberta, 1944.

Cobban, A. "The Enlightenment." In *The New Cambridge Modern History*, vol. 7, *The Old Regime, 1713–1763*, edited by J. O. Lindsay, 85–111. Cambridge: Cambridge University Press, 1963.

Coclanis, Peter A. "Atlantic World or Atlantic/World?" *William and Mary Quarterly*, 3rd ser., 63, no. 4 (October 2006): 725–42.

———. "Drang Nach Osten: Bernard Bailyn, the World-Island, and the Idea of Atlantic History." *Journal of World History* 13, no. 1 (Spring 2002): 169–82.

Colley, Linda. *Captives: Britain, Empire and the World, 1600–1850*. London: Jonathan Cape, 2002.

Cortesão, Jaime. *Alexandre de Gusmão e o tratado de Madrid*. 3 vols. Lisbon: Livros Horizonte, 1984.

———. "Domínio Ultramarino." In *História de Portugal*, edited by Damião Peres, 6:639–760. Barcelos: Portucalense Editora, 1976.

Costa, Leonor Freire. *Império e grupos mercantis entre o Oriente e o Atlântico (século XVII)*. Lisbon: Livros Horizonte, 2002.

———. *O transporte no Atlântico e a companhia geral do comércio do Brasil (1580–1663)*. Lisbon: Comissão Nacional para as Comemorações dos Descobrimentos Portugueses, 2002.

Costa, Leonor Freire, and Mafalda Soares da Cunha. *D. João IV*. Lisbon: Temas e Debates, 2008.

Costa, Leonor Freire, Pedro Lains, and Susana Münch Miranda. *An Economic History of Portugal, 1143–2010*. Cambridge: Cambridge University Press, 2016.

Costa, Leonor Freire, and Maria Manuela Rocha. "Merchant Networks and Brazilian Gold: Reappraising Colonial Monopolies." In *Redes y negócios globales en el mundo ibérico, siglos XVI–XVIII*, edited by Nikolaus Böttcher, Bernd Hausberger, and António Ibarra, 143–69. Madrid: Iberoamericana, Frankfurt am Main: Vervuert, 2011.

Costa, Leonor Freire, Maria Manuela Rocha, and Tanya Araújo. *O Ouro do Brasil*. Lisbon: Imprensa Nacional–Casa da Moeda, 2013.

———. "Social Capital and Economic Performance: Trust and Distrust in Eighteenth-Century Gold Shipments from Brazil." *European Review of Economic History* 15, no. 1 (2011): 1–27.

Costa, Leonor Freire, Maria Manuela Rocha, and Paulo B. Brito. "The Alchemy of

Gold: Interest Rates, Money Stock, and Credit in Eighteenth-Century Lisbon." *Economic History Review* 71, no. 4 (2018): 1147–72.

Costa, Leonor Freire, Maria Manuela Rocha, and Rita Martins de Sousa. "O ouro cruza o Atlântico." *Revista do Arquivo Público Mineiro* 41 (2005): 71–86.

Couto, Jorge. "D. João V." In *História de Portugal*, edited by João Medina, 7:243–67. Amadora, Portugal: Clube Internacional do Livro, 1995.

Cunha, Fanny Andrée Font Xavier da. "Ensino e difusão das ciências técnicas de D. João V à revolução francesa." In *Portugal no século XVIII de D. João V à revolução francesa—Congresso Internacional*, 411–18. Lisbon: Sociedade Portuguesa de Estudos do Século XVIII, Universitária Editora, 1991.

Cunha, Mafalda Soares da, and Nuno Gonçalo Monteiro. "Que casas são 'grandes casas'?" In *História da vida privada em Portugal: A idade moderna*, edited by José Mattoso and Nuno Gonçalo Monteiro, 202–43. Lisbon: Temas e Debates, 2011.

———. "Velhas formas: A casa e a comunidade na mobilização politica." In *História da vida privada em Portugal: A idade moderna*, edited by José Mattoso and Nuno Gonçalo Monteiro, 396–423. Lisbon: Temas e Debates, 2011.

Cunha, Norberto Ferreira da. *Elites e académicos na cultura portuguesa setecentista*. Lisbon: Imprensa Nacional–Casa da Moeda, 2000.

Delaforce, Angela. "Lisbon 'This New Rome,' Dom João V of Portugal and the Relations Between Rome and Lisbon." In *The Age of the Baroque in Portugal*, edited by Jay A. Levenson, 49–79. Washington, DC: National Gallery of Art, 1993.

Diamond, A. S. "Problems of the London Sephardi Community, 1720–1733—Philip Carteret Webb's Notebooks." *Transactions (Jewish Historical Society of England)* 21 (1968): 39–63.

Dias, Luís Fernando de Carvalho. *Os lanifícios na política económica do conde da Ericeira*. Lisbon: Soc. Inds. de Imprensa, 1954.

———. "Luxo e pragmáticas no pensamento económico do século XVIII." In *Boletim de Ciências Económias*, edited by José Joaquim Teixeira Ribeiro, 5:73–144. Coimbra, Portugal: Faculdade de Direito, 1956.

Disney, A. R. *A History of Portugal and the Portuguese Empire*. Vols. 1–2. New York: Cambridge University Press, 2009.

D. João V: Conferências e estudos comemorativos do segundo centenário da sua morte (1750–1950). Lisbon: Câmara Municipal, 1952.

Donovan, Bill M. "Commercial Enterprise and Luso-Brazilian Society During the Brazilian Gold Rush: The Mercantile House of Francisco Pinheiro, 1695–1750." PhD diss., Johns Hopkins University, 1990.

———. "Crime, Policing, and the Absolutist State in Early Modern Lisbon." *Portuguese Studies Review* 5, no. 2 (1997): 52–71.

Duro, António Rodovalho. *História do toureiro em Portugal*. Lisbon: Antiga Casa Bertrand-Livraria Editora, 1907.

Dutra, Francis. "Ser mulato nos primórdios da modernidade portuguesa." *Tempo* 30 (2011): 101–14.

Elliott, John. "Afterword: Atlantic History; A Circumnavigation." In *The British Atlantic World, 1500–1800*, edited by David Armitage and Michael J. Braddick, 253–70. New York: Palgrave, 2002.

Falcon, Francisco José Calazans. *A época Pombalina: Política econômica e monarquia Ilustrada*. São Paulo: Editora Ática, 1982.

Farnsworth, Cacey, and Pedro Cardim. "Mulheres negras protestam em Lisboa em 1717." In *Resistências: Insubmissão e revolta no império português*, edited by Mafalda Soares da Cunha, 217–24. Alfragide: Casa das Letras, 2021.

Ferrão, Leonor. "Lisboa barroca da restauração ao terramoto de 1755: Desenvolvimento urbanístico, os palácios e os conventos." In *O Livro de Lisboa*, edited by Irisalva Moita, 239–82. Lisbon: Livros Horizonte, 1994.

Fisher, Harold Edward Stephen. "Lisbon, Its English Merchant Community and the Mediterranean in the Eighteenth Century." In *Shipping, Trade and Commerce*, edited by P. L. Cottrell, Derek Howard Aldcroft, and Ralph Davis, 23–44. Leicester, UK: Leicester University Press, 1981.

———. *The Portugal Trade: A Study of Anglo-Portuguese Commerce, 1700–1770.* London: Methuen, 1971.

Fonseca, Célia Freire A. "Comércio e Inquisição no Brasil do século XVIII." In *Inquisição: Ensaios sobre mentalidade, heresias e arte*, edited by Anita Waingort Novinsky and Maria Luiza Tucci Carneiro, 195–202. Rio de Janeiro: Expressão e Cultura, 1992.

Fonseca, Jorge. *Escravos e senhores na Lisboa quinhentista.* Lisbon: Edições Colibri, 2010.

———. *Escravos no sul de Portugal, séculos XVI–XVII.* Lisbon: Editora Vulgata, 2000.

———. *Religião e liberdade: Os negros nas irmandades e confrarias portuguesas (séculos XV a XIX).* Ribeirão, Portugal: Edições Húmus, 2016.

França, José–Augusto. *Lisboa: História física e moral.* 2nd ed. Lisbon: Livros Horizonte, 2009.

———. *A Reconstrução de Lisboa e a arquitectura pombalina.* 3rd ed. Lisbon: Biblioteca Breve, 1989.

Francis, Alan David. "The Anglo-Portuguese Alliance in the 18th Century." In *600 Years of Anglo-Portuguese Alliance,* 31–35. London: BBC, Her Majesty's government, Canning House, [1960?].

———. *The Methuens and Portugal, 1691–1708.* Cambridge: Cambridge University Press, 1966.

———. *Portugal 1715–1808: Joanine, Pombaline and Rococo Portugal as seen by British Diplomats and Traders.* London: Tamesis, 1985.

Fuente, Alejandro de la. *Havana and the Atlantic in the Sixteenth Century.* Chapel Hill: University of North Carolina Press, 2008.

Gallas, Fernando Disperati, and Alfredo O. G. Gallas. *O barroco no reinado de D. João V: Arquitectura, moedas e medalhas.* São Paulo: Gallas Disperati Serviços Empresariais, 2012.

Games, Alison. "Atlantic History: Definitions, Challenges, and Opportunities." *American Historical Review* 111, no. 3 (2006): 741–57.

García, Arturo Morgado. "Los caminos de la esclavitud en el Cádiz de la modernidad (1650–1750)." *Historia Social*, no. 67 (2010): 3–21.

———. *Una metrópoli escalvista: El Cádiz de la modernidad.* Granada, Spain: Universidad de Granada, 2013.

Gash-Tomás, José L., and Susana Münch Miranda. "Imperial Economies." In *The Iberian World: 1450–1820*, edited by Fernando Bouza, Pedro Cardim, and António Feros, 431–48. New York: Routledge, 2020.

Gauci, Perry. *Emporium of the World: The Merchants of London, 1660–1800.* London: Hambledon Continuum, 2007.

Gelderblom, Oscar. *Cities of Commerce: The Institutional Foundations of International Trade in the Low Countries, 1250–1650.* Princeton: Princeton University Press, 2013.

Geremia, Claudia. "L'Inquisizione spagnola nelle Isole Canarie: Tracce di stregoneria Africana, XVI–XVIII sec." PhD diss., Università di Firenze, 2022.

Gerzina, Gretchen. *Black England: Life Before Emancipation.* London: John Murray, 1995.

Godinho, Vitorino Magalhães. "Portugal and Her Empire, 1680–1720." In *The New Cambridge Modern History*, vol. 6, *The Rise of Great Britain and Russia, 1668–1715/25*, edited by John Selwyn Bromley, 509–39. Cambridge: Cambridge University Press, 1970.

———. "Portugal and the Making of the Atlantic World: Sugar Fleets and Gold Fleets, the Seventeenth to the Eighteenth Centuries." Translated by Dale Tomich. *Review (Fernand Braudel Center)* 28, no. 4 (2005): 313–37.

Gonçalves, Paula Alexandra Grazina. "Usos e consumos de tabaco em Portugal nos séculos XVI e XVII." Master's thesis, Universidade Nova de Lisboa, 2003.

Grafe, Regina, and Jorge M. Pedreira. "New Imperial Economies." In *The Iberian World: 1450–1820*, edited by Fernando Bouza, Pedro Cardim, and António Feros, 582–614. New York: Routledge, 2020.

Greene, Jack P., and Philip D. Morgan, eds. *Atlantic History: A Critical Appraisal.* Oxford: Oxford University Press, 2009.

Griffin, Patrick. "A Plea for a New Atlantic History." *William and Mary Quarterly* 68, no. 2 (April 2011): 236–39.

Gschwend, Annemarie Jordan, and Kate J. P. Lowe, eds. *The Global City: On the Streets of Renaissance Lisbon.* London: Paul Holberton, 2015.

Guedes, João Alfredo Libânio. *História administrativa do Brasil.* Vol. 4, *Da Restauração a D. João V.* 2nd ed. Edited by Vicente Tapajós. Brasília, Brazil: Fundação Centro de Formação do Servidor Público, 1984.

Guichard, François. "Le Protestantisme au Portugal." *Arquivos do Centro Cultural Português* 28, no. 1 (1990): 455–82.

Guimarães, J. Ribeiro. *Summario de varia história: Narrativas, lendas, biographias, descripções de templos e monumentos, estatísticas, costumes civis, políticos e religiosos de outras eras.* Vol. 3. Lisbon: Rolland & Semiond, 1873.

Hamm, Brian. "Between the Foreign and the Familiar. The Portuguese, the Inquisition, and Local Society in Cartagena de Índias, 1550–1700." PhD diss., University of Florida, 2017.

Hancock, David. *Oceans of Wine: Madeira and the Emergence of American Trade and Taste.* New Haven: Yale University Press, 2009.

Hansen, João Adolfo, Marcello Moreira, and Caio Cesar Esteves de Souza. "Nota sobre a 'sátira geral a todo o reino, e governo de Portugal." *Teresa: Revista de Literatura Brasileira* 17 (2016): 167–90.

Hanson, Carl A. *Economy and Society in Baroque Portugal, 1668–1703.* Minneapolis: University of Minnesota Press, 1981.

———. "Monopoly and Contraband in the Portuguese Tobacco Trade, 1624–1702." *Luso-Brazilian Review* 19, no. 2 (1982): 149–68.

Hatfield, April Lee. *Atlantic Virginia: Intercolonial Relations in the Seventeenth Century.* Philadelphia: University of Pennsylvania Press, 2007.

Henriques, Isabel Castro. *Os Africanos em Portugal: História e memória, séculos XV–XXI.* Lisbon: Mercado de Letras Editores, 2011.

———. *A herança Africana em Portugal.* Lisbon: CTT Correios de Portugal, 2009.

Hespanha, António Manuel. *As vésperas do leviathan: Instituições e poder político, Portugal século XVII.* Coimbra, Portugal: Livraria Almedina, 1994.

Hondius, Dienke. "Black Africans in Seventeenth-Century Amsterdam." *Renaissance and Reformation* 3, no. 2 (2008): 87–105.

Israel, Jonathan. *The Dutch Republic: Its Rise, Greatness, and Fall, 1744–1806.* Oxford: Oxford University Press, 1995.

———. *Empires and Entrepots: The Dutch, The Spanish Monarchy, and the Jews, 1585–1713.* London: Hambeldon Press, 1990.

Kamen, Henry. *Philip V of Spain: The King Who Reigned Twice.* New Haven: Yale University Press, 2001.

———. *The Spanish Inquisition.* New York: New American Library, 1965.

Kolfin, Elmer, and Epco Runia, eds. *Black in Rembrandt's Time.* Amsterdam: The Rembrandt House Museum, 2020.

Kooi, Christine. *Calvinists and Catholics During Holland's Golden Age: Heretics and Idolaters.* Cambridge: Cambridge University Press, 2021.

Labourdette, Jean-François. "L'ambassade de Monsieur de Chavigny á Lisbonne (1740–1743)." *Bulletin du centre d'historie des espaces atlantiques*, 1st ser. (1983): 27–80.

———. *La nation française a Lisbonne de 1669 a 1790: Entre colbertisme et liberalisme*. Paris: Fondation Calouste Gulbenkian Centre Culturel Portugais, 1988.

Lahon, Didier. "Da redução da alteridade a consagração da diferença: As irmandades negras em Portugal (séculos XVI–XVIII)." *Projecto História* 44 (June 2012): 53–83.

———. "Eles vão, eles vêm: Escravos e libertos negros entre Lisboa e o Grão-Pará e Maranhão (séculos XVII–XIX)." *Revista Estudos Amazônicos* 6, no. 1 (2011): 70 99.

———. "Esclavage, confréries noires, sainteté noire et pureté de sang au Portugal (XVIe et XVIIIe siècles)." *Lusitânia Sacra*, 2nd ser., 15 (2003): 119–62.

———. "Esclavage et confréries noires au Portugal durant l'ancien régime (1441–1830)." 2 vols. PhD diss., Ecole des Hautes Etudes en Sciences Sociales, 2001.

———. "O escravo Africano na vida económica e social Portuguesa do antigo regime." *Africana Studia* 7 (2004): 73–100.

———. "Exclusion, integration et métissage dans les confréries noires au Portugal (XVIe–XIXe siècles)." In *Negros, mulatos, zambaigos: Derroteros Africanos en los mundos íbericos*, edited by Berta Ares Queija, and Alessandro Stella, 275–311. Seville, Spain: Escuela de Estudios Hispano-Americanos, Consejo Superior de Investagaciónes Cíentificas, 2000.

———. *O negro no coração do império: Uma memória para resgatar, séculos XV–XIX*. Lisbon: Secretário coordenador dos programas de educação multicultural, Ministério da Educação, Casa do Brasil, 1999.

Large, Joshua, and Juan Camilo Miranda. "British Slaves in Early Modern Portugal." *Revista de Estudos Anglo-Portugueses* 23 (2014): 151–79.

Law, Robin. "Ethnicities of Enslaved Africans in the Diaspora: On the Meanings of 'Mina' (Again)." *History in Africa* 32 (2005): 247–67.

Levenson, Jay A., ed. *The Age of the Baroque in Portugal*. Washington, DC: National Gallery of Art, 1993.

Lobato, Manuel. "A Guerra dos Maratas." In *Nova história militar de Portugal*, edited by Manuel Themudo Barata, Nuno Severiano Teixeira, and António Manuel Hespanha, 2:317–29. Rio de Mouró, Portugal: Círculo de Leitores, 2004.

Lodge, Sir Richard. "The English Factory at Lisbon: Some Chapters in Its History." *Transactions of the Royal Historical Society*, 16 (1933): 211–47.

———. "Historical Revision: LXV—the Methuen Treaties of 1703." *History*, n.s., 18, no. 69 (1933): 33–35.

———. *The Private Correspondence of Sir Benjamin Keene, K.B.* Cambridge: Cambridge University Press, 1933.

Lopes, Maria de Jesus dos Mártires. *Goa setecentista: Tradição e modernidade, 1750–1800*. 2nd ed. Lisbon: Universidade Católica Portuguesa, 1999.

López-Cordón, M. Victoria, and Nuno Gonçalo Monteiro. "Enlightened Politics in Portugal and Spain." In *The Iberian World: 1450–1820*, edited by Fernando Bouza, Pedro Cardim, and António Feros, 475–99. New York: Routledge, 2020.

Lough, J. "France Under Louis XIV." In *The New Cambridge Modern History*, vol. 5, *The Ascendancy of France, 1648–1688*, edited by Francis Ludwig Carsten, 222–47. Cambridge: Cambridge University Press, 1964.

Lourenço, Maria Paula Marçal. *D. Pedro II: O pacífico (1648–1706)*. Lisbon: Temas e Debates, 2010.

Lourenço, Maria Paula Marçal, Ana Cristina Pereira, and Joana Troni. *Amantes dos reis de Portugal*. 7th ed. Lisbon: A Esfera dos Livros, 2008.

Lousada, Maria Alexandre. "Nova formas: Vida privada, sociabilidades culturais e emergência do espaço público." In *História da vida privada em Portugal: A idade moderna*, edited by José Mattoso and Nuno Gonçalo Monteiro, 424–56. Lisbon: Temas e Debates, 2011.

Lydon, James G. *Fish and Flour for Gold, 1600–1800: Southern Europe in the Colonial Balance of Payments*. Philadelphia: The Library Company of Philadelphia, 2008.

Macaulay, Rose. *They Went to Portugal*. Middlesex, UK: Penguin Books, 1985.

———. *They Went to Portugal Too*. Manchester: Carcanet Press, 1990.

Macedo, Jorge Borges de. "Absolutismo." In *Dicionário da história de Portugal*, edited by Joel Serrão, 1:12–13. Porto, Portugal: Livraria Figueirinhas, 1992.

———. "D. João V." In *Dicionário de história Portuguesa*, edited by Joel Serrão, 3:399–401. Porto, Portugal: Livraria Figueirinhas, 1992.

———. "Do poder absoluto ao absolutismo de estado: A sociedade e as suas formas de expressão: As invasões e a resistência nacional." In *Grande Enciclopédia Portuguesa e Brasileira–Atlas histórico*, edited by Fernando Capela, 351–53. Lisbon: Editorial Enciclopédia Limitada, 1991.

———. "Nobreza." In *Dicionário de história de Portugal*, edited by Joel Serrão, 4:392–94. Porto, Portugal: Livraria Figueirinhas, 1992.

———. *Problemas de história da indústria Portuguesa no século XVIII*. Lisbon: Associação Industrial Portuguesa, 1963.

Madureira, Nuno Luís. *Cidade: Espaço e quotidiano, Lisboa 1740–1830*. Lisbon: Livros Horizonte, 1992.

Mandrou, Robert. *L'Europe "absolutiste": Raison et raison d'etat, 1649–1775*. Paris: Fayard, 1977.

Marques, António Henrique Rodrigo de Oliveira. *História da Maçonaria em Portugal*. Vol. 1. Lisbon: Editorial Presença, 1990.

———. *History of Portugal*. Vol. 1, *From Lusitania to Empire*. New York: Columbia University Press, 1972.

Marques, Pedro João. *Portugal e a escravatura dos Africanos*. Lisbon: Imprensa de Ciências Sociais, 2004.

Martínez, María Elena. *Genealogical Fictions: Limpieza de Sangre, Religion, and Gender in Colonial Mexico*. Stanford: Stanford University Press, 2008.

Martins, António Coimbra. "Estrangeirados." In *Dicionário de história de Portugal*, edited by Joel Serrão, 2:466–73. Porto, Portugal: Livraria Figueirinhas, 1992.

Martins, Jorge. *Portugal e os Judeus*. Vol. 1. Lisbon: Nova Vega, 2006.

Matias, Elze Maria Henny Vonk. *Guia ilustrativo das academias literárias portugueses dos séculos XVII e XVIII*. Vol. 1. Lisbon: n.p., 1995.

Matos, Gastão de Melo de. "Lisboa na restauração." In *Lisboa: Oito séculos de história*, edited by Gustavo de Matos Sequeira, 2:437–66. Lisbon: Câmara Municipal, 1947.

Matos, Luís Lopes, and Maria Cristina Neto. "Cemitério Inglês." In *Dicionário da história de Lisboa*, edited by Francisco Santana, 252. Sacavém, Portugal: Quintas, 1994.

Mauro, Frédéric. "La bourgeoisie portugaise au XVIIe siècle." *XVIIe siècle* 40 (1958): 235–57.

Maxwell, Kenneth. *Conflicts and Conspiracies: Brazil and Portugal, 1750–1808*. New York: Routledge, 2004.

———. "Eighteenth-Century Portugal: Faith and Reason, Tradition and Innovation During a Golden Age." In *The Age of the Baroque in Portugal*, edited by Jay A. Levenson, 103–31. Washington, DC: National Gallery of Art, 1993.

———. *Pombal: Paradox of the Enlightenment*. Cambridge: Cambridge University Press, 1995.

McLachlan, Jean O. *Trade and Peace with Old Spain, 1667–1750: A Study of the Influence of Commerce on Anglo-Spanish Diplomacy in the First Half of the Eighteenth Century*. Cambridge: Cambridge University Press, 1940.

Mendes, Rui Manuel Mesquita. "Comunidade Flamenga e Holandesa em Lisboa (séculos XV a XVIII): Algumas notas históricas e patrimoniais." *Ammentu: Bollettino Storico e Archivistico del Mediterraneo e delle Americhe* 7 (July–December 2015): 57–90.

Menezes, Avelino de Freitas de, org. *Nova história de Portugal*. Vol. 7, *Da paz de restauração ao ouro do Brasil*. Edited by Joel Serrão and A. H. de Oliveira Marques. Lisbon: Editorial Presença, 2001.

Molesky, Mark. *This Gulf of Fire: The Destruction of Lisbon, or Apocalypse in the Age of Science and Reason*. New York: Alfred A. Knopf, 2015.

Monteiro, Henrique Jorge Coutinho de Almeida. "A população Portuguesa por 1700." Master's thesis, Universidade de Porto, 1997.

Monteiro, Nuno Gonçalo. *O crepúsculo dos grandes: A casa e o património da aristocracia em Portugal (1750–1832)*. Lisbon: Imprensa Nacional–Casa da Moeda, 1998.

———. *D. José: Na sombra de Pombal*. Lisbon: Temas e Debates, 2008.

———. "Identificação da política setecentista: Notas sobre Portugal no início do período joanino." *Análise Social* 35, no. 157 (2001): 961–87.

———. "A secretaria de estado dos negócios do reino e a administração de antigo regime (1736–1807)." In *Do reino à administração interna: História de um ministério (1736–2012)*, edited by Pedro Tavares de Almeida and Paulo Silveira e Sousa, 23–38. Lisbon: Imprensa Nacional–Casa da Moeda, 2015.

Moreno, Isodoro. *La antigua hermandad de los negros de Sevilla: Etnicidad, poder y sociedad en 600 años de historia*. Seville, Spain: Universidad de Sevilla, 1997.

Mota, Isabel Ferreira da. *A academia real da história: Os intelectuais, o poder cultural, e o poder monárquico no século XVIII*. Coimbra, Portugal: Edições MinervaCoimbra, 2003.

Murteira, Helena. "A cidade capital e o conceito moderno de espaço urbano: Lisboa, Paris e Londres." In *Actas do colóquio internacional universo urbanístico português, 1415–1822*, edited by Walter Rossa, Renata Araujo, and Hélder Carita, 461–71. Lisbon: Comissão Nacional para as Comemorações dos Descobrimentos Portugueses, 2001.

———. *Lisboa da restauração às luzes*. Lisbon: Editorial Presença, 1999.

Neto, Maria de Lourdes Akola da Cunha Meira do Carmo da Silva. *A freguesia de Nossa Senhora das Mercês de Lisboa no primeiro quartel do século XVIII: Ensaio de demografia histórica*. Lisbon: Centro de Estudos Demográficos, 1967.

———. *A freguesia de Santa Catarina de Lisboa no primeiro quartel do século XVIII: Ensaio de demografia histórica*. Lisbon: Centro de Estudos Demográficos, 1959.

Neto, Maria de Lourdes Akola da Cunha Meira do Carmo da Silva, Bernardino de Lima Remédio, and Maria Margarida Rodrigues Remédio. "A freguesia do Santíssimo Sacramento de Lisboa no primeiro quartel do século XVIII: Ensaio de demografia histórica." *Revista de Estudos Demográficos* 50 (2013): 91–126.

Novinsky, Anita Waingort. *Inquisição: Inventários de bens confiscados a Cristãos Novos, fontes para a história de Portugal e do Brasil (Brasil-Século XVIII)*. Lisbon: Imprensa Nacional–Casa da Moeda, Livraria Camões, 1977.

O'Flanagan, Patrick. *Port Cities of Atlantic Iberia, c. 1500–1900*. Burlington, VT: Ashgate, 2008.

Olival, Fernanda. "Os lugares e espaços do privados nos grupos populares e intermédios." In *História da vida privada em Portugal: A idade moderna*, edited by José Mattoso and Nuno Gonçalo Monteiro, 244–75. Lisbon: Temas e Debates, 2011.

———. *As ordens militares e o estado moderno: Honra, mercê e venalidade em Portugal (1641–1789)*. Lisbon: Estar Editora, 2001.

———. "Rigor e interesses: Os estatutos de limpeza de sangue em Portugal." *Cadernos de Estudos Sefarditas* 4 (2004): 151–82.

Oliveira, António Braz de. "As execuções capitais em Portugal num curioso manuscrito de 1843." *Revista da Biblioteca Nacional* 2, no. 1 (1982): 109–27.

Oliveira, Francisca Maria Castilho Pacheco França de. "A freguesia de São Cristovão de Lisboa no primeiro quartel do século XVIII." Honors thesis, Universidade de Lisboa, 1965.

Oliveira, Ricardo de. "As metamorfoses do império e os problemas da monarquia portuguesa na primeira metade do século XVIII." *Vária História* 26, no. 43 (2010): 109–29.

Ortiz, Antonio Domínguez. *Historia de Sevilla: La Sevilla del siglo XVII.* Seville, Spain: Universidad de Sevilla, 2006.

Paice, Edward. *Wrath of God: The Great Lisbon Earthquake of 1755.* London: Quercus, 2008.

Paiva, José Pedro. *Bruxaria e superstição num país sem "caça às bruxas," 1600–1774.* Lisbon: Editorial Nóticias, 1997.

Palma, Nuno, and Jaime Reis. "From Convergence to Divergence: Portuguese Economic Growth, 1527–1850." *European Historical Economics Society Working Papers in Economic History,* no. 137 (August 2018): 1–51.

Paquette, Gabriel. *The European Seaborne Empires: From the Thirty Years' War to the Age of Revolutions.* New Haven: Yale University Press, 2019.

———. *Imperial Portugal in the Age of Revolutions: The Luso-Brazilian World, c. 1770–1850.* Cambridge: Cambridge University Press, 2013.

Pedreira, Jorge Miguel de Melo Viana. "Costs and Financial Trends in the Portuguese Empire, 1415–1822." In *Portuguese Oceanic Expansion, 1400–1800,* edited by Francisco Bethencourt and Diogo Ramada Curto, 49–87. New York: Cambridge University Press, 2007.

———. "Diplomacia, manufacturas e desenvolvimento económico: Em torno do mito de Methuen." In *O Tratado de Methuen (1703): Diplomacia, guerra, política e economia,* edited by João Vidigal, 131–56. Lisbon: Livros Horizonte, 2003.

———. "Os homens de negócio da praça de Lisboa de Pombal ao Vintismo (1755–1822): Diferenciação, reprodução e identificação de um grupo social." PhD diss., Universidade Nova de Lisboa, 1995.

———. "Indústria e atraso económico em Portugal, 1800–1825." Master's thesis, Universidade Nova de Lisboa, 1986.

———. "Os negociantes de Lisboa na segunda metade do século XVIII: Padrões de recrutamento e percursos sociais." *Análise Social* 27 (1992): 407–40.

———. "To Have and to Have Not, the Economic Consequences of Empire: Portugal 1415–1822." *Revista de história económica* 16 (1998): 93–122.

Pedreira, Jorge Miguel de Melo Viana, Leonor Freire Costa, Nuno Palma, and Jaime Reis. "The Great Escape? The Contribution of the Empire to Portugal's Economic Growth, 1500–1800." *European Review of Economic History* 19 (2014): 1–22.

Pereira, Fernando António Baptista. "Lisboa barroca da restauração ao terramoto de 1755: A vida e mentalidade do espaço, do tempo e da morte." In *O Livro de Lisboa,* edited by Irisalva Moita, 343–62. Lisbon: Livros Horizonte, 1994.

Pereira, José Fernandes, and Paulo Pereira, eds. *Dicionário da arte barroca em Portugal.* Lisbon: Editorial Presença, 1989.

Pereira, Luísa Villarinho. "Ourives franceses, lapidários e engastadores de pedraria na Lisboa do século XVIII: Seu contributo na arte e na evolução das mentalidades." *Ammentu: Bollettino Storico e Archivistico del Mediterraneo e delle Americhe* 7 (July–December 2015): 104–13.

Peres, Damião, ed. *História de Portugal.* Vol. 6. Barcelos, Portugal: Portucalense Editora, 1976.

Phillips, William D. *Slavery in Medieval and Early Modern Iberia.* Philadelphia: University of Pennsylvania Press, 2014.

Pieroni, Geraldo. "Outcasts from the Kingdom: The Inquisition and the Banishment of New Christians to Brazil." In *The Jews and the Expansion of Europe to the West, 1450–1800,* edited by

Paolo Bernardini and Norman Fiering, 242–54. New York: Berghahn Books, 2001.

Pijning, Ernst. "Passive Resistance: Portuguese Diplomacy of Contraband Trade During King John V's Reign." *Arquipélago História*, 2nd ser., no. 2 (1997): 171–91.

Pimentel, António Filipe. *Arquitectura e poder: O real edifício de Mafra*. Lisbon: Livros Horizonte, 2002.

———. "Les grandes entreprises du roi D. João V." In *Triomphe du baroque*, 34–41. Brussels: Fondation Europalia International, 1991.

Pinto, Virgílio Noya. *O ouro brasileiro e o comércio anglo-português: Uma contribuição aos estudos da economia atlântica no século XVIII*. São Paulo: Companhia Editora Nacional, 1979.

Polónia, Amélia. "Dinâmicas comerciais e interacções sociais: Os portos de Lisboa e Porto nos séculos XVII e XVIII." In *La ciudad portuaria atlántica en la historia: Siglos XVI–XIX*, edited by José Ignacio Fortea Pérez and Juan E. Gelabert, 243–80. Santander, Spain: Universidade de Cantabria, 2006.

———. *Estudos em homenagem a João Francisco Marques*. Porto, Portugal: Faculdade de Letras da Universidade de Porto, 2001.

Polónia, Amélia, and Francisco Mangas, eds. *Mobilidades: Olhares transdisciplinares sobre um conceito global*. Porto, Portugal: CITCEM, 2021.

Ponte, Mark. "Black in Amsterdam around 1650." In *Black in Rembrandt's Time*, edited by Elmer Kolfin and Epco Runia, 44–59. Amsterdam: The Rembrandt House Museum, 2020.

Postlethwayt, Malachy. *The Universal Dictionary of Trade and Commerce*. Vol. 1. 3rd ed. London: n.p., 1766.

Prestage, Edgar. *Chapters in Anglo-Portuguese Relations*. Westport, CT: Greenwood Press, 1971.

———. *The Mode of Government in Portugal During the Restoration Period*. Lisbon: Instituto Para a Alta Cultura, 1949.

———. *The Royal Power and the Cortes in Portugal*. Watford, UK: Voss and Michael, 1927.

Raminelli, Ronald. "Impedimentos da cor: Mulatos no Brasil e em Portugal c. 1640–1750." *Vária História* 28, no. 48 (2012): 699–723.

———. "'Los límites del honor': Nobles y jerarquías de Brasil, Nueva España y Perú, siglos XVII y XVIII." *Revista Compultense de Historia de América* 40 (2014): 45–68.

———. *Nobrezas do novo mundo: Brazil e ultramar hispânico, séculos XVII e XVIII*. Rio de Janeiro: Editora FGV, 2015.

Rau, Virgínia. *Subsídios para o estudo do movimento dos portos de Faro e Lisboa durante o século XVII*. Lisbon: Academia Portuguesa de História, 1954.

Reginaldo, Lucilene. "'África em Portugal': Devoções, irmandades e escravidão no reino de Portugal, século XVIII." *História* 28, no. 1 (2009): 289–319.

Remedios, Joaquim Mendes dos. "Depois da restauração de D. João IV." *Biblos* 4, nos. 3–4 (1928): 87–121.

Ribeiro, Mário de Sampayo. "El-rei D. João, o quinto, e a música no seu tempo." In *D. João V: Conferências e estudos comemorativos do segundo centenário da sua morte (1750–1950)*, 65–90. Lisbon: Publicações Culturais da Câmara Municipal de Lisboa, 1952.

Rijo, Delminda. "Escravos e libertos na sociedade de Lisboa do século XVII: Fragmentos de existências." In *Mobilidades: Olhares transdisciplinares sobre um conceito global*, edited by Amélia Polónia and Francisco Mangas, 275–306. Porto, Portugal: CITCEM, 2021.

———. "Os escravos na Lisboa joanina." *Cultura, Espaço, e Memória* 3 (2012): 111–29.

Rijo, Delminda, Fátima Aragonez, and Francisco Moreira. "A freguesia de Santa Justa na transição para o século XVIII: História, demografia, e sociedade." In *Família, espaço, e património*, edited by Carlota Santos, 95–121. Porto, Portugal:

Centro de Investigação Transdisciplinar, 2011.

Rodrigues, Teresa. *Cinco séculos de quotidiano: A vida em Lisboa do século XV aos nossos dias.* Lisbon: Edições Cosmos, 1997.

Rossa, Walter. *Beyond Baixa: Signs of Urban Planning in Eighteenth Century Lisbon.* Lisbon: Ministério da Cultura, Instituto Português do Património Arquitectónico, 1998.

———. "Lisbon's Waterfront Image as an Allegory of Baroque Urban Aesthetics." In *Circa 1700: Architecture in Europe and the Americas*, edited by Henry A. Millon, 161–85. Washington, DC: National Gallery of Art, 2005.

Rossini, Gabriel Almeida Antunes. "As pragmáticas Portuguesas de fins do século XVII: Pólitica fabril e manufatureira reativa." *Saeculum— Revista de História* 22 (January–June 2010): 117–35.

Rothschild, Emma. "Late Atlantic History." In *The Oxford Handbook of the Atlantic World, 1450–1850*, edited by Nicholas Canny and Philip Morgan, 634–48. Oxford: Oxford University Press, 2011.

Russell-Wood, Anthony John R. "Black and Mulatto Brotherhoods in Colonial Brazil: A Study in Collective Behavior." *Hispanic American Historical Review* 54, no. 4 (1974): 567–602.

———. "God and Mammon: Ecclesiastical Participation in the Flow of Bullion from Brazil to Portugal During the Reign of Dom João V." In *Portugal no século XVIII de D. João V à revolução francesa— Congresso Internacional*, edited by Maria Helena Carvalho dos Santos, 191–209. Lisbon: Sociedade Portuguesa de Estudos do Século XVIII, Universitária Editora, 1991.

———. "Portugal and the World in the Age of Dom João V." In *The Age of the Baroque in Portugal*, edited by Jay A. Levenson, 15–29. Washington, DC: National Gallery of Art, 1993.

Santana, Francisco. *Bruxas e curandeiros na Lisboa joanina.* Lisbon: Academia Portuguesa de História, 1997.

———. "Processos de escravos e forros na Inquisição de Lisboa." *Ler História* 13 (1988): 15–30.

Santarém, Visconde de (Manuel Francisco de Barros e Sousa). *Quadro elementar das relações políticas e diplomáticas de Portugal com as diversas potências do mundo.* Vol. 5. Paris: J. P. Aillaud, 1845.

Santos, Raul Esteves dos. *Os tabacos: Sua influência na vida da nação.* Vol. 1. Lisbon: Seara Nova, 1974.

Saraiva, António José, H. P. Salomon, and I. S. D. Sassoon. *The Marrano Factory: The Portuguese Inquisition and Its New Christians, 1536–1765.* English edition. Leiden: Brill, 2001.

Saunders, A. C. de C. M. *A Social History of Black Slaves and Freedmen in Portugal, 1441–1555.* Cambridge: Cambridge University Press, 1982.

Scarano, Julita. "Black Brotherhoods: Integration or Contradiction?" *Luso-Brazilian Review* 16, no. 1 (1979): 1–17.

Schneider, Susan. *O marquês de Pombal e o vinho do Porto: Dependência e subdesenvolvimento em Portugal no século XVIII.* Lisbon: A Regra do Jogo, 1980.

Schwartz, Stuart B. *All Can Be Saved: Religious Tolerance and Salvation in the Iberian Atlantic World.* New Haven: Yale University Press, 2008.

———. "Plantations and Peripheries, c. 1580–1750." In *Colonial Brazil*, edited by Leslie Bethell, 67–144. Cambridge: Cambridge University Press, 1987.

———. *Sugar Plantations in the Formation of Brazilian Society: Bahia, 1550–1835.* Cambridge: Cambridge University Press, 1985.

Sequeira, Gustavo de Matos. "A cidade de D. João V." In *D. João V: Conferências e estudos comemorativos do segundo centenário da sua morte (1750–1950)*, 41–64. Lisbon: Publicações Culturais da Câmara Municipal de Lisboa, 1952.

———. *Encyclopédia Pela Imagem: História do trajo em Portugal.* Porto, Portugal: Livraria Chardron, Lello & Irmão, n.d.

Sequeira, Gustavo de Matos, and Luiz Pastor de Macedo. *A nossa Lisboa*. Lisbon: Portugália Editora, [1940?].

Serrão, Joaquim Veríssimo. *História de Portugal*. Vol. 5. 2nd ed. Lisbon: Editorial Verbo, 1982.

Serrão, Joel. "Conspecto histórico da emigração Portuguesa." *Analise Social* 8, no. 32 (1970): 597–617.

Serrão, José Vicente. "O quadro humano." In *História de Portugal*, edited by José Mattoso, 4:49–69. Lisbon: Editorial Estampa, 1993.

Shaw, L. M. E. *The Anglo-Portuguese Alliance and the English Merchants in Portugal, 1654–1810*. Brookfield, VT: Ashgate, 1998.

———. *Trade, Inquisition, and the English Nation in Portugal, 1650–1690*. Manchester: Carcanet Press Limited, 1989.

Shillington, Violet Mary, and Annie Beatrice Wallis Chapman. *The Commercial Relations of England and Portugal*. New York: Burt Franklin, 1970.

Sideri, Sandro. *Trade and Power: Informal Colonialism in Anglo-Portuguese Relations*. Rotterdam, The Netherlands: Rotterdam Up, 1970.

Silva, André Duarte Martins da. "A Básilica patriarcal de D. João V, 1716–1755." Master's thesis, Universidade Nova de Lisboa, 2018.

Silva, Filipa Ribeiro da. "O tráfico de escravos para o Portugal setecentista: Uma visão a partir do despacho dos negros da Índia, de Cacheo, e de Angola na casa da Índia de Lisboa." *Saeculum: Revista de História* 29 (2013): 47–73.

Silva, Maria Beatriz Nizza da. *D. João V*. Rio de Mouro, Portugal: Círculo de Leitores, 2006.

Silva, Maria Júlia de Oliveira e. *Fidalgos-mercadores no século XVIII: Duarte Sodré Pereira*. Lisbon: Imprensa Nacional–Casa da Moeda, 1992.

Sim, Teddy. *Portuguese Enterprise in the East: Survival in the Years 1707–1757*. Leiden: Brill, 2011.

Smith, David Grant. "The Mercantile Class of Portugal and Brazil in the Seventeenth Century: A Socio-Economic Study of the Merchants of Lisbon and Bahia, 1620–1690." PhD diss., University of Texas at Austin, 1975.

———. "Old Christian Merchants and the Foundation of the Brazil Company, 1649." *Hispanic American Historical Review* 54, no. 2 (1974): 233–59.

Smith, Robert C. *The Art of Portugal: 1500–1800*. New York: Meredith Press, 1968.

———. "The Building of Mafra." *Apollo* 97 (1973): 360–67.

Soares, Mariza de Carvalho, and Jerry D. Metz. *People of Faith: Slavery and African Catholics in Eighteenth-Century Rio de Janeiro*. Durham: Duke University Press, 2011.

Stanwood, Owen. *The Global Refuge: Huguenots in an Age of Empire*. New York: Oxford University Press, 2020.

Stella, Alessandro. *Histoires d'esclaves dans la péninsule ibérique*. Paris: École des Hautes Études en Sciences Sociales, 2000.

Sucena, Berta de Moura. "Corpo, moda e luxo em Portugal no século XVIII." Master's thesis, Universidade de Lisboa, 2007.

Sweet, James. *Domingos Álvares, African Healing, and the Intellectual History of the Atlantic World*. Chapel Hill: University of North Carolina Press, 2011.

———. "The Hidden Histories of African Lisbon." In *The Black Urban Atlantic in the Age of the Slave Trade*, edited by Jorge Cañizares-Esguerra, Matt D. Childs, and James Sidbury, 235–47. Philadelphia: University of Pennsylvania Press, 2013.

———. "Slaves, Convicts, and Exiles: African Travelers in the Portuguese Atlantic World, 1720–1750." In *Bridging the Early Modern Atlantic World: People, Products, and Practices on the Move*, edited by Caroline A. Williams, 193–202. London: Taylor and Francis, 2009.

Tinhorão, José Ramos. *As origens da canção urbana*. Lisbon: Editorial Caminho, 1997.

———. *Os negros em Portugal: Uma presença silenciosa*. Lisbon: Caminho, 1988.

———. *O rasga: Uma dança negro-portuguesa*. São Paulo: Editora 34, 2006.

Torres, José Viega. "Da repressão religiosa para a promoção social: A Inquisição como instância legitimadora da promoção social da burguesia mercantil." *Revista Crítica de Ciências Sociais* 40 (October 1994): 109–35.

Vianna, Larissa. *O idioma da mestiçagem.* São Paulo: Editora Unicamp, 2007.

Vieira, Carla da Costa. "Família, perseguição, e mobilidade: O caso da família Medina." *Erasmo* (2014): 43–57.

———. "Mercadores Ingleses em Lisboa e judeus portugueses em Londres: Agentes, redes e trocas mercantis na primeira metade do século XVIII." *Ammentu: Bollettino Storico e Archivistico del Mediterraneo e delle Americhe* 7 (July–December 2015): 114–32.

———. "As 'Relações Judaicas' de Sebastião José de Carvalho e Melo." *Cadernos de Estudos Sefarditas* 14 (2015): 227–80.

Villiers, John. "Portuguese Society in the Reigns of D. Pedro II and D. João V, 1680–1750." PhD diss., University of Cambridge, 1962.

Von Germeten, Nicole. *Black Blood Brothers.* Gainesville: University of Florida Press, 2006.

Walker, Timothy. "Sorcerers and Folkhealers: Africans and the Inquisition in Portugal (1680–1800)." *Revista Lusófona de Ciência das Religiões* 3, no. 5–6 (2004): 83–98.

Whiteman, Anne. "Church and State." In *The New Cambridge Modern History*, vol. 5, *The Ascendancy of France, 1648–1688*, edited by Francis Ludwig Carsten, 122–48. Cambridge: Cambridge University Press, 1964.

Wilkinson, Richard. *Louis XIV.* New York: Routledge, 2007.

Wittkower, Rudolf. "Art and Architecture." In *The New Cambridge Modern History*, vol. 5, *The Ascendancy of France, 1648–1688*, edited by Francis Ludwig Carsten, 149–75. Cambridge: Cambridge University Press, 1964.

Wohl, Hellmut. "Portuguese Baroque Architecture." In *The Age of the Baroque in Portugal*, edited by Jay A. Levenson, 139–61. Washington, DC: National Gallery of Art, 1993.

Xavier, Ângela Barreto. *A invenção de Goa: Poder imperial e conversões culturais nos séculos XVI e XVII.* Lisbon: Imprensa de Ciências Sociais, 2008.

Index

Italicized page references indicate illustrations. Endnotes are referenced with "n" followed by the endnote number.

absolutism
  African interests and, 36
  Atlanticization and, 123, 124, 156, 161
  cultural change and, 123, 141–47, 161
  estrangeirados on, 128
  intellectual reform and, 147–51, 161,
    196n245
  João V and, 36, 53, 55, 82, 122–30, 151–57, 161
  Louis XIV and, 126, 152, 191n7
  nobility impacted by, 126–28
  Philip V and, 126, 152, 191n7
  religious impacts of, 136–40, 154–55
  urban transformation and, 11, 123, 130–36,
    163
Afonso VI (king of Portugal), 43, 73, 79, 80,
  125, 181n81
African populations
  agency of, 11, 24, 28–34
  Atlanticization of Lisbon and, 15–16, 21,
    28, 37, 160
  in baroque period, 22–28, 34, 37
  brotherhoods/confraternities for, 16,
    29–37, 140, 171n125, 171nn128–29,
    171n150, 172n177

  cultural influences of, 14, 34–37, 90, 163
  demographic changes and, 16–21
  free, 8, 15, 20, 24–29, 37, 89
  Iberianization of, 16, 28, 31, 37–38, 160
  interracial relationships, 27
  mandingas and, 87–90, 95
  marriage and, 20, 26–27, 170n99
  Mina, 21, 31–32, 36–37, 87–88, 99, 185n20
  in Mocambo neighborhood, 8, 26
  mulattoes, 15, 21, 25–30, 34, 35, 37, 171n143
  music and dance of, 23, 34–36
  natural reproduction of, 16, 18–20, 27, 37
  See also enslaved persons; slave trade
Afro-Brazilians, 15, 34–37, 72, 87–90, 95,
  162–63, 184n154
Águas Livres Aqueduct, 133–34, 157, 160, 163
Amsterdam
  African populations in, 21
  consumption patterns in, 141
  religious tolerance in, 54
  sources of wealth in, 11
Andrade, Patrício, 89–90
Andreoni, Giovanni Antonio. *See* Antonil,
  André João

Angovi, Florence, 63
Anne (queen of England), 60
Antonil, André João, 98, 99, 115
Armitage, David, 3
Asia
  enslaved persons from, 21
  "shoestring empire" in, 154
  spice trade in, 2, 17, 99–100, 108, 121
  See also specific countries and cities
Atlanticization of Lisbon
  absolutism and, 123, 124, 156, 161
  African populations and, 15–16, 21, 28, 37, 160
  Anglo-Portuguese relationship and, 11, 40, 41, 68
  baroque period and, 135, 144, 156, 157, 161
  cultural changes resulting from, 144
  diversity and pushback as elements of, 68–69, 161
  economic consequences of, 97–98, 106, 119–22, 144, 161
  Inquisition and, 94–96, 161
  interplay with Iberianization, 16, 37–38, 160
  religious consequences of, 72, 90, 94–96
  tobacco industry and, 99
Atlantic world
  diversity present within, 2, 5
  economic fluctuations in, 10, 161
  Europe as "blind spot" within, 4
  as field of historical study, 1, 3–4
  slavery's intensification within, 28
  See also North Atlantic; South Atlantic; *specific locations*

Bahia, Luís da Sylva, 83
Bailyn, Bernard, 4, 163
Baretti, Giuseppe, 20, 27, 38
baroque period
  African populations in, 22–28, 34, 37
  Anglo-Portuguese relations during, 62
  architecture during, 135–36, 151
  Atlanticization and, 135, 144, 156, 157, 161
  blood purity during, 27–28
  decline in Europe, 154
  popular culture in, 34–35
Bas, Jacques Philippe le, *162*
Belangé, James, 66
Benedict XIII (pope), 138
Bichi, Vincenzo, 138, 139

Black populations. *See* African populations
blood purity, 27–28, 82, 127–28
Bluteau, Raphael, 26, 60, 99, 147
bolsas de mandinga, 87–90, 95, 95
Botelho, Manoel, 27
Boxer, Charles Ralph, 8, 111, 188n114
Braun, João Henrique de, 63
Bravo, António Correia, 76, 79
Brazil
  brotherhoods in, 30–32
  diamonds from, 10, 40, 49, 51, 86, 95, 113–15, 121, 124
  Dutch merchants in, 44, 48
  emigration to, 24, 108–9, 115, 122, 166n41, 188n114, 189n172, 189–90n177
  English merchants in, 42, 48–49
  gold discovered in, 10, 17, 22, 24, 40–41, 47, 86, 95, 100, 112, 121, 125, 166n41
  New Christians from, 85–86, 161
  postrestoration focus on, 45
  slave trade and, 10, 16–21, 28, 37, 100, 108, 160
  War of the Spanish Succession and, 47, 48, 112, 140
  See also Afro-Brazilians; sugar industry; tobacco industry
Brazil Company, 73, 74, 76–78, 100, 124
Brereton, William, 93
Brochado, José da Cunha, 23, 56, 96, 101, 109, 124, 139–41, 147, 153
Brockwell, Charles, 94, 195n185
brotherhoods and confraternities
  Black, 16, 29–37, 140, 171n125, 171nn128–29, 171n150, 172n177
  Corpo de Deus procession and, 140
  functions of, 29, 31, 170–71n123
  mixed-race, 29–31, 171n143
  revenue sources for, 32–33, 172n177
  Rosary, 29–30, 33, 36, 172n177
  statutes governing, 30, 31
  wealth resulting from gold trade, 114
  women in, 28–30, 171n150
bullfighting, 7–8, 22–23, 34, 36, 169n61
Burnard, Trevor, 2
Burnett, Thomas, 51, 66, 84, 114, 152

Cádiz
  brotherhoods in, 29, 30
  colonial commerce and, 11
  English merchants in, 56

enslaved persons in, 20, 168n42
population statistics, 7
Caldas, Pedro Álvares, 76
Carlos, Francisco, 74, 76
Castelo Branco, Manuel Garcia de, 89
Castelo Branco, Mariana Bernarda Serafina de, 89
Castres, Abraham, 39, 67, 126
Castro, Damião António de Lemos Faria e, 142
Catarina (daughter of João IV), 42, 107
Catholicism
  absolutism and, 136–40
  conversion to, 62 66, 72, 92, 178n192, 185n1
  Corpo de Deus procession and, 140
  Council of Trent and, 59, 177n160
  England and, 53, 90
  mandingas and, 87, 88
  on marriages of enslaved persons, 26
  number of clergy in Lisbon, 8
  persecution of followers, 176n113
  War of the Spanish Succession and, 46
  See also brotherhoods and confraternities; Holy Office; Inquisition; Jesuits
Cervantes, Miguel de, 1, 3
Charles I (king of England), 41
Charles II (king of England), 42
Chaves, Diogo de, 74
Clement X (pope), 80
Clement XII (pope), 139
Cobban, A., 196n240
Col, Catherine, 93
Colbatch, John, 9, 93, 101
Colbert, Jean-Baptiste, 102, 128
Compton, Charles, 50–51, 55–58, 92
Compton, John, 63
confraternities. *See* brotherhoods and confraternities
Corbiere, Anthony, 55
Corpo de Deus procession, 140
Corte-Real, Diogo de Mendonça, 57, 131, 139, 140, 173n3
Cortesão, Jaime, 189n151
côrtes (parliament), 43, 73, 75, 79–80, 125
Costa, Gaspar Lopes da, 83
Costigan, Arthur, 11
Council of State, 125, 126, 128, 137, 191n18
Council of Trent, 59, 177n160
Coustos, Jean, 93–94

Cox, Thomas, 5, 6, 23, 60, 101, 119
Cromwell, Oliver, 41
Cunha, Luís Álvares de Andrade e, 25
Cunha, Luís da
  on Brazilian gold, 113–15
  on English merchants, 49
  on foreign influences, 141–42
  on Inquisition, 82, 84–86, 94
  on João V's absolutism, 128–29
  on lack of trained navigators, 148
  on military expeditions to India, 154
  on South Atlantic empire, 155, 198n305
  on women in religious orders, 116

David, Thomas, 62
Delaval, George, 55–56, 60
diamonds, 10, 40, 49, 51, 86, 95, 113–15, 121, 124
Donovan, Bill, 22, 49
Duclos, Roland, 103, 116
Dugood, William, 93
Duro, António Rodovalho, 169n61
Dutch. *See* Netherlands
Du Vernay, François, 44, 50, 53

Edict of Fontainebleau (1685), 43, 55, 116
Elliott, John Huxtable, 1
England
  alliance with Portugal, 2, 11, 39–43, 46–47, 68, 129–30, 160, 174n58
  Brazil and, 42, 48–49
  Catholicism and, 53, 90
  Civil Wars in, 41
  commercial rise of, 41–44, 68, 173n5
  economic competition with Portugal, 10
  enslaved persons harbored by, 39–40, 84, 173n3
  gold exports from Portugal, 49–53, 67
  João V's absolutism and, 129–30
  merchants in Lisbon, 39–44, 46–58, 68, 110, 146
  New Christians aided by, 81, 83–84, 93
  Portuguese dependence on foodstuffs from, 100–101
  Protestantism and, 46, 53, 59–68, 90
  slave trade and, 18, 19
  urbanization rate, 7
  wool industry in, 47–48, 84, 103–6, 110, 117
  See also specific cities

INDEX   221

Enlightenment, 85, 128, 149–51, 196n240
enslaved persons
  baptism of, 19, 168n33
  in baroque period, 22–28, 34
  in brotherhoods/confraternities, 29, 30,
    32–34, 37
  bullfighting and, 22–23, 34, 169n61
  confiscation of, 72, 74, 91, 96
  conversion to Catholicism, 92
  demographic changes and, 16–21,
    168n23
  ethnic backgrounds of, 19, 21
  kidnapping of, 17, 167n12, 168n33
  mandingas and, 87–89, 95, 183–84n153
  marriage and, 20, 26–27, 170n99
  in Mocambo neighborhood, 8, 26
  natural reproduction of, 18–20, 27
  purchase price for, 16, 17, 32
  runaways, 26, 39–40, 84, 173n3
  as wage earners, 23–25
  See also slave trade
Ericeira, Count of, 34, 97, 102–9, 121
estrangeirados (the foreignized), 128–29, 149
Estrées, Jean d', 148
ethnicity. *See* race and ethnicity
Europe
  as "blind spot" within Atlantic world, 4
  decline of baroque in, 154
  port capitals of, 3, 68, 162
  See also specific countries and cities

Fanshaw, Charles, 45, 61, 64, 105, 107
Fernandes, Manuel, 77, 78
Ferreira, António, 75
Ferreira da Costa, André, 28
Fielding, Henry, 23
Fisher, H. E. S., 174n58
Fonçequa, Maria de, 27
Fonseca, Jorge, 171n125
France
  Catholicism in, 46
  commercial interests of, 41, 43–44, 173n5,
    173n12
  economic competition with Portugal, 10
  merchants in Lisbon, 43–44
  New Christian families in, 84
  Spanish-Portuguese restoration war
    and, 43
Freemasonry, 93–94
Fuente, Alejandro de la, 4

Galway, Lord, 48, 60, 178n209
Gamboa, José de, 83
Games, Alison, 3
Geddes, Michael, 81
George II (king of England), 39
glasses (spectacles), 144, 195n185
Godin, Robert, 116–17
Godinho, Francisco de Abreu, 78
Godinho, Vitorino Magalhães, 73–74, 111,
  168n22
gold
  contraband trade in, 113, 114, 189nn151–52
  discovery in Brazil, 10, 17, 22, 24, 40–41,
    47, 86, 95, 100, 112, 121, 125, 166n41
  emigration to Brazil due to, 24, 115,
    166n41
  English exports from Portugal, 49–53, 67
  import capacity in relation to, 110, 112
  Mina Africans' ability to discover, 21
  political power of monarchy and, 124
  remittances in, 33, 113–15, 144, 189n170,
    191n220
  shipments to Lisbon, 19, 33, 47, 49–50,
    112–18, 141, 168n22, 188n144
  transformation of mercantile class due to,
    119–21
Gomes, Ignácio, 89–90
Gomes, Manoel, 89
Gorani, Giuseppe, 126–27
Granier, Samuel, 93
Griffin, Patrick, 2–3
Guedes, António, 89
Guimarães, João de Castro, 119, 190n210
Gulston, Ralph, 48
Gusmão, Alexandre de, 113, 120, 126, 129,
  153, 189n152
Gusmão, Bartolomeu de, 148
Gusmão, Luisa de, 73

Hacksaw, John, 65
Hanson, Carl A., 186n58
Hardwick, Joseph, 54
Hatfield, April Lee, 4
Hay, Edward, 48
Hervey, Augustus, 58, 67, 142
Holbech, Francis, 102
Holy Office
  arrests made by, 85, 86, 92–93
  confessions heard by, 15
  confiscations by, 71, 72, 85–86, 96

heretics and, 61, 76
mandingas and, 89
manufacturing program and, 108
papal suspension of, 80
restoration of, 80–81, 92
See also Inquisition
Houssaye, Noah, 54
Huguenots, 43, 55, 66, 116, 186n62
Hutchinson, Allen, 63

Iberianization, 16, 28, 31, 37–38, 160
India
  imperial focus on, 1, 2
  military expeditions to, 154
  slave trade and, 18, 21
  tobacco industry and, 99
  travel from Lisbon to, 9
Innocent XI (pope), 80
Inquisition
  Atlantic scope of, 94–96, 161
  autos-da-fé held by, 8, 61, 81, 93–94,
    182n90
  bailiffs for, 28, 92
  Catholic converts and, 63, 64
  confiscations by, 73, 74, 86, 91
  criticisms of, 85, 86
  demise under Marquis of Pombal, 72
  financial resources for, 73, 86
  Freemasonry and, 93–94
  independence of, 125
  João IV and, 72, 94
  João V and, 72, 82, 85–86, 128, 151,
    177n185
  mandingas and, 87–90, 95, 95
  manufacturing programs and, 108,
    188n110
  New Christians and, 73–86, 94, 108, 161,
    182n90
  Pedro II and, 77–78, 80, 86, 94, 125, 151
  Protestants and, 90–93, 95–96
  reform efforts, 76–80, 151, 180n46
  resurgence of, 11, 71–76, 82–86, 96,
    161
  trial records from, 80, 182n88

James II (king of England), 90
Jenefer, James, 58, 62
Jesuits
  on African populations, 18, 33
  Brazil Company established by, 73

East India company proposed by, 76–79,
  100, 180n46
São Roque church of, 136
Jews and Judaism
  anti-Semitic prejudice against, 78
  blood purity and, 27–28
  conversion to Catholicism, 72
  See also New Christians
João IV (king of Portugal)
  Brazil Company and, 73
  côrtes (parliament) and, 125
  independence movement begun by, 136
  Inquisition and, 72, 94
  New Christians and, 73, 75
  restoration of, 2
  treaties made by, 41–42, 44
João V (king of Portugal)
  absolutism and, 36, 53, 55, 82, 122–30,
    151–57, 161
  Atlanticization under, 2
  Black brotherhoods/confraternities and,
    32–33, 36, 140, 172n177
  Catholic Church under, 136–40
  cemetery granted to Protestants by, 61
  Council of State under, 126, 128, 137
  cultural changes under, 123, 141–47, 161
  descriptions of, 123, 155
  diplomatic corps of, 146–47, 196n216
  emigration laws issued by, 115
  English merchants and, 55, 57, 58, 146
  gold and, 49, 52, 112–16, 188n144
  imitation of Louis XIV, 124, 131, 144, 154
  Inquisition and, 72, 82, 85–86, 128, 151,
    177n185
  intellectual reform under, 147–51, 161,
    196n245
  interracial relationships of, 27
  on kidnapping of children, 65–66
  manufacturing programs of, 53–54, 116–17
  marriage to Maria Anna, 22
  Methuen Treaty enforced by, 48
  modernization efforts of, 5
  monumental building by, 123, 133, 136, 154,
    161, 198n13
  paralytic attacks suffered by, 120, 149,
    195n196
  religious fanaticism of, 53, 155, 195n196
  romantic relationships, 142–43
  urban transformation under, 123, 130–36
  on women in religious orders, 116

INDEX

223

José I (king of Portugal), 33, 160
Judaism. *See* Jews and Judaism
Junta da Administração do Tabaco (Tobacco Administration Council), 86, 98–99, 124
Juvarra, Filippo, 131, *156*

Kennedy, Andrew, 62
Kingsley, George, 64

Lahon, Didier, 31, 167n12, 171n129, 171n143
leather goods, 106, 116, 117
Leffever, Thomas, 48, 52
Lisbon
  Atlantic dependency of, 11, 45–47, 175–76n112
  brotherhoods/confraternities in, 16, 29–34, 171n125, 171n129, 171n143
  consumption patterns in, 141–44
  cultural changes in, 11, 123, 141–47, 161
  danger and disorder in, 8–9, 25–26, 56–58
  demographic changes in, 2, 16–21
  design and function, 5–8, 134, 163
  earthquake in (1755), 6, 14, 56, 60, 134, 159–60, 166n41, 198n13
  emigration to Brazil from, 24, 109, 122, 166n41
  English merchants in, 39–44, 46–58, 68, 110, 146
  French merchants in, 43–44
  gold shipments to, 19, 33, 47, 49–50, 112–18, 141, 168n22, 188n144
  intellectual reform in, 147–51, 161, 196n245
  map prior to 1755, *12*
  modernization of, 5, 121, 136
  native-foreigner conflicts in, 54–59
  New Christians in, 59, 71–86
  popular culture in, 16, 34–37
  population statistics, 6–8, 166n41, 166n57
  post-1668 Atlantic transformation, 10–14
  Protestants in, 59–68, 90–94, 160–61, 177–78n185
  religious tension in, 59–68, 74, 78–79, 91
  social life in, 66–67, 179n225
  urban transformation of, 11, 123, 130–36, 163
  yellow fever outbreak (1723), 134–35, 152
  See also African populations; Atlanticization of Lisbon; baroque period; Catholicism; manufacturing program

Littleton, Edward, 45
London
  commercial prominence of, 11
  consumption patterns in, 141
  enslaved persons in, 20–21
  financial markets in, 51
  New Christians in, 83, 84
  religious tolerance in, 54
  as slave trade port, 17
  urban conditions in, 6, 9
Louis XIV (king of France)
  absolutism and, 126, 152, 191n7
  Catholic Church under, 138
  Edict of Fontainebleau (1685), 43, 116
  João V's imitation of, 124, 131, 144, 154
  warlike mentality of, 153
Lumley, Thomas, 55, 64–65
Luzia, Grácia, 15, 16, 34

Macedo, Duarte Ribeiro de, 100, 102, 103, 106
Macro, Cox, 34–35, 65, 67, 99
Madrid, Treaty of (1750), 154
Mafra, construction of palace-convent at, 131–33, 153
Magalhães, Sebastião de, 33
Magalotti, Lorenzo, 9, 49
Mahony, Helena, 63
mandingas, 87–90, 95, *95*, 183–84nn153–154
Manuel (brother of João V), 31
Manuel (king of Portugal), 72
manufacturing program
  beginnings of, 45, 81, 101–6
  demise of, 47, 82, 108–9, 111–12, 121
  for leather goods, 106, 116, 117
  in peripheral parishes, 7
  Pombal and, 101, 186n38
  revitalization of, 53–54, 97, 116
  for silk, 103, 116–17
  sumptuary laws and, 47, 103, 111, 190n182
  for woolens, 104–5, 116, 117
Maria Anna of Austria, 22, 33, 178n192
Marques, António Henrique Rodrigo de Oliveira, 191n3
Matias, Maria Henny Vonk, 196n245
Matta, João da, 89
Maynard, Thomas, 54–56, 58, 63–64, 74–76, 81–82, 90–92, 102, 104–7
Mello, Francisco de Pina e de, 159
Melo, Francisco Manuel de, 8–9

224   INDEX

Melo, Jorge Fonseca de, 92
Melo, Nuno Álvares Pereira de, 151
Melo, Sebastião José de Carvalho e. *See* Pombal, Marquis of
Mendes, Francisco, 83
Meneses, Alexandre de Metelo de Sousa e, 146
Meneses, Francisco Xavier de, 150
Meneses, Rodrigo de, 79
Merveilleux, Charles Frédéric de
  on *autos-da-fé*, 61
  on bullfighting, 36
  on clothes in João V's closet, 147
  on enslaved persons, 22
  on manufacturing program, 117
  natural history museum established by, 149
  on nobility's loss of power, 127
  on opposition to João V's proposed trip, 146
  on Protestants in Lisbon, 177–78n185
  on urban transformation, 131–33
Methuen, John, 46, 47, 66, 91, 93
Methuen, Paul, 46, 56, 57
Methuen Treaty (1703), 40, 47–48, 53, 68, 106, 109–12, 121
Milner, John, 49–50, 65–66
Milner, Tempest, 146
Mina Africans, 21, 31–32, 36–37, 87–88, 99, 185n20
Miranda, António de, 142
Mogadouro, António, 74
monetary policy, 106–9
Montagnac, Jacques, 50, 116–17
Montchevreuil, René de Mornay, 49
Monteiro, Henrique Jorge Coutinho de Almeida, 166n57
Montgon, Charles Alexandre de, 5
Moors
  blood purity and, 27–28
  capture of enslaved persons by, 19, 168n33
  at Corpo de Deus procession, 140
  enslavement of, 21, 173n3
  piracy and, 19, 50, 114
mulattoes, 15, 21, 25–30, 34, 35, 37, 171n143
Murteira, Helena, 6

Netherlands
  Brazil and, 44, 48
  Catholic persecution in, 176n113

  commercial interests of, 41, 44, 173n5, 173n12
  economic competition with Portugal, 10
  Holy Office's tenure in, 96
  Protestantism and, 46, 177n159
  spice trade and, 2, 17
  urbanization rate, 7
  See also specific cities
Neuburg, Maria Sofia de, 22
New Christians
  Brazilian, 85–86, 161
  confessions by, 74, 75, 180n32
  East India company proposed by, 76–79, 94, 100
  English aid given to, 81, 83–84, 93
  expulsion of, 72, 75–76, 81
  Inquisition and, 73–86, 94, 108, 161, 182n90
  manufacturing programs and, 104, 188n110
  as merchants, 71–76, 81, 84–86, 94, 98, 108, 121
  parish church desecrated by, 59, 74
  persecution of, 71, 76, 81–86, 92, 94, 121
  Spanish, 72, 83
  use of term, 72
Nine Years' War (1688–97), 17, 110
Nolan, Patrício (Patrick), 18–19
North Atlantic
  competing economies in, 54
  focus of Atlantic world historiography on, 1
  interplay between interests in South Atlantic and, 98, 121
  overlapping influences of, 11, 68, 72, 162–63
  Portugal's reliance on nations of, 41
  religious influences from, 2, 72, 95
  slave trade in, 17
  See also specific locations

Oliveira, Cristovão Rodrigues de, 20
Oliveira, Francisco Xavier de, 85
Oliveira, Nicolau de, 20

Pádua, Manuel de Gama de, 76
Paim, Roque Monteiro, 75
Paquette, Gabriel, 175–76n112
Parry, Francis, 62, 64, 75–76, 78, 80, 92, 97, 104–5
Pedreira, Jorge Miguel, 85, 190n209, 194n157

INDEX   225

Pedro II (king of Portugal)
  Atlanticization under, 2
  Black brotherhoods/confraternities and,
    32, 33
  on blood purity investigations, 28
  Brazilian revenues and, 17
  côrtes (parliament) and, 43, 73, 75, 79–80,
    125
  Council of State under, 125, 191n18
  economic interventions, 98, 100, 103, 105,
    106
  engagement in street fights, 26
  enslaved persons and, 19, 25, 33, 168n33
  Inquisition and, 77–78, 80, 86, 94, 125, 151
  interracial relationships of, 27
  limitations on royal power of, 124–25
  marriage to Maria Sofia, 22
  modernization efforts of, 5, 136
  monetary policy under, 107, 108
  New Christians and, 75–79, 81
  seizure of throne from Afonso VI, 43, 73
  War of the Spanish Succession and, 45–46
Pedroso, José Francisco, 87–88, 95
Peebles, John, 62
Penso, Fernando de Morales, 85
Penso, Fernão Rodrigues, 74
Peralta, Manoel de, 83
Pereira, José Francisco, 88–89
Pereira, Mendo de Fóios, 80
Pereira, Tomás, 27
persecution. See religious persecution
Philip V (king of Spain), 45, 126, 138, 152,
    191n7
Pinheiro, Francisco, 19, 22, 34, 49, 119–20,
    167n12, 190n210
Pinheiro, Manuel Lopes, 71
piracy, 19, 50, 114, 175n181
Pombal, Marquis of (Sebastião José de Carva-
    lho e Melo)
  East India company proposed by, 120
  English dependency and, 176n112
  Inquisition's demise under, 72
  Lisbon's rebuilding overseen by, 160, 163
  manufacturing program and, 101, 186n38
  monopoly company of, 100, 185n21
  on New Christians, 83–84
  New Conquests of, 154
  reform efforts of, 12
Porto
  baroque period in, 136

brotherhoods in, 29, 30, 172n177
commercial dominance in, 173n5
emigration to Brazil from, 24, 109
English merchants in, 49, 62, 110,
  174–75n68
enslaved persons in, 91
Holy Office covering, 182n103
importance as regional port, 11
population statistics, 7
travel from Lisbon to, 9
wine industry in, 11, 111
Portugal
  alliance with England, 2, 11, 39–43, 46–47,
    68, 129–30, 160, 174n58
  côrtes (parliament) in, 43, 73, 75, 79–80,
    125
  Council of State, 125, 126, 128, 137,
    191n18
  dependence on foodstuffs from England,
    100–101
  economic depression in, 45, 74
  emigration to Brazil from, 24, 108–9,
    115, 122, 166n41, 188n114, 189n172,
    189–90n177
  in Franco-Hispanic alliance, 46
  independence movement in, 2, 17, 41, 125,
    136
  monetary policy in, 106–9
  navy of, 130, 147–48, 196n223
  political union with Spain (1580–1640), 2,
    41, 100, 135
  Protestants in, 59–68, 90–94, 160–61,
    177n159, 177–78n185
  restoration war (1640–68), 5, 13, 17, 41, 43,
    73, 107, 136
  revenue from overseas empire, 124, 191n3
  spice trade and, 2, 17
  urbanization rate, 7
  See also absolutism; Brazil; Catholicism;
    India; slave trade; specific cities and rulers
Postlethwayt, Malachy, 119
Poyntz, William, 52–53
Protestantism
  burial practices, 60–61
  conversion to Catholicism from, 62–66,
    178n192, 185n1
  Edict of Fontainebleau on, 43, 55, 116
  England and, 46, 53, 59–68, 90
  Inquisition and, 90–93, 95–96
  persecution of followers, 55, 61–62

226   INDEX

in Portugal, 59–68, 90–94, 160–61, 177n159, 177–78n185

War of the Spanish Succession and, 46

Pyrenees, Treaty of the (1659), 43

race and ethnicity
  blood purity and, 27–28, 82, 127–28
  of enslaved persons, 19, 21
  intermixing, 2, 16, 27–28, 37, 160
  prejudice based on, 16, 25, 27–28, 37
  See also African populations

religion
  absolutism and, 136–40, 154–55
  Afro-Brazilian, 72, 87, 95
  Atlanticization and, 72, 90, 94–96
  freedom of, 42, 71
  North and South Atlantic influences on, 2, 16
  tolerance of, 54, 79, 116, 161, 181n75
  See also Catholicism; Jews and Judaism; Protestantism

religious persecution
  of Catholics, 176n113
  of New Christians, 71, 76, 81–86, 92, 94, 121
  of Protestants, 55, 61–62

Ribeira, Luís Álvarez, 55

Ribeiro, José, 89

Rosário, António, 10

Rosary brotherhoods and confraternities, 29–30, 33, 36, 172n177

Rothschild, Emma, 3

royal absolutism. *See* absolutism

Russell, John, 53

Sanches, Ribeiro, 85

Sanderson, Thomas, 67

Santa Maria, Agostinho de, 41

Santana, Francisco, 183–84n153

Saussure, César de, 123, 135, 143–44, 146

Scarburgh, Charles, 91, 107

Schwartz, Stuart, 181n75

Sebastião (king of Portugal), 150, 169n61

Serrão, José Vicente, 189–90n177

Seville
  Black brotherhoods in, 29
  colonial commerce and, 11
  English merchants in, 56
  Holy Office in, 96
  population statistics, 7

silk, 103, 105, 116–17, 140, 142–44, 186n62, 195n185

Silva, António José da, 86

Silva, Filipa Ribeiro da, 18

Silva, José Soares da, 153

Silveira, Brás da, 126

slave trade
  asiento contract, 107–8
  Atlanticization of, 16–18, 28, 37
  Brazil and, 10, 16–21, 28, 37, 100, 108, 160
  demographic changes and, 2, 16–21
  economic depression and, 74
  expansion of, 10, 16–18
  sugar industry and, 17, 21
  tobacco industry and, 21, 99, 185n20
  See also enslaved persons

Smallwood, James, 91

Smith, David Grant, 75

Smith, Robert C., 136

Soares, Domingos, 27

Sousa, Luís da, 182n88

South Atlantic
  competing economies in, 54
  convergence of interests in, 40
  interplay between interests in North Atlantic and, 98, 121
  overlapping influences of, 11, 68, 72, 162–63
  postrestoration focus on, 41, 45
  quadrangular trade network in, 42
  religious influences from, 2, 16, 72, 90
  slave trade in, 17
  See also specific locations

Spain
  brotherhoods in, 29, 30, 32
  Catholicism in, 46, 139
  New Christians from, 72, 83
  political union with Portugal (1580–1640), 2, 41, 100, 135
  restoration war (1640–68), 5, 13, 17, 41, 43, 73, 107, 136
  revenue from overseas empire, 191n3
  slave trade and, 107–8
  urbanization rate, 7
  See also specific cities

spectacles (glasses), 144, 195n185

spice trade, 2, 17, 99–100, 108, 121

Stanwood, Owen, 186n62

Stert, Arthur, 127

Stevens, John, 5, 6, 8

sugar industry
economic depression and, 74
New Christian merchants in, 86
price declines in, 98, 120–21
restoration war financed by, 73
slave trade and, 17, 21
sumptuary laws, 47, 103, 111, 190n182
Sweet, James, 36
Swift, Willoughby, 107
Swinton, John, 60–61

Taboado, Catarina, 27
Tavares, Francisco, 89
Tellez, Balthazar, 18
Tinhorão, José Ramos, 36–37
tobacco industry
administration council, 86, 98–99, 124
Atlanticization and, 99
economic depression and, 74
illegal operations within, 99
price declines in, 45
production increases, 98
revenue provided by, 99, 124, 191n3
slave trade and, 21, 99, 185n20
snuff production, 98–99
Tours, François de, 6, 25
trade imbalances, 45, 106, 110–12, 120
treaties. *See specific names of treaties*
Tyrawly, Lord, 50–64, 67–69, 84, 93, 99,
129–32, 145, 155

Verney, Luís António, 149
Vidal, Cécile, 2
Vieira, António, 73, 76–77, 79–81, 100, 105,
125
Vieira, Carla, 92

Viganego, Pietro Francesco, 112–13, 138, 145,
148, 152–53, 178n209
Villiers, John, 190n199
Voltaire, 155

War of the Spanish Succession
alliances in, 46–47
Brazil during, 47, 48, 112, 140
desertion by soldiers during, 152
emigration to Brazil during, 166n41
expenses from, 146, 147
Methuen Treaty during, 40, 47
Pedro II during, 45–46
royal absolutism following, 124, 125
slave trade during, 108
Williamson, Joseph, 97
wine industry, 11, 47, 49, 101, 108, 110–12,
174n57
Wohl, Hellmut, 136
women
in brotherhoods/confraternities, 28–30,
171n150
clothing styles for, 141
dancing restrictions on, 35
emigration to Brazil, 115
Inquisition and, 93, 94
in religious orders, 116, 142–43
in silk industry, 103, 116
wool, 47–48, 84, 103–6, 110, 116, 117, 186n58,
188n110
Worsley, Henry, 54, 63, 66, 84, 86, 93, 146

yellow fever outbreak (1723), 134–35, 152

Zuzarte, Francisco, 13

www.ingramcontent.com/pod-product-compliance
Ingram Content Group UK Ltd.
Pitfield, Milton Keynes, MK11 3LW, UK
UKHW040759250125
453985UK00002B/12